Institute of Social and Religious Research

PROTESTANT COOPERATION
IN AMERICAN CITIES

H. PAUL DOUGLASS

Protestant Cooperation In American Cities

By

H. PAUL DOUGLASS

Author of "Church Comity", "The Church in
the Changing City", "1000 City Churches", etc.

NEW YORK
INSTITUTE OF SOCIAL AND RELIGIOUS RESEARCH

PREFACE

For nearly a decade the Institute of Social and Religious Research has carried on studies in the field of the city church; and these have given it extensive contacts with church federations and councils of churches. Its first urban study, the St. Louis Church Survey, was made in formal coöperation with the federation of that city. In nearly all its urban projects the federations have constituted a chief source of existing data concerning organized religion, and local contacts have usually been arranged through them. All told, a great deal of assistance has been received from federation workers, and exceedingly pleasant relationships have been established with them.

From these contacts, the Institute acquired a considerable understanding of the federation movement. It discovered, for example, that it is much more difficult to set up and carry out a survey in a city that has no federation than in one in which the federated churches are accustomed to respond to common leadership, where the machinery of common action already exists, and where considerable amounts of information concerning the total Protestant situation are likely to be found. And very early it discovered a wide-spread desire on the part of federation workers to have a critical study of their movement made by some impartial outside agency.

Communications from the field to the office of the Federal Council of Churches had urgently voiced this desire before the present inquiry was undertaken. These quotations from one of them fairly represent the general attitude.

> I should like to make this suggestion which you can pass on to the Committee if you think best; that the whole field of church coöperation is badly in need of research and investigation. * * * We are squarely up against the problem. We cannot much longer put off facing the problem of effective church coöperation. I realize that no doctrinaire method or system is going to prove sufficient; but what are we going to do about Councils of Churches, Councils of Religious Education, Young Men's Christian Associations, and Young Women's Christian Associations all covering the same field in large part and in many places competing with a positively institutional, if not selfish, spirit? Are our Councils of Churches functioning? Is it possible for the Young Men's Christian Association to lead off in church coöperative work? If so, where does the Young Women's Christian Association come in?

18051

What about Councils of Religious Education which are created by delegates from churches and with budgets about as big as the churches together will raise, yet with purely specialized programs?

It would be an immense task to have a thorough survey of the whole field of church coöperation, but I do not see how we can go along much farther without the confusion increasing unless we face this issue squarely. The Federal Council is doing nothing about it, so far as I am able to see. * * *

This is the subject which weighs the heaviest with me. I shall be glad to hear what your conference decides upon.

Similar suggestions for a study of the movement had been actively canvassed in meetings of the Association of Executive Secretaries of Church Federations prior to 1926; and the demand was focused in the 1926 meeting of the Federal Council's Executive Committee in Minneapolis. The Information Service [1] reported upon that occasion as follows:

This year's meeting was organized on a conference basis, the general subject being church federation in the local community. The several phases of the Federal Council's work were successively discussed in their bearing upon the program of the local church federations. It became evident that a thorough study of the local federation or church council in its relation to denominational bodies, coöperating agencies, and other community resources is very much needed. Among the points developed in conference were the following:

The organization of the religious forces in a community should proceed, not in accord with stereotyped procedure, but in accord with the situation encountered, and advantage should be taken of leadership already established no matter what organization may have it—the church council, home missions councils, the Young Men's Christian Association, the council of religious education or some other agency.

Women's missionary organizations are in general remote from understanding of and participation in federation work. It was reported that the strongest women's work is found where their organizations are separate and autonomous, but there is a tendency for them to relate themselves more clearly with councils of churches. It was reported also that the Council of Women for Home Missions is shortly to be affiliated with the Federal Council of Churches.

A Young Women's Christian Association representative pointed out that the churches frequently ignore the body of experience and technical knowledge which that organization has gained. * * * She pointed out that competitive enterprises and duplication are not only unfortunate but are becoming difficult because money is getting scarce for such undertakings and we should be thankful that money is not so readily available as to encourage unnecessary and competitive work.

---

[1] Issue of December 18, 1926.

These quotations suggest the character of the concrete problems on which it was believed a fresh study of the coöperative movement would furnish light. The Institute was asked informally whether it might undertake responsibility for the desired investigation; and consultation with national religious leaders, especially with officers of the Federal Council of Churches, showed that such a study would be welcomed in the most responsible quarters. That it would be timely was indicated by the fact that the federations as a group were just completing two decades of existence, which might well be regarded as constituting an experimental period. Besides, nearly a decade had elapsed since the end of the World War and the collapse of the Interchurch World Movement, with which one era of coöperation obviously culminated. This, it was believed, afforded sufficient time to determine the general character of the present era. Finally, it was hoped that all persons seriously concerned for the welfare of the Church would be vitally interested in an attempted reappraisal of the coöperative movement.

CHARACTER AND LIMITATIONS OF THE PROPOSED STUDY

The proposal, as it was formally brought before the Institute, was for an investigation of organized Protestant coöperation limited in the following ways:

It was to be confined primarily to the larger cities, but was to draw incidental illustrations from other communities.

It was to center upon fully organized church federations and councils of churches employing paid executives, but to give incidental attention to other types.

While other agencies of organized Protestant coöperation as well as federations were to be studied, these others were to be approached on the side of their contacts, coöperative or competitive, with the federations.

The investigation was to take account of temporary coöperation in specific projects, as well as of organized forms of continuous coöperation. It was not to be concerned with national agencies of coöperation, such as the Federal Council, except as they should be found operating directly in local fields and affecting the programs and activities of local federations. It was not to culminate either in a "boosting" document, even though the conclusions should turn out to be conspicuously favorable to the federations, or in a practical manual on "How to Run a Federation." The report was to be an objective and dispassionate presentation and analysis of the facts discovered, with such generalizations as might seem to be justified.

A NARRATIVE OF THE PROJECT

The project was approved in principle by the directors of the Institute in January, 1927, and money was appropriated for an experimental case-study. The Philadelphia Federation was chosen for this purpose, and was studied in the spring of 1927. The results were formulated in a report which was approved by the Institute staff. It was also informally referred to the Association of Executive Secretaries of Church Federations, which voted in favor of having a representative group of federations studied in the same way. In January, 1928, the directors of the Institute authorized the project, which was put into the hands of the writer.

In setting up the study, tentative lists of federations suitable for inclusion were first prepared in conference with persons familiar with the movement. Replies from the federations approached generally evidenced very cordial willingness to permit themselves to be investigated. In a few cases, acute local situations were confessed which could not bear the light of publicity just at the moment. In a few others, it was not possible for the local federation to meet the convenience of the Institute with respect to the dates of the study. Nevertheless, a very representative series of case-studies was completed.

The field force consisted of the project director, assisted by Rev. C. E. Silcox and Rev. Wilbur C. Hallenbeck. The field study occupied in the aggregate about thirty months, an average of six weeks to a federation, and was completed in January, 1929.

BY-PRODUCTS OF THE FIELD STUDY

During the progress of the study, many informal discussions of details and principles of federation work were held with secretaries and committees; and there were also many formal conferences with boards of directors and other committees. At the end of the survey period, tentative reports of criticism and suggestion were rendered upon request in a number of cities. The value of these by-products was recognized in a formal finding of the 1928 meeting of the Association of Executive Secretaries:

> We find that the Councils and Federations of Churches, which the Institute of Social and Religious Research has thus far studied in connection with its scientific investigation of the present status

of Protestant Coöperation in America, report immediate results of
large value to their present programs. The immediate values to
the organizations thus far studied are so significant, and the
promise of advantage to the whole coöperative movement and the
ends which we seek to achieve so apparent, that we call upon the
members of our Association and upon the Councils and Federations of Churches to lend every possible assistance to the Institute
in order to facilitate the publication of the final report.

PUBLISHED RESULTS

The report of the investigation is in two volumes. The first,
entitled *Church Comity: A Study of Coöperative Church Extension in American Cities,*[2] dealt with a single major phase
of federation activity. The present comprehensive report covers
the remainder of the data.

This volume consists of an introductory section and two
main parts. In the introduction an attempt is made to orient
the Protestant coöperative movement within the world of ecclesiastical organization, and special consideration is given to the
problems presented by denominationalism.

In Part I, which is the general report, the practical ideals and
objectives, the structural characteristics, and the functions, activities, means, agents, and resources of the federations are discussed, as well as the relations of city federations to other
Protestant coöperative movements and to the national movement. There is also an attempt to interpret the movement as
part of the evolution of the Protestant social group in America,
and to summarize its characteristics. The general report is
thus intended to reveal the coöperative spirit in organized Protestantism, and the major trends and variations within the coöperative movement. This part of the book is addressed to all
who desire to understand and measure contemporary church
evolution, or who are interested in present-day religion as
organized for action.

Part II, the technical report, is particularly intended for the
use of federation workers and their critics. In it the leading
federations are compared on many points. It reports upon
practical administrative details as related to the internal organization of federations, to their committee system, their employed
workers, and their finances and publicity; and it contains technical analyses of the major phases of federation programs. It
shows and compares the reactions of constituencies to the federations. While it is not a manual of practice, the technical report
furnishes many of the essential materials of a working guide to

---

[2] Institute of Social and Religious Research (New York, 1929), 181 pages.

the conduct of federations. It is followed by an appendix containing certain statistical data and methodological notes.

GENERAL METHOD AND SPIRIT OF THE INVESTIGATION

The main data of the present investigation were gathered in a series of institutional case-studies. Careful schedules of information sought from each federation were prepared with a sequence of topics which has been substantially followed in the structure of the report. The case-studies covered about three-fifths of the active church federations in the major cities, and accordingly constituted an exceedingly adequate sampling. The generalized results, in the main, are descriptive and analytical rather than statistical. Certain measurable aspects of federation work have, however, been quantitatively investigated; and statistical results on these points are believed to be exceedingly significant.

The report is fundamentally factual; and in the main, facts and events are allowed to speak for themselves. Rarely have motives been ascribed to men or to movements. At certain points, however, where motives were fairly self-intrusive, it seemed safe to attempt to penetrate below the phenomena and to register the impressions of the investigator as to the inner forces at work.

Evaluation of particular results has in a large measure been implicit in the comparison of one federation with another. Certain deeper questions of the value of the entire movement, and of the significance of its major activities, have also been formulated and the writer's opinion indicated; but with no claim of having reached a final verdict. Such items of methodology as appeared to be too complicated for sufficient explanation in the text are dealt with in the appendix.

CONTENTS

PART I: THE GENERAL REPORT

CHAPTER   PAGE

Preface... v

I. Introduction................................... 3

II. Denominationalism and Religious Partisanship.... 22

III. The Church Federation Movement............... 40

IV. Claims and Recognitions....................... 56

V. Form and Structure of Church Federations........ 76

VI. Membership and Participation................... 89

VII. Coöperative Activities......................... 104

VIII. The Constituents' Judgments upon Current Programs... 127

IX. Agencies, Resources and Methods............... 139

X. Affiliation of Other Interdenominational Organizations....................................... 155

XI. Present Limits of Federative Coöperation........ 182

XII. Forces Unifying and Enlarging the Federation Movement...................................... 203

XIII. Currents and Eddies of Federation Thinking....... 228

XIV. Organizational Characteristics of the Federations... 254

XV. Some Larger Meanings of the Church Federation Movement...................................... 272

PART II: THE TECHNICAL REPORT

XVI. The Committee System......................... 291

XVII. The Paid Staff................................ 309

XVIII. Evangelism................................... 329

CHAPTER   PAGE

XIX. Religious Education............................ 345

XX. Social Service................................... 371

XXI. Social Service (continued)....................... 402

XXII. Coöperation by Protestant Women.............. 435

XXIII. Finances and Facilities......................... 448

XXIV. Promotion and Publicity....................... 471

APPENDICES

I. Organization of the Roman Catholic Archdiocese of New York....................................... 483

II. The Investigation of Religious Distance............. 484

III. Frequency of Particular Items in Federation Programs, by Major Departments............................ 490

IV. Constituents' Judgments Regarding Federation Programs.. 495

V. Bibliography...................................... 496

INDEX....................................... 499

TABLES

TABLE   PAGE

I. Distribution of Church Federations, by Size of Cities.................................... 4

II. Specified Faiths and Denominations Ranked According to Degree of "Distance" Felt Toward Them by Protestant Constituents of Church Federations. 26

III. Specified Faiths and Denominations Ranked According to Degree of "Distance" Felt Toward Them as Measured by Specified Criteria............. 29

IV. Degree of "Distance" Felt Toward Other Faiths and Denominations by Constituents in Certain Cities..................................... 34

V. Degree of "Distance" Felt by Certain Sex- and Status-Groups Toward Other Faiths and Denominations.................................... 35

VI. The Work of the Federation as Understood by Constituents of the Philadelphia Federation...... 68

VII. Sense of Obligation of Constituents to Coöperate in 17 Federations, by Cities.................. 70

VIII. Sense of Obligation of Constituents to Coöperate in 16 Federations, by Denominations........... 72

IX. Proportion of Protestant Denominations, Churches and Church-members in Three Cities Formally Belonging to Church Federations............. 95

X. Departments, Standing Committees and Commissions in 23 Church Federations.............. 105

XI. Standard Activities in Federation Programs, by Departments of Work....................... 108

XII. Ranking of 26 Federations According to Scope of Program.................................. 109

XIII. Ranking of Items of Service Programs According to Constituents' Judgments Regarding Appropriateness and Importance, in 16 Federations.... 120

TABLE   PAGE

XIV. Constituents' Judgments Regarding Appropriateness and Importance of Programs of 17 Federations, by Cities............................... 128

XV. Ranking of 17 Federations According to Constituents' Judgments Regarding Appropriateness and Importance of Programs................... 128

XVI. Constituents' Judgments Regarding Appropriateness and Importance of Programs of 10 Federations, by Denominations...................... 130

XVII. Ranking of 12 Denominations According to Judgments of Their Members Regarding Appropriateness and Importance of Their Federations' Programs...................................... 132

XVIII. Constituents' Judgments Regarding Appropriateness and Importance of Programs in 5 Federations, by Classes of Constituents............... 133

XIX. Constituents' Judgments Regarding Appropriateness and Importance of Certain Elements of Federation Programs.............................. 134

XX. Classification of Paid Workers of 21 Federations... 147

XXI. Meetings and Attendance of Various Federation Committees................................. 296

XXII. Composition of Various Federation Committees... 298

XXIII. Characteristics of Members of Various Federation Committees................................. 299

XXIV. Distribution of Members of Various Federation Committees, by Years of Committee Membership and by Number of Other Federation Committees in Which Membership Is Held.......... 301

XXV. Size of Paid Staff in 21 Federations............. 309

XXVI. Ranking of Items of Evangelism Programs According to Constituents' Judgments Regarding Appriateness and Importance, in 17 Federations.... 341

XXVII. Ranking of Items of Religious Education Programs According to Constituents' Judgments Regarding Appropriateness and Importance, in 15 Federations...................................... 366

TABLE   PAGE

XXVIII. Constituents' Judgments Regarding Appropriateness and Importance of Phases of Social Service, in 16 Federations............................. 418

XXIX. Sources of Income in 20 Federations............ 449

APPENDIX TABLES

1. Denominational Distribution of Federation Constituents Who Replied to the "Religious Distance" Questionnaire.. 486

2. Comparison of Nine Relationships According to Degree of Religious "Distance" Attached to them by Protestant Constituents of Church Federations with Respect to Members of Other Faiths and Denominations.............. 487

3. Specified Relationships With Other Faiths and Denominations Ranked by Cities According to Degree of "Distance" Felt... 488

4. Specified Relationships With Other Faiths and Denominations Ranked by Denominations According to Degree of "Distance" Felt.................................... 489

5. Constituents' Judgments Regarding Appropriateness and Importance of Programs in 17 Federations, by Cities.... 495

6. Constituents' Judgments Regarding Appropriateness and Importance of Programs in 10 Federations, by Denominations... 495

CHARTS

CHART   PAGE

I. Proportion of Cities of Given Populations Having Church Federations, 1929 5

II. Index of Religious "Distance" Felt by Protestant Constituents of Church Federations Toward Members of Specified Faiths or Denominations 28

III. Index of "Distance" Felt by Protestant Constituents of Church Federations Toward Members of Specified Faiths and Denominations with Respect to Marriage and the Presidency of the United States 30

IV. Average Score of Religious "Distance" Felt by Protestant Constituents of Church Federations of Specified Denominations Toward Members of Other Faiths and Denominations 32

V. Average Score of Religious "Distance" Felt by Protestant Constituents of Church Federations of Specified Status and Sex Toward Members of Other Faiths and Denominations 35

VI. Comparison of Sense of Obligation to Coöperate in Church Federation Proposals Felt by Their Constituents in 16 Cities 71

VII. Comparison of Sense of Obligation to Coöperate in Church Federation Proposals Felt by Constituents of Specified Denominations in 16 Cities 73

VIII. Distribution of Judgments of Constituents with Respect to the Importance and Appropriateness of Current Programs—17 Church Federations 129

IX. Distribution of Judgments of Constituents with Respect to the Importance and Appropriateness of Current Church Federation Programs—12 Denominations 131

X. Distribution of Judgments of Constituents of Church Federations with Respect to the Importance and Appropriateness of Specified Elements of Their Programs 135

CHART   PAGE

   XI. Comparative Attendance of Members of Specified Types of Church Federation Committees............ 297

  XII. Women Members on Specified Types of Church Federation Committees................................ 299

 XIII. Occupation of Members of Specified Types of Church Federation Committees.......................... 300

 XIV. Distribution of Judgments of Church Federation Constituents with Respect to Importance and Appropriateness of Specified Elements of Social Service Programs— 16 Federations................... 420

  XV. Distribution of Annual Income According to Source— 20 Church Federations... 450

PART I

THE GENERAL REPORT

Chapter I

INTRODUCTION

In entering upon the study of organized Protestant coöperation in cities, the first step is obviously to identify and locate the phenomena with which one has to do.

THE PHENOMENA OF COÖPERATION

The antecedents and the practical objectives of the present study predetermined it to approach Protestant coöperation from the standpoint of the interdenominational federations and councils of churches of the major cities. The study was undertaken largely because the federations asked for it, and in the hope that it would throw light upon their practical problems. The federations conspicuously constitute the chief institutional expression of urban coöperation in its interchurch phase, and in every way furnish a natural place for beginning.

THE CHURCH FEDERATIONS: NUMBER AND LOCATION

In the city federations, coöperation is organized in the same sense that the Protestant church generally is organized, namely: out of denominational units, under paid professional leadership, and for the immediate purpose of carrying on a program of religious advocacy and activity. The study was limited to cities, because in no other type of community is Protestant coöperation generally organized in this sense. Indeed, coöperation in this highly institutionalized form is characteristic of only the largest cities.

DISTRIBUTION BY SIZE OF CITY

This is shown in Table I, which distributes the forty-three local church federations reported by the Federal Council of Churches in May, 1929, according to the size of cities in which they are found.

The outstanding evidence of this table is that the proportion of cities in which there are federations very rapidly decreases with decreased size. All cities of over half a million have federations; nearly all cities of 300,000 have them. But less than half the cities of from 150,000 to 300,000 population have federations, and a mere fraction of those below 150,000. Further-

3

more, the proportion that has to make shift with only part-time paid leadership is increasingly high as population diminishes. Fully organized Protestant coöperation is then a phenomenon of the cities, and especially of the metropolitan city. It definitely goes with the complexity of the church of the large city, and it is doubtless complexity that has called it forth. It represents a demand that, up to the present, has been able to find permanent backing and support chiefly in the great centers of population.[1]

TABLE I—DISTRIBUTION OF CHURCH FEDERATIONS, BY SIZE OF CITIES

POPULATION*	NUMBER OF CITIES		
	In U. S.	Having Federations	With Part-time Secretaries Only
Total	138	43	10
50,000 to 100,000	60	6	1
100,000 to 150,000	31	5	3
150,000 to 200,000	13	5	3
200,000 to 300,000	10	5	2
300,000 to 500,000	10	8	1
500,000 to 1,000,000	9	9	0
1,000,000 and over†	5	5	0

* 1925 estimate.
† Counting Brooklyn as a separate city because it has its own federation.

REGIONALITY

It must also be noted that the distribution of city federations is distinctly regional. They are relatively most frequent in the cities of the north-central and western states, somewhat less frequent in the northeastern states, and nearly absent from the southern and south-central group. Except for cities included in larger metropolitan areas, the only city of over 300,000 population lacking a federation is New Orleans. Of cities of from 100,000 to 300,000 population, two-thirds of the north-central and western and two-fifths of the north-eastern have federations; but this is true of only one of the eight southern cities of this size; and no smaller southern city has a federation.

DISTRIBUTION OF FEDERATIONS STUDIED

Of the forty-three urban church federations thus accounted for, nineteen were studied intensively.[2] The Massachusetts State Federation was also studied intensively for the sake of comparison. Limited first-hand studies were made of federations in

---

[1] For proof of the heavy death-rate of federations in the smaller cities, see p. 51.
[2] Baltimore, Boston, Brooklyn, Chicago, Detroit, Indianapolis, Massachusetts State, Minneapolis, New York, Oakland, Philadelphia, Pittsburgh, Portland, Me., Rochester, Sacramento, San Francisco, St. Louis, Washington, Wichita, Youngstown.

five other cities,[3] and in the same way the Ohio State Federation was studied. Six more federations were investigated by the use of uniform schedules in formal interviews with the secretaries, and the remainder by means of reports and data secured from Federal Council headquarters.

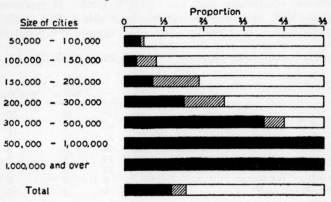

CHART I

Proportion of cities of given populations having Church Federations, 1929

In these federations, coöperation reveals itself as a set of organizations—that is to say, as institutionalized. Much of the spirit of coöperation was in existence in discontinuous and unsystematic form before it became thus established. In taking on definite objective expression and evolving typical forms, federation thus indicates an advanced phase of coöperative association; though probably not the final one.[4]

---

[3] Cleveland, Columbus, O., Dayton, Louisville, Toledo.

[4] *Designations.* The organizations under discussion have two major designations. The older designation was "Church Federation," or "Federation of Churches." This is now slightly less frequent than the term latterly more popular, namely, "Council of Churches." These two designations have been adopted by nearly nine-tenths of the entire number of organizations.

The term "federation" naturally implies something more formal and permanent than a mere council, something based upon more definite agreements; and the recent greater tendency to use the later term may reflect a certain reaction in emphasis. The study, however, could trace no difference in particular claims, nor generally in form of organization, nor in practical authority between the group of organizations called federations and those called councils.

THE MEANING OF COÖPERATION FOR THE ULTIMATE PARTICIPANT

When one consults the rank and file of the men and women of the churches who constitute the constituencies of federations, one finds another aspect of the phenomena strongly insisted upon.

Over 2,800 constituents replied to questionnaires concerned explicitly with the programs and activities of their federations. They constituted a fair cross section of the ultimate participants in these coöperative processes.[5] The most significant aspect of the answers was the fact that these constituents showed themselves relatively disinclined to discuss the more concrete and organizational aspects of federation work. Instead, they constantly and characteristically ran off into expressions of attitude and judgment concerning the underlying issues of church life and fellowship, issues not directly suggested by anything in the questionnaire. Philadelphia constituents, for example, were asked directly, "What do you understand to be the present *work* of the federation?" Only 15 per cent. of the replies referred to any phase of its work; all the rest concerned the major meanings and relationships of the movement, and not any of its particular activities.

The total evidence was exceedingly strong as to the plane of thinking habitually occupied by federation supporters. To them, at least, the federation movement is a symbol of profound tendencies in the Christian church; consequently, it is regarded and judged very much less by what it is and what it is doing than by what it suggests and what it may or may not become as a modifying tendency in the life of the Church.[6]

Three northern organizations designated themselves "The Federated Churches." This term apparently indicates an effort to disavow any organization in addition to, or separate from, the churches themselves. On the other hand, a southern organization now defunct called itself "The League of Churches." Another, formerly the "Committee on Church Coöperation," now appears as "The Christian Council." These sectional variations in terminology probably reflect the already recognized inability of the South to go as far in organized coöperation of the churches as other parts of the nation have found it possible to do.

[5] For forms of questionnaire see Ch. IV, p. 69.

[6] Two similar and illuminating instances of the unwillingness of the average churchman to think of federation or church unity in precise terms of organizational responsibilities and activities have recently come within the author's experience. Both at the last quadrennial session of the Federal Council, and at the Institute of Religion promoted by the Christian Herald in June, 1929, strenuous efforts were made by the projectors of the program to direct the thinking of the participants to a so-called functional approach to the problem. A list of concrete objects which it was believed could better be carried out by the Protestant forces working coöperatively than by separate denominations was first made; then it was proposed to discuss ways of securing those specific objects. Third, the existing coöperative agencies were to be explored with a view to deciding which is best suited to undertake the objects agreed

IDEALIZING FORMULAS AND UTTERANCES

Recognition of federation as a symbol of Protestant religious unity and fellowship also finds expression in official formulas and utterances. Thus, when the earlier phases of the coöperative movement came to crystallization in the establishment of the Federal Council, a constitution was adopted the preamble of which read:

> Whereas, in the providence of God, the time has come when it seems fitting more fully to manifest the essential oneness of the Christian churches of America in Jesus Christ as their divine Lord and Saviour, and to promote the spirit of fellowship, service, and coöperation among them, the delegates * * * do hereby recommend the following Plan of Federation.

Whether or not subsequent performance has justified the initial assertion, this attempt to establish an inclusive Christian institution upon a declaration of common experience, faith, and purpose aptly reflects the historic genius of the Church. All its inaugural statements take the form of a testimony or manifesto. The institution of a civil government sometimes employs the same device, as witness the familiar preamble of the Declaration of Independence. This is the way in which the Church habitually initiates what it thinks to be significant movements.

In the case of the Federal Council, the impulse to testify to the spiritual conviction underlying federation was obviously accentuated by a consciousness of the epoch-making character of the event. This quality has consequently carried over unequally into the localized and more commonplace moods in which the individual federations were established. Seven of them, however, out of the twenty-one cases studied, adopted the Federal Council preamble with minor modifications. Ten more expressed themselves "not in entire forgetfulness" of the high mood of testimony. The phraseology of their constitutions implies that the practical coöperation of the churches which they seek is the realization of a common·moral and religious ideal. Only four constitutions employ a thoroughly cooled-off formula that asserts the mere practical advantage of coöperation with-

---

upon. In both cases the discussion consistently and persistently shied off from the functional approach and repeatedly returned to the discussion of generalities. In other words, the coöperative agencies are regarded as symbols of the will to coöperate rather than as carefully devised instruments for the carrying out of coöperative ends. They are favored on general principles rather than because they are doing well what can best be done in common. Equally they are opposed on general principles by those who do not find them acceptable symbols of cherished ideals, and not because they are doing their work poorly.

out explicit reference to some underlying vision of a better relationship among Christians.

In such unmistakable terms, the federation movement formally defines itself as more than an organization; and this consciousness is unquestionably pervasive even when unexpressed.

Moreover, local federations have their own high moments illuminating the vaster emotional spaces within which formal declarations find place. Such a moment, recapturing the fine rapture of the original impulse of coöperation, finds eloquent expression in the following "charge" delivered to the new secretary of the Greater Boston Church Federation by the president of the organization in 1923.[7]

It is not easy to determine the precise authority with which we install you as the Executive Secretary of the Churches and Religious Organizations of Greater Boston. We represent a large number of the churches, who through their delegates and through their offerings have created this organization, and in theory we represent all the churches of the metropolis, other than those of the Roman communion, for united coöperation in those concerns that we cannot care for in separation or that we can care for with an immense increase of spiritual power and influence by united counsels, by united action, and by united service. But we are persuaded that our authority is both deeper and broader than this, in that we believe that this organization springs from a common consciousness, and increasing sense and desire for fellowship, that is rising to new strength and purpose throughout the whole household of faith, and we judge that spirit of fellowship to have its origin in Him who said, "He that is not against us is for us" and whose prayer was that we all might be *one* with the unity that He had with the Father.

We, therefore, are representing many different creeds and traditions, but united in one common objective, and we trust in one divine spirit of life, commission you to conceive, with us, such plans as will unite us according to our several abilities and convictions, to direct our thought to those great trusts for which we have a common responsibility, to cultivate the spirit of fellowship amongst us by which we can demonstrate to the world that we are one in more and greater things than those in which we differ, and to lead the whole Church in that comprehensive service of this great city's life, that will make manifest that we also have laid down our lives for the world.

In the name of the Lord Jesus Christ, the Great Head of the Church, and by such authority as has been named, I declare you, George Lyman Paine, to be constituted the Executive of this association of churches, and in token, that, in this commission, we associate ourselves and all for whom we may rightly speak, in the same aim, sharing the same responsibility, pledging ourselves to service in the same cause, we offer you the right hand of fellowship,

[7] Rev. Ernest G. Guthrie, D.D.

praying for the divine blessing and power upon you, and the whole Church of God in this place.

Coöperation as expressed in the federation movement is thus an external and active aspect of a situation in which the holding of ideals and values in common by the members of the coöperating group constitutes the inside. These ideals and values furnish the subjective accompaniments of coöperative experience and also supply its logical cause. People belonging to a group coöperate just for the reason that they possess common ideals and emotional tendencies.

In the particular case of the church federations, common ideals find continuous and varied expression. The movement is not old enough for them to be taken for granted—young love must be vocal and keep using the language of affection. One cannot do justice to the present coöperative tendency until one thoroughly appreciates the vigor of this necessity. And one who leaves phenomena of this order out of account will do scant justice to the federation movement.

COÖPERATION AS PRACTICED

The central phenomenon of Protestant coöperation in American cities must be identified however, not with its established organizations on the one hand, nor in flights of idealization on the other, but in the actual body of coöperative behavior in which Protestants are engaged. Behavior, in the scientific sense, is not to be contrasted with thought. Rather it is made up, in the first place, of a more or less definite common body of thought; of the varying attitudes of Protestants of various communions toward one another; of tentative gestures and experimental measures of coöperation which are by no means established as habits and which show a high percentage of failures; of shifting methods determined by processes of trial and error.

The more systematic forms which coöperative behavior takes are too varied to be illustrated in advance. Their story occupies the body of the report, especially the sections on membership and participation, activities, agencies, methods and resources. These deal objectively with the mass of coöperative facts, which are often in contrast both with the organizational form and the sentimental claim.

The outstanding character of the phenomena of actual behavior is that it is rapidly changing as fresh adjustments are reached as a result of practical experiment. This also reflects the relative youth of the movement of organized coöperation.

Here is something in the making, a tendency rather than a completed achievement, something the significance of which is by no means comprehended when chief attention is given either to its organized forms or to its glorious visions. Not the treasure, nor yet the earthen vessels, reveal the essence of the fact, but rather the processes whereby the treasure is progressively placed in the vessels and then poured forth from them again.

This cautionary analysis is the more necessary because it is relatively easy to observe, measure, and record the more completely institutionalized and static expressions of the coöperative movement; while the study of its indefinite and shifting forms is hard. This inclines indolent and superficial minds to see in it "just another organization." And it is of course, conceivable that some one will decide at the end of the investigation that its being "just another" is actually the only fact that has significance. But it would be most stupid and vicious injustice so to decide before beginning. Wherever the values of the phenomena may lie, the phenomena themselves include the three elements enumerated: (1) a central body of coöperative behavior very much in flux; partially expressed (2) by organized federations; and (3) related to, and in part reflecting, large and general ideals concerning a certain unity and fraternity which befits the Christian church.

The Viewpoint

With respect to coöperation in any of its expressions, the present investigation has endeavored to maintain a consistently scientific viewpoint. It has caught the Church, so to speak, in the very act of creating a new order out of its separate organizations. The spectacle may be pleasing to any particular observer, or displeasing. Here is obviously a phase of the age-long controversy between variety and unity in religion. Men are still willing to do each other to death over these revered abstractions. But the scientific observer must not permit any prejudice to array his sympathies on one side or the other.

Even as related to the concrete reality of the Christian church, a scientific study must be exactly as much on the side of diversities of manifestations as on that of the unity of spirit —not because both are assumed to have a common source, but because both are experienced as facts which should be judged by their results alone.

If a real and vital diversity should appear in the midst of a barren and arbitrary unity, science would want it to have a chance to express itself fully and to show its implications. If, on the contrary, an actual and substantial ground of unity should arise to challenge a set of accidental and meaningless variations artificially and stupidly propagated, science would be equally curious to get it out into articulate utterance and self-manifestation. There are four, sometimes five, kinds of Plymouth Brethren in American cities, each constituting a separate denomination according to Census definition. Science is on the side of any vital differences which any one of them may embody. She can have no objection, however, if some other interest goes about suppressing merely repetitious perpetuations of unreal complexity or unreal unity. On her own account she is equally zealous to explore the possibilities of any genuine impulse in either direction.

In this sense only can science be interested in promoting results of any proposals for the advocacy or support of any cause. She can only ask, 'Is the phenomenon vital? Does it appear to be the expression of something operating strongly or significantly beneath the surface? Has it deep roots?' If so, science will very much wish to promote it to the point of getting it expressed adequately. And this is the attitude of the present study.

THE HYPOTHESIS

Absence of bias, of course, does not preclude one from entertaining an hypothesis.

Now, concerning the movement of organized Protestant coöperation in the United States, it is probably a safe hypothesis that it is the expression of evolutionary processes far more ultimate than any mere ecclesiastical reorganization. Parallel with marked processes of secular integration, there has gone on a development towards homogeneity in all the older and major religious bodies of Protestantism. This is a fact more profound than any of the deliberate devices used to foster coöperation or to hasten unity. It harmonizes with the trend toward sameness and standardization of life now so widely recognized as a fateful symptom of the tendencies of our nation and our times.[8] It explains the more or less superficial charge that we are coming to have "chain-store religion."

It has not fallen within the scope of the present study to explore at length the history and course of this deeply significant movement. This has been done recently in a group of competent studies showing how the diverse elements of Protestantism originated, the lines in which they have evolved, and finally,

---

[8] For example, see Bertrand Russell, "Homogeneous America," *Outlook and Independent*, February 19, 1930.

how they have increasingly come to coöperate.[9] The results of this evolution have had elaborate concrete illustrations in the author's series of first-hand studies of the city church made for the Institute of Social and Religious Research; and these studies inevitably supply his background in the present investigation.

For the religious faiths of the city have been imported from many quarters. They have come along with immigrant people from every "tribe and kingdom and nation." Each new element has brought its traditional religious pattern and has proceeded to found its churches and supplementary institutions accordingly. Some of these institutions have survived; many have died; nearly all have moved at least once; and a majority have hard times just ahead if they are not already experiencing them in the flux and struggle of the city's growth.

Meanwhile, the natural assimilating processes have gone forward—recently with accelerated speed. Immigration has been greatly limited. "Self-Americanization" has bettered all the deliberate efforts of Americanizers; and the children of the diverse migratory streams are less far apart, culturally and economically, than their fathers were. The rancor of difference is reduced perhaps even more than the objective fact. But the ecclesiastical forms that grew up out of the original situations continue, though in considerable measure they have ceased to reflect actual human religious attitudes or valid grounds of present segregation in the community.

One striking evidence that religious differences are not really what they purport to be is the fact that the actual memberships of the more representative city churches are denominationally heterogeneous. They draw from many different denominations. In a recent sampling of down-town churches, from 20 to 75 per cent. of members received by letter (as the majority were) were found coming from denominations other than the one to which the church belonged, the average being approximately one-third. A neighborhood survey found 8 per cent. of the Protestant families in an urban district representing mixed denominational allegiance. Some members of the family went to one church and others to another. In spite of surviving denominational differences, the great central body of Protestant adherents—all but a small fraction recognizing one another as evangelical in faith—feels a definite unity in contrast with its

---

[9] Bass, *Protestantism in the United States* (New York: Crowell, 1929). Niebuhr, *The Social Sources of Denominationalism* (New York: Holt, 1929). Slosser, *Christian Unity* (New York: Dutton, 1929).

attitude toward non-Protestants. It is this large measure of essential religious homogeneity that underlies the movement of organized coöperation.

IDENTIFICATION OF MAJOR PROBLEMS

This preliminary analysis makes it possible to identify with certainty the major problems that underly the local coöperative experiments of urban Protestantism.

These experiments stress two points: the better coördination of the activities and functions of the separate units that make up the entire church—its local congregations and secondary agencies, denominational and interdenominational; and the adjustment of the conflicting interests of groups within the larger group, in this case the denominations within the inclusive Protestant fellowship.

The struggle of civilization to keep from being run down by its own material facilities is one of the most familiar phenomena of contemporary human experience. The danger is equally great with respect to the social machinery devised by the modern age to govern human relationships and to accomplish the collective purposes of groups and classes of men. Vast aggregations of specialized institutions and agencies have been brought forth for these ends. Only by ceaselessly scrapping the outworn ones and by continually amalgamating and reintegrating the survivors can man save himself from being ousted by their sheer multiplying mass.

This struggle is most acutely evidenced in the realms of business and industry. Here such combinations as trusts, labor unions, chain stores, branch banking systems, super-systems of transportation and of power distribution, constitute gigantic, though often merciless and uncomprehending, efforts to reduce the disorderly multiplicity of social machinery to manageable order.

The compulsion to keep out of the way of its own machinery or to perish rests with equal urgency upon the Church. Anyone who is even superficially familiar with the facts must be staggered by Protestantism's present organizational variety and complexity, especially in cities; and must be perplexed by what may be called its incidentally but inherently competitive character as contrasted with the purposeful competition of sects that will have later discussion.

Here then is simply the Church's particular version of the age's tendencies. With respect to the total situation that coöperative experiments are trying to influence, the overtopping fact is, first, that it is one of unparalleled complication. Whether the denominational or the coöperative agencies themselves are considered, the American city is a veritable jungle of religious organizations. Minor integrating movements have grown up so rapidly that the cry now goes up: "There are already as many interdenominations as denominations." The growing homogeneity of the Protestant group lifts the fact of complexity into consciousness and exposes its futility. But it does not in itself remedy complexity. All the practical readjustments still remain to be made. The coöperative movement is a series of efforts actually to put such readjustments into effect as will reduce the existing complexity and give an ordered unity to the situation.

A second major problem, that of conflict, is coördinate in importance with that of complexity. The fields of social readjustment are always red, but never more so than in the realm of religion. This is true in the present case, even though partisanship as expressed in denominations is largely a survival, fighting only a half-hearted rear-guard action. The conflicting elements in the situation then, as well as the inherent complexity, stand close to the heart of the problem. Here again, coöperation enters actually to reduce conflict.

One gets a certain light on both problems by asking how far the coöperative experiment has come in dealing with them. Though young in organizational history, the modern movement of coöperation has a considerable perspective; and even within its narrower limits one may note the course and tendencies of its brief career.

These, then, are the three elements of necessary background for the present investigation—the coöperative experiment of modern Protestantism is confronted by the immense complexity of religious organization in the American city, and by the surviving religious partisanship entrenched in the denominational order, and has gone forward a little way in about a quarter-century of articulate history.

COMPLEXITY OF URBAN RELIGIOUS ORGANIZATION

How profoundly complex the situation in the cities is from the standpoint of religion can be disclosed only by an actual inventory and classification of the Protestant religious organizations. In the present investigation, such a process was carried out in more than twenty cities. It supplemented previous censuses and surveys, and utilized all existing directories of religious agencies.

The many thousands of organizations thus reviewed belong

to five orders: local churches; denominational agencies as locally organized; interdenominational agencies; non-ecclesiastical extensions and allies of the Church; and national or regional administrative machinery centering in cities.

This enormous massing about the city church of varied ecclesiastical agencies and their extensions and allies, creates a situation worlds away from that presented by the town and the village. No longer is the local church the only religious agency of the community. Protestantism in the city is pre-eminently a larger church consisting of many local congregations and parishes plus a vast and enlarging array of supplementary and superlative organizations. These further complicate the situation created by the many varieties of local churches and their individual involvement with the other constructive forces of the city. The variations and relationships of these local churches, adding to the vast network of organized religious activity above the level of the individual church, constitute the chief characteristics of the urban religious situation.

The five orders of organizations entering into this complexity are now to be briefly described one after another.

LOCAL CHURCHES

Taking the fifty largest cities in the United States (1920) as representative of the most distinctively urban group, one finds in them nearly eighteen thousand local churches. Each one maintains a worshipping congregation and constitutes a religious fellowship. These are the legally recognized corporate units of organized religion.

Three-fourths of these churches are Protestant. Their average membership (omitting members under thirteen years of age) is three hundred and forty-five. This gives approximately one church for every seventeen hundred population of probable Protestant antecedents. All but 12 per cent. of these churches possess edifices of their own with accompanying facilities exclusively devoted to worship and parish activity.

Somewhat less than one-fifth of the total number of Protestant churches have over one thousand members each, and may be called large; but the most frequent and characteristic Protestant church is a small one with between one hundred and two hundred members only. Its Sunday-school enrollment is not as large as its church-membership. It has a single paid professional minister; it spends less than three thousand dollars annually, and owns property worth not over thirty-five thousand dollars. It is thus a relatively feeble institution. Most of the churches with large memberships have programs correspondingly elaborated beyond the average; and possibly one-tenth have made some deliberate effort at special social adaptation of their services to the needs of their immediate communities.

Possibly from a fourth to a third of all Protestant city churches (and virtually all Catholic churches) have at least a second paid worker. In the case of Protestant churches, the most frequent assistant is a secretary, a visitor, or an ordained assistant pastor. Professional directors of religious education are few; but a scattering of specialists in business, educational, recreational, or social work make up the larger multiple staffs.

These churches have parishes that overlap and intermingle unbelievably. They exchange constituencies back and forth. Their practical fortunes are profoundly interrelated, as the report on comity impressively revealed. Not infrequently they are definitely competitive. Their workers—often duplicating one another—are continually crossing paths and sometimes crossing purposes. Even if there were no more to urban ecclesiastical confusion than this welter of local churches the situation would be cluttered enough.

DENOMINATIONS

American cities of one hundred thousand population and upward have an average of from twenty to fifty Protestant denominations, the number varying according to the size of the city, with over one hundred in Chicago and New York. The number is not larger because many of the smaller American sects are so rural that in most cities they have no churches.

A denomination implies an elaborate set of machinery for the supervision and control of local churches: First, agencies of local church government as such, for example, a district superintendent or similar official supervisor; second, a wide range of denominational organizations with limited functions, such as a minister's association for the discussion of common problems; a church-extension board to found churches, find their ministers and render them financial aid; agencies to raise money for missions and for the operation of this or that church bureau or commission. Finally a full-fledged denominational system will include specialized agencies for religious education, for young people's work, for women's interests, and possibly for men's, to say nothing of a denominational club or "social union."

In what precedes, only that machinery has been described which is regarded as necessary to assist the local churches in the functions they undertake to perform parochially. But a

denomination also has collective undertakings that go beyond
the field of the local church. Thus it habitually maintains
denominational schools and philanthropies. Schools may range
from kindergartens to universities and theological seminaries.
The philanthropic equipment of the stronger denominations in
typical cities consist of a children's home, a home for the aged,
some form of temporary shelter for strangers or needy adults;
also, some agency of poor relief. In the smaller denomination
this list is cut in two, and in the very largest it is increased
by a half through the inclusion of such specialized agencies as
homes for convalescents or incurables.

While the church in the village is simply the local congregation, the church in the city is also this complex group of overhead organizations and of ecclesiastical activities that do not
take local parochial form. The thirteen major denominations
of St. Louis, for example, show a combined total of forty-nine
overhead organizations, including thirteen ministers' meetings,
seven church-extension societies, fourteen denominational organizations of women, and ten of young people, besides an extensive
group serving miscellaneous interests. There were in addition
forty-five denominational social agencies, including twenty-eight
children's, old people's and other homes, eight hospitals, and
nine schools of major rank.

INTERDENOMINATIONAL ORGANIZATIONS

In metropolitan centers nearly every area of the Church's
activity that has been denominationally organized has also its
interdenominational version. Coöperative effort itself, up to
date, has not diminished, but has rather added to, the complexity
of the situation. Organizations of this type constitute the particular field of the present investigation.

The oldest of the interdenominational agencies are the unions
or alliances of Protestant ministers organized for mutual fellowship and counsel.[10]

Next came interdenominational organization in the realm of
religious education. Its accumulated machinery includes not
only comprehensive councils of religious education, but numerous older, and sometimes not fully integrated, agencies like
Sunday-school associations, superintendents' associations, graded
unions and adult Bible-class leagues.[11]

Women's interchurch organizations most frequently take the
form of interdenominational missionary unions or social-service

---

[10] Pp. 158-9.
[11] P. 162.

agencies, one or both of which are to be expected in the typical city.[12]

The typical city will also have its interdenominational leagues of young people, and perhaps, also, of men's brotherhoods. Formerly there were also interdenominational committees on church extension, but virtually all of these have been absorbed in church federations.

Generalizing, one sees that all the major special fields of interchurch interest, as well as the chief areas of age-, and sex-differentiation, are thus covered interdenominationally.

The church federation movement is at the same time the most exalted of interdenominational movements in conception, and the most comprehensive in actual achievement. It undertakes to manifest the essential oneness of the Christian churches through an all-sided program of activity and fellowship, while all others occupy but limited special fields. It is inclusive in genius and undertakes to combine in a given city all of the forms of inter-denominational service into a single organization. In this effort it is not always successful. The degree to which any given federation has actually succeeded in comprehending the interchurch interests in its community, figures as one of the most crucial issues throughout the following investigation.[13]

THE CHURCH'S NON-ECCLESIASTICAL EXTENSIONS AND ALLIES

Beyond the 14,000 local Protestant churches and the denominational machinery in the largest cities, and beyond those interchurch agencies that follow ecclesiastical forms, spreads the vast realm of the Church's extensions and alliances. The city has developed a supplementary network of non-ecclesiastical organizations, ministering not in behalf of groups of churches but as independent and self-perpetuating associations of people of Christian spirit and goodwill. These associations render service to peoples and needs beyond the ordinary scope of the local church's methods and activities, and beyond the agencies of the single denomination. Some of these organizations have received formal ecclesiastical approval as specialized arms of the Church. All look to the Church for moral backing and are financially supported by the Protestant constituency. These allies and extensions of the Church in cities are in general affiliated with national Christian movements, sometimes as branches, more often as autonomous subsidiaries. In either case, their local relationships are complicated by the fact of their larger

[12] P. 169.
[13] P. 180.

ties. Exceptional examples are purely local, like the Seamen's Institutes of certain coast cities.

Chief among churches' extensions and allies, historically speaking, are the Young Men's and Young Women's Christian Associations. The names of these agencies directly reveal their specific concern with particular age-, and sex-groups. A group of reform agencies occupying special fields, like the Lord's Day Alliance, Anti-Saloon League, and Women's Christian Temperance Union, have also always stood very close to the Protestant churches. Bible societies deserve special mention. In addition to the denominational philanthropic agencies, there have developed in different cities Protestant hospitals, protectories, etc. St. Louis, for example, has a total of seven such non-ecclesiastical Protestant agencies.

Certain non-sectarian agencies (which may or may not be similarly related to other faiths) are so frequently identified with Protestant churches that they stand as accepted allies and reinforcements. Illustrations are the Boy and Girl Scouts movements and the Camp Fire Girls, with large numbers of local units under church sponsorship and direction.

The Sunday-school movement nationally considered, though listed in the interdenominational group of agencies, occupies an intermediate position at present. Its status is partly non-ecclesiastical and partly ecclesiastical. It is in process, however, of basing itself more definitely upon authorized denominational action; and is thus working over toward the ecclesiastical group.

Administrative Machinery, National and Regional

A multiplicity of district, state, and national offices and boards of the denominations through which the Church at large is administered, are concentrated in cities and add a final element to the complexity of the urban religious situation.

Their number varies greatly from city to city. On the one hand stand the ecclesiastical capitals, the largest cities together with certain others determined by geography or special advantage. Besides New York, Philadelphia, and Chicago, this group includes Boston, St. Louis, and San Francisco—natural centers for New England, the Southwest, and the Pacific coast respectively, also Washington, as the national capital, and Indianapolis, which ranks beyond its size as the headquarters of denominations whose strength is largely concentrated in the middle and border states. Such cities bear the weight and complexity of the greatest aggregations of urban ecclesiastical machinery.

Still beyond the widest reaches of Protestant coöperation lies the field of coöperation external to Protestantism; first with public agencies such as the schools, philanthropies, and welfare departments of cities, and with voluntary agencies engaged in social service. Of special importance are the contacts and methods of coöperation with councils of social agencies and with the community chest movement. Finally comes the field of interconfessional coöperation; for example, between Protestants and Catholics, Jews and Christians. Both of these fields have brought forth special agencies or agency contacts.[14]

COMPLEXITY OF SUBURBAN RELIGIOUS ORGANIZATION

What is true of city centers is frequently even more true of the outlying communities within metropolitan areas. Suburban residential communities in which Protestantism is strong, frequently reveal an unnecessary wealth of religious organization. It is not unusual to find them sustaining local ministers' associations, local councils of churches, local councils of religious education and local women's interchurch associations, two or more of which are quite generally found in one place. This is to say that the Protestant organizations that most habitually get together in urban federations may remain apart in the much smaller tributary communities. The suburbs thus share the city's organizational complications without always achieving even its partial remedies.

SUMMARY

All the machinery of the church visible, as it exists in the American city, has come to pass according to no general plan and no unity of Protestant purpose. What the city presents is a vast spectacle of churches and allied agencies accidentally founded as to numbers, locations, and distribution. There is a plethora of religious institutions. It could not be otherwise so long as the process of accretion went forward without any realignment and reintegration to match the successive phases of the needs of the rapidly changing city. No rational intelligence would plan such religious institutions of the city as have resulted from the crude struggle for survival. To undo the unreason of the past, and now to substitute a system of religious organizations in the American city, thus becomes a major problem of a generation that is attempting the reconquest of its civilization and of itself in urban terms through the greatest experiment of

---

[14] P. 213.

all times. The issue in its most essential aspects presses upon the Church and would do so entirely aside from any conflicts of special denominational ambitions and purposes.

That the problem belongs to the situation and not merely to Protestant stupidity is evidenced by the complicated internal organization of the Roman Catholic church in the same cities.[15] The problem exists within denominations quite as truly as it does among them. Every communion knows its own competition of "cause" with "cause." The Church in cities has come to perform a large number of different functions in the name of religion. According to the principle of functional specialization in civilization, these have seemed to call for specific agencies.

In a large measure it is in response to the challenging needs of the modern city that these wheels within wheels have come into being; and many of them are honest, though uncoördinated, attempts to meet exigent needs.

No matter, then, in whose hands they may be, the diversified forms of the Church and of religious effort in the modern city constitute a complicated mass of partially antagonistic machinery, which greatly needs to be made into some sort of a system. The church-federation movement with which this book is primarily concerned, is first of all an attempt to substitute such a system for the existing chaos.

---

[15] Appendix I.

Chapter II

DENOMINATIONALISM AND RELIGIOUS PARTISANSHIP

The complexity of organized Protestantism in cities is increased tenfold by its denominational divisions. The persons and the movements responsible for operating the major part of the bewildering organizational machinery are denominational; and their characteristics are what make the machinery work as it does.

Undoubtedly the sharpness of their competition has been greatly mitigated by the passage of time. If the projectors of many of these agencies had it to do over again, they would not now start them in their present competitive forms. At best, however, denominations are the armies of the different faiths. Their machinery developed out of denominational differences; their moods are keyed to the pitch of conflict; their prevalent attitudes bear the brand of such differences and moods even when not definitely created by them. Much of the earlier spirit survives. Any proposal for the effective coöperative coördination of the existing machinery and agencies has to reckon with resistances deep-rooted in the emotional attitudes of religious bodies. Has not God revealed himself in special fullness to each? Is not each, therefore, better than the rest?

There is a certain inevitability of denominational conflict so long as denominationalism exists even in its milder forms. This inevitability discovers itself upon three levels:

(1) The mere effort to define itself and to maintain a consciousness of self-identity compels a denomination to stress its differences from others. It must differentiate itself more or less sharply from all other denominations. It must develop a sense of distance between itself and them. So much is involved in the mere psychological experience of a man or denomination in being an individual.

(2) This necessary differentiation for the sake of self-identity is promptly rationalized into arguments for maintaining the difference felt. The denomination must perpetuate itself for the

22

sake of some mission or other to which it has been appointed for the sake of the generation and the world. It is conscious of possessing unique values, at least historical ones. The sect cannot possess the modesty of the decent average human being. It must exaggerate its original feeling of self-appreciation to enforce the alleged importance of these values for others.

(3) Only finally and only partially does the sense of denominational difference eventuate in the actual clash of direct competitive purposes. As soon, however, as a denomination has acquired a strong sense of self-importance and of the immense value of its contribution to the world, it must inevitably push on to make its enterprises succeed in potential or actual conflicts with those of others. Partisanship thus inevitably embitters the complexity of the urban religious situation.

THE CENTRAL PROBLEM

Consequently the problem of Protestantism in cities is not the simple one of reorganizing so as to retain no more institutional complexity than is demanded by the principle of specialization. The faiths and denominations characteristically feel distinct from, superior to, and in more or less definite conflict with one another. They are not willing to give up the specialized functional activities that are under their own auspices. The immediate problem therefore is to affect so much of the more efficient reorganization as denominationalism and religious partisanship will permit.

Here then is the crux of the federation movement, or of any other version of Protestant coöperation: the breaking down of the will to be organizationally separate and the substitution of the will to be united—at least to some extent and in certain matters. For denominationalism is a massive fact—an enormous force in the thinking and feelings of men. But it works unequally. The denominations do not start from the same point. Some are greatly handicapped; and the reaction of any one of them to the particular appeal or challenge of the federation movement can be measured only in terms of the facility or difficulty which preëxisting differences insert into the situation.

DENOMINATIONAL BARRIERS

How far will denominationalism allow coöperation to go, and to what matters may it be extended? It will require the whole story of the federation experiment to answer this query in detail.

FUGITIVE ILLUSTRATIONS OF EXTREME DENOMINATIONALISM

On the one hand, there is real danger of overemphasizing the virulence of denominationalism as judged by its more extreme expressions.

As the investigation was a scientific study, there was no effort to collect non-representative views. Fugitive examples of attitudes were, however, forced upon it. Some of these may serve to illuminate the temper of violent religious partisanship, and will be useful so long as they are not misinterpreted as representing the average.

Thus in indicating that he believed the Minneapolis Federation was a misrepresentative movement and that the fact that the federation recommended something was "a good reason for not doing it," a Lutheran minister wrote as follows:

> 2 Cor. 6, 14: "Be ye not unequally yoked together with unbelievers, etc." is the main reason why I answer as above. The Federal Council is simply a means whereby certain take-in-everybody Protestants try to yoke together unconverted Jew, Mary-worshipping Roman Catholic, Christ-hating Unitarian. According to the peculiar Modernist mind, that is possible and desirable. Another reason is Dr. S. Parkes Cadman, who states: "With us every bath is a baptism and every meal a communion." Perhaps he did not say that for the Council, but I do not think that *anything he* may say would represent my view.

Another expression of an extreme denominational position making coöperation impossible, is found in the response of the Southern Baptist Pastors' Conference of Louisville, Ky., to the proposed common evangelistic use of Lent:

> To THE LOUISVILLE MINISTERIAL ASSOCIATION,
>   LOUISVILLE, KENTUCKY.
> DEAR BRETHREN:
>   In view of the recent action of the Louisville Ministerial Association in approving a pre-Easter program suggested for use by the various Evangelical Churches of the city, we, the Baptist Pastors' Conference of Louisville, Ky., desire to state that it is not possible for us to coöperate in such a program because of the reasons indicated below:
>   1—We hold that the teachings of the New Testament seem to discourage the observance of any special season or days except Sunday, as indicated in the letter to the Galatians, 4:10: "Ye observe days and months and seasons and years. I am afraid of you lest by any means I have bestowed labor upon you in vain." And again in Col. 2:16.
>   2—The practice of the New Testament churches does not seem to warrant such observances.
>   3—The term Easter seems to be of Heathen origin, derived from the Goddess of Spring, and the Dawn; also the word Lent has a

similar origin (The Spring), and though they apply to the forty days of fast preparatory to the observance of Easter, we cannot feel that such seasons merit special recognition more than other times.

4—On account of the formality and ritualism that has developed in connection with its observance, the laxity in moral conduct following the temporary restraint, the display of fashions that the occasion encourages, we question whether or not the cause of Christ, in all His simplicity, is greatly enhanced.

5—We trust that our position on this matter, which is virtually that held by the [Southern] Baptist denomination at large, will be accepted as a matter of principle which we cannot violate.

Adopted by unanimous vote of the Conference in session February 27, 1928.

Such utterances sound ominous for coöperation. But merely quoting them does not tell how frequent their sentiments are, nor how typical. One does not know from how many denominations similar ones could be drawn, nor against how many and whom they would be directed.

In the present study, therefore, an attempt was made to measure objectively the strength of the sense of barrier or distance between various members of the Protestant groups habitually coöperating in federations, and between them and persons of other faiths and denominations.

THE DIRECT INVESTIGATION OF RELIGIOUS DISTANCE

The instrument used for this investigation and the method of its use will be found in Appendix II. It compared the degree of the feeling of religious distance felt by representative groups of federation members with respect to members of twenty-two faiths and denominations.

The list appears in Table II. It was selected with a view to including the more familiar examples of all major varieties of organized religion existing in the United States which would naturally be considered in average religious thinking. Various methods of measuring the results in terms of the degree of religious distance felt by members of any faith or denomination were possible. As a first basis of measurement, complete disinclination to coöperate with persons of other faiths or denominations in any of the relationships listed was taken as the basis of measurement and given a theoretical score of 100. The actual distance-score of each faith and denomination consequently became some fraction of this theoretically perfect score of total antipathy. The atheist got over 50 per cent. of the total possible antipathy which he would have received if every federation constituent had declined to have anything to do with him

in any relationship whatever. The Methodist got only half of
1 per cent. of antipathy by the same measurement.

Two separate sets of measurements were taken: one calculated religious distance on the questionnaires of 1,002 Protestants in five cities (Boston, Chicago, Detroit, Washington and
Wichita) with reference to nine social and religious relationships
selected from the total list of fifteen.[1] The other calculated
religious distance from 778 questionnaires from four cities (Minneapolis, Pittsburgh, Rochester and St. Louis), with reference
to the entire list of fifteen relationships as they appeared in
the questionnaire, the nine previously measured being included.[2]

The results of these two measurements as related to the
twenty-two faiths and denominations are shown in Table II.
The first column indicates the standing of each faith or denomination for the five cities, and the second column for the four
cities.

TABLE II—SPECIFIED FAITHS AND DENOMINATIONS RANKED
ACCORDING TO DEGREE OF "DISTANCE" FELT TOWARD
THEM BY PROTESTANT CONSTITUENTS OF CHURCH
FEDERATIONS

| FAITH OR DENOMINATION | PER CENT. OF POSSIBLE DISTANCE | |
	5 Cities 9 Relationships	4 Cities 15 Relationships
Atheist	51.6	43.5
Mohammedan	43.8	35.6
Buddhist	43.5	36.0
Mormon	37.1	30.7
Spiritualist	25.7	18.5
Roman Catholic	25.0	15.7
Jew	22.0	17.6
Greek Orthodox	17.2	11.5
Christian Scientist	16.8	12.0
Unitarian	11.7	9.5
Adventist	11.4	6.1
Universalist	9.2	6.6
Pentecostal	6.5	2.8
Salvation Army	2.5	1.3
Protestant Episcopal	2.0	.4
Disciple	1.9	.6
Lutheran	1.8	.6
Friend	1.4	.5
Baptist	.8	.2
Congregational	.7	.3
Presbyterian	.6	.2
Methodist Episcopal	.5	.2

These results, generally speaking, are exactly what would
have been expected. The atheist is by definition "a man with-

[1] Listed in Appendix II.
[2] The denominational distribution of replies in the two groups of cities is
shown in Appendix Table 1.

out a God." He is farthest away in the sympathy of religious people, and is most largely left outside the pale of fraternal relationships. "Heathen" faiths, represented by the Mohammedan and the Buddhist, constitute the next most distant group. The Mormon and Spiritualist rank next, presumably because they are regarded as essentially non-Christian cults. The other four religious groups toward whom a more than average feeling of distance is registered are the Roman Catholic, Jewish, Greek Orthodox, and Christian Scientist.

Toward other faiths and denominations as a whole the questionnaires yield a distance-score of 15.9 in five cities, and one of 13.0 in the four cities. All groups that can possibly be classed as Protestant (unless Spiritualist and Christian Scientist are to be so classified), evoke a less than average feeling of distance. Within the Protestant ranks as thus statistically defined, a distinctly greater degree of antipathy is nevertheless shown toward denominations that the majority of the persons who filled out the questionnaire regarded as not orthodox (Unitarian and Universalist), or as irregular or eccentric (Adventist, Pentecostal and Salvation Army). Within this latter group, however, the degree of distance varies considerably.

Finally, even within the group of regular evangelical denominations, a feeling of distance appreciably greater than toward others is registered toward those that stress liturgy or distinctive historic origins (Protestant Episcopal, or Lutheran) and those that hold some determinative attitude toward religious ordinances(Baptist, Disciple, and Quaker) not held by the majority. The least distance is felt toward the large and well-established Protestant denominations that are evangelical but hold no strongly distinctive emphasis either in the realm of observance or of doctrine.

All told, the feeling of distance among denominations actively associated with the Federal Council of Churches and habitually coöperating in city church federations is relatively negligible. This explains why they are so generally found in these organizations.

Comparison of the distance-scores against even these denominations shows, however, rather large proportionate differences. Thus, the score of 1.9 against the Disciples is more than twice the score of .8 against the Baptists.

The two entirely separate measurements are in interesting and convincing agreement.[3] The distance-score for the nine

---

[3] Appendix Table I.

relationships was greater than that for the fifteen. This is explained by the fact that the fifteen included a larger proportion of non-compromising relationships, like coöperating with persons of other religion in community-welfare movements with

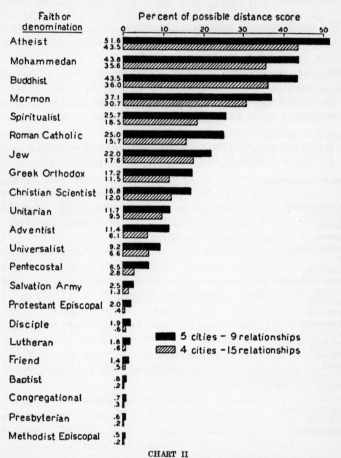

Faith or denomination | Per cent of possible distance score

Atheist 51.6 / 43.5
Mohammedan 43.8 / 35.6
Buddhist 43.5 / 36.0
Mormon 37.1 / 30.7
Spiritualist 25.7 / 18.5
Roman Catholic 25.0 / 15.7
Jew 22.0 / 17.6
Greek Orthodox 17.2 / 11.5
Christian Scientist 16.8 / 12.0
Unitarian 11.7 / 9.5
Adventist 11.4 / 6.1
Universalist 9.2 / 6.6
Pentecostal 6.5 / 2.8
Salvation Army 2.5 / 1.3
Protestant Episcopal 2.0 / .4
Disciple 1.9 / .6
Lutheran 1.8 / .6
Friend 1.4 / .5
Baptist .8 / .2
Congregational .7 / .3
Presbyterian .6 / .2
Methodist Episcopal .5 / .2

■ 5 cities — 9 relationships
▨ 4 cities — 15 relationships

CHART II

Index of religious "distance" felt by Protestant constituents of Church Federations toward members of specified faiths or denominations

respect to which little feeling of distance arose. Only slight differences appear, however, in the ranking of the faiths and denominations on the two sets of measurements. On the longer list of relationships, for example, Mohammedans and Buddhists exchanged places, the Jews rose and the Catholics sank one place in the scale. There were also certain shifts of position in the group that habitually coöperates. All told, however, the close correspondence of results is extraordinary, considering that the data were drawn from different cities and that somewhat different measures were used.

MARRIAGE AND THE PRESIDENCY

The same general feeling of distance found in respect to the total relationships measured is discovered by a comparison of returns from 1,002 constituents in five cities on two separate items, viz: willingness to marry persons of other faiths and denominations, and willingness to vote for them for President of the United States. This is shown in Table III, which should be compared with Table II.

TABLE III—SPECIFIED FAITHS AND DENOMINATIONS RANKED ACCORDING TO DEGREE OF "DISTANCE" FELT TOWARD THEM AS MEASURED BY SPECIFIED CRITERIA

FAITH OR DENOMINATION	PER CENT. OF POSSIBLE DISTANCE WITH RESPECT TO	
	Marriage	Presidency
Mohammedan	72.8	64.4
Buddhist	71.0	63.7
Atheist	68.5	66.1
Mormon	67.2	52.1
Roman Catholic	55.2	39.8
Jew	54.0	23.7
Spiritualist	42.3	21.3
Greek Orthodox	39.0	22.2
Christian Scientist	27.1	10.4
Adventist	21.5	7.4
Unitarian	16.9	5.5
Universalist	12.5	3.9
Pentecostal	9.0	2.3
Salvation Army	4.7	1.3
Lutheran	2.0	.1
Friend	1.6	.4
Protestant Episcopal	1.3	.1
Disciple	1.1	.2
Baptist	.8	.0
Congregational	.4	.0
Methodist	.4	.09
Presbyterian	.3	.04

There is considerably more hesitancy to marry a person of another faith than to vote for him for the Presidency.[4] But at this point very suggestive differences appear in detail. With respect to marriage, it is not the atheist who is most discriminated against, but the alien. The atheist, however, still remains the last man for whom a religious person would vote for president.

---

[4] For measurement by relationships, see Appendix Table 2.

On both measurements, the Mohammedan, Buddhist, atheist and Mormon occupy the bottom of the scale. Next come the Jew and the Catholic, who were ahead of the Spiritualist in the

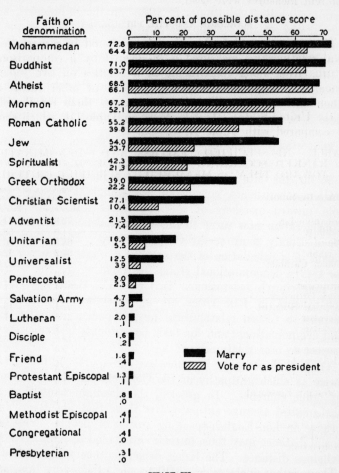

Faith or denomination	Per cent of possible distance score
Mohammedan	72.8 / 64.4
Buddhist	71.0 / 63.7
Atheist	68.5 / 66.1
Mormon	67.2 / 52.1
Roman Catholic	55.2 / 39.8
Jew	54.0 / 23.7
Spiritualist	42.3 / 21.3
Greek Orthodox	39.0 / 22.2
Christian Scientist	27.1 / 10.4
Adventist	21.5 / 7.4
Unitarian	16.9 / 5.5
Universalist	12.5 / 3.9
Pentecostal	9.0 / 2.3
Salvation Army	4.7 / 1.3
Lutheran	2.0 / .1
Disciple	1.6 / .2
Friend	1.6 / .4
Protestant Episcopal	1.3 / .1
Baptist	.8 / .0
Methodist Episcopal	.4 / .1
Congregational	.4 / .0
Presbyterian	.3 / .0

■ Marry
▨ Vote for as president

CHART III

Index of "distance" felt by Protestant constituents of Church Federations toward members of specified faiths and denominations with respect to marriage and the Presidency of the United States.

general showing but fell below him on the two criteria under discussion. With respect to willingness to marry, the Jew and the Catholic rank very near together; but there is very much greater objection to the Catholic as president than to the Jew.

Irregular and non-orthodox Protestants occupy the middle of the scale in much the same order as in the general showing. There is the same appreciably greater disinclination to enter into the relations specified with members of bodies that represent distinct liturgical tendencies or stress on the ordinances, while only shades of the feeling of distance emerge between the denominations that have the largest relative representation in the sample.

One also notes a great easing-up of prejudice with respect to irregular Protestants in the matter of the Presidency; on the other hand, there is nearly as great objection to voting for, as there is to marrying, the Buddhist, Mohammedan, or atheist.

DENOMINATIONAL DIFFERENCES IN THE FEELING OF RELIGIOUS DISTANCE

So far, the data presented have shown the attitudes that federation constituents, considered as a single Protestant group, hold toward members of specified faiths and denominations. Consideration now turns to the separate denominations. Some are distinctly more sectarian than others. This is shown by means of a calculation of the average distance-score per person for twelve denominational groups representing the constituencies of nine church federations. In Chart IV, the results for 778 constituents in four cities are again shown separately with respect to fifteen relationships toward persons of other faiths and denominations; and for 1,002 constituents in five cities with respect to nine relationships.[5]

On this showing the extremes are far apart. Lutherans have twice as much antipathy as the Congregationalists to members of other churches. In general, the denominations that show the greatest average antipathy are those that find their historic origins in non-English-speaking stocks of people. Vestiges of social distance may thus, in their cases, tend to reinforce strictly religious distance. The larger denominations stand exceedingly close together at the middle of the scale. Judged by this sample, Baptist, Presbyterian and Methodist manifest very similar reactions. The least feeling is registered by denominations that have traditionally professed religious breadth and inclusiveness.

A comparison of the two sets of measurements reveals a strong tendency to agreement; but in the five cities, Methodists and Episcopalians register less distance-feeling than do Disciples.

---

[5] For list of cities and distribution of cases by denominations p. 486.

DISTANCE-FEELING BETWEEN PARTICULAR DENOMINATIONS

A calculation of the way in which each denomination distributes its feelings of antipathy or fraternity among other denominations, involved statistical processes too extensive for formal presentation. With respect to any denomination one may, however, by taking the total distance-score as a base, quickly read off from the results, in terms of deviations from the average, a list of other denominations whom it especially loves in contrast with those whom it tends to hate. The results

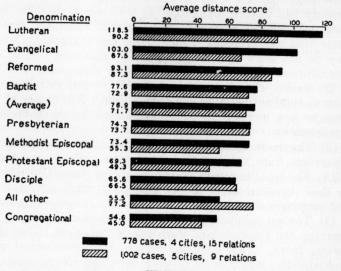

CHART IV

Average score of religious "distance" felt by Protestant constituents of Church Federations of specified denominations toward members of other faiths and denominations

of this process, as worked out for the 1,780 Protestant constituents in nine cities, may be generalized as follows:

(1) Mild antipathy is mutual. Those regular Protestant denominations that are set by the majority at a single step's distance—according to hypothesis, on account of their special stress on liturgy or observance—reciprocate. In turn, they show a slight but appreciably increased antipathy to the denominations that constitute the bulk of the membership of the federation movement. It is a speculative question how cause and effect are interrelated in bringing about this result. Specifically, however, the Episcopalian and the Lutheran are harder on the Baptist, the Congregationalist, the Presbyterian and the Metho-

dist, than these latter denominations are on one another. But the Lutheran and the Episcopalian discriminate to an equal extent against one another. The Episcopalian also shows notable antipathy to the Quaker, presumably because the forms of religious worship of the two are so antithetical.

(2) With regard to the non-evangelical Protestant bodies, the sterner judgments come from the more Calvinistic sources, or from religious bodies whose antecedents are non-English-speaking. On the other hand, the most easy attitudes toward non-evangelicals are held by denominations with which these formerly had historic affiliations; or with which they are intimate geographical neighbors. The returns strikingly demonstrate that the orthodox dislike those non-evangelicals whom they do not know by direct neighborly experience. Small denominations that are not distributed widely throughout the cities of the nation, and that are predominantly rural in experience, show unusual antipathy to non-evangelicals. This dislike of the stranger is a sociological phenomenon even before it becomes a religious one.

(3) The more rigid and Calvinistic bodies also feel wider separation from the irregular Protestants. From a different angle, Episcopalians register themselves as especially adverse to those irregular sects whose religious services are informal and seemingly disorderly.

(4) Toward members of the Greek Orthodox church, on the contrary, the Episcopalians alone among Protestant bodies show special favor. This doubtless reflects the ecclesiastical good understanding which exists between these two communions.

(5) Protestant antipathy to Jews runs very equally from denomination to denomination. Toward Catholics, however, the Lutheran and the Episcopalian are appreciably more favorable than are other Protestants. The Disciples are most aggressively opposed.

(6) Five groups, the atheist, the Mohammedan, the Buddhist, the Mormon, and the Spiritualist, are especially singled out for antipathy by all regular Protestants such as make up federation constituencies. With respect to these, no significant denominational tendency appears. They are disapproved cordially and with one accord.

While the explanations suggested by the above six paragraphs are confessedly open to question, they get substantial reinforcement from facts that are to come out in the later evidence. The denominations with virtually no antipathy to one another are just the ones that habitually and fully coöperate in federations. Those with slight antipathy—but enough to be felt—coöperate irregularly and partially. Those that the sterner majority frown upon, get included in federations only in regions where these major denominations are ecclesiastically weak, or where, as especially in New England, their attitudes have notably been tempered to greater liberality. In brief, the consistency of the two sets of phenomena becomes impressive. This point deserves and will have further comment.

HOW CITIES DIFFER WITH RESPECT TO RELIGIOUS DISTANCE-FEELING

Table IV ranks nine cities according to the degree of religious distance actually felt by their federation constituents toward all faiths and denominations other than their own; and in each case indicates the degree in terms of its per cent. of the highest possible distance-score.

TABLE IV—DEGREE OF "DISTANCE" FELT TOWARD OTHER FAITHS AND DENOMINATIONS BY CONSTITUENTS IN CERTAIN CITIES

5 CITIES—9 RELATIONSHIPS		4 CITIES—15 RELATIONSHIPS	
City	Per Cent. of Possible Score	City	Per Cent. of Possible Score
Total	15.2	Total	11.7
Chicago	13.8	Rochester	9.0
Boston	14.9	St. Louis	11.1
Washington	15.8	Minneapolis	11.3
Detroit	16.4	Pittsburgh	14.9
Wichita	18.9		

As is explained in another paragraph, the nine relationships were limited to those that carry strong feeling of distance; consequently the average score is larger in the five cities than in the four. While, therefore, the two groups cannot be compared, the total showing suggests that in some cities the coöperating Protestants are appreciably more liberal than those in other cities in their fraternal feeling towards persons of other faiths and denominations.

The average Wichita and Pittsburgh Protestant has about 50 per cent. more antipathy to members of churches other than his own than has the average Chicago or Rochester Protestant.

Some shadow of explanation for such differences may be found in the current reputation of the cities and of the geographical divisions they represent. Thus the cities of the northern Atlantic states, along with Chicago, tend to show smaller average distance-scores, while those of the Southwest and the Northwest, together with that staunch Presbyterian center, Pittsburgh, tend to show higher scores.

VARIATIONS AS RELATED TO SEX AND TO ECCLESIASTICAL STATUS

A tabulation of returns according to the sex and ecclesiastical status of those responding was carried only far enough to show that these were significant factors in the situation. Since, however, the fundamental question was that of the prevailing attitude of the constituency of a given federation whatever the composition of that constituency might be, the measurement of

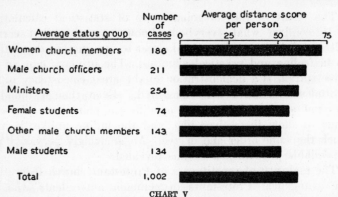

CHART V

Average score of religious "distance" felt by Protestant constituents of Church Federations of specified status and sex toward members of other faiths and denominations

differentiation by sex and status fell to secondary importance. On the 1,002 cases in five cities the showing was as follows:

TABLE V—DEGREE OF "DISTANCE" FELT BY CERTAIN SEX- AND STATUS-GROUPS TOWARD OTHER FAITHS AND DENOMINATIONS

Sex- and Status-group	Number of Cases	Average Distance-score per Person
Total	1,002	60
Ministers	254	60
Male Church Officers....................	211	64
Other Male Church-members............	143	51
Women Church-members	186	72
Male Students (college and theological)..	134	51
Female Students (college)...............	74	55

The tendency, it will be noted, is for ministers to show considerably greater antipathy to members of other churches and denominations than their male church-members do, except when the latter are church officers. Women church-members show more antipathy than any male group and go far beyond the average. The cases of 208 students were included to show the influence of age and of the more modern attitudes presumed to characterize the younger generation. Their distance-scores fall well below the average. Male students, however, exactly equal the distance-score of male church-members who are not officers; while women students, like women church-members in general, show more antipathy than the corresponding male group.[6]

SUMMARY OF FACTUAL FINDINGS

The result of the foregoing series of statistical calculations is to confirm what everybody knows, namely: that certain faiths and denominations stand closer to one another than others do in feeling and practical affinities. The primary gain of the investigation is a demonstration of the great consistency of the attitudes that have been measured. Even though found in different areas and compared on different points, the like continue to show themselves like, and the unlike unlike, in very much the same order and degree. An amazingly pervasive and dependable phenomenon is thus revealed.

The majority of constituents of Protestant church federations are evangelical Protestants of common antecedents who lay no great and distinctive stress on liturgies or ordinances. Others with similar antecedents holding the same doctrine, but with special stress on certain forms of worship and observances, stand at just a little distance from this central core. Non-evangelical Protestants stand appreciably further, irregular Protestants, largely new and erratic, still further. Next come Christians who are not Protestants; then Jews, next heathen, and finally men of no faith. This is the established general order whatever the Protestant denomination, whether the measurement is made in four cities or in five different cities, and whether nine or fifteen relationships are considered.

Second, some denominations are more liberal and others less liberal in their attitudes toward other faiths and denominations. But though the average sense of distance thus varies, the ranking of the faiths and denominations with respect to whom distance is felt remains substantially the same. The more liberal

---

[6] Further occupational and age-variations would doubtless be found by further use of the religious-distance questionnaire. Thus a group of Philadelphia social workers registered the relatively low average score of 53, while members of a young-people's society, not college students, returned the high average of 75. Apart from higher education, youth is not necessarily liberalized.

A differentiation between the religious-distance feelings of rural and city Protestants is also probable. A small sampling of Ohio rural ministers yielded the extreme average distance-score of 77.

denomination simply has for each one a little less, and the conservative denomination a little more, feeling of distance.

Third, there is a considerable and generally consistent variation in the intensity of the feeling of distance from region to region (as measured by the location of cities) and among classes of constituents.

Fourth, with all this consistency, striking variations appear at specific points. Thus, in the comparison of distance-feeling in respect to marriage and to the Presidency, a highly specific objection to a Catholic President appeared which shifted the general position of this communion in the distance-scale.

Finally, an examination of the denominations severally in their attitudes toward members of other individual denominations show specific affinities and antipathies that go to make up the more or less liberal or conservative total attitude of each.

GENERALIZATION

All the phenomena just summarized reveal greater or smaller degrees of like-mindedness. Each denomination registers a maximum of like-mindedness on the part of its own members. Denominations differ greatly in the degree of unlikeness which they actually feel toward other denominations. In contrast with irreligious people, all religious denominations are presumably like-minded. The degree and limitations of like-mindedness are what the investigation has revealed.

Religious unlikeness expresses itself overtly in denominationalism and religious partisanship. These phenomena signify that religious groups have unequal capacity and readiness for coöperation on the instinctive level. That is to say, he that starts to do anything coöperatively at once meets resistances at least equal to the instinctive unlikeness of the elements he seeks to combine.

These elements are undoubtedly capable of great modification by various forms of propaganda and education. But this the investigation was not in a position to measure. How the same 1,780 constituents would fill out the same questionnaire after attending an interdenominational conference on church unity, and how they would fill it out after attending a fundamentalist convention or conclave of the Ku Klux Klan, remains yet to be discovered. The inconsistent attitude, already noted, toward voting for a Catholic as President unquestionably reflected the stress of propaganda during the presidential campaign.

Here then is the central difficulty in the coöperative movement, one with which it must always reckon, but concerning which it is by no means powerless.

Conclusions as Bearing Upon the Problem of Protestant Coöperation

Comparing the statistical results of the formal questionnaire with the fugitive expressions of extreme sectarian spirit quoted earlier, one is enabled to say with finality that such extreme attitudes are not characteristic of the constituencies of church federations as a whole. They represent individual extremes, or else express group attitudes which of themselves keep those who hold them outside the habitual ranks of coöperators.

On the other hand, a close correspondence between the habitual behavior of federations and the attitudes confessed by their constitutencies is equally demonstrated. As will be shown, certain churches are habitually included in the movement of organized Protestant coöperation, while others are excluded; and there is unequal actual participation even of those nominally included. The denominations falling in each of these groups actually show corresponding intervals of the feeling of separation when statistically placed by means of the distance-scale. This is almost certainly a case of cause and effect. Whatever a federation does by way of denominational inclusion or exclusion, it does by reason of the prevailing attitudes of its constituencies toward other faiths and denominations.

The wider gaps measured on the religious distance-scale show what faiths and denominations are too far off in the feeling of constituencies to be brought within the practical scope of the coöperative movement at present.

The middle ranges on the religious distance-scale reveal a debatable zone where the degree of unlikeness is not entirely unsurmountable. These denominations may and do coöperate in part; and the degree of their coöperation varies with the regions in which their cities are located, and presumably with the objective success and promotional shrewdness of the particular federation with which they have to do.

Finally, one finds a substantially interchangeable nucleus of denominations whose felt differences are so slight that they scarcely need to be considered from the standpoint of coöperation in federations. Even these differences, however, may widen or narrow from city to city and situation to situation. The most successful federations know how to minimize local causes of friction, and how to exalt the emotional unity that already exists.

PRACTICAL FEDERATION PROBLEMS

From the standpoint of the maintenance and operation of the federation movement, a policy for meeting the situation is already obvious. A federation must begin by organizing the most like-minded elements of Protestant constituencies; it should continue by securing partial affiliation from the only moderately unlike until the habit of coöperation is established and greater likeness is achieved; it should seek for points of temporary and occasional coöperation with the radically unlike, especially in matters in which all religious people tend toward similarity, as opposed to non-religious ones. These policies will undoubtedly result in a modification of the acuteness of the distance-feelings themselves, to a point which only experience can determine. The practical degree to which such modification will be pushed must depend ultimately upon how the spiritual ideal of unity is evaluated in comparison with the ideal of variety as involving separate organizational ends, and the degree to which variety is finally conceived of as comprehended within a more inclusive unity.

Chapter III

THE CHURCH FEDERATION MOVEMENT

The preceding chapters have introduced Protestant coöperation generically as a spirit and tendency greater than any and all the organized forms into which it has poured itself. The problems of the urban church and of civilization that have chiefly impelled and conditioned the development of coöperation, namely, institutional complexity and religious partisanship, have been analyzed and in part measured. Up to this point, the historic church federation movement has been used only as illustrative of coöperation. Now, however, the study turns directly to the institutional development of the movement. It is, therefore, the story of the origin and evolution of the local church federations that furnishes the theme of the present chapter.

The investigation of these federations, which constitutes the core of this study, was essentially one of contemporaneous institutions. Consequently the historical phase of the study is deliberately limited, and passes lightly over a labyrinthine array of antecedent factors. It recognizes in the movement of organized Protestant coöperation no seamless robe, but rather a patchwork of various fabrics and textures. Whether seen in the light of one or another of its original motives or in its present-day variety, the movement appears as a coat of many colors. Furthermore, some of the original tints have faded; the dominant colorings have not always remained the same.

It therefore becomes necessary to deal very summarily with a highly complicated and, at the same time, shifting body of phenomena. The present section constitutes such a summary. It compresses within bold outlines what is judged most necessary for one to know in order to understand the church federation movement. It seeks, not to narrate organizational happenings at length, nor by particular dates with reference to particular personalities, but rather to disclose vital turning points of the movement's evolution. Its primary function is to sensitize the attitudes of the reader toward the organization as a living movement of the present.[1]

---

[1] In addition to the recognized literary authorities in this field, the sources drawn upon in the preparation of this historical sketch are of six sorts:

ORIGINS AND COURSE OF DEVELOPMENT

The more remote origins of the modern church federation movement may be discerned in various proposals for organized Protestant coöperation, especially in frontier missionary work, during the first half of the nineteenth century. Its most immediate forerunner was the Evangelical Alliance. This agency was nationally organized in the United States in 1867 as an extension of an earlier world-movement in which American religious leaders had shared. Under its auspices local Alliances were organized in various states and cities, and interchurch coöperation, both in its evangelistic and social service aspects, was established.

Aside from these movements, whose influence locally was generally ephemeral, the agencies most directly related to church federations were alliances or unions of Protestant ministers established in numerous cities. These organizations were primarily fraternal and professional. They were not representative of the churches as such and had no ecclesiastical standing. The Baltimore Ministerial Union, for example, in 1885 announced its purposes and limitations as:

> The cultivation of a more intimate acquaintance and the promotion of fraternal feeling among the various evangelical bodies, the discussion of questions affecting the general Christian life of our City and the securing of united and harmonious action in evangelical and moral enterprises. No matter affecting the distinguishing practices or tenets of any denomination or church represented in the Union shall at any time be brought forward for discussion or action unless by unanimous consent.

Many of the ministerial unions, however, magnified their responsibility and undertook to act somewhat continuously in behalf of the Protestant churches; and many coöperative projects

---

(1) Scattered records primarily in the shape of minutes of organizations; (2) fugitive historical summaries prepared in the regular course of the work of a number of federations; (3) systematic annals such as are published by the Massachusetts State Federation and more briefly by the Rochester Federation; (4) formal histories of which that of the Cleveland Federated Churches presents the most significant example. Two other types of sources emanate from the national federation movement. These include (5) the classified lists of local federations accompanied by brief information in the successive issues of the *Yearbook of the Churches* published by the Federal Council, and finally (6) such general summaries as those found in Sanford's *History of the Federal Council of Churches*, and in *Christian Unity: Its Problems and Possibilities*, compiled by the Committee on the War and the Religious Outlook. A recent brief historical sketch, treating of the federation movement exclusively from the standpoint of the Federal Council as an organizing agency, appeared in the *Church Council News Letter*, a publication of the Federal Council, in May, 1929.

of significance were carried out under their auspices.[2] When therefore, federations came to be formed in cities, the original point of contact on the part of their promoters was naturally the ministerial union. Thus the Chicago Federation in its earliest phase included no laymen, its membership consisting of delegates from coöperating denominational ministerial associations. It was therefore a federation, neither of churches nor denominations, but simply of ministers.

While local federations were most often the children of ministerial unions, other indigenous agencies have had important part in fostering and getting them organized locally. These agencies have been primarily those under lay control, including Young Men's Christian Associations in a number of cases, together with an occasional civic or moral reform movement. Such impulsion at the hand of the extensions and allies of the Church, when the direct representatives of the Church failed to move coöperatively, stands forth as a noteworthy feature in the story of origins.

HISTORICAL SUMMARY

The story of the federations naturally revolves about the founding of the Federal Council of the Churches of Christ in America (1908) as its pivotal point.

With reference to this event, the story divides itself into eight epochs, three preceding it and five following.

(1) Remoter beginnings of coöperation push back indefinitely into the nebulous fraternal impulses of Protestant Christianity in America. They culminated, as has already been noted, in the Evangelical Alliance. (2) The period immediately preceding the organization of the Federal Council of Churches was occupied by a preliminary organization called The National Federation of Churches (1900-1905), under whose auspices local federations were actively promoted. (3) The third period (1905-1908) covers the years between the adoption of the plan of the Federal Council and its ratification by the national gatherings of the constituent denominations in consequence of which the Council came into full being in 1908.

(4) Immediately following the establishment of the Federal Council came a well-marked period during which it promoted branch federations in states and cities (1908-1912). (5) A fifth period following the breakdown of this policy, was initiated by the activities of the Men and Religion Forward Movement.

[2] For statement of present relations between ministerial unions and church federations, see pp. 158 ff.

Its results were conserved within the Federal Council under the auspices of a Commission on Federations. This commission, from 1915 on under the secretaryship of Rev. Roy B. Guild, D.D., was responsible for the establishment of the most important local organizations.

(6) The World War (1918-1919) constituted a sixth period characterized by the influence of special war-time commissions and the focussing of church federation effort upon expanded coöperative movements comprehending all constructive agencies of communities. These stimulated the organization of new federations in many cities.

The more recent past (1919-1929) falls into clearly distinguishable subdivisions. (7) The first, characterized by a distinct slowing up of new local organizations, terminated in the resignation of Dr. Guild in 1924. This was followed (8) by the contemporary period marked by a similar dearth of new organizations; but also by renewed effort, understanding and appraisal, and a mustering of resources for a new start.

HISTORY BY EPOCHS

The significant story of increasing Protestant coöperation falls within the framework just sketched. It has now to be told briefly for the more important periods.

THE IDEALS AND INSTITUTIONS OF THE FOUNDERS

The Evangelical Alliance was an international fellowship of Protestant churches through delegated representatives. It held meetings from country to country. It was a gesture of unity, a testimony to the general instinct of fraternity. As a practical movement it was loosely conceived and on such broad lines that questions of its implications for the general ecclesiastical life did not quickly emerge. It proposed a brief creedal statement of the evangelical faith, and undertook certain declarations of common conviction on moral questions; it brought Protestant world-sentiment to bear upon the ills of oppressed minorities in eastern European countries; it engaged sporadically in international works of mercy.

EFFECT OF THE EVANGELICAL ALLIANCE ON CHURCH POLICIES

The attempt to apply ideals stressed by the Evangelical Alliance to local American situations may be traced in early action with respect to comity as related to church extension. The matter was discussed at length, for example, in the *Pres-*

byterian Monthly Record.[3]   The discussion had particular reference to competition between Presbyterian and Congregational churches. The article noted that forty small places in Iowa had both Congregational and Presbyterian churches. A subsequent article in the same magazine cited sixty-nine places in Illinois and twenty-three places in Michigan,[4] each of which had a Congregational and a Presbyterian church, and stated that in these three states there were eighty-five places with both Congregational and Presbyterian churches where neither church had a membership of more than sixty. A plan put in operation to deal with this particular form of overlapping was not at the outset particularly successful. The Presbyterian Board, in its Annual Report for 1877,[5] reported that the plan was ineffectual. The plan was, however, quoted in the *Presbyterian Monthly Record* for November, 1874,[6] and was favorably noted by the General Assembly in 1875.

ATTITUDE TOWARD CHURCH UNITY

Because it covered the whole of Christendom and did its thinking on a scale so vast as manifestly to make any corresponding organizational unity out of the question, the Evangelical Alliance was the more able to concern itself with ideals of unity. The reunion of churches consequently was one of its repeated themes of discussion for over thirty years.

Only during the last years of the Evangelical Alliance was this ideal expressed within practical terms of ecclesiastical order or polity, or enunciated as a possible formula for concrete realization. What is recognized as a classic statement of such a formula was made by the veteran Philip Schaff at a meeting of the Alliance held in Chicago coincidentally with the World's Parliament of Religions in connection with the Columbian Exposition in 1893. In his address on the "Reunion of Christendom," Dr. Schaff declared for a federal type of union, defined as follows:

> Federal or confederate union is a voluntary association of different churches in their official capacity, each retaining its freedom and independence in the management of its internal affairs, but all recognizing one another as sisters with equal rights, and coöperating in general enterprises, such as the spread of the gospel at home and abroad, the defence of the faith against infidelity, the elevation of the poor and neglected classes of society, works of philanthropy and charity, and moral reform.

---

[3] Issue of November, 1873, p. 349 ff.
[4] Issue of November, 1873, p. 349 ff.
[5] P. 637.
[6] Pp. 321 ff.

THE SOCIAL GOSPEL

While the Schaff formula may be taken as the culmination of the main stream of Evangelical Alliance thinking, it by no means expressed the special convictions that dominated the active leaders of the movement during the decade immediately preceding the organization of the Federal Council. Nothing is more plain than that these men regarded Christian unity, not merely as an end glorious in itself, but more as an effective means to what they had most at heart, namely, the social applications of religion. From 1890 on, and through all the years during which the Federal Council movement was taking on shape under their very hands, the officials of the Evangelical Alliance and the organizers of parallel efforts directly antecedent to the movement were in the forefront of agitation for a new "social gospel" and among the most forceful advocates of its claims. They had been moved by the "bitter cry" of the poverty and sickness of the city masses, and stirred by the scandalous misgovernment of American cities. Characterizing the national conference of the Evangelical Alliance in 1887, its then secretary, Dr. Josiah Strong, wrote:

> This movement sprung from a recognition of the perils which threaten our Christian and American civilization, and the great social problems which press for solution. It is believed that the Gospel of Christ affords the only safeguard from these perils, and the only solution of these problems. But how is it to be applied? A very large proportion of the people, 'the masses,' do not enter the churches. The leaven which alone can leaven the lump is not mingled with the meal. If the people will not come to the churches, the churches must go to the people.

The typical viewpoint was pointedly expressed in the slogan of the 1887 conference "National Perils and Opportunities," rephrased for the 1889 conference as "National Needs and Practically Applied."

Dr. Strong focalized his interpretation of the Church's social mission in his classic volume *Our Country,* and later in *The Challenge of The City.*

The diffusion and attempted local application of similar convictions as to the social implications of the Gospel led, in the early nineties, to the development of somewhat numerous institutional churches in cities. Their leaders united in 1895 in founding The Open and Institutional Church League. The League's platform included the following pronouncements:

> As the body of Christ, the open or institutional church aims to provide the material environment through which His spirit may

be practically expressed. As His representative in the world, it seeks to represent Him psychically, intellectually, socially and spiritually to the age in which it exists.

Thus, the open or institutional church aims to save all men and all of the men by all means, abolishing so far as possible the distinction between the religious and the secular, and sanctifying all days and all means to the great end of saving the world for Christ.

While the open or institutional church is known by its spirit of ministration rather than by any specific methods of expressing that spirit, it stands for open church doors every day and all the day, free seats, a plurality of Christian workers, the personal activity of all church members, a ministry to all the community through educational reformatory and philanthropic channels.

The Open Church League had direct organizational connection with the earliest city federation, that of New York City; and its secretary, Dr. E. B. Sanford, became the organizing official of the National Federation of Churches and the first executive of the Federal Council after its organization.

What the National Federation of Churches was thinking and talking about in the years just preceding the Federal Council appears from the report of its proceedings in 1905. Its interests as there expressed covered coöperative religious activities in evangelism, city missions, and the establishment of institutions for sailors in seaport towns; also in special religious effort on behalf of students in state universities, and correspondence with Protestant bodies in Europe.

But a far longer list of addresses and discussions concerned social issues. In the field of public morality, these covered marriage and divorce, Mormonism regarded as a menace to the American home, Sabbath observance, commercialized recreation, and the liquor traffic. Political corruption was denounced, and the return of the Bible to the public schools advocated. Matters of public charity and of the Church's care for the poor were actively discussed. Specific attention was given to child labor, immigration, tenement-house reform, strikes and lock-outs, and prison reform. Finally, ecclesiastical interests and relations were involved in discussions of comity in home missions, union for foreign-mission work, and a closer alliance of the young people's movements, the Young Men's Christian Association, the Young Women's Christian Association, and the Women's Christian Temperance Union, with the Church. The report of Dr. Washington Gladden, as permanent chairman of the executive committee, spanned a wide range of issues from most detailed suggestions of how to district cities so that the care of the "Church's poor" might be attended to without duplication, to the all-inclusive declaration that the churches have responsibility for resisting oppression and securing freedom "for humanity in every part of the world."

All this signified that the aggressive leadership of the coöperative movement was beginning to vision the Church as having a mission greatly conditioned by the distinctive features of the modern world. The characteristics of the age were being viewed somewhat objectively. They were being subjected to analysis and interpreted as a series of evils which the Church has to combat. The first impulse was to attempt to meet them by the practical missionary devices then current, including emphasis upon organized personal evangelization. Gradually, however, emphasis came to be directed to two things; first, the large-scale betterment of social conditions; and, second, the remedying of administrative evils. These were novel emphases for the Church, not at that time adequately stressed by any body of opinion in the nation. It thus turned out that, by way of the slums and through the method of muck-raking, these leaders of the coöperative movement made a recognized place for themselves among the pioneers of the American social thought.

In such hands, social motive was the primary dynamic of coöperation. So great a challenge could be met only by united effort. It was simply assumed that a socially motivated church could not be sectarian. Such conviction coalesced with more general impulses toward greater religious unity which had incarnated themselves in the Evangelical Alliance. The difference was that these leaders were primarily concerned with unity for the sake of power to meet the social challenge of the city and of the nation. This they sought without waiting for an organic union of churches; and thus they anticipated most hopefully from the various forms of federative coöperation of churches culminating in the historic church federation movement.

LOCAL FEDERATIONS ANTEDATING THE FEDERAL COUNCIL

As a product of the new social movement within the Church, the New York City Federation was established in 1895; and in the following year came under the long-continued and epoch-making secretaryship of Dr. Walter Laidlaw. Partly as indigenous movements, but partly because of aggressive promotional campaigns of the national agencies preceding the Federal Council, long lists of similar organizations now began to be reported. The states of New York, Ohio, and Rhode Island were formally organized in 1900 and 1901 respectively. Albany, Detroit, Chicago, Jersey City, Hartford, Portland (Maine),

Rochester, Schenectady, Syracuse, Toledo, and Utica are among
the points where the evangelists and organizers of the new
movement supposed that they had effected permanent local
organizations.[7] But of all the federations named, those of
Massachusetts and New York City are the only ones that have
had a continuous life under paid leadership from the time of
their foundation.

ORGANIZATION OF THE FEDERAL COUNCIL

The phenomena of the coöperative movement, national and
local, run hand in hand. It is pertinent, therefore, to account
movements resulting in the establishment of the Federal Council
as essential to the story of the present localized movement.

The work of the National Federation of Churches went forward
from 1900 under an influential committee maintaining a salaried
staff and able organs of publicity. It culminated in 1905 in an
interchurch conference on federation, held in New York City,
which formally adopted the scheme of organization for the Federal Council, subject to the action of the constituent ecclesiastical
bodies. The favorable action of a majority of the more important ones was secured during the next three years; and the Federal Council was accordingly fully organized in 1908.

As in similar cases where a movement has passed over into an
institution, there is much in the story to make one question
whether the organizational climax did not signify a spiritual
anticlimax. It is perfectly evident that as the federations developed, its quality was modified. It did not harden into institutional forms without straining out something of its original
genius. In its more fluid stages its leadership had rested in
prophetic hands. With the establishment of the Federal Council
it was transferred to a place within the ecclesiastical system and
became an adjunct to the existing denominational order. Shortly
before the final merging of the Evangelical Alliance in the new
federation organization, its distinguished secretary, Dr. Josiah
Strong, had withdrawn from its leadership. His primary interest
was in the social gospel. This could be only a minor part of the
general coöperative concern as dominated by average church-
leadership. He was too single-hearted for the transitional years
through which the movement he had directed was getting back
upon the main track of official acceptabilty. In short, the adjustment of the coöperative movement to a national scheme of fed-

---

[7] In response to the question, "When was your federation organized?" few
cities now cite these earlier dates. They do not recognize the continuity of
their present organizations with those founded in this period.

eration based strictly upon denominational representation and a formal delegation of authority, implied a radical shifting of mood. The movement was set back to the position, and compelled to take the pace, of the slower of the denominations and of the regions they represented. More and more stress was laid on official denominational agreements in the establishment of local federations and in the conduct of the various departments of the general work. However, the change of mood was not complete. There are many evidences that the earlier and later spirits have continuously struggled and are still struggling within the movement.

How many city federations were actually and vitally alive at the date of the founding of the Federal Council cannot be ascertained exactly from published data.[8] It is clear, however, that there were very few *bona-fide* ones. Consequently, the significant history of the diffusion of the movement concerns primarily the subsequent two decades.

PROMOTION OF LOCAL FEDERATION BY THE FEDERAL COUNCIL

The first wave of organization, simultaneously with, or directly promoted as the result of, the establishment of the Federal Council, included federations in Chicago, Portland (Maine), Philadelphia, and St. Louis, soon followed by those of Baltimore, Boston, Columbus, and Louisville. Cleveland organized in 1911 in a somewhat independent attitude. On the other hand, Indianapolis, organizing in 1912, was one of the few federations formally to declare itself a branch of the Federal Council of Churches.

The second phase of federation under Federal Council auspices was marked by the abandonment of the effort to found branches of closely predetermined pattern, and by more scattering organizations generally of smaller cities than those covered by the first wave. In this phase the development of suitable local programs was greatly stimulated by the inventories of community need undertaken under the Men and Religion Forward Movement.

THE WORLD WAR

The World War inserted a hiatus into the federation movement. During the war-years preceding American participation in the conflict, almost no federations were founded. The results of the first phase of experience were, however, gathered up into

---

[8] Sixteen state federations "and commissions" were reported, in contrast with only six fully organized ones which exist today according to the Federal Council 1929 list.

a manual of methods, and the movement began to register its permanent traits.

With the entry of the United States into the war, on the contrary, a rapid expansion of the federation movement began. The forces of the Federal Council, associated with others, pressed the organization of War Councils of Churches. In these Councils, the ecclesiastical viewpoint was largely held in abeyance, and other agencies such as Young Men's Christian Associations and Young Women's Christian Associations were temporarily associated with the churches in the effort to promote national morale and to meet those acute religious and moral situations in cities that arose with the expansion of the military establishment, war-time industries and the moral stress and temptation of the period. Nearly one-third of the existing federations take their origins from the three years, 1918-1920. They include Boston, Detroit, Kansas City, Rochester, Washington, and Wichita.

THE RECENT PAST

The period of recent history exhibits two phases; the first, following the expansion, is again marked by rapid decline in organizations. A few new federations, however, date from this period, including those of Minneapolis and San Francisco, which were established in 1922.

The last five years—1924-1928—have been marked by administrative changes in the personnel and machinery by which the Federal Council promotes local federations, by an almost complete cessation of the forming of new organizations, and by the lapsing of a considerable number of those that originated in earlier periods. Eight of the nine federations dating from the post-war period do not maintain full-time secretarial leadership. This strikingly demonstrates an era of diminishing returns.

No complete historical record of local federations from the beginning has ever been compiled. The foregoing history has accordingly been drawn in the main from data afforded by federations that still survive. These, however, have constituted the backbone of the movement, and their story is a sufficient indication of the epochs through which the whole has evolved.

TRENDS OF EVOLUTION

THE TYPICAL LIFE-CYCLE

Turning to a closer analysis of histories of individual federations, it is obvious that only those originating in the first wave of organization have had sufficient time to show typical cycles of development. Their stories, however, tend definitely to fall into four periods.

In the earlier years, during which they were generally served by voluntary or part-time secretaries, the movement as such had not developed either typical methods or accepted leadership. The promotional influence of the Federal Council had to be continuously exercised, and the older coöperative agencies generally persisted in the cities side by side with the federations. This phase was followed in the majority of cases by a period of actual or virtual lapse. As earlier workers disappeared, the organization ceased to function actively, and much of its work reverted to the Ministerial Alliances or fell apart into the hands of committees organized for separate interest. This tendency was fortunately counteracted by the Men and Religion Forward Movement which culminated in a plan of "conservation," in the terms of which the divergent emphases tended to become unified and standardized in a single coöperative ideal.

The third phase was founded in the sharpened emphases and tightened organization of the war-period. This gave way in turn to the recent period of typical development, during which aims and methods have been measurably defined, limitations recognized, and standards glimpsed. In short, the surviving federations have now begun to find themselves.

Running through these evolutionary cycles of the older organizations, certain trends may be discovered which are fairly characteristic of the movement as a whole.

PROGRESS SELECTIVE RATHER THAN INCLUSIVE

(1) The movement has suffered many failures, measured by the frequent lapse or extinction of federations. Progress has been selective rather than inclusive.

As reported by the Federal Council in May, 1929, the official list of city church federations employing paid leadership for full-time or part-time, includes forty-three cities.[9] At least half as many more federations have been reported in the same category at different times since 1920. These have either lapsed entirely, have ceased to employ paid workers, or are no longer functioning as federations. Several more have had to accept greatly diminished status and narrowed programs, involving either the substitution of a part-time for a full-time executive or the employment of much cheaper leadership than formerly, generally by the substitution of a woman secretary for a man.

---

[9] P. 4.

More than half of these lapsed federations were located in cities of under 200,000 population. The most obvious explanation is that smaller cities find it difficult to secure the necessary financial support for a full-fledged federation program. This generalized explanation is, of course, greatly modified by other factors, among which the quality of leadership is outstanding. But, whatever the cause, there has been a sharp division between the fit and the unfit from the standpoint of survival.

RAPID GROWTH OF SURVIVING ORGANIZATIONS

(2) Relatively speaking, exceedingly rapid growth in backing and resources as well as in scope of program, has been registered by most of the surviving federations. Thus the Indianapolis Federation increased the number of churches supporting it by two and a half times between 1920 and 1928; the Philadelphia Federation had five times as many supporting churches, and seven times as many individual contributors, in 1928 as in 1921. As a whole, the present federations are much more considerable and substantial institutions than an equal number would have been at any earlier period.

AMALGAMATION OF PREVIOUSLY INDEPENDENT MOVEMENTS

(3) A significant part of this growth is owing to the amalgamation of previous agencies with the federation movement. Certain federations from the first definitely sprang from the convergence of previously organized movements. Thus, the Pittsburgh Federation had three roots: first, an interdenominational evangelistic committee dating back to the Wilbur Chapman campaign of 1904, and maintaining a salaried superintendent in its latter years; second, a comity committee consisting of the paid church-extension representatives of the major denominations, whose main emphasis had been upon coöperative understandings in work with foreigners in downtown districts and in the newer suburbs; and third, the Christian Social Service Union, "an agency of the churches and Ministerial Union," which had originated in the Men and Religion Forward Movement and existed for several years as a militant force for social betterment and law enforcement. An editorial in the Pittsburgh *United Presbyterian* noted these three separate lines of organized interdenominational work, commented upon the overlapping character of their appeal to the churches for support, and commended a proposition for combining them in a federation which should be supported through "regular denominational channels." This was accomplished in 1915. Combinations of

organizations previously separate became federations in other cities.

With respect to the movement as a whole, the most conspicuous phenomena of the immediate past are the very numerous amalgamations with federations of agencies that remained separate during the earlier years of coöperative progress.[10] Such amalgamations, or combinations coming short of full amalgamation, have been particularly frequent with councils of religious education and interchurch organizations of women. Such adjustments commonly turn these previously independent agencies into self-administering departments of federations.

EVOLUTION OF PROGRAMS FROM ORIGINAL GERMS

(4) In the large sense, virtually everything found in the activities of federations today was implicit in the earliest definitions of purpose and objective. Indeed, the outstanding characteristics of the movement in its inception were the inclusiveness of its interpretation of Christianity and its stress upon the social gospel as complementary to evangelism and religious culture. But within this broad field, emphasis has shifted from time to time.

As already noted, social service carried over into the earlier church federations little of the original mood of prophetic enthusiasm and expectation, and in the earlier years was not translated directly into their programs. Social-service movements rather tended to appear independently in separate cities and under men of lesser intellectual and spiritual stature than the great originators. When these secondary leaders first come into view, one finds them busy with this or that bit of organization or agitation for reform or constructive legislation. Such independent organizations for social service were in a number of cases later gathered up under the federation banner, as were numerous others similarly organized in behalf of separate social interests. On the whole, however, neither the platforms nor the work of the earliest federations laid great stress upon social service.

By the end of the first decade of the federation movement, however, social service had firmly re-established itself as a generally recognized phase of federation work.

Other comparisons of the earlier with later phases of specific activities appear in connection with discussions of the departments of federation work in subsequent chapters. A major

---

[10] P. 155.

difference in content of program is the considerably greater stress given to moral-reform movements in the pre-war period of federation history, and its considerably more naïve attitude toward social work and community surveys as means of guidance for coöperative programs. In the post-war period, on the other hand, interest in interracial and international justice and goodwill have been relatively magnified.

Again, different federations naturally have stressed different aspects of coöperative work. Thus, the Massachusetts State Federation was primarily devoted to comity and the prevention of overlapping of local religious organizations. The Portland, Maine, organization grew out of the Gypsy Smith evangelistic campaign, and was an attempt to conserve the community values of that movement. New York was for many years primarily interested in the evangelization and Americanization of foreigners, and in geographical and statistical studies of the population with this end in view. The original sub-committees of the Philadelphia Federation included religious education, Sabbath observance, public morality, economic problems, and finances. The earliest federations thus started with one-sided emphases which they later proceeded to elaborate under generous formulas growing out of the inclusive spirit of the movement.

CAPITALIZATION OF EXPERIENCE

(5) The organizational characteristic of the more recent period is the capitalization of successful experience. A small group of effective federation secretaries has been developed. As a voluntary professional group, the Association of Executive Secretaries has much to do with setting the effective standards of this later development. In consequence, the more recent plans and activities of the federations have been developed through discussion and correspondence, and definitely represent pooled experience. Some of the more recent federations have been created according to patterns worked out elsewhere. They thus had the advantage of lessons learned from past mistakes, have started with the full round of normal development, and have quickly come to include a wide range of coöperative agencies.

DISCONTINUITY OF RECENT LEADERSHIP

(6) One of the crucial factors entering into success or failure of any movement is the quality of professional leadership. In the case of the federations, the capitalization of experience has been greatly hindered by the discontinuity of this leadership.

Of present federation secretaries, only five entered the work before 1920. Nine have been continuously employed since that date in the same positions, while two more have changed fields but have remained in the secretaryship. Seven additional secretaries have survived since 1923. All told, sixteen out of forty-three have had a tenure in their present positions longer than the average pastor in the city ministry with whom it is most nearly fair to compare them.

These sixteen secretaries are survivors of an even hundred persons who have been reported as secretaries at one time or another since 1920. Eighty-two of the hundred have now passed out of federation ranks. Since half as many federations have lapsed during this period as survived to the end of it, a partial explanation of the discontinuity of leadership is immediately at hand. But even beyond this instability of the institutions which they serve, the secretaryship has borne the marks of professional tentativeness. Beyond a very slender nucleus, no permanent group of federation secretaries has been evolved.

SUMMARY

Whatever else is true, then, here is history still in the making. The federation movement needs no apology for being young. Yet all the more for this reason it needs painstaking contemporaneous scrutiny in order that analysis and measurement may show whether it has promise beyond what its brief historic trends have had time to reveal. To this further phase of investigation the present report now turns.

Chapter IV

CLAIMS AND RECOGNITIONS

The coöperative behavior of the Protestant churches is far more significant than any or all of their pronouncements about coöperation. The big fact is that the churches join federations and continue to belong to, support and participate in them. It is of but secondary moment that they also talk about, and try to explain this, their conduct. From the standpoint of the reader, however, it will be simpler to begin by letting the federations speak for themselves; just as one hears a man's story before cross-examining him or undertaking an independent check-up of his statements.

Cleverly conducted federations, like all similar institutions, use a variety of methods of interpreting themselves and presenting their claims to the world. These are expressed both officially and unofficially. Officially, they find utterance in formally adopted statements of purposes and objectives, with their sanctions, implied or expressed, as contained in constitutions and platforms; in representative expositions of federation philosophy; and also in promotional and "selling" arguments. Lacking formal dignity, these latter types of expression are marked by a certain authority of immediacy and realism, born either of financial necessity or of controversy. They are thus, on the one hand, cases of special pleading and, on the other hand, revelations of vital logic and working philosophy.

Unofficially, the coöperative attitude is expressed in various utterances of constituents showing what aspects of the federation movement they recognize and apprehend, and what they approve or disapprove as appropriate and rightly belonging to the movement. Certainly what the constituents see it to be, what they judge it as, is quite as much of the essence of the movement's reality as are its platforms or even its organizational structure and current activities.

The chapter accordingly deals first with official claims and pronouncements; then with less formal official representations; and finally with the reactions of constituencies, both favorable and unfavorable, to the total coöperative situation of which the federations' self-interpretation is of course only a part.

OFFICIAL PRONOUNCEMENTS

In starting to discover what the federations say for themselves, an initial difficulty occurs in distinguishing between their several separate voices and that of the Federal Council as the official mouthpiece in the general movement. As in investigations of local federations, the study is bound primarily to consider their own utterances. On the other hand, their historical and present relationships with the national agency make it certain that they have been stopped from elaborating their claims as much as they would have if they had not had the Federal Council to think and talk for them. They recognize the Council as the chief spokesman of the group as a whole; and what it says comes so near to being what they mean, that they see little need of correcting or supplementing it.

At the same time, it seems clear to the writer that the Federal Council does not say exactly what the federations mean; chiefly in that it often says more than they feel. The divergence, in brief, is less one of formula, than of mood.[1] The local federations are dominated by a more work-a-day type of imagination. They have been so chastened by hard experience that their feelings are less exalted. They are on the firing-line, not comfortably at headquarters. They are not stirred to rhapsody in great assemblages, nor by the sense that they are uttering epoch-making words. Their consciousness is humbly realistic, their expression correspondingly restrained. They are so near to the edge of failure that it is not easy for them to think of themselves more highly than they ought to think. For these reasons the present investigation was doubly committed to learning what federation is from the federations themselves, even though the Federal Council's version is also important and partially a substitute for local utterances which it inhibits.

ANNOUNCED OBJECTIVES

The most formal and official way in which federations have explained and elucidated their purposes is through their constitutions. Sixteen constitutions have been systematically compared. These, their basic official statements, ought sufficiently to indicate the range of the concrete objects and purposes which the federations are pursuing.

The sixteen constitutions enumerate a total of fifty-four specific objectives. To what extent these are really distinct from one another is concealed by the obvious uncertainties of language.

---

[1] Pp. 229 ff.

Certain differentiations nevertheless are fairly clear and may be summarized.

Of separate objectives, interchurch coöperation for fellowship, evangelism, or service are professed by twelve federations, while comity in church extension is made a specific objective by eight. This latter objective is most pointedly expressed in the constitution for the Massachusetts Federation of Churches, as follows:

> The object of this Federation shall be to promote coöperation and comity, and prevent waste in the organization and maintenance of churches in Massachusetts.

Next in frequency come mixed formulas to the effect that the object of federation is to promote unitedly the religions, moral, and social welfare of the community. The Portland, Maine, Federation, for example, contents itself with a general statement of this sort. Four federations say that their object is to coöperate with "other religious organizations," and four that it is to coöperate with "religious movements of the community." The distinction intended is apparently between permanently and formally established agencies and the more temporary type of religious campaign. Four federations mention the fostering of community-betterment movements as distinct from religious movements. The Minneapolis Federation has developed a formula combining all three items just enumerated, as follows:

> Its general purposes shall be to promote religious organizations, and to foster religious movements and education for community betterment.

Four federations use some such formula as "The object of this federation is to promote the application of the law of Christ to all the relations of life." One says that it exists "for united and aggressive action upon religious and social questions." Three say that the federation is a movement for the welfare of the churches, without stating wherein such welfare consists. Only a single, lone federation declares that it exists to carry on a body of interdenominational work. This omission of concrete content from the list of objectives is made up for in part by certain enumerations of work which have later mention.

While the average federation enumerates three or four concrete objectives without much evidence of real comprehensiveness, of

balance in statement, or of correspondence to the actual scope
of its program, a few, by combining some element of general
manifesto with specifications as to programs, have managed to
achieve a certain dignity and fullness of suggestion in their
statements. Thus, the St. Louis constitution reads:

> Its objects shall be to express the Christian fellowship of the
> churches of this city acknowledging Jesus Christ as Divine Lord
> and Saviour; to bring these churches into united service for Christ
> and the world; to secure their concerted efforts in matters affecting
> the religious, moral and social welfare of the people; and to pro-
> mote the application of the teachings of Christ to the relations
> of life.

PROPOSED ACTIVITIES LISTED

Still another group of federations—among which are those of
Buffalo, Oakland and Philadelphia—enumerate long lists of specific functional interests along with general objectives. The
Philadelphia Federation says that it was "formed to promote the
welfare of comity and coöperation of the Christian churches in
Philadelphia and vicinity." Other objects specified are (1) promotion of coöperation in evangelism; (2) closer relations among
churches of various denominations and among religious agencies;
(3) consolidation of superfluous churches, the release of church
property and the transfer of equities to other centers; the establishment of churches wherever needed, but the discouragement of
duplication; (4) law enforcement, touch with the courts and
police; coöperation with government relative to the enforcement
of the eighteenth amendment; (5) Sabbath observance; (6) world
peace; (7) industrial peace.

COMMON SOURCES AND ELEMENTS

In comparing constitutional statements of objective, one notes
the influence of the "model constitution" advocated by the Federal Council during its earlier years, and the borrowing of later
constitutions from older ones. Federations copy one another's
phraseology without much discrimination. All told, these formal
statements of objective are relatively blind apart from the study
that is to follow of the conceptions which average men actually
draw from (or in spite of) them, apart also from the study of
concrete federation activities and of the specific sanctions and
purposes which are attached to them. What one would gather
who had no evidence other than the formal statements is: (1)
that coöperation is the more or less undefined good which is
sought; (2) that avoidance of competition in church extension

is a major goal; (3) that coöperation with religious organizations and movements of the community other than ecclesiastical is an outstanding objective; and (4) that the social applications of religion are to be unitedly promoted.

FEDERATIONS AND CHURCH UNITY

A much debated article in the constitution of the Federal Council declares that it was established "to express the fellowship and Catholic unity of the Christian Church." In adopting the preamble of this constitution as their permanent basis of union, as several federations have done, nearly all have omitted this reference to church unity. An interesting variant is introduced by the Detroit constitution which substitutes the clause "anticipating a closer union in the future." No other direct acknowledgment of church unity as an objective appears in any constitution.

OFFICIAL EXPOSITIONS

Federations define themselves by means of official expositions as well as in authoritative basic declarations such as the last paragraphs considered. What they say through this medium is not, however, a single harmonious word. Among the hundreds of pieces of promotional literature that are issued monthly, and the thousands of addresses annually delivered by officials, one seeks in vain for a typical utterance so strong and compelling as to serve as an adequate formula for the total fact. Dealing as the federation does with virtually the total round of Protestant church concerns, its problem of exposition is almost like that of getting the whole compass of the Christian religion into a single statement. Promoters simply put forward what they think is the best foot, considering a given time or circumstance. Their tone in the main, is naturally conciliatory and defensive: "Our objective is to supplement sectarian and parochial expressions of Christianity by expressions of Christian coöperation"; or "The federation is not a program-building agency, nor a super-church, but an organization for fellowship in service, in spite of theological differences." These obviously are not complete or critical utterances; and it is highly significant that while the federation movement has made considerable progress toward the exposition of its program,[2] it should have done so little unitedly toward a statement of its philosophy. There is a real paucity of recent authoritative formulations. One suspects that this is

---

[2] For example, in Pittsburgh and Cleveland.

because in the present state of coöperation it is much easier to agree upon concrete measures than upon theoretical statements.

FUNDAMENTAL PRINCIPLES IN COÖPERATIVE WORK

The experience of local federations has, however, been systematically pooled at various times by the studies of commissions: and the main features of a common working philosophy have been shaped, notably by the "Church and Community Convention" held in Cleveland in 1920 under the joint auspices of the Commission on Councils of Churches of the Federal Council of the Churches of Christ in America and the Association of Executive Secretaries of Church Federations. There were fifty executive secretaries at the time of the Convention. The results of such processes, though now a decade old, may still serve as the best authoritative summary of federation principles as localized:[3]

THE CHURCHES IN SIMULTANEOUS COMMON ACTION

Whenever there are two or more churches in a community, there at once appear certain purposes and certain activities common to all or to a majority of the local churches, which may be more advantageously and more effectively realized if carried on in coöperation or simultaneously. The arrangement for such coöperation requires some kind of interchurch committee or council. These activities may be as simple as the preparation for a union Sunday-school picnic or as complex as the conduct of a highly organized every-member canvass, house-to-house visitation, or evangelistic campaign. All that this principle involves is a plan by which the churches can carry on simultaneously and in full harmony the activities which the churches are all caring for separately, and which they would carry on each in its own way were it not for the very decided advantage of getting action at one and the same time on the same objective by all the churches in the community.

Coöperative and United Church Action. In developing the spiritual resources of a community, in maintaining the highest moral ideals, and in establishing justice and righteousness on the earth, certain forces need to be released and certain attacks made against centralized and organized evil which require more or less highly specialized machinery in order to express in thought and action the will of the churches. These activities, being general and community wide, are beyond the effective control of any one church or denomination. Corrupt morals and domestic relations courts, unbridled and segregated vice, corruption at the city hall, and coöperation in constructive programs with civic or other social agencies for the common good are all problems with which no one church can deal effectively. Furthermore, simultaneous action by individual denominations will not produce the necessary moral and spiritual momentum and force to meet such needs. This is largely due to the fact that separate denominations, however effectually

---

[3] P. 49.

organized, can find few or no points of contact with such problems. Such contacts must be made by a single highly organized and specialized agency. In order to be effective from the churches' point of view, this agency must speak for and in behalf of all of the churches as constituent units.

It is through such interchurch activity that the churches become what would be technically known as a community or social force. There is a difference between the force and influence of the churches acting independently and separately in a community and the churches of a community becoming an effective social force. . . . Such an organization has force:—

a. When in its organization and management there is direct and accredited representation by all the constituent bodies.

b. When it expresses in thought and action the will of the entire group.

The only effective democratic principle is the development of common thought and common ideals. There is a fallacy in majority action as well as in mob rule. Centralized agencies representing large, self-conscious, and forceful units can only gain the confidence of the community and really exercise effective social control when they actually speak the common mind and act for the entire group.

As society becomes increasingly complex and as the forces of evil become more highly organized and centralized, the churches, as the guarantors of the world's moral and spiritual values, must learn how to express themselves in thought and action in a comparable manner.[4]

Stripped to skeleton form, the above statements of principle apparently mean to assert that simultaneous effort of separate denominations under a common plan constitutes the germ of the federation movement: but that a common plan is not sufficient. The effective exercise of the Church's influence in the modern world requires a highly organized special agency speaking for the constituent church units under a system of representation, which, however, in order to be genuine must actually "speak the common mind" as well as take action passed by a majority of votes.

SLOGANS AND SALES TALK

Federations also turn out by the hundreds those types of forceful, condensed expositions or "snappy" statements which constitute the dialect of modern publicity effort. Though there is considerable evidence of fraternal borrowing from one another, such expositions have infinite variety which cannot be adequately illustrated. The following are offered as typical examples.

---

[4] Guild (ed.) *Community Programs for Coöperating Churches*, (New York: Association Press, 1920), pp. 5 and 6.

An announcement in display type occupying a full page in the annual publication of a federation:

THE FEDERATION OF CHURCHES' AIMS

To increase the efficiency of Protestant activities through church coöperation.

To economize financial expenditures by avoiding undesirable duplication.

To provide adequate Christian ministry for every Protestant resident.

To bring a personal evangelistic invitation to every non-church member.

To make systematic religious instruction available to every Protestant child.

To provide suitable training for church and Sunday-school workers.

To have the community life dominated by Christian ideals.

A page from a promotional leaflet accompanying a financial appeal:

SEVEN REASONS WHY *YOU* WANT TO BE A SUPPORTER OF THE FEDERATION OF CHURCHES

1. You believe the Christian religion is the great solvent of personal and social problems.

2. You are not satisfied with the manifold divisions in the church.

3. You hold that coöperation in the other realms social, political, business, is economical and efficient.

4. You see many tasks which the individual church, or even the denominations, cannot carry alone.

5. You know that competition, unmodified by coöperation, is wasteful and unchristian.

6. You have seen church life in our city improved through the work of the Federation of Churches.

7. You look forward to the answer some day of the prayer of Christ "that they all may be one."

In a third example, a running summary of a federation's work in its weekly publication presents it as: a *visible symbol* of the unity of the Christian forces; a *center* for planning and promoting joint Christian enterprises; a *headquarters* for reliable information about church activities; a *voice* of the churches on great world issues; a *counselor* in the location of new church enterprises; a *sponsor* for united Protestant religious services; an entrusted agency for the development of week-day religious education; a *promoter* for vacation schools; a *director* of the community training schools; a *friendly service* in behalf of delinquent boys and girls; a *bond* between the churches and social agencies; a *representative* of the churches in public relations; an *agent* in conducting religious services in public institutions.

Here are thirteen things which this federation desires its constituency to see in it. It emphasizes each of the thirteen by printing it in heavy type.

The chief notes sounded by federation sales-talk as judged by these examples are familiar ones of efficiency, economy, adequacy, system, inclusiveness, dominance, and ideal unity; in contrast with division, competition, and consequent weakness.

How the Federations Impress Their Constituencies

What the rank and file of Protestant constituents see in a city federation is an organization calling itself by this name which they know to reflect certain coöperative purposes and undertakings of the Protestant denominations, to be carried out by certain machinery which they probably understand but vaguely, and to be personalized in certain professional agents and designated representatives with whom they are more or less familiar. They have never seen the constitutions, and rarely come within the range of an official exposition. Occasionally they get a piece of publicity matter or hear sales-talk. They understand that certain functions of the churches are being carried on in common, but have only a dim notion of what these are and how they are conducted. What then do the individuals who make up the Protestant body think of the phenomena thus slenderly presented and partially understood? What has history, plus emotional advocacy, plus the formal documents, plus experience with the federation as a going concern, said about the movement to its constituency? How have its ultimate supporters, the individuals behind the churches, come to define the federation in their own minds as a result of an incomplete registering from all the sources of information and impression? How do they value their federations?

In the most vital sense, the only answer is that to be found in the behavior of these constituents. The degree to which the denominations and churches to whom the individual constituents belong have actually accepted membership, and undertaken coöperation in federations, tells what the thinking of constituents comes to. No other evidence with respect to thinking is so weighty as is the evidence of conduct.

HOW CONSTITUENTS' REACTIONS WERE SECURED

But the investigation also created opportunity for free expression of the individual thought of constituents relative to their federations. In connection with the circulation of schedules by means of which certain more exact data were sought, opportunity was also afforded for expressions of personal opinion and constructive suggestions as to federation work. Thus, at the end of the questionnaire used in an attempt to register the constituent's sense of obligation to coöperate in carrying out representative proposals of his federation,[5] a note was added as follows: "It is not assumed that any one of these statements will exactly reflect your position on the above matter. Please, therefore, write here a third statement expressing your position as accurately as you can in four lines or less." Blank spaces were provided for answers in response to this invitation.

In connection with still other schedules relating specifically to the programs of federations,[6] further opportunity was offered for the constituent to make constructive suggestions as to what a given federation was doing or should do.

Replies to these invitations for expressions of opinion were supplemented by numerous spontaneous communications in which the feelings of constituents overflowed. Some of these expressions were quite long. In the main, however, the body of thinking secured in this way was brief and pointed because of the limited space offered for expression. While the direction and scope of the answers was doubtless somewhat influenced by the contents of the accompanying questionnaires, there was no direct limitation either as to the form or the scope of the answers. The situation rather challenged and stimulated free discussion. The more general results or reactions thus secured are now to be summarized.

CONSTITUENTS' REACTIONS SUMMARIZED

Being essentially casual and representing varying degrees of articulateness in response to a chance incentive, the following expressions do not discover the whole mind of any constituent. At the most slighting valuation, however, this body of data is believed to constitute a very significant array of opinion. It has been organized in fidelity to clues seemingly inherent in the material itself.

Beginning with the most indefinite apprehension of the movement, there comes first of all a wholly indefinite and indiscriminate type of approval. Federation is a good and Christian thing, and as such should be supported. The following are typical expressions of this mood:

[5] P. 69.
[6] P. 127.

My willingness to coöperate comes in the feeling that it is a duty to fall in line with the leaders of a good work.

I should be willing to coöperate in any way that would bring Christ closer to the people of Minneapolis.

The Federation's aims may not work out as expected, but let us get started with something along this line. I am ready to do my part.

Would support any Christian movement for mankind's betterment, regardless of sponsor.

The use of such phraseology of course does not necessarily mean that the writer was incapable of more penetrating thought, but merely that this was all that the particular occasion evoked.

AN ACCEPTED COMMON AGENCY

Again federations are approved of on de facto grounds. They are our enterprises; valuable community movements; assets to our churches; we therefore stand up for them as we do for the other efforts of our home town: we are not knockers and do not cultivate the critical spirit. The following are fairly typical expressions of this characteristic mood:

Look to the Council for leadership in city-wide religious affairs.

I regard the Federation of Churches as representative of all Protestant denominations in our community, and feel that if it is to function effectively each church must respect all proposals of the Federation and support them as far as it reasonably can do.

I believe that the best advance can be made by trying out the plans which the Council offers after deliberate consideration in the light of Rochester's needs.

Should consider Federation's findings as representing best moral sense of community and as such entitled to hearty support.

The Council is the authorized spokesman in community projects for my denomination and thus deserves my coöperation.

A CURE FOR COMPETITION

As would be expected, a good many constituents regard federation primarily as an interdenominational movement mitigating the evils of sectarian strife and allowing Protestantism again to respect itself in that mutual Christian regard is now shown between its several branches. A casual group of constituents' utterances from this general standpoint follows:

I would coöperate in any movement to bring the different denominations more closely together and to make all more tolerant toward one another.

Usefulness of denominational boundaries is a thing of the past. Until something better materializes the Federation should receive our unswerving support.

The presence of so many denominations in a community, some of which are very closely related, without some means of drawing and working together, is certainly undesirable, not to say unthinkable, in our day.

I believe in coöperative Christianity. It is too late in the world's progress for any church to hold itself aloof from other churches. Such aloofness would be proof to me of something wrong about that church.

The future of our churches depends upon a closer federation and less denominational conflict. I would coöperate with the Federation with this hope in mind.

The power of the Catholic Church is partly due to its having a strong centralized government. The weakness of Protestantism is that it has had no such thing in the past.

Protestants are wasting their resources by too much overlapping.

I am in favor of any organized movement of the entire Christian Church conducted in a Christ-like way without abuse of those who may differ from.

A real sense of relief from the acknowledged shame of denominational competition, and of joy in possessing visible expressions of harmony and coöperation, breathes through many of these expressions.

FIVE PRACTICAL REASONS FOR FAVORING FEDERATION

Other expressions single out some special feature of the federation movement and focus attention upon it. Most of the features stressed fall generally under five categories:

First, "union is strength"; coördinated effort is more effective.

Second, coöperation is efficient. "The great systems of chain stores have proven success by giving bigger and better service. Religious team-work means bigger and better things for Christ."

Third, federation means goodwill. It fosters "a harmonious working together of our Protestant church-members"; "it creates good feelings between denominations and tends to break down walls between them."

Fourth, federation is enlarged service. "It enables us to carry out broader programs of Christian work in the community."

Finally, federation is fraternity; "it is the truest expression of brotherhood among Protestant churches."

An occasional reply takes on a still more mystical glow and

speaks of fellowship in the realm of religious experience as heightened by the collective effort at practical coöperation.

All told, then, what the constituent sees in his federation is either a sort of area of glorified haze; or else something nearer to the heart's desire, ecclesiastically speaking, than our present sectarianism is; or, finally, an organization possessed of such popular virtues as strength, efficiency and enlarged service.

RETURNS FROM PHILADELPHIA CONSTITUENTS

In the case of the constituents of the Philadelphia Federation, the procedures previously described were varied by the circulation of a post-card asking specifically, "What do you understand to be the present work of the Federation?" The question being uniform, it was possible to tabulate the replies; first, according to the aspects of the federation which constituents recognized, and, second, according to classes of constituents. The results are shown in Table VI.

TABLE VI—THE WORK OF THE FEDERATION AS UNDERSTOOD BY CONSTITUENTS OF THE PHILADELPHIA FEDERATION

Aspect	Number of Replies	No. Times Indicated by		
		Ministers	Laymen	Laywomen
Total Tabulable Responses	235	151	55	29
Coöperative Agency (Indefinite)	67	35	23	9
Agency of Comity	54	31	13	10
Voice of Protestantism	25	23	2	0
Administrative Agency for Common Work	22	18	3	1
Movement Toward Church Unity	20	17	2	1
Expression of Fellowship	19	10	3	6
Bureau of Information and Clearing House of Plans	18	13	4	1
Indefinite Approval of Federation	10	4	5	1

Most of these aspects would be likely to impress the constituents of any federation. It is noteworthy that all classes of respondents substantially agreed in the ranking they gave to the several aspects recognized. Of those definitely discriminated, for example, comity ranked first with all classes. The most striking discrepancy was with respect to federation as an expression of fellowship. This aspect was ranked last by the ministers, but first by the non-professional women, and second by the women as a group. The ministers perhaps stood nearer to the practical operations of the movement and were consequently able to judge it more precisely and less sentimentally. On the other hand, ministers were much more alive to the relationship of federation to church unity than was either lay group.

The Moral Authority of Federations

The data just summarized give a rough indication of the nature and range of those qualities of federations that stand out in the minds of federation followers. They show what characteristics are most commonly fixed upon by the understanding when federations speak for themselves. It was, however, thought important also to register in more systematic fashion, and in generalized form, the degree of constituents' loyalties toward their federations. The device used for this purpose was a questionnaire entitled "Sense of Obligation to Coöperate in Carrying Out the Representative Proposals of the Federation." The name of the particular federation was inserted and questionnaires, each with an explanatory letter, were mailed to a representative list of supporters of fifteen federations with a request that out of ten statements of attitude, they check the two that most nearly corresponded to their personal positions. A copy of the questionnaire follows:

Sense of Obligation to Coöperate in Carrying Out the Representative Proposals of the Federation or Council of Churches in Your Community.

1. The fact that the Federation (or Council) proposes it a good reason for not doing it.
2. The Federation (or Council) a misrepresentative movement; not desirable to coöperate with it.
3. Federation's (or Council's) proposals are understood to be mere gestures; practically negligible.
4. Would coöperate if convenient and advantageous—no obligation because Federation (or Council) proposes.
5. Would feel some obligation in matters in which it is customary for the Federation (or Council) to act.
6. Would feel obligation if assured of very adequate consultation with constituency in advance and probably approval of my denomination.
7. Would feel considerable obligation unless in conflict with position of my denomination or sentiment of my own church.
8. Would strain a point to coöperate for the sake of supporting an important movement.
9. Recognize representative character of Federation (or Council) and would feel strongly obligated to support it as the corporate expression of the Protestant movement in the community.
10. Regard consensus as registered in the Federation's (or Council's) proposals as morally authoritative for coöperating churches of the community.

This questionnaire follows a type familiar to psychological investigation. Its peculiarity is that a person answering is given an opportunity to choose among several answers. The underlying theory is simple. People do not use the identical words in the same sense, nor is it certain that anyone of a series of statements will exactly reflect the attitude of any individual. Free expressions of opinion are not directly comparable nor susceptible of tabulation, and no expression in previously fixed form may be exactly true. A questionnaire in the form presented on the contrary is both comparable, tabulatable and flexible. In the particular case as has been shown, those responding to the questionnaire indicated the two statements out of the series of ten which most nearly corresponded to the attitudes felt with respect to their federation. As will be observed, the series of statements was arranged so as to constitute an ascending and descending scale for measuring loyalty toward its representative proposals. The trend of the answers was believed to indicate, for each city, something of the degree of practical authority which its federation had achieved over the minds of their supporters. The combined answers were thought to tell something of the same thing for the group of federations.

These questionnaires were replied to by 3,047 constituents of the seventeen federations. The results of their responses are summarized in the following table in which the ten numbers at the head of the percentage distribution columns correspond to the ten questions on the questionnaire.

TABLE VII—SENSE OF OBLIGATION OF CONSTITUENTS TO COÖPERATE IN 17 FEDERATIONS, BY CITIES

City	No. of Constit- uents Replying	No. of Replies	Distribution of Proposals on Scale Per Cent.									
			Total	1	2	3	4	5	6	7	8	9	10
Total	3047	5800	100	*	*	1	5	6	7	12	24	33	12
Baltimore	195	343	100	0	*	0	7	3	10	14	24	31	11
Boston	183	330	100	*	1	2	6	9	10	13	27	26	6
Chicago	300	582	100	0	0	*	4	6	7	13	22	35	13
Detroit	177	337	100	0	*	1	4	5	5	13	26	34	12
Indianapolis	29	60	100	0	0	0	7	5	2	11	25	35	15
Minneapolis	230	445	100	*	*	0	6	5	6	11	27	32	13
New York	239	465	100	*	*	*	7	5	9	13	23	32	11
Oakland	157	313	100	0	0	*	4	6	11	8	21	32	18
Philadelphia	189	344	100	1	2	2	6	6	12	15	22	25	9
Pittsburgh	181	354	100	1	1	1	5	4	6	15	22	35	10
Portland, Me. ...	44	86	100	0	0	0	3	12	3	6	25	34	17
Rochester	217	431	100	1	0	0	4	7	6	8	25	34	15
St. Louis	199	387	100	1	*	1	7	6	6	10	23	33	13
Washington	225	396	100	*	1	1	4	6	8	11	21	34	14
Wichita	188	349	100	*	0	0	4	5	4	9	25	37	16
Youngstown	132	261	100	0	0	1	4	4	4	11	22	35	19
Mass. State	162	317	100	0	1	2	8	6	8	17	21	31	6

* Less than five-tenths of 1 per cent.

The most outstanding feature of the above showing is that, in all but one of the seventeen federations, number 9 was chosen more often than any other answer, as reflecting the position of constituents. This answer read: "We recognize the representative character of the Federation and feel strongly obligated to

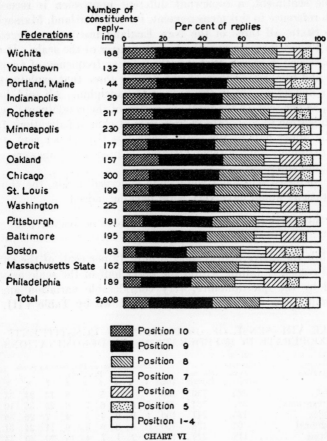

CHART VI

Comparison of sense of obligation to coöperate in Church Federation proposals felt by their constituents in 16 cities

support it as the corporate expression of the Protestant movement in the community."

Adding answers nine and ten together as representing the extremes of favorable sentiment, and ranking the sixteen federations accordingly, one finds four federations occupying the upper quarter of the scale; viz., Youngstown, Wichita, Portland, and

Indianapolis. According to the responses, the constituents of these federations have the most loyal feelings toward them. On the other hand, Baltimore, Massachusetts State, Pittsburgh, and Boston trail at the bottom of the list. If the lower half of the scale (answers 1-5) is considered as reflecting the zone of unfavorable sentiment, a somewhat different impression is received. With reference to this measurement, Boston, Portland, Massachusetts State, all three of the New England institutions, together with Philadelphia occupy the lowest quarter of the scale. It will be observed, however, that it is the relative frequency of answers four and five, rather than of one, two or three that explains this low standing, except in the case of Philadelphia. All told, however, 88 per cent. of the total expression of the constituents' sense of obligation to coöperate in proposals of church federations falls in the upper half of the scale, while less than 2 per cent. take the extremely unfavorable attitudes expressed in answers one, two, and three.

If confessed sentiment completely governed action, the church federations would have very solid backing indeed.

DENOMINATIONAL VARIATION IN SENSE OF OBLIGATION TO COÖPERATE

While the above figures showed only 12 per cent. of the entire 5,800 responses falling within the lower half of the scale as supplied by the questionnaire, very considerable variation among denominations was revealed. This is shown by Table VIII.

TABLE VIII—SENSE OF OBLIGATION OF CONSTITUENTS TO COÖPERATE IN 16 FEDERATIONS, BY DENOMINATIONS

DENOMINATION	No. of CONSTITUENTS REPLYING	No. of REPLIES	Total	DISTRIBUTION OF PROPOSALS ON SCALE PER CENT.									
				1	2	3	4	5	6	7	8	9	10
Baptist	385	750	100	*	1	*	5	5	8	13	24	33	11
Congregational	381	734	100	0	0	1	6	7	6	23	35	10	12
Disciples	125	241	100	1	0	0	4	5	4	7	26	36	17
Evangelical	65	128	100	0	0	0	6	5	6	11	24	31	17
Lutheran	118	229	100	1	2	1	7	4	15	20	20	23	7
Methodist Episcopal	643	1216	100	0	*	*	5	6	6	10	24	34	15
Presbyterian	507	966	100	*	1	1	5	6	7	11	22	34	13
Protestant Episcopal	158	294	100	*	1	1	11	9	12	14	25	20	7
All Other	426	777	100	*	0	1	4	6	7	15	24	31	12

* Less than five-tenths of 1 per cent.

The results of the preceding calculation may be summarized as follows:

When the five questions constituting the lower half of the scale are considered, the showing for most of the denominations closely approximate the average. The Disciples are slightly more favorable than the average; Congregationalists appreciably less favorable; Lutherans considerably less favorable; and Episcopalians very much less so. One is led to recognize one wing at least of these denominations as distinctly critical or antagonistic. Twenty-two per cent. of the representatives of the communion last named take positions in the lower half of the scale.

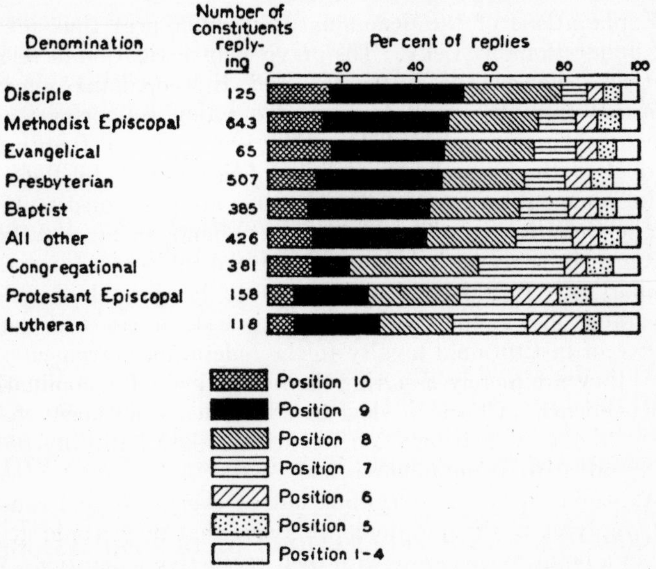

CHART VII

Comparison of sense of obligation to coöperate in Church Federation proposals felt by constituents of specified denominations in 16 cities

Considering the other end of the scale, it will be noted that answer eight, rather than answer nine, is the modal position for Congregationalists and Episcopalians. That is to say, more persons of these denominations assert that they "would strain a point to coöperate for the sake of supporting an important movement in the community," than take any of the other of the nine positions. They are unwilling, however, to voice their sense of obligation as strongly as the majority do.

Considering question seven alone, an exceptional inclination is seen among the Congregationalists and Lutherans to choose this expression of attitude. One-fifth or more of constituents from these bodies would feel considerable obligation to coöperate with federations unless their proposals were in conflict with the positions of their own denominations or the sentiment of their individual churches.

Considering answer ten, which asserts that a consensus of Protestants as registered in the Federation's proposals is morally authoritative for the coöperating churches, the Disciples and Evangelical constituents took the strongest position, followed by Methodists; while the Lutherans and Episcopalians were most unready to acknowledge this attitude.

Explanations of the denominational differences thus revealed are unquestionably risky. The previous investigation of religious distance showed the Lutherans and Episcopalians somewhat removed from the main body of federation supporters; and a subsequent paragraph will show they are also more than usually critical of the concrete programs of federations. As their attitudes come out in the present table, they are thus consistent.

The Congregationalists, on the other hand, so far as religious distance is concerned, belong to the central core of federation supporters. But they also turn out to be critical of concrete programs, just as they hesitate, on this test, to assert an average degree of institutional loyalty to the federation movement. Perhaps they are merely asserting their traditions of denominational independence. Churches slow to acknowledge authority to any central body in their own denominations might naturally be slow to accord it to an interchurch body.

At worst, however, sixty-nine out of every hundred constituents replying to the questionnaire assert that they would at least strain a point to coöperate with their respective federations, while forty-five in every hundred acknowledge even stronger obligations to loyalty. If this is more than lip service, it indicates a very impressive degree of practical authority on the part of federations over the minds of their constituencies.

SUMMARY

The chief ways in which federations present and assert their claims have now been reviewed, and suggestive indices of constituents' reactions to these claims have been brought forward. The resulting impression is inevitably one of considerable incoherence. The data presented do not furnish even a consistent skeleton upon which to build an understanding of the federation movement; they could not do so because the movement is still highly experimental and its type unfixed.

So far as it is legitimate to furnish in advance a clue to the outcome of a study, the reader should be helped by the preliminary analysis in Chapter I. To that extent the writer was willing to help him. At the present point, however, the reader must be content to take directly from the mouths of federations and their constituents, what they say about the movement. He will thus be forced to recognize the inherent complexity of the phenomena. This will challenge him to press on to the consideration of more objective aspects of the federation movement, waiting till the end of Part I for such generalization as the variety of the facts permits.

Chapter V

FORM AND STRUCTURE OF CHURCH FEDERATIONS

The federation movement is voluntary. Local units of religious organizations—churches or denominations—enter into free associations. These associations bear names implying that the units, while retaining their separate identities, combine for limited purposes. It is obviously necessary to consider this fundamental aspect of the movement; and, first of all, to discover the exact nature of the specific acts or processes of association, and the consequent group-life that takes this particular form.

THE NATURE OF THE ASSOCIATION INVOLVED IN FEDERATION

First of all, a federation is identified with some community. It is an association of churches or other religious agencies that constitute a natural geographical group. As a political unit defined by legal boundaries, a city is of course a mere accident. Socially defined, it consists of a metropolitan center with its suburbs, the unity of which is now officially recognized by the United States Census in its statistics of metropolitan districts.

In the practical definitions of their geographical fields, virtually all federations go beyond the limits of their respective cities. Most of them constitutionally recognize the suburbs as within their jurisdiction. Three of them, Boston, New York, and St. Louis, specify the greater or metropolitan city in their titles. Four more, Cleveland, Louisville, Pittsburgh and Rochester, identify the county as the area of their responsibility. Nine more name themselves the federations of a city "and vicinity."

Still others, federations that have failed to give constitutional recognition to the suburbs, have nevertheless undertaken formal responsibility for them through the method of compacts. Philadelphia, for example, has an agreement with the State Council of Churches whereby it undertakes to function in suburbs within the state of Pennsylvania.[1]

---

[1] Examples of difficulty over an indefinite decision as to the responsibility of federations in their suburbs are found in a companion volume of this report, *Church Comity* (New York: Institute of Social and Religious Research, 1929), pp. 100 and 104.

All told, then, city federations generally attempt to make their geographical areas correspond to the vital social fact of the metropolitan district. At the same time, some are by no means conscious of what is involved in this fact; and most have failed to make their geographical claims good in the sense of really getting the more distant churches into full working association and in developing appropriate forms of ministry in the remoter suburbs.

AN ASSOCIATION WITH LIMITED OBJECTIVES

A federation is an association for certain purposes and not for others. This is invariably implied in the constitutional statement of objectives; it may also be expressed in connection with the incorporation, in which case a formal statement of the scope of the proposed organization is required to satisfy legal requirements; or it may be set forth defensively, as in occasional cases apparently attempting to forestall suspicion on the part of the constituent churches. Thus the Youngstown Constitution reads:

> No provision of this Constitution, or action taken by the governing board or Executive Committee, shall be interpreted as interfering with or limiting the action of any individual church or denomination.

Cleveland and Indianapolis virtually duplicate this phraseology.

PRIOR ALLEGIANCES NOT AFFECTED

Such a statement implies that the association of churches in a federation does not affect the prior relationships and allegiances of the member units. This is the undoubted intent of the movement as a whole. So universally is it taken for granted as not often to appear in set terms; but it is written indelibly in the basic structure of the organization.

UNITS OF ASSOCIATION

In view of the vast number of forms in which the Church has come to exist in cities, and of the extent and variety of its ecclesiastical extensions and allies as set forth in a preceding chapter,[2] it is not strange that federations have found room to vary their decisions as to the types of organizations that may associate under their auspices.

---

[2] P. 14.

PRIMARY UNITS

The major trend of such decisions is, however, unmistakable: church federations are primarily associations of ecclesiastical units.

But ecclesiastical units may be larger or smaller, broader or less inclusive. Precisely which of the ecclesiastical entities may enter into this type of association? Out of what organizational elements are church federations formed?

From this standpoint, two distinct types of federations have evolved. Federations are usually associations of local church congregations. This was true in fifteen out of twenty cases examined in detail. Four, on the other hand, were associations "of the denominations as locally represented"; that is to say, of ecclesiastical units immediately above and including local churches,—such as presbyteries, conferences, classes, etc., rather than of local churches as such. The Greater New York Federation constitutes a third variant. Certain denominations may and do designate delegates to its governing body; but this federation is not composed of local churches, nor does it define itself as, and technically it is not, an alliance of denominations as such.

The two major types of federations, however, do not actually represent completely different alternatives. Some of the distinctive features of each enter into the other. Neither can be understood without recognition of this fact, which tends to explain why both succeed.

RECOGNITION OF LOCAL CHURCHES WHEN THE DENOMINATION IS
THE UNIT OF MEMBERSHIP

Cities whose federations make the denomination rather than the local church the unit of membership, have without exception recognized the need to give partial authority to direct representatives of local congregations. Thus Chicago and Detroit provide for annual meetings of delegates from local churches, at which meetings the work of the year is reported. These congregational representatives elect part of the directors or of the delegates at large in the governing body. A formal report of a special committee of the Pittsburgh Council reported in 1920 that "the Council of Churches would be strengthened by providing representation of some kind from each congregation"; but this recommendation was not formally carried out. The New York Federation recognizes representatives of local churches as non-voting members.

In this way the local church returns to the federation via the back door whenever it has been forbidden the front entrance.

ORGANIZATIONAL RELATIONS WITH DENOMINATIONS AS LOCALLY ORGANIZED

On the other hand, federations composed of local-church units are not able to escape close organizational relations with denominations as locally organized. Presbyteries, conferences, and classes represent ecclesiastical units on this level. They intervene between the local congregation and the general overhead denominational organization, superior to the one and subordinate to the other.

The names of these intermediate units vary with denominations, and the nature of their authority varies with denominational polities. But whatever their form, it is the denomination as locally represented by them with which the federation in fact has to do. Thus, while in the case of a non-coöperating denomination a few individual churches may join the federation, the majority always follow the denominational cue.

But beyond this, constitutional recognition of the denominational unit is shown, especially in two ways; first, federations constituted of local churches as units frequently admit secondary memberships on the part of organizational representatives, among whom denominational dignitaries and executives are the most frequently recognized. City mission societies, which represent their denominations in specific and limited functions, are also given organizational membership by three federations. As it works out, therefore, a denomination is likely to be represented by the delegates of its local churches, and in addition by its bishop, district superintendent, or city-extension executive. Two federations go so far as to give full membership to resident denominational officials as such—apparently on the theory that their permanently representative character is inherent in their office. If these officials are not directly admitted to membership in the federation as such, they are frequently accorded constitutional place on governing boards and executive committees.

Finally, in one or two cases, federations receive direct support from certain central denominational treasuries, although membership is by local churches.

GEOGRAPHICAL JURISDICTION OF FEDERATIONS AND DENOMINATIONS AS LOCALLY ORGANIZED

Special difficulties attach to relationships with denominations as locally organized when their jurisdictions do not correspond geographically to those of the federations. Four possibilities are present.

First, all denominational jurisdictions might exactly correspond to that of the federation which usually covers the city and its immediate suburbs. This rarely happens.

Second, the city may be so large that some of the denominations have subdivided it. There will then be more than one organization in a number of denominations with which the federation has to come to terms. Thus New York City has to deal with two Episcopal bishops, three or four Methodist district superintendents, two presbyterial executives and the like.

Third, the city and suburbs may be under different and sometimes opposing denominational jurisdictions.

Fourth, a denomination may be so weak that it has no supervisory unit closely corresponding to the city, or the city and suburbs. In such a case its unit next above the local churches is likely to cover a large district predominately rural, or even an entire state. Consequently the denominational executives will not be closely enough identified with the city to enter into continuous and intimate relationship with the federation and its workings; while they are still near enough to be sensitive over their prerogatives and to interfere where they ought to coöperate.

As it appears to the investigators, one of the chief problems of a federation in a small city is the lack of a body of resident denominational executives whose work is practically limited to the city. This prevents the establishment of the closely knit ties, and the continuous face-to-face coöperation on the part of executives, which are responsible for much of the success of federations in the larger cities.

SECONDARY MEMBERSHIP AND REPRESENTATION OF NON-ECCLESIASTICAL ORGANIZATIONS

In addition to the determining structural features of federations, which are invariably built up out of ecclesiastical units, a secondary group of features represents the part that non-ecclesiastical types of religious organization play in them. Some federations provide directly for the membership of these organizations in their central body. The non-ecclesiastical member organizations elect delegates to this body on equal terms with others. Other federations concede non-ecclesiastical organizations direct representation without first technically giving them organizational status as members.

Thus in six cases out of twenty, federations admit both churches and "other religious organizations." The latter, in three of the cases, are specifically made to include the Y.M.C.A and Y.W.C.A.. Detroit accords like status to the Minister's Union.[3] Boston goes so far as to include philanthropic agencies at the discretion of the directors; and when such agencies exist under religious auspices, they might apparently seek membership under the broad formulas of some of the other federations. Boston even makes all of the numerous local federations of the greater city members of the general federation in coördinate standing with local congregations. Rochester provides that the federation "may invite other organizations in coöperative affiliation." But only Wichita establishes full basic equality of churches and organizations that are not churches; its membership consisting of any evangelical "church or Christian association" that may wish to join. Nine federations in all thus recognize non-ecclesiastical member-agencies, in addition to those that include church organizations in other than their parochial and directly denominational form.

The genius of the federation movement thus reveals itself. It is intended in principle to include as coöperators organizations of whatever form religion has assumed in the modern city, or else to absorb them into itself. Ecclesiastical forms have numbers, antiquity, and prestige behind them. They moreover show no disposition to be absorbed. This compels the movement to make them structurally basic, and generally leaves other (and absorbable) types of organization to find membership on a secondary basis.[4] But it does admit these other types in a backhanded way when it can not do so straightforwardly.

FORM, NATURE AND CONSEQUENCES OF THE ACT OF ASSOCIATION

So far, the discussion has concerned those who associate themselves in federations. The next step is to consider the form and nature of the act of association through which they enter into their new status. This act is more or less clearly characterized in the constitutions of about two-thirds of the federations studied. While not too much should be made of differences of phraseology, their variations are probably not unimportant. The most frequent type of formula used in defining membership is

---

[3] Some federations have virtually independent women's departments or Councils of Religious Education operating under their own by-laws. These affiliated organizations frequently recognize non-ecclesiastical agencies as members just as federations themselves do.
[4] P. 155.

that it consists of such churches as "shall agree by voting, according to their authorized methods" to enter into the federation. Obviously mere variants are: "Churches which shall officially decide to unite"; or which "vote to enter"; or which "elect to coöperate." Still other constitutions say that members are such churches as accept the constitution and by-laws.

In contrast with these formulas, which apparently conceive of federation as permanently bringing a member church or organization into a new status, are those that hinge membership upon specific and recurrent acts of coöperation which may not necessarily be continued. Thus the Oakland constitution reads: "A coöperating church is hereby defined to be any Protestant evangelical church which coöperates by electing delegates to and participating in the financial support of this Council."

Elaborating on this later issue, the Washington constitution specifies: "Each member church in the Federation is expected to make some contribution each year. . . . When any church fails to make a contribution for two successive years, despite requests that it do so, it may be dropped from the roll at the discretion of the Executive Committee." Louisville has a somewhat similar provision.

Such federations apparently abandon the conception that the status of member churches as federated is permanently established by some act of joining, and think rather of their association as consisting in recurrent specific vital acts of participation.

PROVISIONS FOR WITHDRAWAL

One-fifth of the federations studied went so far as to embody in their constitutions provisions for the voluntary withdrawal of members. Their union is not indissoluble. A church (or denomination) may honorably discontinue its relationships after due written notice, qualified in one case by the provision that all financial obligations must have been discharged. It is not clear from the evidence whether this reflects a cherished theory of the inherent right of secession or merely a concession to reluctant candidates for membership.

PROVISIONS FOR LIMITED PARTICIPATION

Analogous qualifications often appear, providing terms of limited association for churches that do not desire to accept fellowship in the total work of a federation. These provisions are generally phrased negatively: providing that a church that does not feel willing to coöperate in some part of a federation's program may be excused from responsibility with respect to that part upon formal action and application in writing; and that it shall not forfeit membership on that account. The Minneapolis Federation, on the contrary, puts the matter positively as follows: "Any church may affiliate in any one department or project of the federation. It may designate the department of work in which its funds shall be invested."

It will be discovered later how prevalent is the fear of being drawn into some form of union for which the churches are not ready. This may explain such provisions for limited participation and for easy exit as have just been described.

REPRESENTATIVE PERSONS

Whatever be a federation's theory as to the inherent nature of the bond of association into which its members enter, membership is actively realized through representative persons and what they do. A typical formula is: Each church shall be represented in the federation by its pastor, etc.

REPRESENTATION OF INDIVIDUAL CHURCHES

The constitutional representatives of the individual church generally consist of the pastor and a minimum of two or three lay persons, with additional representation for every 200 or 300 church-members beyond the first unit. In three cases, on the other hand, representation is equal, whatever the churches' size. Only two federations, those of Oakland and St. Louis, do not recognize the pastor as such. An Oakland church could fill its list of delegates and exclude its pastor. In St. Louis all resident ministers, whether or not they are pastors, get membership in the federation by virtue of their denominational standing; but not as representatives of their respective churches.

The requirement of some lay representation is almost universal; and the application of the constitutional formulas assures an average of three or more laymen to one clergyman. In six of the twenty cases examined, the constitution required that delegates should include a certain proportion of women. In a seventh, it was specified that delegates might be either men or women; in an eighth, it was "recommended" that one of the two be a woman. Nearly half of the federations thus provided for women delegates from local churches in such terms that their numbers would range from one-fifth to two-fifths of the total. Where the proportion was not fixed, a minimum was sometimes mentioned as "not less than five women." [5]

_____
[5] P. 172.

Constitutional provision for organizational membership of other agencies besides churches and denominations, obviously carries the right of representation by such member-agencies. The number of delegates permitted them varies from one to five per organization; but no common trend as to number is observable. In most cases the particular religious organizations admitted to membership are not listed, their choice being left to the discretion of the governing body of the federation. Of religious organizations definitely specified, the most frequent are minister's unions (in five cases), the Y.M.C.A. (in three cases), and the Y.W.C.A. (in three cases). Whether or not they admit non-church organizations to direct membership, federations sometimes provide for the membership of persons who are virtually *ex officio* representatives of other agencies. Thus, Brooklyn admits as members "such officials as shall be nominated by their denominations." Other federations admit resident connectional officials—bishops, Y.M.C.A. and Y.W.C.A. general secretaries, the presidents of ministers' unions. One federation goes so far as to elect delegates at large "as representatives of non-member churches."

One must, of course, note that it would be more logical not to bring non-delegated individuals into what is essentially an association of organizations, but rather to widen the organizational membership so as to allow members to designate as their delegates the classes of persons just enumerated. Obviously, federations are trying to bring into their ranks a wide range of influential officials whose favor is important, whether or not their membership is logically on a parity with that of the basic organizations.

ADMINISTRATIVE MACHINERY

The comprehensive discussion of administrative machinery logically belongs in the sections that deal with the means by which federations do their work. The subject finds preliminary mention here to give a better understanding of these organizations. Apparently in the attempt to overcome the local infelicity of having a federation of churches, and then of permitting direct membership by the representatives of a large number of agencies that are not churches, nearly half the federations make a purely verbal distinction between the organization itself and a "council" through which it operates. The basic membership of the council in every case consists of exactly those delegates and other members who constitutionally make up the organization. The additional members commonly consist of the elective officers and members of boards of directors or executive committees, together with denominational executives, representatives of such organizations as the Y.M.C.A., Y.W.C.A., and so forth, when they have not received direct membership in the federation itself. Three federations add chairmen of standing committees to the council. In extreme cases, the council may add any suitable person as a corresponding member upon a two-thirds vote. However, as has been seen, the majority of federations do not take advantage of this method, but boldly mix organizations of different types and representative persons in their basic memberships.

In addition to the central body of representative persons, all federations have additional administrative agencies, commonly called directors or executive committees, which actually operate the work of the organization. Sometimes there are two such bodies, a larger and more formally representative group and a smaller executive group. Terminology varies, but the distinction between those two types is clear. The one determines the scope and general policy of the agency—its major financial plans and responsibilities—and employs its general agents; the other administers the policies in detail as they have been determined.

BOARDS OF DIRECTORS

This study will use "board of directors" as the generic term for the first type of administrative agency. Such boards commonly consist of the general officers of the federation, frequently including the chairmen of standing committees and commissions, together with an average of about twenty members at large. In three cases, it is required that these members at large be selected according to "proper denominational distribution," while in the remainder no specification is attached. Very rarely a specified proportion of laymen is required, and in rare cases there is some additional requirement for the inclusion of women. *Ex officio* membership in boards of directors is frequently accorded to non-church religious organizations, including the Y.M.C.A. (three cases), the Y.W.C.A. (three cases), and in a few cases other organizations. Where federations maintain separate women's departments, some representative of those departments is commonly included in the board of directors, while in the case of Washington the entire executive committee of the women's department is included.

EXECUTIVE COMMITTEES

"Executive committee" will be used as the generic term for the smaller and secondary administrative agency that is found only in the larger federations. Bodies of this type ordinarily have fewer than a dozen members and are likely to include only the president of the federation *ex officio* and a group of members at large with respect to whom no required ground of selection is indicated. Sometimes, on the other hand, the body of federation officers constitutes the executive committee. Where only one general administrative body exists, the federation itself, in its annual or other stated meetings, is likely to attempt to handle general policies; but in such cases it will probably turn out that executive committees come to have, on the whole, larger powers than they do in other cases.

DEPARTMENTS, COMMISSIONS AND COMMITTEES

Of the strictly functional characteristics of the church federation movement, the most outstanding is that its major activities are departmentalized or put into the hands of standing committees and commissions. Departments, however, are relatively few. The details of this committee system will be considered in connection with the discussion of the federation program item by item.[6] For the sake of completing the picture of the essential form and structure of federations, it is necessary, however, to include the more general constitutional methods by which these bodies are created, and the basis of the selection of their memberships.

Federation constitutions commonly specify that their governing boards may determine the major departments of work and may set up committees or commissions to carry them on. In a minority of cases, the departments and commissions are specified in constitutions or by-laws. Despite this latter tendency, no other structural aspect of federations has shown so great a change over a period of years. Old committees are abandoned with scant courtesy and new ones added, sometimes without much recognition of constitutional forms. In brief, internal organization as related to particular aspects of work is very much in flux.

Inasmuch as governing boards determine the departmentalization of federation work, it is very natural that they should select the heads and other members of the committees. In three cases out of twenty, however, the committee chairmen are elected at the annual meeting, along with the other officers; and, as has

---

[6] P. 291.

been seen, the position of these chairmen is very frequently magnified by giving them membership on executive committees. In
a few cases the chairman is specifically charged with nominating
the other members of his committee, and usage very generally
accords him this privilege. The basis of selection is rarely specified. St. Louis, however, requires that committee membership
should be distributed equitably among the coöperating denominations; and in a few other cases the appointing bodies are told
to keep denominational representativeness in mind. As it works
out, however, chairmen and executive secretaries are apt to be
excessively mindful of the denominational composition of committees; and sometimes representativeness at this point is made
to outweigh competency and effective interest.

DISTRICT FEDERATIONS

The conception that groups of neighboring churches representing a distinct district or community ought to coöperate in matters
of immediately local concern, is constantly reiterated, sometimes provided for on paper, occasionally experimented with; but
it is nowhere effectively realized in a system of district councils,
such as the theory calls for. The idea, however, has been partly
realized in the very limited fields of religious education.

Eight out of twenty federations studied with respect to this
point made constitutional provision for, or recognized the existence of, subordinate district federations or councils.[7] Several
constitutions specify that individual churches may belong to such
councils without impairing their memberships in the city-wide
body. The size and unusual political composition of New York
City explain the peculiar subdivision of its federation work
through borough organizations. The Brooklyn Federation in its
relation to the Greater New York Federation presents an additional and exceptional example of organizational decentralization. Its constitution provides that it shall accept such representation in the Greater New York Federation as may be accorded
it, but without recognizing the New York Federation as administratively responsible for Brooklyn. Constitutional provision for
district federations is frequent; but in only a few cases are they
actually being maintained. They are being deliberately soft-
pedalled by a number of federations that have written it into
their fundamental documents.

---

[7] Baltimore, Boston, Massachusetts State, Minneapolis, New York, Rochester, and Washington; also Brooklyn with reference to Greater New York.

SUMMARY

Considered in all the formal aspects that have now been investigated, the church federation movement presents itself as essentially a congregational and low-church phenomenon. In the large majority of cases it originates in, and continues as, a voluntary association of local congregations of various denominations. This association implies in the main the moral consent and coöperation of the denomination as locally organized, but not generally its formal denominational action. National membership of denominations in the Federal Council of Churches may be interpreted as implying authorization to local churches or denominational units to form local federations; but no formal action to such effect has generally been taken. These characteristics permit churchmen generally—whatever be their own ecclesiastical polities—to think of the type of association involved in federation as a working convenience rather than as an organic expression of the unity of the participating churches.

The council of denominations established by the formal action of locally authoritative bodies of the coöperating communions, originated in Pittsburgh. Here churches maintaining a congregational polity are relatively feeble. The successes elsewhere of this type of federation appear to the writer to be due to the instinct of strong personalities (employed as denominational executives) for domination in the interchurch movement, rather than to the inherent ecclesiastical tendencies of the movement itself. At least the denominations as locally organized in the great American cities have not generally created federations. Had they done so, the movement would in some respects have been stronger. Its practical outcome locally might not have been very different, but its implications for further evolution would have been quite other than they are. At the same time, neither the congregational nor the denominational version of voluntary local association could, of course, have fundamental or creative ecclesiastical authority for those who conceive the church locally as something created by virtue of the sanction of historic national or world-bodies, whose permission is necessary to give validity to any lesser ecclesiastical movement. In brief, the federation movement, as to its constitutional form and structure, does not wear the organizational aspect of a formal movement for church unity.

Chapter VI

MEMBERSHIP AND PARTICIPATION

Whether because of, or in spite of, what federations claim
for themselves, but obviously in some recognition of these claims
as standing for common ideals, many churches and religious
agencies join, support, and participate in local federations. This
is the most vital single measure of coöperation, the most adequate test of the success of the coöperative movement.

How successful, then, are the existing federations from the
standpoint of securing backing as organizations? Weighed in
the crude but convincing scales of membership and participation, have they established themselves as truly and adequately
representative of the Protestant forces which they are presumed
to include?

Before it is possible to use this test, it must be determined
what part of the Protestant forces they are presumed to include.
This is to raise the question of eligibility.

ELIGIBILITY

One who had independently measured the differences in feeling and attitude among faiths and denominations, could have
prophesied in advance which of these religious bodies probably
could, or could not, be effectively included in any practical
coöperative movement.[1] But he could not be certain without
a more exact understanding of the nature of the actual coöperative undertaking. He could not anticipate the exact terms in
which differences would express themselves, nor how formal
statements of eligibility might be modified by usage, by virtue
of factors not included in his prior measurements.

A report of the investigation of these matters must therefore
precede any statement of actual membership and participation
on the part of Protestant forces.

GROUNDS OF ELIGIBILITY

The only admitted grounds of eligibility are theological.

The majority of church federations, twelve out of twenty cases
examined, constitutionally limit their membership to evangelical

---

[1] P. 26.

churches. In ten of them the term "evangelical" was directly used; in two more the requirement was made by implication: either the preamble of the constitution was couched in strongly evangelical terminology, or the terms of membership were made the same as those of the Federal Council of Churches.

In three more cases, membership was limited to Protestant churches. This left only five cases, those of the Portland (Maine), Boston, Massachusetts State, New York City, and Rochester federations, in which no theological limitations were specified. In the first three and the last, as will be later shown, denominations not usually counted as evangelical have actual membership. In the case of New York, non-evangelicals along with all other small denominations, are virtually ruled out of voting membership by a constitutional requirement as to denominational size as a basis of representation.

One observes that the only federations erecting no theological requirements are located in New England and in the Northeast. Those making only the Protestant limitation are in larger cities of the North; while those making the evangelical limitation also include all cities studied in the Middle Atlantic states, and in the interior toward the South and West, Minneapolis being the single exception. In brief, theological conditions of eligibility for federation membership are regionally determined. This agrees with what was found about regional tendencies in connection with the sense of religious distance.[2]

MODIFICATIONS OF ELIGIBILITY BY USAGE

No precise definition is attempted by any federation of such terms as "Protestant" or "evangelical" when used to indicate the conditions of membership.

Usage, however, sometimes broadens and sometimes narrows the original intent of organizations at this point. The more inclusive coöperative undertakings of the World War period swept into the federation fold certain bodies that had previously been excluded. Philadelphia, for example, has ignored its ultra-evangelical membership requirements and includes Unitarians. Moreover, as will be shown,[3] a wider interpretation of eligibility is sometimes given by one department of a federation than by another.

Usage, on the contrary, sometimes shuts out religious bodies that are not constitutionally proscribed. The measurement of religious distance has already shown that certain sects that

---

[2] P. 34.
[3] Pp. 161 and 179.

appear to the Protestant majority to be peculiar or erratic are set off in feeling as distinct from the central group. Some of these bodies are technically both Protestant and evangelical. About others, questions might be raised. As a matter of fact, denominations of this type are generally not cultivated as constituents of federations, nor are they equally sought as active members. If deeds instead of words are to be considered, these churches fail to be eligible. This may be true locally even of churches whose national bodies are included in the Federal Council.[4]

The case of Negro churches is analogous but different. They are unquestionably Protestant and characteristically evangelical. They have national membership in the Federal Council and there is nothing in the constitution of any federation studied that prevents them from having full and complete membership. In point of fact, however, there is hardly a city in which their churches are in full and active membership in any such proportion as the churches of the participating white denominations; while in most cities Negro churches are not in active membership at all. How far this may be due to their own sense of solidarity in contrast with the white churches, coupled with lack of development in the coöperative spirit, and how far it results from lack of fraternal cultivation and from the sense that they are not wanted, the investigation is not in a position to say. In the large, however, usage leaves the Negro churches out of organized federation fellowship; and this may be true of federations that carry on active work *for* Negroes, or that maintain commissions on interracial good will that include Negro members.

LIMITATION OF ELIGIBILITY AND SIZE OF PROTESTANT GROUP

In any effort to calculate what per cent. of eligible churches actually have memberships in the federations, the statistician must decide whether or not to define as eligible those bodies that are excluded by established usage.

By how much does their exclusion weaken the federation movement numerically? The answer is, not very much. This point was investigated in a typical series of cases. The exclusion in any city of churches historically regarded as non-evangelical does not make more than about a 2 per cent. difference in the possible strength of a federation. More significant numerically is the group of denominations regarded by

---

[4] Infra.

the majority as irregular and erratic, which are merely ignored or rendered ineligible by usage, though not by constitutional provision. These sects are generally small and young. They represent numerous denominations, and about 7.5 per cent. of the churches in large cities, but include proportionately few members. Taking Wichita as a typical smaller city, one finds 8 denominations, 12 churches, and 1,423 members in this ignored group. Taking St. Louis as representative of larger cities, one finds 33 denominations, 63 churches, and 6,674 members in the same classification. But the exclusion of this group makes a less than 4 per cent. difference to the Protestant body in Wichita, and less than a 6 per cent. difference in St. Louis.

Even the practical exclusion of the great Negro denominations generally makes a small percentage difference, since Negroes do not constitute any very large proportion of the population in the major cities of the North. Even in Washington, where the proportion of Negroes is greatest, their omission, in addition to that of the irregular and erratic sects, reduces the eligible Protestant constituency only to 90 per cent. of the whole. All told, the churches of from 93 to 95 per cent. of Protestants in most of the great American cities are not shut out from federation membership either by constitutions or by custom.

Membership in Church Federations

The next practical problem is to discover how far the practically eligible constituency is won for actual federation membership. Of all those whom the federation wishes to include, how many are unwilling to be included, either because they are opposed to the federation idea or do not feel that the work of the particular federation merits their coöperation?

As has already been noted, there are two forms of primary membership in church federations; sometimes the unit is the local church and at other times the denomination. Secondary memberships of organizations other than churches need not be considered in the present connection. It is necessary therefore, to ask what proportion of churches and constituents are covered by each of these types of primary memberships in typical cases.

Membership by individual churches is almost always expressed by the appointment of delegates to the governing body of the federation.[5] But making stated contributions to support is also sometimes a constitutional requirement for membership, and is

---

5 P. 83.

inherently so significant a measure of participation that the facts have also been studied from this point of view.

Even with respect to delegates, a considerable number of federations make no real effort to fulfill the requirements of the constitution. There is no official list of member churches; or if there is, it is not up to date. Names of delegates that have not been renewed for very long periods, are allowed to stand. Only by positive revolt can a church once enrolled, get itself crossed off the membership list. In other words, the theory of membership is completely scrapped in practice; and the federations really consider current participation only as a ground of membership.

SUCCESS IN SECURING MEMBERSHIP

Disregarding those federations that do not really try to secure formal memberships, a sufficient series of cases was examined to yield a rough generalization as to degrees of success in this endeavor. The less successful federations get about 20 per cent. of the fully eligible churches on their formal lists of members. Normally successful federations in large cities do about a half better than this, and get in the neighborhood of 30 per cent.; while successful federations in the smaller cities get from 50 to 60 per cent.—presumably because they often have much smaller fields to cultivate relative to their working forces.

This showing in terms of proportions of churches may seem to suggest a rather feeble movement. Local opinion, however, almost always turns upon the character of the churches and the number of church-members they represent. Figures on this point were only in part available. In a considerable series of cases, however, it appeared that the member churches were invariably much larger than the average. Thus the Greater Boston Federation included only 19 per cent. of the churches that usage makes eligible. But church constituency represented by these member-churches was 50 per cent. greater. Rochester member churches equalled only 30 per cent. of the total number of eligible churches; but the church-membership represented was twice as great. The average membership of the member churches in Wichita was 315; of the non-member churches only 125.

An element of uncertainty enters into all these figures by reason of the equivocal position of the suburban churches. Even when federations, according to their constitutions, profess to include the suburbs, it is almost uniformly recognized locally that the remoter churches, whether in the suburbs or in the less accessible portions of cities, are not generally available for membership. Political lines do not really define the phenomena. Some suburbs are nearer than some parts of the cities themselves, both geographically and socially speaking. What the figures as previously presented therefore mean is that of geographically available churches, whether urban or suburban, approximately the proportions stated are found in federation memberships.

DENOMINATIONAL COMPARISONS

Within each city a calculation of the relative proportion of the churches and of the members of each denomination formally connected with the federation as an organization, is justifiable. Such a comparison between cities, however, is not justifiable for reasons that will be obvious. The locally unimportant denominations are not equally cultivated, especially if their churches are so feeble as not to yield much support. Consequently, denominations that stand in the forefront of the movement in one city may be only slightly connected in another. On the other hand, one of the frequent phenomena of federations is a very high percentage of membership on the part of several small denominations that are closely allied with the general federation movement. The only fair classification accordingly, appears to be one that divides the denominations into the habitually coöperating ones, in contrast with those that coöperate partially and with those that rarely coöperate at all. Again, the fully coöperative group divides between those denominations that are widely distributed throughout the cities and the country, and those that are strongly localized. To the widely distributed and habitually coöperating group belong the Baptist, Congregational, Disciple, Methodist and Presbyterian denominations. These constitute the backbone of the federation movement. Examples of denominations that generally coöperate in cities where they exist, are the Methodist Protestant, Reformed, and United Presbyterian. When in a given city, a federation gets a strong majority of the stronger churches of the denominations just enumerated, it is in a position to feel that it is measurably solving the problem of mobilizing its normal constituency.

DIRECT DENOMINATIONAL MEMBERSHIP

When the denomination is the unit of membership rather than the individual church, the measurement of the extent of membership becomes a much more straightway problem statistically. The proportion of eligible denominations, churches and members that have actually come into the membership of the leading federations organized on this basis is shown in the following table:

TABLE IX—PROPORTION OF PROTESTANT DENOMINATIONS, CHURCHES AND CHURCH-MEMBERS IN THREE CITIES FORMALLY BELONGING TO CHURCH FEDERATIONS

CITY	PER CENT. BELONGING		
	Denominations	Churches	Church-members
Chicago	17	43	38
Detroit	26	52	83
Pittsburgh	20	54	45

This calculation from the 1926 Census of Religious Bodies is limited to churches within the respective cities, and all denominations are assumed to be Protestant that are neither Roman nor Greek Catholic, Jewish nor non-Christian. Because of the frequent massing of Protestants in suburbs the showing in some of the above cases would have been distinctly better if suburban areas had been included.

The question of eligibility is also disregarded. Membership is reckoned from the standpoint of the federation as such, even though some of its subsidiaries may have a different basis.

From this standpoint the preceding table reveals at best a relatively small per cent. of Protestant denominations belonging to church federations. The omission is of no great importance, provided the major denominations are included. As between Chicago and Detroit, however, the difference in number of member-denominations works out as a striking difference in the strength of the federation in terms of churches, and of members as well. Specifically, the Detroit Federation is relatively much stronger than the Chicago Federation because it includes four Lutheran denominations instead of one, the Protestant Episcopal Church, and one considerable Negro denomination which Chicago does not include. The surprisingly small proportion of Protestant church-members represented by the Chicago Federation is in general explained by the unusual average size of these omitted churches.

While the results in Detroit and Pittsburgh are very close with respect to denominations and churches, they are far apart with respect to members, largely for the reason that in Pittsburgh Lutheran churches are outside of the federation and Negro denominations have only partial and secondary membership.

The peculiar basis of organization of the Greater New York Church Federation makes a comparative statement as to its membership's strength impossible. Its board of directors includes representatives from nine out of more than one hundred Protestant denominations, the larger ones all being represented. But since the federation was not instituted, nor the directors appointed, by formal denominational action, no one can say precisely how many of the more than half a million members of Protestant churches these represent.

A somewhat similar case is that of the Massachusetts State Federation, which receives delegates from about one-fifth of the Protestant denominations, including all the larger ones. These represent 78 per cent. of the total Protestant church-membership. The representatives of these denominations are officially designated; but in their character as representatives they can scarcely be regarded as standing as close to the churches as do representatives in federations to which local churches appoint their own delegates.

CASE STUDY OF FEDERATION MEMBERSHIP

How difficult a matter it is to discover the proportion of churches and members formally represented by delegates in a federation, may best be seen in a single case.

As reported to the Federal Census of Religious Bodies in 1926, a city of about 130,000 population (exclusive of very important industrial suburbs, the social relationships of whose populations to the central city cannot be accurately determined) had nearly 90,000 church-members in 134 churches.

Of these members, approximately 51,000 were Protestants, divided among forty-five denominations.

The church federation limited its membership to evangelical churches but without defining the term "evangelical." Two or three denominations with an aggregate of between 500 and 600 members, were excluded as belonging to denominations commonly labelled "non-evangelical." But the federation proceeded in addition, to ignore twenty churches of fifteen denominations regarded as unusual, erratic, and non-coöperative in spirit. The aggregate membership in this group was about 2,000. It included, for example, the Holiness, Spiritualist, and Salvation Army organizations.

Usage also prevented any effective membership on the part of Negro churches with some 2,000 members. This reduced the Protestant forces in the terms of which the federation thought about its success or failure, from forty-five denominations to twenty-six, from ninety-six churches to sixty-nine, and from 50,000 members to about 46,000.

This residuum still represented 93 per cent. of the total Protestant body. Starting with this as the effectively eligible group, 80 per cent. of its membership was regarded as coöperative and 20 per cent. as self-excluded. This non-coöperative element comprised 38 per cent. of the church organizations of the eligible group. The average coöperative church had 610 and the average non-coöperative church only 240 members.

In the last analysis, the federation membership actually represented about 37,000 of the 51,000 Protestants. Of the 14,000 that stood outside of the federation, some 4,500 were excluded by constitution or usage. The rest were self-excluded.

Since all the larger denominations other than one Lutheran synod were coöperative; since the federation occupied important advisory and service relations toward the Negro churches; and further, since the Sunday-school teachers and pupils even of the non-coöperative and excluded bodies, participated to a considable extent in religious-education activities, the federation looked upon itself as essentially representative of the organizable part of the Protestant forces. It had no sense of failure, and little urgency of conscience, with respect to the situation.

This was a tenable position as regards the city. The federation, however, lists separately fifteen suburban churches, some of which share in religious-education activities, or are otherwise coöperative in spirit. The suburbs also sometimes figure in comity cases. But for this city, no clear definition of its responsibility for suburban territory exists. No one has fully inventoried the suburban churches and membership; and no one would claim that the federation was as adequately representative of the total metropolitan district as it is of the central city. This situation is common to practically all cities. Such are the complications that make any appraisal of the significance of formal membership difficult.

At worst, however, formal membership does not say the last word. One turns, therefore, to consider other aspects of membership and participation.

FINANCIAL PARTICIPATION OF CHURCHES

As the chapter on Finance will show, federations do not get most of their money directly from churches.[6] Nevertheless, all federations are in part dependent upon such direct gifts; and financial support constitutes one of the most definite tests of organizational participation. One may say that the acid test

---

[6] P. 449.

of federation membership is whether it causes a church deliberately to transfer money out of its treasury into the treasury of the federation.

Many churches that will not do this, contribute to one or more phases of the federation work through their subsidiaries, particularly the parochial women's and young people's organizations. Thus in the case of Washington, only seven Baptist churches contributed directly, but five more had organizations that contributed. Hospitals, religious education, and women's departments are most likely to get financial backing from churches that will not support the federation as such.

Because these secondary types of support are not always credited to the individual churches, it is not possible to tell exactly how many churches support federations either directly or indirectly. Certain comparisons limited to those churches that contribute directly, are nevertheless illuminating. In fifteen cases studied from this viewpoint, the proportion of Protestant churches thus contributing ranges from virtually none to over two-thirds. In more than half the cases, more than a tenth, but not as many as a fourth, of the Protestant churches had made direct contributions in the year preceding the study. In just a third of the cases, more than a third of these churches had supported the federation after this fashion. As in Table IX these comparisons are based on all Protestant churches. Cities vary greatly in the proportion of foreign, Negro and erratic churches which must be recognized as unpromising sources of financial support. But even leaving the significance of these factors somewhat indefinite certain rough conclusions appear warranted.

First, of course, a large independent income from individuals, or from community funds, reduces the necessity of dependence on churches. But whenever such is not the case, a federation must rally a considerable proportion of churches to its financial support if it is to escape failure.

The showing is in striking commentary upon the relative weakness of the average Protestant church. Many individual churches are so weak that their contributions scarcely seem worth the time and effort that must be spent in cultivation and solicitation. Federation officers find that they can get money in faster by appealing to selected individuals than to the great majority of the smaller churches. From the standpoint, however, both of financial support and loyalty, it appears most important to consider financial participation as the vital test of organizational health. Not nearly so many churches support federations financially as belong to them technically through signing the membership roll and sending delegates. On the other hand, it should be noted that occasionally a church that feels twinges of conscience over its non-participation will contribute a small sum and have nothing else to do with the organization.

PARTIAL MEMBERSHIP

But neither membership nor contributor's lists tell the whole story. The preceding study of federation constitutions [7] has shown somewhat frequent provision for partial membership. Presumably experience has proved the necessity of this measure in dealing with the denominations that are less ready to commit themselves to the full implication of the federation movement. Usage, moreover, has extended this method of association beyond its constitutional bounds. Particularly is this true of federations that have built into their structure previously independent organizations, like councils of religious education and women's departments. These, with young people's organizations, are the most frequent points at which the practice of partial membership occurs.

Partial membership may exist under either type of basic membership. Thus in the Chicago Church Federation, which consists of denominational units, six denominations that belong to the Council of Religious Education do not belong to the federation. These include three of the major Negro bodies. One additional denomination belongs to the young people's department and one to the women's department. In many federations that have local churches as their units, a membership list quite different from that of the federation itself appears in the departments enumerated. Not only churches constitutionally excluded as non-evangelical, but churches self-excluded on other grounds, frequently appear.

CAUSES OF PARTIAL MEMBERSHIP

Among the causes of this discrepancy is the fact that larger geographical areas are sometimes more effectively served by the subordinate phases of activity than by the federations as such. Thus in Philadelphia the women's department has included churches in the New Jersey suburbs which do not figure in any other activity of that federation. Councils of religious education, often originating on a county basis, also find it easier to associate the fringe of rural churches in specific activities than

---

[7] P. 82.

federations do to include them in more general aspects of work. Again, a slightly larger range of denominations belongs to the national organizations promoting religious education than belongs to the Federal Council. Churches of denominations that are not thus in national coöperative relations may find it difficult to accept full membership in the local federation, but not difficult to take definite place in subdivisions of the work. In short, belonging to a Council of Religious Education has smaller general ecclesiastical significance. Its implications are less exacting. It does not appear to commit a church to entangling alliances, or to a possibly premature tendency towards church unity. Summarizing the point, a higher percentage of the churches of the less coöperative denominations, and a wider range of denomination, are frequently found in the membership of the departments of federations, especially departments of religious education, women's, or young people's departments, than in the central federations themselves. This situation has been constitutionally legitimatized in some cases, and is found in a good many more.

PARTICIPATION WITHOUT MEMBERSHIP

Virtually all federations include the total body of Protestant ministers in their mailing lists; and all general interchurch plans are communicated alike to members and non-members.[8] Churches that utterly repudiate federation authority even practice partial comity in church extension. A united evangelistic campaign may in a district draw in the churches and denominations that do not care to recognize formal federation leadership. Information in many lines, helpful services, and a share in particular projects are also open to, and frequently make appeal to, churches that have no technical relationship to coöperative organizations.

MEASURING TOTAL PARTICIPATION

While it is impossible systematically to distinguish in the data between habitual and merely occasional coöperation, the evidence makes it certain that this marginal realm of participation without membership greatly extends both the usefulness and the power of church federations. Consequently an attempt was made in a representative series of cases to estimate what proportion of really eligible churches actually participated in fairly significant coöperative projects year by year. The results

---

[8] See the companion volume, *Church Comity,* pp. 49 and 53 f.

again showed federations falling into two clearly distinguishable groups, the relatively unsuccessful and the relatively successful. The former, typically getting but 20 per cent. of the eligible churches on their membership lists, secured stated participation in some form from 45 to 55 per cent. The latter, getting 30 per cent. of the eligible churches upon their membership lists, secured practical participation from 80 to 95 per cent. This latter figure appears to stand for the normal effectiveness of the successful federation, while the former reveals immaturity or dangerous weakness.

Measured in this way, the single departments, which go beyond the federation in scope of formal membership, invariably failed to equal it in effective total participation. Thus a federation in a small city got 62 per cent. of its churches into active membership. The women's department of the same federation surpassed this record and got 79 per cent. of the churches; but the participation of churches, counting all phases of the work, included 85 per cent. of them.

HABITUALLY NON-COÖPERATIVE ELEMENTS

The foregoing review of membership and participation in church federations makes possible a generalized statement with respect to the habitually non-coöperative Protestant elements. Within the Protestant group that is desired and freely admitted to such organized fellowship, five conditions tend to keep churches and denominations out of the fold:

(1) The first condition is the adverse general attitude of certain denominations. The deliberate refusal of some of them to associate themselves with the Federal Council of Churches, and the limited association of others, is familiar and has already been alluded to. Without attempting an adequate analysis of their motives, it is superficially clear that the self-excluded denominations are primarily those that have historic antecedents alien to those of the central group of coöperating Protestant bodies, or else those that cherish a special doctrine of the church and the ministry. They are nationality churches that are, or recently were in part at least, non-English-speaking. Or else they entertained distinctive conceptions of the nature of the church and the proper terms on which those more inclusive organizational fellowships that look toward church unity may be undertaken. Not only when denominations are the units of federation membership, but when local churches are, the attitudes of these denominations are absolutely consistent. They show distinct regional variations. Their representatives are

among the aggressive leaders of federation movements in certain cities, while in others they stand entirely outside. Again, in a given city, a few of their churches may actively belong to the federation, while the majority do not. Throughout the country as a whole, however, and in the attitudes of the majority of churches from city to city, these denominations stand aloof from the main coöperative tendency.

(2) Again, in federations that are composed of individual churches, those that represent the extreme right or left wing of denominational theological attitude may withhold themselves from membership, even when the majority of their own communions are strongly coöperative. This was found to be true of the fundamentalist churches in certain cities.

(3) Again, within the denominations that habitually coöperate, individual churches of alien antecedents are regularly absent from the membership list. Thus a foreign-speaking Methodist or Baptist church is likely to constitute an exception to the habitual coöperation of those denominations.

(4) Weak churches of the coöperating denominations are also apt not to belong to the federation. The reasons for this are fairly obvious. Even the small financial obligation that is felt to be implied in membership serves as an inhibition; while, on the other hand, the federation finds the little church scarcely worth cultivating. Coöperation has its rewards. The important church or minister gets recognition by being appointed to influential positions in the federation. This attraction is not open to the humbler church.

(5) Finally, as has already been noted, the remoter churches geographically speaking—especially those of the suburbs—do not find their way into federation memberships in due proportion.

SUMMARY

All told, then, the practical test of success in getting members is felt to be that of securing a strong minority of the larger churches of the more important denominations for formal membership, together with a considerable majority of their churches for some form of Protestant participation.

The history of the federations has shown that they stand in varying degrees of development, and while the study of membership has been contemporaneous, the data, taken all together, throw light on the typical succession of stages through which the federations go in this matter. Thus the majority of successful federations experienced a rapid growth in organizational membership following the war. Some of the ones established later have not reached this period of rapid growth, but are likely to in the normal course of successful development. As soon, however, as the larger churches of the more important denominations are absorbed, a federation feels that it has reached the point of diminishing returns. The time and effort necessary to win and to cultivate the large marginal group of feeble, alien, and remote churches is disproportionate, considering how little they can bring to the federation. Leaders feel the burden of more urgent responsibilities. Violent charges of neglect sometimes follow from this policy. Federations, however, tend to satisfy their consciences with the fact that participation and service-benefits are open to all equally, including the less desirable elements from the membership standpoint, and that a large majority are found somewhere within the scope of actual participation.

SPECIFIC CONCLUSIONS

It seems fair to conclude that the instinct of the federations in this matter is essentially right. Coöperation rather than formal membership is, and of right ought to be, the heart of coöperative movement. On the other hand, ecclesiastical authority and representativeness, both with respect to the positions taken and the actions carried on by federations, theoretically demand a larger degree of formal affiliation on the part of denominational and parochial units than is habitually secured.

It is fair also to conclude that the unequal participation of churches and denominations grows logically out of the situation, and that its continuance in some degree is to be expected.

The various stages of half-way membership, and participation without membership, are genuine reflections of the series of positions which various ecclesiastical bodies occupy—some nearer to, and some further from, the characteristics of the federation as determined by the central coöperating group.

It seems justified as a final conclusion that the typical successful federations of the most important cities have really gathered up within themselves the consensus and coöperation of a large majority of the bodies of Protestants in their respective communities. The affiliation of the component units is not uniform in degree even in respect to the matters undertaken as central concerns; and at no point is it without limits. This statement will be clarified when the study of federation activities in detail is reached.[9]

---

[9] Chapters XI and XII.

Chapter VII

COÖPERATIVE ACTIVITIES

The present chapter summarizes what federations actually do under the impulses, through the forms, and by means of the organizations revealed in the three preceding chapters; and at the end an attempt is made to explain why federations do these things and not others.

The carrying on of interchurch activities is undoubtedly the most revealing phase of coöperative behavior in American cities. It shows Protestantism actually functioning unitedly. It is the broadest aspect of organized coöperation, especially as activities are shared by a considerable section of the Protestant group that does not formally adhere to the organized movement.

The attempt is here made primarily to classify the coöperative activities centering in federations, to show their range, their characteristics, and their larger relationships. Their more detailed description and discussion is reserved for Part II, The Technical Report.

SCOPE OF FEDERATION PROGRAMS

For the most part, the internal organization of church federation is functional; and the most direct evidence as to the functional scope of the movement is consideration of the departments and standing commissions or committees through which it does its work. A study of these agencies as such comes in another chapter. They are listed here because they indicate the major fields within which federation activities fall. The number of federations operating in each field is also given.

Twenty-three federations were compared on this point. The results are shown in Table X.

Eighteen other committees were found represented in only one federation each, and four others in not more than two each.

As the table brings out, federations are organized primarily according to fields of service-activity, and secondarily according to the essential means they use to perpetuate themselves and extend their influence. With women and young people, however, organization on age-, and sex-lines supersedes organization on a functional basis. Women's or young people's departments, how-

104

ever, maintain their own subcommittees, in large measure duplicating the fields of the federations themselves.

TABLE X—DEPARTMENTS, STANDING COMMITTEES AND COMMISSIONS IN 23 CHURCH FEDERATIONS

Number of
Federations Having

I. TYPE OF SERVICE ACTIVITY

Evangelism and Religious Work	23
Comity	22
Religious Education	22
Social Service	19
International Relations	18
Interracial Relations	13
Political Action, Legislation or Law Enforcement	12
Industrial Relations	6
Court, Hospital or Other Institutions	5
Missions	3
Radio	3
Rural or County Affairs	3
Moral Reform	2
Sabbath Observance	2

II. MEANS OF ADVOCACY AND SUPPORT

Finance	13
Publicity	12

III. AGE- OR SEX-DEPARTMENTALIZATION

Women's Department	12
Young People's Department	8

RELATIVE FREQUENCY OF FIELDS OF ACTIVITY

Evangelism, comity, religious education, social service, and international relations constitute the big five of federation activities. Of the twenty-three federations studied on this point, the one in Louisville omits only a comity committee and the one in Boston only a religious-education committee. Of the four federations that do not maintain social-service committees, all have committees whose duties are limited to one or another special phase of social-service work. These, with the cultivation of Christian attitudes with respect to interracial relations, political action, legislation, and law enforcement, constitute the fields of activity entered upon by more than half the federations studied. The diminishing frequency of special organized provision in other fields means that the matters covered by them have less stress, but rarely that they are entirely omitted by the majority of federations.

Finance and publicity are represented by standing committees in more than half the federations. But whether they are so represented or not, these necessary interests obviously can not be absent from any federation scheme. The tendency to age-, and sex-departmentalization in women's or young people's departments is characteristic of the larger federations and radically conditions the carrying on of many activities.

FREQUENCY OF PARTICULAR ACTIVITIES

While the foregoing summary of the prevailing divisions of federation work serves to suggest its general scope, a really adequate knowledge of what the work covers requires a listing and analysis of specific activities as sustained by the individual organizations.

The instrument used in securing this information was a uniform check-list derived from a preliminary study of the published summaries of activities of representative groups of federations and supplemented during the earlier field studies. This process eventuated in a master-list of 204 activities carried on by two or more federations. These were classified by departments in harmony with the prevailing usage as set forth in the previous section. The current work of twenty-six federations was then checked against this list, and the frequency of each activity in their combined program was calculated.

A current activity was defined as something that had been in actual operation within the year preceding the study. Distinctions of both quantity and quality were ignored, except that no federation was credited with an activity unless it had been developed to a reasonable extent in comparison with that federation's own characteristic activities or with corresponding activities of other federations.

The results of this check-list as relating to certain major departments of work are shown in Appendix III, which indicates the number and proportion of federations that maintain each of the enumerated activities classified according to the prevailing divisions of work.

By the inspection of these tables, the student of the federation movement is enabled to distinguish between the habitual and the exceptional elements of federation programs, and to discover the relative vogue of numerous activities. The items appearing with average or greater frequency are described and discussed in connection with the presentation of major departments of work in subsequent chapters. It will be a sufficient summary at this point to note that a federation that confined itself to activities found in two-thirds or more of all similar organizations would have the following evangelistic program: (1) hold Lenten or Holy Week services; (2) supply pulpits for

coöperating churches; (3) hold conferences on evangelism; (4)
make comprehensive plans for community evangelistic campaigns; (5) conduct home-visitation evangelistic campaigns;
and (6) hold interdenominational Good Friday services. Its
single religious-education activity would be the conduct of a
training school for vacation-school workers. The only social-
service activities currently carried on by more than two-thirds
of the twenty-nine federations are: (1) the promotion of the
coöperation of churches with the social agencies of the community; (2) agitation for reform on specific issues; (3) general
publicity for, and (4) the advocacy of, specific measures of international goodwill. No separate women's activities would be
included in a program common to more than two-thirds of the
federations. There would, however, be a comity committee with
activities of two or three types, the particular forms of which
are not listed comparably in the present showing.[1]

No single principle determines the frequency or infrequency
of a given activity within any department of work. Only the
roughest generalization seems possible. The most that can be
said is, first, that all federations tend habitually to promote
the interest in, and the acceptance of, certain ideas about each
general field of activity through the usual publicity resources,
and with respect to its special constituency. It thus correlates
the practical attitudes, and may try to bring the work of the
separate denominations under a common administrative plan
or agreement. In the second place, all federations tend to find
under each department of work, one or more particular tasks
which they carry out under their own auspices. Thus, for
example, habitual activity in the realm of religious education
includes the highly general matter of promoting better religious-
education administration, and the highly specific one of maintaining the federations' own training schools. Similarly, one
finds under evangelism a comprehensive interpretation and advocacy of the ideal through conferences and the particular federation activities in connection with the celebration of Holy
Week. A typical federation thus has two lines of effort and
engages in both at the same time. One deals with particulars,
the other with general functions in each field of service. One
correlates denominational work, the other operates interdenominational work flying the federation banner.

Within the broad field of activities thus charted, has the
typical federation achieved a well-developed program which has

---

[1] Douglass, *Church Comity* (New York: Institute of Social and Religious
Research, 1929), pp. 44–48.

both range and substantiality? Or is the tendency to enter
many fields nominally and to occupy them but poorly? Such
questions can be answered only by a direct measure of the range
of activity of each federation, in order to discover what is average and typical for the group as a whole.

SCOPE AND VARIETY OF FEDERATION PROGRAMS COMPARED

The cumulative check-list of 204 activities already described
enables one to compare federations by means of a count of the
number of items under each division of work found in the program of each. The results of this process are generalized in
Table XI, which shows in total and by departments the maximum and minimum number of activities carried on by any one
federation, and calculates the median.

TABLE XI—STANDARD ACTIVITIES IN FEDERATION PRO-
GRAMS, BY DEPARTMENTS OF WORK

DEPARTMENT	IN 26 FEDERATIONS	NUMBER OF ACTIVITIES PER FEDERATION		
		Maximum	Minimum	Median
Total	204	138	14	79
Religious Education	25	18	0	9
Evangelism	28	23	2	11
Comity	18	12	0	6
Social Service	20	12	0	5.5
Legislation and Law Enforcement	18	16	1	6.5
Court Work	6	6	0	2.5
Hospital Service	4	4	0	2
Industrial Relations	4	4	0	2
Racial Relations	8	8	0	5
International Relations	11	10	0	4.5
Finance	10	7	1	3.5
Publicity	19	16	1	6
Women's Department	9	9	0	5
Service and Miscellaneous Functions	24	21	1	12

According to this measurement, the federation with the broadest program (138 standard activities) was carrying on somewhat
more than two-thirds of the 204 activities reported by any two
or more of the twenty-six federations, while the median organization was carrying on 39 per cent. of them.

FEDERATIONS RANKED BY SCOPE OF PROGRAM

The federations might have been ranked according to the
proportion of the total number of activities that each one was
carrying on. It is more accurate, however, first to score each
separately according to its relative standing in each department
of work, and to arrive at a final ranking by calculating the

number of times a given federation stands in the first, second, third, or fourth group. This method avoids the obvious uncertainty of a ranking on the basis of the mere presence or absence of activities, that may have been defined in somewhat different ways. All it attempts is to group together federations operating programs of similar scope. The results of this method are shown in the following table, which lists the federations alphabetically within each group.

TABLE XII—RANKING OF 26 FEDERATIONS ACCORDING TO SCOPE OF PROGRAM

	Above Average		Below Average
Highest Fourth	Buffalo Chicago Detroit Indianapolis St. Louis Wichita	Just below Average	Minneapolis New Bedford Oakland Philadelphia San Francisco Youngstown
	Kansas City		New York
Just above Average	Baltimore Pittsburgh Rochester Sacramento Toledo Washington	Lowest Fourth	Boston Brooklyn Louisville Mass. State New London Portland

In considering this list, one discovers very little correlation between the scope of the federation's program and the size of the city in which it is located; and not much between the scope of program and the size of the Protestant constituency or of the federation's staff or budget. Probable causes of greater narrowness or greater expansion will be brought out when the program is discussed in its several departments.[2] They will naturally be found in the realm of unpropitious beginnings, unfriendly environment, or failure to make good in practice, with a consequent decline of institutional scope.

It is, however, important to notice that about three-fifths of the federations have highly inconsistent rankings. They do not reach the position shown, because all or a strong majority of their departments tend to be broad, or to be narrow, in scope as the case may be.

The least inconsistent federations are those that stand either at the top or at the bottom of the list. Thus those in Buffalo, Chicago and Detroit—also, the one in St. Louis in slightly less

[2] Chapters XVI ff.

degree—rank high in almost all aspects of their programs, while those in Boston, New London, and Portland have consistently a low rank. In the cases of the Minneapolis, Brooklyn, Louisville, and Massachusetts State federations the degree of inconsistency is relatively small. They rank where they do on the general tendencies of their programs, though a few aspects place them higher and a few lower.

The standing of all the remaining federations is highly inconsistent. Those in Indianapolis, Wichita, Kansas City, Washington, Rochester, Toledo, Baltimore, Paterson, and Sacramento have some weak departments in spite of which they stand relatively high. Those in Youngstown, New Bedford, Philadelphia, San Francisco, Oakland, and New York have some strong departments, in spite of which they stand below the average in their general tendencies.

In the study of the individual cases it is generally easy to identify the particular handicap, or the particular advantage, that puts a federation below or above its natural level. Comity, for example, does not flourish south of Mason and Dixon's Line.[3] This affects Baltimore, Washington, and Wichita adversely. Minneapolis interprets certain aspects of the church's social duty in a distinctly narrow manner.[4] The rivalry of other agencies of religious education narrows the possible program in this field in a considerable number of cities; examples are Philadelphia, Pittsburgh, and Washington. In its evangelistic program, Philadelphia represents a lapse in coöperation: this federation now shows a narrower set of evangelistic activities than it formerly maintained. On the other hand, the Louisville program is strengthened by unusually strong evangelistic activity; as is the New York program by its comity, the Pittsburgh program by its social service, and the Wichita and Toledo programs by their religious education.

The above showing fairly represents the relative expansion of federation programs in the several cities compared. It should be clearly understood that the comparison does not show the degree of intensiveness with which any department is developed as measured, say, by the number of hours of paid-workers' time devoted to it, or the amount of money expended; nor does it raise any question of the quality of the work. The federations are merely compared with respect to the scope and variety of their total programs.

---

[3] Douglass, *Church Comity*, p. 10.
[4] P. 247.

PROBLEMS FOR CONSIDERATION

As cities vary so greatly in size, as well as in the strength of their Protestant constituencies, they obviously cannot expect federation programs of equal magnitude. The scope of its program consequently does not indicate whether the more fully developed federation has larger or smaller general influence in its community than has the less developed one. There is some reason to think that successful enterprises in the smaller cities have relatively a considerably stronger grip on the situation than have the larger enterprises in the larger cities.

CHARACTERISTIC FEDERATION ACTIVITIES BY MAJOR DEPARTMENTS

The next step toward an understanding of federation activities must be some sort of a logical classification of them.[5] Administrative logic has already been implied in the list of departments of federation work. What is needed now is a classification that will more distinctly reveal the inherent qualities and relations of the individual activities. The attempt to present such a classification was deferred until after the frequency-data had been presented, because only a false impression would be given by printing organized lists of activities without showing which were really established practices of the movement and which were exceptions. But the frequency-lists mix all sorts of activities without regard to affinity. It is time, then, to try to fit together all activities whose frequency warrants their treatment as belonging to the movement, and to show systematically how

[5] Unlike those of other major departments, the federation program of comity does not consist of a group of discrete activities constituting the advocacy and practice of Christianity on the part of the coöperating Protestant forces. Comity does not have to do with individuals but with churches. It saves no one, serves no one. Instead it merely makes the institutional way straight and its rough places plain.

When comity is not incidentally engaged in such service activities as giving ecclesiastical information and advice to those who request it, it consists of a series of procedures directed either to the avoidance or adjustment of denominational conflict in the establishment, location, removal and conduct of churches (negative comity); or to coöperative church planning of non-competitive institutions so devised, placed, and sustained as to meet the needs of the city (positive comity).

In negative comity, the sequence of steps is (1) receipt of information (formal or informal) concerning some conflict or adjustment situation; (2) consideration of the case (formal or informal); (3) reference to individual or committee; (4) investigation; (5) conference with parties of interest; (6) report of results; (7) action on report; (8) efforts to get decision adopted.

In positive comity, the necessary sequence is (1) urgency and survey of defective conditions; (2) strategic plan for religious institutions; (3) communication of the plan to the constituency (publication, publicity, etc.); (4) efforts to get the plan adopted.

See the companion volume of the report, *Church Comity*, especially Chapter V.

particular activities fall into certain fairly consistent federation programs in all the more frequent departments of work.

THE PROGRAM OF EVANGELISM

The most familiar evangelistic method of the church at large is to gather people into congregations for religious services. But to do this coöperatively, obviously implies joint planning.

(1) This is the logical starting point of the evangelistic program—joint planning may be merely coördinative, as when the denominations counsel together but do not undertake actual joint operations, or administration, as they must when they set up types of evangelistic activity under the federation's own auspices.

(2) Next, it is necessary to inform and inspire the leaders and more active participants in whatever is planned. Evangelistic conferences and "retreats" in which individuals come into religious rapport and are personally committed to the program, constitute a logical second step—and one frequently taken in some form, sometimes through occasions for clergy and laymen separately. (3) Again the participation of laymen in evangelistic campaigns, or of the clergy in concerted technical measures, requires special training. Training devices accordingly must enter into a rounded program.

(4) The rank and file of the church will also be asked to intensify their private religious observances, and means are furnished them for the cultivation of the devotional life.

(5) Now, at length, come its most frequent and conspicuous features, namely, public evangelistic services. As to time, the most characteristic services are seasonal, associated with Lent, Holy Week and Easter; or with the summer vacation. Most of them are regularly recurrent; others, however, are associated with special campaigns. A minority of services are directed to the evangelization of limited or special classes of people; sometimes children or young people; sometimes casual crowds on the streets or in public parks; sometimes the inmates of institutions.

(6) Parallel with public services goes on the evangelism of individuals, in which the church has always had representatives at work. In the federation program, this is often carried on simultaneously by hundreds of workers over large areas of the city as a feature of highly organized campaigns.

(7) In connection with both services and personal evangelism, goes on the distribution of the Scriptures and of religious literature.

So far, all the items of the federation program of evangelism have long been familiar to religious practice. Two relatively novel items complete the list.

(8) Federations frequently undertake somewhat technical surveys to locate and measure evangelistic need and opportunity.

(9) Finally they use the new evangelistic device of radio broadcasting.

The nine types of activities enumerated constitute the apparently permanent features of a typical program of evangelism now emerging in the practice of federations.

THE PROGRAM OF RELIGIOUS EDUCATION

A recognized pattern for a community program has been evolved by the technical agencies of religious education. It is assumed to cover the four major fields of (1) the church Sunday school, (2) vacation church schools, (3) week-day religious instruction, and (4) leadership training.

In addition it will include (5) possible separate provision for religious education in the home. (6) It will make, in all aspects of the program, age-adaptations to the Christian culture of children, of youth and of adults. It will commonly institute committees for the administration of these divisions of the field; and where possible will head them with professional experts. Finally it will include (7) practical service-activities, such as a bureau of information and advice and a reference library, and will supply the contacts, stimulus, and general promotional advocacy and publicity for the whole movement. (8) Its relations to the state and national agencies of religious education will involve it in further activities of coöperation and support.

As unevenly developed by the federation, a religious-education program on these lines is likely to involve at least coördinating or promotional activities in most of the fields enumerated, and the operations of training processes in some of them. In view of the greater precision of educational techniques and practice, this program is more clear-cut and more nearly standardized than that of evangelism, or indeed of any other department of federation work.

THE PROGRAM OF SOCIAL SERVICE

The social-service program, on the contrary, is the least well-established and the most problematical. The concrete interests handled by general social-service committees are exceedingly varied; while the number and range of fields, identified by the organization of separate committees, further establish the complexity of the larger whole.

A principle of classification for the items of the social-service program of federations may however be found in a series of facts that give such work its broadest conditioning.

(1) In the first place, it is concerned with a federation of churches, and not merely one of social agencies. Social agencies have their work to do; but they are not sent to proclaim a gospel. The Church, on the contrary, has the historic function of preaching quite as much as of practicing. It has to make the world helpful as well as to be helpful in the world. It is the Church's mission to be both a voice and a hand.

(2) In these two capacities the Church, as federated, has to do with different publics. It preaches to the community, to its own special constituency, and in important senses to the state. It practices by assisting the social agencies to serve needy people, and by serving such people directly under its own auspices. Its preaching takes the forms of agitation, of propaganda, sometimes of education. Its practice as related to social agencies may involve efforts to modify and improve their condition as well as to work with them as they are. Its practice, as related to its own social work, may be institutional in form or non-institutional.

(3) Entirely apart from these strictly logical possibilities, some phases of social service are actually emphasized by federations as a group, while others are minimized.

TYPES OF SOCIAL-SERVICE ACTIVITY

In the following outline of the social work of federations, those functions that fall on the side of preaching come first, the less developed having prior mention, then the highly developed functions, namely, the advocacy of specific social ideals before their own constituencies, and propaganda directed toward influencing the activities of government.

Similarly, on the side of practice, the relatively slight work of federations under their own auspices comes first; then the extensive forms of coöperation with voluntary social agencies, and with the state.

The distinctions thus defined are of course not absolute. Preaching and practice interpenetrate, and functions set down under one head exhibit secondary characteristics which show that they are related to another. Finally are added certain technical functions, together with others that reach beyond the strict confines of the social field. These comprise a third major division within the classification scheme now to be presented.

Advocacy of General Social Ideals

Federations regularly, though almost always incidentally, preach a social gospel. It is ordinarily a somewhat nebulous gospel. They proclaim general Christian ideals of social relationships by this or that method, but with little system, continuity or originality. In but one case was this function performed so consciously and effectively as to be counted a regular activity. This does not signify that the ideals underlying social service do not have to be continuously rekindled at the original altar of religion. It simply means that keeping social service alive is not regarded as primarily the responsibility of federations. It is rather left to the constituent churches and denominations.

The Attempt to Influence the Action of Government

A frequent and highly stressed type of activity has for its essence the attempt to focus Protestant group-sentiment upon the conduct of government. Agitation arouses this sentiment so as to bring pressure upon the political processes or personalities of the city, state, or nation from the standpoint of Christian ideals. Such effort may direct itself to influencing the actions of citizens, either as individuals as expressed, for example, in voting; or as groups organized for purposes of propaganda or education. In the latter case, such group-action may concern itself either with legislation, that is to say, with the passing or preserving of laws in furtherance of moral and social welfare; or it may focus upon administration, of which agitation for law enforcement is the outstanding illustration.

Education of Social Attitudes Involving Larger Group-Relationships

Again, certain federations stress the guidance and modification of attitudes of their constituents toward the larger group-relationships of man. Such effort chiefly concerns (a) relationships within the economic order, of which industrial conflicts reveal the dynamic core; (b) relationships within and between racial groups, of which prejudice and the infliction of disabilities afford the most superheated examples; or (c) relationships between nations, which largely concentrate upon issues of war and peace.

SOCIAL WELFARE ACTIVITIES

Non-institutional Social Service

Only occasionally, but in the aggregate under a wide variety of forms, have federations undertaken family and individual case-work divorced from systematic institutional ministries. Again, they have sometimes instituted rather simple measures for neighborhood or community betterment. Social service of this more direct and unpretentious type is apt to characterize the feebly developed programs of the smaller federations. It also figures as a by-product of some of the larger programs. But work in these areas is left, in the main, to denominations and individual churches rather than undertaken coöperatively.

Institutional Service

An occasional federation operates social-welfare institutions under its own auspices; for example, a community center or a home. In very rare instances, the establishment of new inter-denominational institutions were under discussion.

Participation in the Work of Voluntary Social Organizations

In contrast with the very limited work under the direct auspices of federations are the activities which the typical federation is likely to undertake in coöperation with the existing voluntary social agencies of the community. Sometimes these agencies are non-sectarian, sometimes denominational. They may be individually assisted, or the federation's coöperative relationships may be with the representative Council of Social Agencies. Participation in the work of social agencies sometimes takes forms other than coöperative, as when federations attempt to correlate Protestant social agencies.

Coöperation with the Institutionalized Social Activities of Government

A narrow group of activities, but an important and expensive one, involves the coöperation of federations with the state. Here the agencies concerned are not voluntary but governmental. Such coöperation is found particularly in courts and prisons where federations maintain representatives acting as probation officers and pastors and chaplains.

TECHNICAL AND MARGINAL ACTIVITIES

Social Education, Research, and Technical Services

Outside the field of preaching, yet not partaking of the nature of direct social service, lie the formal educational and technical activities of a few federations. These conduct systematic educational classes, or carry on social research into the needs of some class or community; or they make technical investigations of other social institutions with reference to their worthiness to receive public support.

Borderland Activities

Finally, social service is not the only concern of federations. There are many borderland activities which involve it and other aspects and departments of work at the same time; as, for example, when church-extension surveys raise problems of community welfare, or when missions take the form of institutional work for a foreign-speaking population through methods which are essentially social. Again, pastoral ministries often come to recognize that they involve social case-work. Education, either carried out formally in classes or more informally as in extension institutes, may deal with social themes; as, for example, sex-hygiene. Religious services themselves sometimes figure as primarily social activities; as, for example, when they get their significance from some specific occasion like the celebration of a community or national holiday. The outreach of social service into such overlapping fields is a necessary part of the total scheme. In addition, many experiments that cannot claim any general significance have been entered upon by individual federations.

Virtually everything in the realm of social service that is currently undertaken by any considerable number of church federations falls somewhat naturally within one or another of the above classifications which thus serve to define summarily the scope and content of the field.

PROGRAMS OF WOMEN'S DEPARTMENTS

Generalizing as to the kinds of service underlying the specific activities of women's departments, one finds the interchurch organization of women carrying on five characteristic types of work: (1) It advocates, more or less systematically, Christian ideas and causes before its distinctive public of church women, particularly the cause of missions; (2) it raises funds and contributes goods for various philanthropic purposes; (3) it performs personal service in a variety of fields of social work primarily as a volunteer; (4) it carries on formally organized educational processes of rather small magnitude, education in the main being retained by the separate denominations; (5) it administers occasional pieces of social work and shares in the administration of still other work carried on by the federations with which it is affiliated.

Scope of Women's Departments' Programs

Missionary activities are the most frequent and characteristic of undertakings for the group of women's organizations as a whole; and some of the older types that originated as missionary movements have never broadened their programs beyond this. The most frequent phases of social and community service appear in less than half the women's organizations studied; and the great majority of activities are found in less than one-fourth of the cases. This indicates that, except for the original missionary interest, there is no strong common tendency running throughout the entire group of organizations. Up to date, coöperative women have simply caught on here and there to some rather chance aspect of the total coöperative program which was available in a given case.

SERVICE-FUNCTIONS OF FEDERATIONS

The thing which the federation does more often than any other is to furnish information. The majority of communications received by it, either by mail or telephone, begin, "Can you tell me . . ." or "How can I find out . . ." One who sits casually in a federation office is impressed and amused by the variety of subjects concerning which the federation is questioned in the name of religion.

Many requests come from other constructive organizations in the community. For example, the Historical Society wants to know which is the oldest church in a certain district and the date of its founding. An official charged with making an address of welcome at a religious convention on behalf of the Protestant churches must be told how many there are in each denomination and what is their numerical strength. The federation's directory of addresses of pastors and churches is used by numerous other interests.

In performing these services, the federation regularly has to refer inquirers to other agencies. It thus functions as an intermediary and redistributing organization in the matter of getting information on to the ultimate consumer.

Naturally a large number of inquiries relate to speakers for various religious meetings. The federation knows the capability and availability of persons who are either eloquent or expert, and is constantly called upon for advice in this connection.

The federation's mailing list of constituents is loaned, under proper safeguards, to important movements that desire access to the churches. In exchange, the federation receives the courtesy of the use of mailing lists of community agencies in other spheres.

The federation's investigation of, and attitude toward, numerous individuals seeking to promote special interests in the religious world amounts virtually to the granting or withholding of Protestant endorsement. Here, for example, is a man who wants to carry on a campaign to induce people to remember Christian institutions in their wills. The object is laudable, but the federation has to decide whether to back and facilitate such a movement in its city at a given time. The individual can, of course, go ahead without regard to the federation; but he finds it much easier when the federation is on his side.

Incidentally, the federation office is looked to for confidential advice on a wide variety of matters. Its officials are accessible people possessed of a large general knowledge of current religious affairs and much wisdom concerning them. They are in relationships of intimate friendliness and confidence with leaders in many departments of denominational religious and civic activity, and have opportunity to influence in detail large numbers of movements with which they are not officially concerned.

Not a few of these service functions involve the general pastoral ministries of friendliness, sympathy, and a spiritual authority; since so many of the inquiries involve acute need of some sort. High on the list of the federation's services accordingly, is the fact that it maintains in its offices kind, patient and good people, as well as wise and decisive ones—people able to deal with these many incidental demands with a due sense of their relative importance and urgency.

A very considerable part of a federation's service functions has to do with agencies outside the community. Federations promote the national programs initiated by the Federal Council of Churches and other bodies serving the Protestant cause at large, such as the International Council of Religious Education and the Religious Education Association; as well as the interests of non-sectarian agencies such as the Peace movement. These relationships have further study in another connection.

A still further set of service activities is involved in the city's role as host to important interests that are not strictly of a religious character. When a city government or Chamber of Commerce is attempting to function in behalf of the whole public, it is likely to call in representatives of the major religious bodies; and this, in the case of Protestantism, generally means the church federation.

Even if the federation movement had no other function, it would justify by such activities a considerable part of the expenditure of time and money in its maintenance. It occupies a pivotal position in facilitating the exchange of information, courtesies, and plans within the great network of agencies essential to the ongoing of our complicated urban civilization.

How Constituents Regard the Service Program of Federations

Judged by responses from constituents of sixteen federations, the somewhat miscellaneous group of service-functions is regarded just about as favorably as the total program.[6] The relative standing of representative aspects of the service program is shown in Table XIII.

TABLE XIII—RANKING OF ITEMS OF SERVICE PROGRAMS ACCORDING TO CONSTITUENTS' JUDGMENTS REGARDING APPROPRIATENESS AND IMPORTANCE, IN 16 FEDERATIONS

ITEM OF PROGRAM	PER CENT. OF JUDGMENT Highly Favorable	Unfavorable
Total Service Items	72.6	7.7
Functions as clearing house of Protestant religious plans	84.5	2.3
Is satisfactorily related to the Protestant Ministers' Union	76.3	4.3
Functions as bureau of religious information	75.0	4.4
Acts as employment agency for church workers	65.8	9.8
Furnishes pulpit supplies to churches	61.0	11.3
Furnishes mailing list to suitable agencies desiring to communicate with the churches	57.5	15.3
Publishes Federation periodical	48.4	13.1

Problems of Federation Programs

It is a question whether the scope, content, and trends of the program as it is emerging, and is coming to be reproduced through imitation, should be allowed to stand for a tentative goal for the movement at large. Shall one assume that the period of initial experiment is probably over, and that most of the possibilities of the movement have been explored? If so, the

---

[6] P. 134.

outline of a standard program may be in sight. Or shall one say that the present program is too narrowly conceived and shows too little balance to constitute a norm when placed in the scales of theoretical value?

Still again, even if the present outline is accepted as revealing a satisfactory general type, may not the average program be improved by the greater specialization in which the particular needs and genius of each city shall express themselves? May not the common purpose and the spirit of unity of the coöperating churches be more vitally realized through conspicuous developments in particular areas of service than by means of a largely uniform program? Is the standard program that is tending to evolve to be regarded, then, as an end to be approached or as a point of departure? This alternative constitutes one of the profoundest challenges of the current federation movement.

WHEN AND WHY PROTESTANTS COÖPERATE

Generalizing with respect to the entire study of federation activities, one is led to a very obvious conclusion; viz: that these organizations are instruments of selective ecclesiastical coöperation. They provide a ready means whereby Protestants may work together in a limited number of undertakings under very special conditions. Compared with possible coöperative activities, the 204 items of the standard check-list—most of which occur infrequently—fail to impress one as at all inclusive. It was never to be presumed, however, that Protestants will wish to coöperate at all points; and no general agreement as to just what activities are to be coöperatively operated has ever been reached.

ABSENCE OF A GUIDING PRINCIPLE OF AGREEMENT

When, then, do Protestants coöperate, and when do they not? The only comprehensive formula supplied by the data is that they coöperate in "the prosecution of work that can better be done in union than in separation." This entirely empty phrase from the Federal Council constitution is echoed time and again in local expositions; but it entirely fails as a guide to concrete decisions. Negatively it assumes that, in the main, the denominations will continue separate and more or less competitive existences. Whatever may be conceded to the realm of coöperation, the major area of the Church's interests is reserved for the several communions. The situation is exactly like that of the nation before the formal establishment of federal government, when coöperation was grudgingly admitted by the states in limited spheres.

How fast then, can the movement go? No general answer is possible. What can best be done together must be determined one issue at a time. The result is dependent upon the accident of the moment. There is no guiding principle. Under these conditions the mood of the movement is purely opportunistic.

Having observed the development of programs, and the conduct of the several activities of the more than twenty federations, the author feels considerable assurance in attempting to generalize as to the conditions under which coöperative activities arise, and in venturing tentatively to explain why Protestants coöperate at these points and not at others.

Negatively speaking, one has first to say that Protestants almost never coöperate for the sheer reasonableness of such action, or because they want to be brotherly. Coöperation at a given time or place always reflects some particular advantage or particular pressure that serves to carry over previously separate activities into a joint program at this point or that.

CONDITIONS OF COÖPERATION

Summarizing positively, one observes that Protestants coöperate when the inhibitions of ecclesiastical control are appreciably reduced, or when the impulse to coöperation is appreciably heightened, either by reinforcement from outside sources or by internal pressure; or when both conditions coincide. Twelve conditions falling under these categories seem to the author to cover virtually the entire range of coöperative activity. Seven show the results of a reduction of ecclesiastical inhibitions; two, the result of the reinforcement of coöperative impulses from outside; and three, the drive of internal pressure. These twelve conditions mark the fields, the climatic situations, and the favoring circumstances in and because of which even the tender plant of united service can flourish. They will now be presented in order:

Ecclesiastical Inhibitions Diminished

(1) Protestants coöperate in spheres where coöperation is a long-accepted habit and where the original motive is obscured by tradition. Here time has worn away the vigor of inhibitions. One cannot trace the origins of these more established coöperative habits with sufficient accuracy to tell whether they were, in their time, caused by special opportunities or pressures, or whether they were born of the energy of great convictions. But

traditional types of interdenominational Sunday-school work, women's interdenominational missionary unions, Sabbath-observance movements and the like, well illustrate this strain in the coöperative movement.

(2) Protestants coöperate when some accepted and unchallenged generality needs particular reinforcement or vital re-statement, and when all measures for carrying out the consequences of re-statement are left to the denominations. Thus even Catholics and Protestants may unite in urging the observance of Good Friday, which they then proceed to observe each in his own separate way. In short, there is no real conflict with the ecclesiastical status-quo.

(3) Protestants coöperate in spheres not previously occupied denominationally. They undertake joint pioneering ventures somewhat frequently. In such cases denominational inhibitions do not as yet exist. The coöperative movement for week-day religious education comes partly under this category. So does the taking of advanced ethical positions in the field of social conflict. Here the new coöperative movement does not clash with what the denominations are already doing, because it is so far in advance of them.

(4) Protestants coöperate in spheres where the type of activity and the characteristics of the persons concerned do not constitute a profitable field for denominational service. This tends to be true of the more self-sacrificing types of missions. Thus the Home Missions Council recently appointed a commission "to consider the feasibility of maintenance by (denominational) boards of joint departments for the conduct of mission work of the type which is not productive from a denominational point of view, such as Indian missions, lumber camps, etc."

There is no profit for the denominations in such ministries, but merely outgo of money and service. This partly explains the willingness to coöperate in court and hospital work, in comity arrangements with respect to the foreign-born, in street preaching and temporary seasonal services. Denominations can build themselves up faster by investing their energies at other points, leaving these difficult types of service to coöperative activity. Coöperation under such circumstances scarcely commands praise as conspicuously virtuous.

(5) Protestants coöperate when the process is not only profitable, but carefully safeguarded as well. In typical comity procedures an officially operated bargaining system exists to regulate competition advantageously. The promised land is parcelled out among the denominations, and each denomination expects

sooner or later to get value received for any concession it may make anywhere along the line. This goes far toward making comity palatable.

(6) Protestants coöperate in areas of activity that are not controlled by the clerical and the ecclesiastical tradition. This is particularly true of movements of women and of young people. Both have anticlerical instincts. They do not feel bound by the claims of regularity as the coöperative movement generally does. Consequently they calmly venture into coöperative commitments whose implications greatly frighten the ecclesiastical mind. It is freer evolution of these age-, and sex-groups that explains considerable reaches of coöperation that would not otherwise occur.

(7) Protestants coöperate where new and poorly established interchurch movements find that they can strengthen themselves by coming under the aegis of some more comprehensive coöperative machinery like a church federation. Such movements bother the denominations less when regulated than they do when independent. The history of the assimilation of other interchurch agencies into the federation shows that it is notably the less stable ones that combine, while the more successful tend to remain aloof. In all the situations so far enumerated, coöperation occurs because the usual inhibitions for one reason or another, are diminished or relaxed.

Re-enforced Coöperative Impulses

(8) Protestants coöperate in situations controlled by forces outside the Church that are willing to recognize a coöperative method of service but will not put up with a sectarian method. This situation is illustrated in radio broadcasting where the owners of the facilities will not bother themselves with competitive sectarian claims; in court work where the administration of justice will not tolerate sectarianism; in the matter of chaplaincies in public institutions for the same reason; and in weekday religious education where public-school authorities generally refuse to countenance or facilitate the movement unless the warring sects get together. At such points the children of the world coerce the children of light into united effort. Certainly not all of the credit, in such situations, can go to the Church.

(9) Protestants coöperate in work requiring an exceptionally exacting technique, the standards of which are set by forces outside the ecclesiastical field. This is true with respect to training schools of religious education; to surveys and statistics, and to the duties of professional social workers. The denomina-

tions separately cannot supply enough leadership in these fields; and work that acknowledged authorities will count respectable can hardly be done without coöperation. Only the pooled resources of the churches can meet the technical demands of the situation at these points. Here again the virtue behind coöperation originates mainly outside the Church.

Coöperation Under Internal Pressure

(10) Protestants coöperate where they find great practical convenience in so doing, coupled with small ecclesiastical implications. Thus coöperation is easy in merely routine services such as the exchange of information, in the operation of employment and service bureaus, in the promotion of national Christian movements, in functioning as a clearing house of plans, in the conduct of temporary seasonal services, etc. When these advantageous conditions pertain, Christians coöperate just as the Gentiles do and for the same reasons.

(11) Protestants coöperate when they feel that only the weight of their united forces can win a particular issue or make a particular plan succeed. This is evidenced by most of the coöperative efforts in the political field, by simultaneous evangelistic campaigns, and by advanced movements in which one feels that one's attempt to interest one's own denomination needs to be backed by the joint action of a representative Protestant body. When Protestantism must speak unitedly in order to have any chance to be heard, it is likely to find a temporary voice.

(12) Protestants coöperate where the high symbolic significance of an occasion requires at least the gesture of united action. Here, for a brief moment, the demands of aesthetic unity govern. The impression that only a united church can make is achieved by means of a very temporary union for a particular occasion. When the occasion is over, the union dissolves and the old order is not greatly disturbed. Interdenominational Holy Week services, and the coöperative celebration of national anniversaries illustrate this situation.

CONCLUSION

Any given example of coöperative activity is likely to be the result of the concurrence of more than one of these conditions. Thus when an activity is at the same time advantageous and incidental, or advantageous and temporary, it is easy to get it into the coöperative program. Each federation gets its going program out of the accident and circumstance by which, in particular communities, a concatenation of forces such as has been described, weakens the denominational barriers allowing coöperation to break through and to assert itself in limited form in this or that sphere.

To explain coöperation that is even so scant and occasional, it is necessary to assume that the previous habits of constituencies and the advantage of the existing agencies are not too greatly disturbed; that denominational leaders are personally friendly, or else are forced by the situation; and that tactful and conciliatory policies are pursued.

Now the habit of committing coöperative responsibilities to church federations has grown rapidly, even under the limitations just shown. It has established a new order of church life and constitutes a vast achievement, an achievement that appears greater rather than smaller when the niggardly conditions under which it has been accomplished are understood.

What will be the next step of evolution? At what point, if at all, will coöperative practices become so well established that the fields of activity which they have generally occupied, under the specially favoring conditions just enumerated, can be identified, defined and, in principle at least, assigned to the federations by action of the national denominational bodies? When shall the selection of activities by a given federation cease to be merely opportunistic, and instead proceed upon the presumption that, if there is a federation at all, it will have a clearly marked set of functions definitely and permanently committed to it?

If the present direction and rate of evolution continue, there may easily be some such an outcome within the next two decades. There is enough consistency in present tendencies toward a common program to suggest at least the probably major spheres of future federation activity, and the probable lines of its further development. Such a program, once established, could be added to by the same process that originally made it possible, and might be expanded by more rational and generous considerations.

Chapter VIII

CONSTITUENTS' JUDGMENTS UPON CURRENT PROGRAMS

The study of the attitudes of constituents toward federations was not limited to the measurement of the sense of obligation to coöperate, which has already been reported upon.[1]

To ascertain also what the constituents thought of their respective federations as functioning agencies, agencies performing specific services in behalf of the coöperating churches, questionnaires were sent out which asked separate judgments with respect to an average of about fifty of the most important items of the current federation program in each city. A uniform scale of judgments was provided allowing a constituent to take one of the five following positions upon each item of the program:

(1) Something which the Federation should not undertake at all.
(2) Questionable.
(3) Permissible but not important.
(4) Somewhat important.
(5) Highly important.

Returns in this form were received from 2,884 persons in sixteen cities. They rendered an aggregate of 134,280 judgments upon specific aspects of federation activities.

A distribution of the answers of these 2,884 constituents is shown by cities in Appendix Table 5.

JUDGMENTS UPON CURRENT PROGRAMS

On the combined showing of these questionnaires, seventy-two out of every hundred constituents held the programs of their respective federations to be highly important. Nineteen per cent. held that they were somewhat important, while only 9 per cent. gave unfavorable judgments indicated by the three positions at the lower end of the scale. These results are presented in total, and for each city, in Table XIV.

---

[1] Pp. 69 ff.

127

TABLE XIV—CONSTITUENTS' JUDGMENTS REGARDING AP-
PROPRIATENESS AND IMPORTANCE OF PROGRAMS OF 17
FEDERATIONS, BY CITIES

		Per Cent. Distribution of Judgments			
CITY	Total	Should Not Undertake	Ques- tionable	Permissible But Not Important	Somewhat Important	Highly Important
Total	100	2	2	5	19	72
Baltimore	100	2	3	8	24	63
Boston	100	4	4	9	29	54
Chicago	100	0	1	5	20	74
Detroit	100	1	2	5	18	74
Indianapolis	100	1	3	5	23	68
Minneapolis	100	1	1	4	14	80
New York	100	2	2	7	23	66
Oakland	100	2	4	6	18	70
Philadelphia	100	4	4	6	20	66
Pittsburgh	100	2	2	4	17	75
Portland, Me.	100	1	2	3	23	71
Rochester	100	1	1	4	19	75
St. Louis	100	1	2	4	15	78
Washington	100	1	2	9	26	62
Wichita	100	0	1	4	17	78
Youngstown	100	0	1	6	18	75
Mass. State	100	2	2	5	20	71

JUDGMENTS BY CITIES

Striking differences in the distribution of judgments were
registered from city to city. A convenient means of comparing
them is furnished in Table XV.

TABLE XV—RANKING OF 17 FEDERATIONS ACCORDING TO
CONSTITUENTS' JUDGMENTS REGARDING APPROPRIATE-
NESS AND IMPORTANCE OF PROGRAMS

FEDERATION	Per Cent. of Highly Favorable Judgments (Position 5)	FEDERATION	Per Cent. of Unfavorable Judgments (Positions 1–3)
Minneapolis	80	Wichita	5
St. Louis	78	Chicago	6
Wichita	78	Minneapolis	6
Pittsburgh	75	Portland, Me.	6
Rochester	75	Rochester	6
Youngstown	75	St. Louis	7
Chicago	74	Youngstown	7
Detroit	74	Detroit	8
Portland, Me.	71	Pittsburgh	8
Mass. State	71	Indianapolis	9
Oakland	70	Mass. State	9
Indianapolis	68	New York	11
New York	66	Oakland	12
Philadelphia	66	Washington	12
Baltimore	63	Baltimore	13
Washington	62	Philadelphia	14
Boston	54	Boston	17

This table shows at a glance cities in which the current federation programs were most favorably regarded, and most unfavorably regarded; and those in which the constituents' attitudes fell nearest to the average. The range of highly favorable judgments, from 54 to 80 per cent.—though noteworthy—is proportionately much narrower than the range of unfavorable

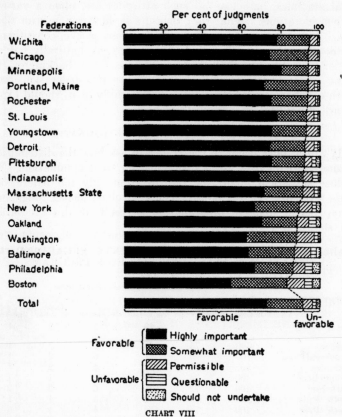

CHART VIII

Distribution of judgments of constituents with respect to the importance and appropriateness of current programs—17 Church Federations

judgments, which is from 5 to 17 per cent. The antagonistic minority is more than three times as numerous, relatively speaking, in Boston as it is in Wichita.

CRITERIA OF JUDGMENT

The particular form of the questionnaire makes it clear that various factors enter into these judgments. Appropriateness and importance both figure as criteria with respect to any item of the program; and it is probable that many a constituent will consider both of these criteria in the light of the present leadership and administration of his federation. Some said as much in comments accompanying the return of their questionnaires.[2]

What the returns yield is therefore a rough measure of practical attitudes, based, as all such attitudes are, upon a variety of considerations. What they measure is, however, a grim reality. A federation, 80 per cent. of whose active constituents think its work as a whole is highly important, naturally has an easier time than one that enjoys only 54 per cent. backing on the same basis; and there will be no surprise if a federation, one-sixth of whose constituents think unfavorably of it, should experience difficulties in administration.

CONSTITUENTS' JUDGMENTS BY DENOMINATIONS

It will at once occur to the reader to ask how the distribution of judgments varies from denomination to denomination. To reduce statistical labor, the returns from only ten federations were tabulated on this point. These involved 99,092 judgments upon specific items of program.[3] The results of this tabulation are shown in Table XVI.

TABLE XVI—CONSTITUENTS' JUDGMENTS REGARDING APPROPRIATENESS AND IMPORTANCE OF PROGRAMS OF 10 FEDERATIONS, BY DENOMINATIONS

DENOMINATION	Total No. of Judgments	PER CENT. DISTRIBUTION OF JUDGMENTS				
		Highly Important	Somewhat Important	Permissible	Questionable	Should Not Undertake
Total	100	73	19	5	2	1
Baptist	100	75	18	4	2	1
Congregational ...	100	70	21	6	2	1
Disciples	100	76	17	4	2	1
Evangelical	100	74	20	4	1	1
Lutheran	100	72	18	6	2	2
Meth. Epis.	100	75	18	5	1	1
Meth. Prot.	100	74	21	4	1	0
Presbyterian	100	74	18	5	2	1
Prot. Epis.	100	67	19	7	3	4
Reformed	100	71	20	4	3	2
United Presb.	100	77	16	2	1	4
All Other	100	71	19	6	2	2

On the combined programs of these ten federations, the distribution of constituents' judgments varied but slightly from

---

[2] Pp. 230 f.

[3] Appendix Table 4. The federations covered by the tabulation were those of Boston, Massachusetts State, Chicago, Minneapolis, Detroit, Pittsburgh, Rochester, St. Louis, Washington, and Wichita.

the results of similar calculations for seventeen federations already shown in Table XV. One per cent. more regarded the program as highly important, and one per cent. less said that a federation should not undertake certain activities. This close correspondence indicates that the more limited sample is probably entirely adequate for its purposes.

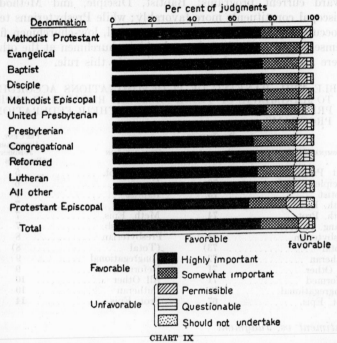

CHART IX

Distribution of judgments of constituents with respect to the importance and appropriateness of current Church Federation programs—12 denominations

Ranking Tables

The denominations, for greater convenience in comparing them, are ranked in Table XVII according to the per cent. of highly favorable and also according to the per cent. of unfavorable judgments.

While the total distribution of judgments for each denominational constituency should first be considered, it is manifestly possible to regard any given denomination, as this table does, from either end of the scale.

The Protestant Episcopal constituents tended not to regard federation programs as highly important; and they also were more definitely critical than those of any other denomination. While all the other denominations stay on the same side of the average in both columns, they fail to show exact consistency. The most that one can say is that—of denominations adequately reported upon—the Congregational, Episcopal and Lutheran constituents express themselves less favorably than the average toward current programs; Baptist, Disciple, and Methodist Episcopal constituents more favorably; while Presbyterians tend to occupy the median position. In general, low-churchmen find themselves at one end of the scale, high-churchmen at the other. There are, however, obvious exceptions to this rule.

TABLE XVII—RANKING OF 12 DENOMINATIONS ACCORDING TO JUDGMENTS OF THEIR MEMBERS REGARDING APPROPRIATENESS AND IMPORTANCE OF THEIR FEDERATIONS' PROGRAMS

DENOMINATION	PER CENT. OF HIGHLY FAVORABLE JUDGMENTS (POSITION 5)	DENOMINATION	PER CENT. OF UNFAVORABLE JUDGMENTS (POSITIONS 1-3)
Unit. Presb.	77	Meth. Prot.	5
Disciples	76	Evang.	6
Baptist	75	Baptist	7
Meth. Epis.	75	Disciples	7
Meth. Prot.	74	Meth. Epis.	7
Evang.	74	Unit. Presb.	7
Presbyterian	74	Presbyterian	8
(Total	73)	(Total	8)
Lutheran	72	Congregational	9
All Other	71	Reformed	9
Reformed	71	All Other	10
Congregational	70	Lutheran	10
Prot. Epis.	67	Prot. Epis.	14

Sentiment vs. Judgment

Head and heart are not always in accord; though, on the whole, they tend to be so as related to the federations.

Minneapolis and St. Louis, which head the list on the score of favorable judgments of program, get slightly less than average expressions of loyalty, as shown by the previous test of constituent's sentiments.[4] Washington, Portland, and Oakland on the other hand, none of which cities carries on work of exceptional scope, rank higher on loyalty than on estimated value of program. All other cities have about the same relative standing on the two tests.

The majority of denominations, too, show close correlation between constituents' sentiments and judgments. This statement applies to Disciples and Methodists, Evangelicals, Con-

---
[4] P. 70.

gregationalists, and Episcopalians. Presbyterian constituents express a degree of loyalty out of proportion to their appreciation of federation programs; but Baptist and Lutheran heads rank federations higher than their hearts do.

DISTRIBUTION OF JUDGMENTS BY CLASSES OF CONSTITUENTS

The working definition of a constituent adopted for the purposes of the investigation was: One listed in the official directory or mailing list of persons statedly cultivated by the federation by the more or less regular means of publicity, by financial solicitation, or by frequent invitation to participate in activities. These lists define the Protestant public which the federation is in systematic communication with a view to support and coöperation. They naturally include officially related persons, as well as all ministers and the important representatives of each practical interest of the federations, whether or not they are connected with member-organizations according to the constitution. The discussion of membership and participation, which showed how little practical significance attaches to mere constitutional definitions, should be in mind at this point.[5]

The different classes of constituents as thus defined indicate different tendencies of attitudes toward federations. Those standing nearest to them by official leadership actually turned out to be, on the whole, the most favorably inclined, as is shown for five cities in Table XVIII.

TABLE XVIII—CONSTITUENTS' JUDGMENTS REGARDING APPROPRIATENESS AND IMPORTANCE OF PROGRAMS IN 5 FEDERATIONS, BY CLASSES OF CONSTITUENTS

Class of Constituents	Per Cent. Distribution of Judgments					
	Total	Highly Important	Somewhat Important	Permissible But Not Important	Questionable	Should Not Undertake
Officers and Committeemen	100	74	19	5	1	1
Members of Member-organizations	100	69	21	6	2	2
Constituents from non-member Denominations	100	60	25	9	2	4

In considering this showing, one notes that officers and committeemen in the five cities are only a little more favorably disposed to the current programs than is the average constituent in the sixteen federations previously considered. But as compared with non-official members of organizations, and with constituents of non-member denominations in their own cities,

---

[5] Pp. 100, 103.

officers and committeemen find decidedly more to commend and
less to criticize. Constituents from non-member denominations,
in turn, are more critical than those of any single denomination,
but somewhat less so than those of the more critical cities as
shown in Table XV.

The constituent from the non-member denomination, however, should not be regarded as representing the rank and file of
genuine outsiders. After all, he is a constituent, a voluntary
participant in one or more of the many federation activities that
are found valuable by many whose denominations do not officially throw in their lot with the federation movement.[6] At the
worst, however, the marginal constituent registered only 15 per
cent. of unfavorable attitudes, as compared with 85 per cent. of
favorable and highly favorable attitudes toward the activities
of his federation.

It was to be expected that constituents would not be equally
favorable to all aspects of the work of their federations. The
actual variations of their attitudes among seven major departments of work as revealed in answers to questionnaires concerning specific activities, is shown in Table XIX. The results

TABLE XIX—CONSTITUENTS' JUDGMENTS REGARDING AP-
PROPRIATENESS AND IMPORTANCE OF CERTAIN ELE-
MENTS OF FEDERATION PROGRAMS

ELEMENT OF PROGRAMS	Total	PER CENT. DISTRIBUTION OF JUDGMENTS				
		Should Not Undertake	Ques- tionable	Per- missible	Somewhat Important	Highly Important
Total Program	100	2	2	5	19	72
Comity	100	2	2	3	13	80
Finance	100	2	2	5	16	75
Religious Education	100	1	2	5	19	73
Women's Department	100	1	2	5	20	72
Social Service	100	2	3	5	18	72
Evangelism	100	1	2	7	22	68
Publicity	100	1	1	6	26	66

CONSTITUENTS' ATTITUDES TOWARD DEPARTMENTS OF WORK
COMPARED

therein tabulated were secured by combining the returns on
specific activities under evangelism, religious education, comity,
finance, etc., and calculating the percentage distribution of judgments for the department as a whole according to the five positions indicated by the questionnaire, viz: (1) the organization
(federation) should not undertake this activity; (2) is questionable whether the organization should undertake this activity;

[6] P. 83.

(3) is permissible but not important; (4) is somewhat important; (5) is highly important.

WHAT THE TABULATION SHOWS

In reflecting upon this table, the first thing to consider is that an average of over 72 per cent. of all constituents held that the total program of their respective federations was highly important. The difference between the 66 per cent. who regarded publicity as highly important and the 80 per cent. who regarded comity as highly important is not greater than might be ex-

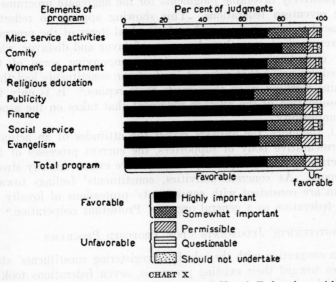

CHART X

Distribution of judgments of constituents of Church Federations with respect to the importance and appropriateness of specified elements of their programs

pected, considering that the former may be regarded as an end of coöperative activity while the latter is but a means.

The second suggestive fact is the somewhat inconsistent showing of the particular items. Comity, which is judged most important on the whole is also regarded with disfavor by a more than average percentage of constituents. Feeling around for an explanation, one might guess that the degree of control of denominational policies implied in comity must necessarily be regarded as significant, but also that it might well be distasteful to those who do not want to coöperate. On the other hand, publicity appears as "somewhat important" to a higher proportion of people than any other element of the program. Perhaps because of its secondary rating, it is objected to by fewer than is any other item. Guessing again as to the relatively small proportion of constituents who regard evangelism as highly important, one suspects that it is the administration of this interest that is in doubt. As a responsibility of the denomination or the local church, evangelism might be expected to stand close to the top.

Adding together the judgments that call the program as a whole important or somewhat important, one gets 91 per cent. of positively favorable judgments for the aggregate programs of the seventeen federations. This showing appears to reflect a somewhat uncritical attitude. Individual items of the program, however, elicit a much wider range of favor and disfavor, while the exceedingly acute comments accompanying some of the schedules prove that some at least of the constituents had their brains working when they made their replies.[7] It is only the consolidation of the average judgment that takes on the aspect of uniformity.

If, therefore, the answers reflect the attitudes of an actually representative body of supporters, the current processes of the federations as a group are proved to have extraordinarily strong support. As concrete activities, constituents' feelings toward them are consistent with constituents' professions of loyalty to the federation as a general organ of Protestant coöperation.[8]

CONSTITUENTS' JUDGMENTS UPON PROPOSED PROGRAMS

In connection with the schedules registering constituents' attitudes toward their existing programs, seven federations took a poll of opinion as to certain specific proposals for enlargement or advance of program. The proposals varied greatly from city to city, and were not sufficiently numerous in any one department to throw comparative light upon attitudes toward novel proposals according to particular fields.

CONTRASTING ATTITUDES

It is highly significant, however, that the prevailing attitude toward new proposals was much less favorable on the whole than that toward existing programs. Thus, a tabulation for thirty items representing new suggestions, showed the following contrast with that for the total program as shown on page 134. Even

---

[7] Pp. 229, 230.
[8] P. 70.

so, just half the judgments regarded the new proposals collectively as highly important.

CONSTITUENT'S POSITIONS	PER CENT. DISTRIBUTION OF POSITIONS	
	Existing Program	Proposed Program
(Number of judgments)	(134,280)	(4,586)
Total	100	100
"Should not undertake"......................	2	4
"Questionable"	2	8
"Permissible but unimportant"...............	5	12
"Somewhat important"	19	26
"Highly important"	72	50

REACTIONS TO SPECIFIC PROPOSALS

The reaction of particular constituencies to specific proposals has a certain suggestive value. Eighty-two per cent. of the St. Louis replies regarded the proposed hospital chaplaincy as highly important, and only 6 per cent. declared it unimportant or inappropriate. Baltimore also had an unusually favorable vote on the proposed juvenile-court worker and hospital chaplaincy. Work of this type tends to be well thought of wherever it already exists. In contrast with these philanthropies, proposals for a director for the religious-education department in St. Louis got only 75 per cent. of highly favorable replies and 12 per cent. of outright opposition. New York City did not fare very well in a vote on a demonstrative church school under federation auspices. Half the New York replies, however, said that the extension of federation organization in the several boroughs of the city was very important, while an additional third held it somewhat important. Eighty per cent. of the Massachusetts replies thought highly of the proposal for closer coöperation between the interdenominational agencies of the state, with the Council of Religious Education largely in mind. Seventy-six per cent. were highly favorable to the organization of an interdenominational conference on politics, economics, and civic responsibility in imitation of the British "Copec." New York's constituency, on the contrary, did not take to the proposed church directory; nor did Rochester to the proposed annual statistical summary of the churches; nor did Baltimore to the proposed religious census. This looks as though the constituencies were not of a mind to spend effort upon statistical records or research. The Rochester constituency was not enthusiastic over sending fraternal delegates to the Trades Union Assembly; nor over the proposed case-work clinic for ministers; nor yet over a social-service secretary. The least popular proposal was that of Rochester for a weekly Protestant newspaper. This was strongly favored by only 16 per cent. of the constituency, while over two-thirds thought it inappropriate or unimportant.

EXPLANATIONS

In incidental expressions of opinion accompanying these data, constituents sometimes indicated that their federations had already entered most of the well-tried fields of activity and had better let well-enough alone. Others said that the federations were not covering satisfactorily what they had already undertaken. In the large, however, the results probably show the natural gap between loyalty to types of work already established and familiar, and habitual disinclination to undertake the additional burdens and expense of responsibilities not forced upon the conscience as already accomplished facts.

Chapter IX

AGENCIES, RESOURCES AND METHODS

The characteristic agencies and resources through which federations carry on their programs have naturally been indicated in connection with the description of the form and structure of such organizations. These factors have now, in the present chapter, to be studied in their distinctive characters, namely, as the functional means whereby the ends of coöperative Protestant activity are secured.

The first phenomenon calling for consideration is the scheme of internal organization through which the various means are related and made to function harmoniously. Then come the separate factors—the conspicuous system of committees, paid, professional leadership, finances, facilities and methods of publicity and promotion. More exhaustive treatment of each of these points is to be found under appropriate headings in Part II. The present chapter merely summarizes the account of the agencies, resources and methods of federations with the general reader in mind.

The Scheme of Internal Organization and How It Works

The chain of processes by which the federation does its work, theoretically begins with some particular action of the organization as an ultimate entity. But since it is impossible actually to assemble and coördinate the total memberships of the federated churches and denominations, it is necessary for them to act through a representative body and through a technique presumed to safeguard and express the separate interests of the coöperating elements.[1] The stated occasion of such representative functioning by the whole body of representatives is ordinarily the annual meeting. The concrete processes through which major representative decisions are made possible in such a meeting are generally as follows: the meeting receives and adopts reports of officers and committees. It elects officers and directors from a slate provided in advance. It hears an inspirational address interpreting some phase of coöperative interest and intended to evoke loyalty and support. It may be asked to con-

---

[1] P. 83.

sider some general aspect of policy that is of direct importance to the constituency and that has had a measure of previous consideration. Shrewd leadership will occasionally give a bit of an issue to thresh over, so that it will not seem that the meeting is merely a rubber-stamping device. Thus a proposal for a simultaneous campaign of evangelism may be submitted on such an occasion. Annual meetings are generally, however, essentially formal occasions in which tacit assent is given to past actions, and the work is committed to new leaders, substantially without discussion. Their significance ordinarily is educational and psychological, not administrative. Even in times of internal crises, the actual outcome of conflict is likely to be determined outside the annual meeting and merely registered in its transactions.

OFFICERS AND DIRECTORS

What the delegates have done in annual meeting is essentially to pass on operating authority and responsibility to a set of unpaid officers and directors. These agents proceed to function through stated meetings, monthly, bi-monthly, or quarterly. The main functions of these groups are as follows: they elect paid professional agents. They institute standing committees and commissions and appoint their members. They receive reports from paid officers and committees. They take action controlling the more general policies of the federation. According to its essential idea—the idea that gives the organization its name—a federation is often a loose alliance of previously existing organizations.[2] The directors spend much effort in fixing the terms of such alliances and in recurrently adjusting relations with their semi-independent subsidiaries. They determine more or less permanent relations between the federation and other non-federating Protestant agencies working in related fields; and they deal with a variety of specific issues relating to one or another of the above functions.

Most of these processes are essentially administrative. In view, however, of the terms of alliance between federations and semi-independent subsidiaries, transactions relating to the latter are coördinative rather than executive. That is to say, the officers and directors are not at liberty to control or operate the work of the subsidiaries, but may merely influence it, through advice or the registering of sentiment, so that it will measurably fit in with the general federation scheme.

---

[2] P. 156.

STANDING COMMITTEES AND COMMISSIONS

Boards of directors in turn delegate authority in limited areas to standing committees and commissions, subject to the general policies adopted and to review by the superior body. Evangelism, religious education, comity, and social service are the major fields thus departmentalized.

Committees and commissions function discontinuously by means of stated and special meetings.

The major functions include the following: committees and commissions frequently extend their own memberships by the election of additional persons interested in the particular fields of work. Each conducts federation work in the field delegated to it, and reports back to the directors. Each may receive reports from, and will generally supervise the work of, any paid specialists who may be employed for service within the committee's particular fields. Each committee is assumed to reflect and to summarize the state of Protestant interest in the area of activity delegated to it, and to do constructive thinking in carrying forward the collective ideals and policies pertaining to this area.

In theory, the function of standing committees and commissions is executive. But the independence of the denominations making up the federation, and the spirit of denominational agents represented in the committees, frequently reduce most of the committee's work from executive to coördinative rank. The work becomes the toggling together into an ostensible unity, of plans and decisions independently arrived at.[3] Again many committees are composed of widely varying elements, in view of whose existence one has to read further functional distinction into the actual committee process. Thus, for example, social-service committees frequently include a considerable group of professional social-service workers as members. These professionals are not intimately representative of churches and church agencies, and the function which they are intended to perform is merely advisory. Only occasionally, however, are they labelled advisors and permitted only to discuss and not to vote on measures. Technically, they generally have full membership with corresponding rights; but these they are not in position to exercise on a parity with other members who represent active responsibility in church and denomination.

Still further, the size and composition of certain committees imply that they are intended to be primarily educational, at

---

[3] P. 122.

least so far as the larger part of their membership is concerned. Their executive function is so slight that the quality of the membership can do little damage. People of no real competency, but possessed of influence or money, are often attached to such committees. The actual purpose is to keep them in touch with federation interests and to secure their loyalty. Practically speaking, these are laudable objectives, though the means employed to secure them is not entirely straightforward. Finally, many committees carry a list of names still more marginal in character—names of persons who are thus willing to lend their weight to a good enterprise in which they have confidence, but who, it is understood in advance, will neither attend nor actively participate in committee affairs.

Such is the variety of function that differentiates committees and commissions when they are realistically interpreted, and not in terms of mere theory.

PAID PROFESSIONAL EMPLOYEES

Parallel with the setting up of committees and commissions, boards of directors employ professional agents to carry out their central policies and to promote and facilitate the work of the subordinate machinery. Strictly speaking, what is delegated to the paid employee is the function of initiative in bringing pertinent matters to the attention of the directors, and of carrying on defined responsibilities in limited areas of work.

Unlike the directors and committees, paid professionals function continuously. They perform routinized service. They receive and refer to the proper representative bodies any matters coming within the authority of such bodies. They devise specific plans and techniques for the performance of the duties assigned to them. In this capacity they are presumed to do much of the constructive and coördinative thinking of the organization. They also make many minor administrative rulings; and sometimes larger ones which, if objected to, get before the authoritive bodies on an issue of confidence in the paid officer. Many of these rulings, however, slip into established usage without controversy; and the body of usages gets the force of law exactly as is true in the case of political governments. Paid officers thus necessarily have great weight in determining the series of decisions by which the work of federations goes forward.

Theoretically, the entire round of functions performed by paid officers is executive, the issues being determined by committees; but the type of leadership actually expected is essentially of a creative sort. It must be followed up by many functions that are primarily educational and promotional, intended to produce loyalty and morale.

Under the formal scheme that has now been sketched, the actual on-going processes of federations occur. The facts are sometimes only remotely related to the supposed hierarchy of responsibility. The following in relation to the various agencies whose work has been outlined shows what kinds of things actually turn out to be most significant in the process, and measures certain of them.

STANDING COMMITTEES AND COMMISSIONS

The actual frequency with which each field of federation is actively organized under a department, commission, or committee has already been shown.[4] It remains to present the varying types of internal organization represented by particular federations.

NUMBER OF COMMITTEES

Omitting boards of directors and executive committees, the 23 federations studied were maintaining a total of 240 standing committees. The number ranged from five in Baltimore and Brooklyn to sixteen in Boston and Chicago, the median being 10. Half the federations maintained from six to eleven committees each.

Types of internal organization, as determined by both the number and the character of the committees, may best be understood with reference to the status of the several fields of service within the federation movement. As has been shown, this is indicated by the frequency of their departmentalization or assignment to standing committees. Some fields of service are so essential as to be represented by committees invariably, or almost invariably. Others are so exceptional as to have committees in only one or two cases.

TYPES OF INTERNAL ORGANIZATION

Considering, then, both the number of committees and the frequency with which they occur in the federation movement, individual federations are seen to fall into three types of organizations.

(1) Federations with a large number of committees, including all of the usual ones, and some of the exceptional ones besides.

---

[4] P. 105.

A few peculiar activities in this case are not enough to throw the typical program out of balance. This type of organization is represented by the Chicago and the Detroit federations.

(2) Federations with an average or small number of committees virtually limited to the invariable or highly frequent fields. These represent the ultra-conservative tendency. They do not divide their work among many agents, and they do only what others are also generally doing. The Cleveland and the Toledo federations fall into this class.

(3) Federations with a small or average number of committees which reach largely into the very infrequent or erratic realms of activity. This is the adventurous group. It agrees with other federations on a few main fundamentals, but beyond that chooses a sphere for itself from realms not often entered by others. The New York and the Boston federations illustrate this tendency.[5]

OVERORGANIZATION AND UNDERORGANIZATION

Whether a given federation is overorganized or underorganized must be determined with respect to the scope of its total program, the magnitude of its work, and the size of its corps of paid workers. Large transactions within a given sphere may justify its subdivision and assignment to a variety of committees; say, for example, five or six within the general sphere of social service. Such subdivision will bring up the total number of committees even though the total range of interests covered by the federation remains narrow. A very high correlation exists, however, between the number of committees and at least two out of the three factors just enumerated. Thus, a federation with many committees is likely to cover a broad scope and carry a larger amount of work, or else to maintain a large staff. Exceptions appearing to indicate underorganization are represented by Baltimore, Pittsburgh, and Toledo. These federations get along with few committees relative to their work. This means that more responsibility is carried by paid executives. Perhaps certain secretaries prefer to keep in their own hands matters that in other cases are turned over to committees. Exceptions appearing to indicate overorganization are found in Boston and San Francisco. In the latter case, some of the perhaps superfluous committees have probably been held over from the day when the budget and staff were much larger.

Whether the average complexity of federation organization

---

[5] See page 109 for discussion of consistency and inconsistency in terms of range of activities.

should be taken as a general norm, is of course debatable. The author indicates in other connections a suspicion that the movement on the whole may be overorganized.[6] One line of evidence bearing upon the question is covered by the study of committee performance in chapter XVI.[7]

EXCEPTIONAL COMMITTEES

Some of the highly exceptional committees are the following:

Two Cases Each	One Case Each
Athletics	Literature
Endorsement of financial appeals	Music
Sabbath observance	Ministers' Meetings
Surveys	Negro work
	Temperance

In most federations, many of these separately listed interests could obviously be made to, and actually do, fall in under other and more frequent committees. They may not signify a broader program, but merely a greater variety of labels applied to the same body of work. It is no secret that the Sabbath-observance committee, for example, is retained because some of the constituents of certain federations are partisans of a particular version of Sabbath observance, and are unwilling to have their interest handled on a parity with other problems of social ethics. Again, activities that federations have taken over from previously existing agencies sometimes demand to be represented by separate committees. This explains, for example, the Men's Bible Class committee in Oakland. Such an activity logically comes under religious education, but the unique history of this particular class compelled the federation to give it a committee of its own. Practical necessity thus explains many of the above exceptions, which tend to heap up additional masses of machinery and add weight to the suspicion of overorganization.

The justification of the exceptional committee is, of course, the value and character of the function it performs in its particular federation. If the federation has a novel function inherently worth performing, it is probably perfectly reasonable to provide separate machinery at least temporarily, and especially when there are insistent practical grounds in so doing.

WOMEN ON FEDERATION COMMITTEES

In spite of the considerable proportion of women found among the church delegates who make up the ultimate personnel of fed-

[6] P. 263.
[7] P. 291.

erations, women members of boards of directors are relatively scarce. On the other hand, the president of a separate but affiliated women's organization, or the officers of such a women's organization where it exists, are usually included among the federation directors. The proportion of women on standing committees differs greatly according to the functions of the committee. Thus, out of 318 members of 60 comity committees, only one per cent. were women; while out of 626 members of 43 social-service committees, 18 per cent. were women.

PAID WORKERS

Twenty-one federations investigated on this point employed, at the time of the study, a total of 131 paid workers who gave continuous service. Sixty-two of these workers were men, and sixty-nine women. The account did not include seasonal employees like vacation-school workers, nor persons employed on honoraria rather than salaries, as is true with a few publicity advisors. Neither did it count teachers in local week-day schools of religious education, even though somewhat closely administered by federations.[8] Four of the 131 workers studied were nominally employed for part-time services, but actually gave virtually full time.

NUMBER AND CLASSES OF PAID WORKERS

The distribution of paid workers according to position is shown in Table XX.

Besides the fact that 53 per cent. of the employed workers are women, three important points deserve mention.

(1) Two-thirds of the federations employ one or more departmental or assistant secretaries.

(2) Somewhat more than two-thirds of all male employees are ordained ministers—these include all but two of the male executive secretaries.

(3) Almost exactly half of all paid workers are employed in the three specialized fields of religious work (evangelism), religious education, and social service; leaving the other half to account for general administration and all minor specializations.

A few points in the classification require further comment. The fourteen office secretaries fall into two groups; first, those belonging to federations so small that the person employed to keep the office may naturally come to control a considerable round of general administrative functions. This situation con-

---

[8] For description of the omitted types of workers, see pp. 351, 355, 478.

trasts with federations in which there are so many subordinate workers that the immediate supervision and coördination of office work is likely to be put in the hands of some person other than the executive secretary. This creates the demand for a second type of office secretary.

TABLE XX—CLASSIFICATION OF PAID WORKERS OF 21 FEDERATIONS

CLASSES	No. of Federations Employing	WORKERS			No. of Ordained Ministers
		Total	Male	Female	
Total	21	131	62	69	43
Executive Secretaries	21	21	18	3	16
Departmental or Ass't Secy's	14	26	18	8	15
Religious Work	2	3	3	0	3
Religious Education	8	8	6	2	6
Social Service	5	5	3	2	1
Other	9	10	6	4	5
Religious-education Supervisors	—	10	3	7	1
Week-day Schools	3	4	2	2	1
Children's Divisions	3	4	0	4	0
Other	2	2	1	1	0
Chaplains	8	9	8	1	8
Court and Social Case Workers	7	14	8	6	0
Women's Department Secretaries	4	4	0	4	0
Office Secretaries	14	14	1	13	0
General Clerical Workers	—	11	0	11	0
General Office	6	8	0	8	0
Financial	3	3	0	3	0
Departmental Clerical Workers	—	13	0	13	0
Religious Education	5	6	0	6	0
Social Service	4	5	0	5	0
Other	2	2	0	2	0
Miscellaneous	8	9	6	3	3
Summary: Number employed in					
Religious Work*	9	16	11	5	
Religious Education	9	24	9	15	
Social Service†	8	24	11	13	

* Including chaplains.
† Not including two women's department, supervisors chiefly concerned with social service.

Again it is to be noted that, on account of the nature of their work, chaplains are rated as religious workers although attached to social institutions and sometimes accounted for under social-service budgets.[9]

Among workers classified as miscellaneous, are included some whose functions are administrative, like occasional directors of athletics; others who are merely specialized office workers, like switchboard operators; and still others who carry on highly exceptional activities such as those of an advertising solicitor attached to a federation publication.

---

[9] See pp. 423 and 456.

In general, the distribution of workers reflects the relative departmentalization of federation functions, except that in the fields of religious education, and of social work in connection with courts and public institutions, the technical demand of the services rendered requires paid workers more frequently than is true of any other departments.

WOMEN IN EXECUTIVE POSITIONS

Women constitute a very considerable proportion of the paid executives of the federations. Of the executive secretaries 3 were women; of the departmental or assistant secretaries, 8, of whom 2 were religious-education directors; of the religious-education department-heads or supervisors, 7; besides, there were 4 secretaries of women's departments. This equals slightly under one-third of all paid workers in strictly executive positions. While it is only fair to state that some of the women executives are employed for reasons of economy both in federations that previously had male leadership and in the fields of religious education, the situation is significant as the resultant of the recognized role of women in the Church and the limited resources of the organizations up to date.[10]

FEDERATION FINANCES

A comparison of the amounts of annual budgets of federations shows, first, that they naturally reflect the size of the city and consequently the magnitude of the Protestant forces which they represent. Second, they are obvious measures of the magnitude of the federation enterprise.

SIZE AND RANGE OF BUDGETS

The annual expenditures of forty-three federations were reported in the *Church Council News Letter* of May, 1928. The story which these figures tell is straightforward and obvious. Budgets ranged from $500 to $132,000. Standing at the bottom of the scale are a fourth of the federations with budgets of only $500 to $3,000. Eight out of eleven of the cities falling in this group have less than 200,000 population; and the group includes no case of a federation employing a full-time paid secretary. The small budgets belong to the smaller cities which do not enjoy the characteristic professional leadership of the movement.

Standing just below the average, came another fourth of the

---

[10] Technical reports on the vocational characteristics and performance of different types of workers appear on pp. 310 ff.

cases, federations with budgets ranging from $3,000 to $8,500. This group again is characterized by the small average size of its cities. At the bottom of this group stand federations employing women secretaries. All the rest, until one comes to the two places at the top of the group, employ only a single paid worker. In other words, here is a group of federations whose budget is largely explained by the fact that the secretary does not have any full-time assistance.

With the fourth of the federations that stand just above the average, budgets range from $13,500 to $29,000. This group starts with cities of a little over 100,000 and ends with Baltimore, Boston, and Philadelphia at the top. Staffs of three and four workers are characteristic. The differences to be noted here are chiefly those of scope of program. Federations that include Councils of Education run financially beyond those in larger cities which do not include such Councils.[11]

The highest fourth of the federations have budgets running from $30,000 to $132,000. The extreme case is that of Greater New York, whose responsibilities in connection with national broadcasting and consequent method of financing are reported in another connection.[12] Excluding New York, the range of expenditures in the upper fourth is substantially from $30,000 to $50,-000, with approximately $35,000 as the average budget. These obviously measure the financial magnitude of the larger federations. Seven out of the ten are in cities of more than three-quarters of a million population, while five out of the ten are in cities of more than a million. Federations in smaller cities which fall within this group have broad programs, including extensive work in religious education under paid leadership.

The median budget of the entire group is $13,500, represented by the Indianapolis Federation. This city of 350,000 population also stands midway between the larger and the smaller cities and has the average staff of three workers.

In the average city, the total budget for united Protestant work as represented by a church federation about equals the minimum budget of a single denominational church of any of the better-organized denominations—a considerably more than average church, but the kind that would probably be thought of as typical of its denomination in a city of a given size. In other words, the amount of financial support which the total Protestant body is at present willing to invest in its coöperative under-

[11] P. 172.
[12] P. 331.

takings merely equals that invested in any one of scores of its single units. Whatever federations do, is done within these financial limitations.

SOURCES OF SUPPORT

Summarizing the sources of federation incomes, gifts from individual churches and from individuals, and incomes from business or services rendered, are found to be the invariable or very frequent ones. Incomes from denominational subsidies, loans or direct transfers of department funds, are found to be moderately frequent. An income from the Community Chest is very infrequent, and in no case is income from endowment reported. Some of the exceptional situations are interesting though not typical. One federation gets the bulk of its income from the sale of tickets for lectures or entertainments. Another is largely supported by loose collections taken at public meetings. Women's departments occasionally contribute heavily in proportion to the total budget. In a few cases, a semi-independent commission has an "angel," a man who virtually finances the commission's entire work out of his own pocket, and who consequently runs it very much to suit himself. Finally, in a very few cases, non-ecclesiastical agencies have given federations small subsidies, as for example, the grant of the Phelps-Stokes Fund to the Washington Federation for local research in Negro social conditions.

EXPENDITURES

When one asks where the money goes, the answer is simple: most of it goes to administrative salaries, to general operating expenses and rent, and to such departments as evangelism, religious education, and social service which are virtually universal, and which frequently employ professional directors. Little money—and that in infrequent cases—goes separately to other departments, either because they are operated inexpensively by volunteers, or else incidentally by paid workers who are carried on central administrative budgets.[13]

FACILITIES

The facilities used by church federations in their major fields of activity—evangelism, religious education, comity and social service—are mainly those borrowed on occasion from the coöperating churches or other agencies in connection with which the federation functions. The only special equipment required by the federation as such is in connection with its function as an

---

[13] For a comparison and discussion of federation finances from the administrative viewpoint, see pp. 454 ff.

administrative center and place of service and information. It consists, in short, of the office and its furnishings.

TENURE

Only one federation (St. Louis) owns its own quarters. The rest are housed in rented or contributed rooms. Three federations receive free quarters from the Y. M. C. A.'s of their respective communities, and several others are charged less than full commercial rates in recognition of the religious character of their work. Classified according to the tenure and character of the quarters occupied, the twenty-three federations investigated on this point are divided as follows:

Tenure		Number of Federations
Rent Commercially in Office Buildings..........		13
Rent in Religious or Social-work Headquarters..		6
Denominational headquarters	2	
Y. M. C. A. central building...................	1	
Council of Social Agencies building...........	2	
Chamber of Commerce......................	1	
Free Rent in Y. M. C. A. Building..............		3
Owns Property		1

The Boston and Massachusetts State federations occupy joint offices and make common use of part of the space. Two other federations share their offices with independent but coöperative women's organizations; and two or three others supply space to separate Protestant agencies doing reform or social work.

Besides the nine federations that are tenants or guests in denominational, Y. M. C. A., or social-agency buildings, two have offices that adjoin the rented headquarters of one or more denominations. Thus almost half the cases illustrate a certain tendency for religious organizations to cluster under the same roof, just as the professions or secular businesses do under urban conditions. Such clustering is obviously a convenience to common constituencies. It adds, moreover, to the prestige and reputation of the Y. M. C. A. or denominational headquarters to have the federation as a tenant. The grant of free rent may tend to create a sense of obligation on the part of the federation's constituency to support the generous landlord. But clustering in adjacent offices does not always mean freedom from competition, as the example of the business world proves all too well. With the religious agencies on the whole, however, the clustering tendency is probably to be taken as a symbol and sort of practical extension of the practice of coöperation.[14]

---

[14] For a discussion of facilities from the administrative standpoint, see p. 464.

PUBLICITY AND PROMOTION

Federations, of course, have to make formal reports to, and otherwise keep in contract with, their constituencies. They must make the best showing they can, and try to commend themselves to supporters of various degrees of intimacy and loyalty. They must, so far as possible, keep in the eye of the general public and magnify their place in the community.

The devices of publicity and promotion by which federations attempt to secure these results are varied. The formal annual report may be an attractively printed summary of the work and a thinly veiled appeal for financial support. Other exigencies and occasions bring forth their promotional literature. The more active departments will issue their own separate stories and appeals.

The methods of promotion and publicity most extensively used are, however, the publication of a regular federation organ and the personal appearance of paid workers before gatherings of constituents. Federation organs range in size and quality from the occasional mimeographed bulletin to the religious family newspaper of a community. Personal contact varies from the rather occasional public addresses of the secretary who is not an attractive speaker to the habitual use by a departmental head of large amounts of time in telling his story from church to church as a means of raising his own salary. In such cases, ability to plead effectively becomes one of the prime qualifications of the position. The average federation organ is a monthly paper of four or eight pages; and the average federation secretary expects to make frequent personal appearances before his constituents in natural course as incidental to the more significant occasions with which they have to do.

Necessarily the chief instrument of contact with the general public is the regular press of the city. The use of the press runs all the way from occasional news reporting to the regular conduct of a weekly federation department in a metropolitan journal. The average case represents aggressive and somewhat systematic cultivation of this means of publicity.

Administrative contacts with constituents are chiefly kept up through notices in the federation organ supplemented by mimeographed communications. Dozens of such communications go out from the average federation office annually in connection with the operation of its program. Mailing lists of the clergy, of religious-education workers, and of laymen representing special interests are continuously cultivated by these means.

A few federations employ part-time publicity directors. In others, promotional methods especially related to finance and public relations are devised and operated through standing committees. As a service-function, certain federations undertake to assist churches and religious organizations with their local individual publicity, or conduct the Saturday church announcement section of city newspapers.

SUMMARY

In sketching the agencies and resources employed by federations, the chapter has simply shown that these organizations possess the ordinary equipment that one has learned to expect from voluntary social agencies in modern cities.

The nearest institutional analogies to federations are city-wide denominational organizations and social agencies. The federations resemble the denominational organizations in that they have to do with ecclesiastical affairs and are composed of ecclesiastical units. They resemble the social agencies in that they do considerable philanthropic work through which clients are served, and which the public is urged to support.

Further observation of likeness and unlikeness to these two types of agencies with respect to the means they use will help to define the characteristics of federations.

(1) In the matter of support, federations, like denominations, get partial support from the organizational units of which they are composed. Social agencies have no corresponding advantage, but are much more frequently endowed.

Like social agencies, federations do not have authority over their supporters but must plead and ingratiate themselves, whereas denominations can exact some financial response from the faithful through apportionments and quotas. But unlike most social agencies in cities, federations with few exceptions do not receive aid from Community Chest funds.

(2) In the matter of property, unlike many denominations, federations do not own their headquarters buildings. Unlike many types of social agencies, they do not possess and operate extensive plants for various forms of service. The probable reasons are that property is the symbol of a permanence which few federations have established, and that federations more often help others with their social work than conduct work of their own.

(3) An important chain of differences both from denominational and social agencies grows out of the fact that the units of

which federations are composed are essentially competitive, and that many departments are very imperfectly integrated with the general organization.

A major department like comity exists to regulate the conflicting interests of member-units. A formerly independent organization, when combined with a federation, often remains unintegrated.

Now the organizational machinery of federations is very extensive for the amount of work they have to do. This is partly because each poorly integrated interest must have separate representation, or because it insists on retaining all its own agencies after it joins the federation. The committee and department system is overstressed. The process is one of aggregation rather than of true organization; and the result is an excess of means relative to ends.

Partly because denominational professionals and clergymen are available for the work, but also because these classes dislike to let power go out of their own hands, federations use voluntary workers in circumstances in which social agencies of similar magnitude and with like technical problems would employ paid ones. Moreover, federations do not grant their paid executives the degree of authority characteristic of such offices either denominations or social agencies, to say nothing of business and industry. While holding these executives responsible for failures, they suspect and fear possible autocracy to the point of not permitting efficiency; subordinate workers are less elaborately and exactingly supervised than are those holding corresponding positions in social agencies.

In brief, the use of means reflects the peculiarities of federations; and these peculiarities in turn rest back upon the characteristics and relationships of the component units.

Chapter X

AFFILIATION OF OTHER INTERDENOMINA-
TIONAL ORGANIZATIONS

The complexity of religious organization in American cities, to which the actual inventory, city by city, bore such an amazing weight of testimony,[1] would not be sufficiently reduced even if all the Protestant churches and denominations were full members of, and in complete coöperation with, their local federations. For federations were not the first interdenominational agencies, nor have they been the last. It has been one of their crucial problems to determine how to adjust themselves to a strong group of previously existing organizations, as well as to those that have kept springing up later, to say nothing of fixing their relations with the multiform extensions and allies of Protestantism that are non-denominational in auspices and non-ecclesiastical in form.

The federation movement early tried to define its proper relationship to these general types of other organizations. Thus, in 1906 Dr. E. B. Sanford, speaking as executive secretary of the National Federation of Churches (the immediate predecessor of the Federal Council of Churches), declared:

> Local federations will have as their mission not so much to initiate or organize special work for special needs, humanitarian, fraternal and civic, as to give counsel, guidance and support to work already inaugurated which secures and retains the commendation of the federated churches.

In harmony with this view, one of the earliest local constitutions, that of the Philadelphia Federation, specified:

> The Federation may work as a unit or through committees;
> * * * it shall have power to foster separate institutions more or less allied, and to coöperate with other constructive institutions.

A considerable proportion of later constitutions state that one of the objects of federations is "to coöperate with other religious organizations" or "with religious movements."[2] Thus, both the high and inclusive ideal of federation as a functional unifying of

---

[1] Chapter I, p. 14.
[2] P. 58.

155

the Protestant church, and the actual expectation of federation constituencies, conspire to assure that these organizations would have to give urgent attention to problems of affiliation.

It is therefore no surprise to find that certain federations originated as amalgamations of previous interdenominational movements; and that the story of most of the others is marked by repeated attempts to work out relationships with other Protestant agencies.

Expansion of this sort is well illustrated by Chicago. In 1917 the Coöperative Council of City Missions became affiliated with, and later merged in, the Commission on Comity. The Night Church in the same year became one of the federation's evangelistic activities. In 1919 the Woman's Church Federation became the Woman's Department of the Chicago Church Federation, while the Young People's Civic League became its Young People's Department.

The files of the average federation secretary disclose lists of organizations which he thinks ought to come into the federation and which he hopes to include some day.

Twenty-five years of history have seen large progress in discovering general tendencies toward affiliation as well as typical sources of resistance to it. With respect to other agencies of the interdenominational type, great progress has been achieved in their actual assimilation into the federation movement. Relationships with these agencies is the theme of the present chapter. The case of the non-denominational extensions and allies of the church is so different that its consideration is reserved for the succeeding chapter.

Types of Adjustment Attempted

The internal structure of federations testifies that the genius of the movement has largely consisted in its capacity to gather up previous interdenominational organizations into the larger unity of its more inclusive movement. Illustrations of this tendency have been met with in virtually every sphere of characteristic federation activity. The consequence, as repeatedly seen, is that federations are overlaid by loosely related departments which were formerly independent agencies.[3]

But in no quarter has the federation's tendency to assimilate previous interdenominational agencies been unresisted. In many cases these agencies have not been satisfied even to continue to live their own life within a more comprehensive organization.

---

[3] P. 99.

It is not strange then, that the whole process has gone faster and farther in some cities than in others; that different solutions have been devised by different federations; and that the outcome is one of incomplete assimilation—a story full of gaps. In the large, however, certain general types of adjustment have been achieved. These it is necessary to understand before taking up the case of the particular agencies.

AFFILIATING DEVICES

In the study of the constitutions of federations, the device of secondary organizational membership was discovered as the basic means whereby the affiliation of other Protestant organizations has been sought. Here are federations of churches. The interdenominational agencies are not churches; but it has been made legal for them to join the federation organization exactly as though they were; or, if not constitutionally invited into organic relationships, their professional representatives have been placed *ex officio* on federation "councils," boards of directors, and executive committees.[4] Under his type of adjustment the federation simply asks the other organization to accept the status and relationship offered. By so doing the other organization approves the federation, which thus gains in prestige. No corresponding obligation is proposed. Nothing is asked of the other organization in return. It is under no obligation to bring its plans to the federation as the instrument of common counsel, nor to modify its program in the slightest degree. Nevertheless, this gesture of affiliation, though its consequences are not separately traceable, may very likely have ministered considerably to the rise of the coöperative spirit in not a few cases.

ACTUAL COÖPERATION

Whether or not another interdenominational organization belongs to the federation, actual coöperation in any particular project is a matter of specific agreement. Agreements, of course, may become fixed habits; as, for example, when the offices of separate organizations are so grouped as to perform the function of a single Protestant headquarters; or when agreements take the form of a permanent division of some field of activity. Freedom from competition is thus achieved; but there is no relief from complication, because each organization maintains its own machinery, raises its own budget, and makes its own separate appeal to a common constituency.

[4] Pp. 80 and 84.

As a matter of fact, however, most of the activity carried on coöperatively by federations and organizations thus loosely affiliated has been discontinuous and relating to separate projects or campaigns. Many coöperative experiments that might have become habitual have rather fallen by the way. Furthermore, the incidental coming together of agencies in separate projects has often revealed the essentially competitive nature of the situation. All are nibbling at some field. None can safely be ignored. Hence, in particular projects they must coöperate; but each agency is all the time wishing that all the rest would withdraw and leave the field in its single responsible hands.

COMBINATION OR INCORPORATION OF ORGANIZATIONS

More fundamental and far-reaching than the affiliating devices or particular phases of coöperation that have been described, are the many cases in which other agencies have combined with, or have become incorporated into, federations with more or less definite provision for maintaining their continued identity within the larger whole.

Of these combinations, some have been merely formal. Under the constitutional provision that gives boards of directors power to set up departments or commissions, a federation simply votes to recognize another agency as its commission, say on religious education or on young people's work. The other agency votes in turn to become such a commission. Then everything proceeds as before. There is no integration of plan or function; and sometimes there is less than no integration of spirit. Israel entirely fails to take possession of the promised land.

On the other hand, many organic combinations have brought previously independent organizations under the free type of federation control characteristic of departments which federations themselves initiate; and under quite as complete a degree of actual control. A vital integration is thus achieved. There is unity of plan and of purpose, and as much reduction of complexity as specialization of function ought to allow. The federation movement has actually made great progress in the successful inclusion of other interdenominational agencies. This story is now to be told in terms of each major agency.

ADJUSTMENTS WITH MAJOR AGENCIES

MINISTERS' UNIONS

An inventory of the current Protestantism of the United States reveals that interdenominational ministers' unions are among the characteristic expressions of the coöperative movement in American cities. Primarily these are unofficial organizations for professional fellowships. Frequently, however, they announce a broad and indefinite sphere of purpose, phrased in the St. Louis constitution, for example, as "The interests of the Kingdom of God in the city and the nation and throughout the world." Thus broadly conceived, ministers' unions afford important instruments for the use of current movements affecting the Protestant churches at large. To meet the demand of such movements, they often create special committees or take other appropriate action. In the realm of moral and social conditions, they traditionally maintain standing committees and pass resolutions attempting to reflect the consensus of Protestant fellowship. They arrange pulpit exchanges, conduct union anniversaries, and sometimes joint evangelistic campaigns; and they frequently constitute a forum for the discussion and initiation of more permanent interchurch projects, such as systems of week-day religious education.

In other words, the ministerial unions often suggest incipient church federations.

Historic Relationships With Federations

In their capacity as instruments of current movements of Protestant concern, it was frequently the ministers' unions that took the first steps toward the present federations.[5] This was the case, for example, in both Chicago and Cleveland.

When a ministers' union has started a federation, a definition of the respective functions of the two bodies is obviously necessary. Under such conditions the Dayton Ministerial Association took the following action in 1915.

> Resolved, 1: That the Dayton Ministerial Association hereafter limit its sphere of activity to matters that concern the ministry as such; and that the monthly meetings be characterized by conference, inspiration and Christian fellowship.
>
> Resolved, 2: That those interchurch activities that depend for their success upon the coöperation of the laymen, be referred to the Federated Churches of Dayton.
>
> Resolved, 3: That the intimate relations subsisting between these organizations be recognized by encouraging each to act in an advisory capacity to the other.

An article in the constitution of the Wichita Ministerial Assosiation provides: "Business shall be wholly incidental. Normally, many business matters shall be referred to the Council of

---

[5] P. 41.

Churches for action." This phraseology suggests some difficulty in making a clear-cut division of responsibility.

Present Relationships

The present relationships of ministers' unions and federations are of two kinds: first, incidental, though often highly significant ones; and second, systematic relations covered by arrangements authoritatively set up. Incidental relations may be complementary, leaving the ministers' union as a forum for discussion and the federation as the machinery of action; or supplementary, as in many cities where the ministers' union votes approval for the more important efforts of the federations; or coördinate, as where the two agencies hold joint meetings or install joint committees.

It is not impossible, however, for the two organizations to be competitive. They sometimes maintain parallel committees, which tends to destroy initiative on both sides; and one agency sometimes thus preëmpts a field which the other would like to enter.

Affiliating Devices and Organic Combinations

To prevent competition and assure a suitable adjustment of the two agencies, many of the constitutions of federations include the ministers' union under some of the affiliating devices already discussed.

But beyond these systematic relationships of organizations that remain separate, the rallying of the body of Protestant ministers for united action has sometimes become a direct function of the federation itself. Thus, in Chicago the Ministers' Union is a commission of the federation operating under the general system of virtual independence, which leaves it substantially in the position of unions elsewhere that have been closely affiliated with federations but not merged in them. In New York and Boston, on the contrary, there are neither Protestant ministers' unions nor regular commissions taking their place. The federations of these cities, however, maintain regular union meetings of ministers, in addition to calling them together for special campaigns.

Functional Unification

The more usual situation is one in which the two organizations are functionally unified but organically independent. The ministers' union becomes an adjunct of the federation in the sense that the federation office is the union headquarters, the federation secretary by established custom serves as its permanent corresponding secretary, and its program and policy in most important issues originate in federation councils.

Characteristics Bearing on Relationships

Ministers' unions are not formally representative of the Church, nor personally representative of its lay element. They suffer the most habitual limitations of the federation movement itself: (1) they do not effectively include ministers of the Negro and marginal Protestant denominations; (2) they ordinarily limit themselves to the evangelical bodies; (3) within them exist theological divisions that render them powerless to come to grips with facts in a good many areas of current interest; (4) attendance represents a mere fraction of the total number of ministers; and (5) frequently there is little continuity of policy or sentiment.

On the other hand, as voluntary organizations without ecclesiastical implications, the unions sometimes include ministers of denominations that will not formally coöperate in the federation itself.

These characteristics suggest a relationship of close affiliation; but one that does not completely merge the ministers' union in the federation. And this apparently is the adjustment most favored by federation secretaries. The reason generally given is that the ministers' union, when independent, is useful as a forum in which matters of Protestant concern can get initial expression and the cruder phases of sentiment can be sensed without involving a representative body in responsible action. The ministers "blow off steam" and relieve otherwise tense situations; they can also express their fraternal feelings best in a voluntary agency of their own.

On the other hand, a non-affiliated or aloof attitude between federations and ministers' unions would be regarded as indicating a failure of the coöperative spirit. The coöperative role of the ministers' union in cities in which federations do not exist, has frequently been discussed. The early officers of the Federal Council believed that the local unions "should take on the functions of a federation, giving opportunity for the direct representation of the churches in such ways as may seem best." This suggestion has been recently renewed,[6] and is doubtless appropriate for smaller communities. A study by the Boston Federation of the functions of many ministers' unions and community federations within the metropolitan area of that city, showed

---

[6] By Secretary John M. Moore of the Federal Council.

very similar functioning in the two types of organizations. The essence of the federation idea, however, is that it provides a representative basis for coöperation in which laymen participate as they do in most other phases of ecclesiastical life, but as they cannot in a ministerial association.

COUNCILS OF RELIGIOUS EDUCATION

In fifty of the seventy-eight cities that had estimated populations of 100,000 and over in 1925, there are either church federations or councils of religious education of the currently acceptable type, or the full equivalent of both.[7] Sixteen cities have federations only, twelve have councils of religious education only, and twenty-seven have both.[8] Small cities show a strong tendency to have only one or the other. Among the larger cities that have federations only, are Los Angeles, Seattle, and San Francisco; while Denver, Jersey City, New Orleans and St. Paul have only councils of religious education. The problem of adjusting relationship thus concerns at present the twenty-seven cities that continue both agencies. The problem becomes specially crucial where the subject has been a matter of discussion or conflict or is now under consideration.

Historic Relationships

Compared with other major interests of federations, the machinery of religious education is given departmental standing three times as often as is that of any other field. This evidence of the distinct, and relatively independent, place within the federation scheme occupied by religious education might well lead one to wonder how it ever got in to start with. Indeed, it is not too much to say that, by whatever means and in whatever degree it has been included, this interest characteristically retains a marked tradition of its own and the control of a quasi-independent means for expression and operation.

Distinctiveness

The reasons for the assertive maintenance of a distinctive role on the part of religious education are chiefly historical. This

---

[7] This figure is arrived at by combining the lists of federations published by the Federal Council, and of councils of religious education published by the International Council of Religious Education, supplemented by the field work of this study. Where county councils of religious education include cities of 100,000 population or over, the council is counted as belonging to the dominant city.

[8] Some of the sixteen cities credited with having federations only, maintain certain interdenominational work in religious education but not enough to be typical of a council of religious education.

interest is, in fact, no more unusual than other activities of federations. But it represents an old phase of organized Protestant coöperation with roots deep in the past. The older Sunday-school movement has a century and a half behind it; the federation movement a scant twenty-five years. As the younger and more inclusive movement has gradually extended itself, it has frequently found the older movement very unwilling to be assimilated, except on its own terms if at all, and generally able to make such terms as perpetuate a large measure of separate life within the larger whole.

The most outstanding fact of the present situation is, nevertheless, that religious education in cities is generally coming under the federation movement. The process is incomplete, and one need not venture to prophesy whether it will ever become universal. Quite obviously, however, it is greatly influenced by a course of evolution that has been going on since the beginning of the present century within the religious-education movement itself; and particularly by three factors.

The New Religious Education

First, the new conceptions of general education and the new pedagogy that have developed have become disturbing elements in the intellectually stagnant and organizationally routinized world of the older Sunday-school associations; for they have often been interpreted as demanding modifications of theology, and of the general outlook upon moral life, as well as upon methods of teaching.

It is beyond the province of this report to characterize the clash of the old and the new in the world of organized religious education except as it directly touches the Protestant movement of coöperation. As a result of this clash, councils of religious education sprang up in a number of cities parallel with the older Sunday-school associations, and a second set of national agencies began to appear. These imposed themselves upon the already complicated mass of religious machinery with which the city church was burdened.

Sometimes a spurious union of the old and the new took place within the same organization. Thus, one Sunday-school association maintained most of its older standing committees, manned chiefly by laymen of the old-guard, while placing religious-education specialists of the new generation in charge of a new group of committees that paralleled and almost entirely duplicated the functions of the old ones. The fact that all these committees existed chiefly on paper was all that prevented a clash.

In brief, religious education, along with activity in other fields, requires the simplification and combination of machinery. It has therefore naturally fallen in with the federation movement, the chief agency of the churches facilitating this result.

Increasing Denominational Control of Religious Education

In the second place, the machinery of religious education was becoming increasingly official. It was getting to represent direct denominational control and more or less of regularity. The older interdenominationalism of the historic Sunday-school movement had been voluntary. Its mood was practical and its genius chiefly promotional. It was assumed to be an organization for the fostering of methods only, and to involve no challenge to accepted thinking, no departure from accepted doctrine. It was managed by laymen, and was hence a movement largely free from ecclesiastical implications. On this basis, it has long been possible for denominations with little mutual sense of religious distance from one another to engage in coöperative activities. The federation movement itself has also been preceded by a similar voluntary coöperative movement.

When, however, the federation movement in its present phase came upon the scene, the situation had so evolved that it inevitably took the form of an interdenominationalizing of denominations. Denominational units and not individuals constituted the federated entities. About fifteen years later, the same change had established itself in the realm of religious education, as is best seen in the new constitution of the International Council of Religious Education. By means of constitutional compromises, the essential denominational control of the movement was secured; and one may safely say that the fact that both movements had come under a common type of control is largely responsible for forcing them together locally.

Independent Movements of Religious Education

While the older and the newer versions of religious education were getting adjusted, and while denominationalism was taking possession of the coöperative machinery of religious education, numerous new fields of religious education were getting themselves organized in many cities. There were already a good many forms of religious education supplementing the Sunday-school associations. Thus, the Young Men's Christian Association and Young

Women's Christian Association often attempted special work in this field. Adding these to the loosely related organizations hanging over from the older era—such as the graded unions, and the adult Bible-class leagues—and bringing in the newer organizations, it turned out to be not unusual for a city to show (1) a historic Sunday-school association, (2) a competing council of religious education, (3) an association for operating daily vacation Bible schools, (4) a committee for week-day religious education and (5) an association of young people's societies—all interdenominational and in addition to the increasing machinery of religious organizations within the denominations.

Such conditions naturally forced issues of coördination and integration to the fore. Not infrequently it proved easier for the competitive agencies of religious education to accept unification under the more inclusive church federation than to get together on their own account. On the other hand, there are many cities in which federations do not exist; and in some, separate inclusive councils of religious education were preferred. Consequently, interdenominational religious education is by no means completely identified with the church federation movement. The Protestant churches have not finally decided officially how they are going to conduct their coöperative activities in this field; but there is a strong tendency for them to do so under the federation banner.

The foregoing statement is intended to supply a necessary background for the study of religious education as it is at present comprehended within the church federation movement, to which the present chapter now turns.

Present Relationships

While the program of religious education tends to uniformity, the relationships with the federation movement under which it is conducted are extremely varied.

Five phases of relationship may be identified, varying from complete control of the religious-education machinery by the federation, to almost entire lack of control.

In the first stage, the federation has a department of religious education corresponding to a council of religious education; or else a previously independent council of religious education has entered into complete organic identity with a federation. This later process is usually accompanied by a revision of the council's constitution. The constitution of the Detroit Council, for example, now reads: "The object of this Council shall be to advance the cause of religious education functioning as the Department of Religious Education of the Detroit Council of Churches." Such councils have exactly the same status as other commissions of federations, most of which enjoy great initiative and liberty of action.

In the second phase, permanent functional identity has been established between the council of religious education and the federation, though the former maintains a technically distinct organization. In this phase the distinction is a mere gesture originally necessary to secure the affiliation of the two organizations, but not significant for their present operation. The federation carries on religious education through the council exactly as though the council were merely a department or commission.

In the third stage, there is administrative integration between a council of education and a federation, while the former maintains real organizational autonomy. In the case of Baltimore, for example, there are joint offices, joint financial measures, an overlapping staff and, in large measure, an integrated policy and range of activities. But the two organizations maintain their respective identities.

In the fourth stage, an entirely independent religious educational organization enters into a compact with a federation to function as its department of religious education. This agreement may have genuine vitality, and the organizations thereafter may present themselves to the public as maintaining the relation defined. This tends to be true, for example, in the case of Indianapolis, where the relation of the local council of churches to the state organization of religious education is so intimate that the local council can not well become merged in the church federation, but where a generous sense of the inclusion of religious education in the scope of the federation is in evidence.

In the fifth stage, such a compact as has been described has degenerated into mere lip service rendered to prevent the idea bcoming a reality. Thus, in Philadelphia the federation and the Sunday-school association mutually voted that the latter was to function as the former's commission on religious education. The Sunday-school association then proceeded to forget the compact. It never reports nor, in any genuine way, represents itself as carrying out the relationship it has adopted.

In contrast with all these stages and degrees in which religious-education organizations are integrated with the federation movement, stand ten cases in which councils of religious education or Sunday-school associations are entirely separate and have no organizational relationship whatever with the corresponding federations of their community. Even in these cases, organized coöperation in particular projects is possible, or even characteristic. For example, the Community Training School for Church School Teachers may be jointly conducted by the two agencies, which then proceed to go their several ways in other activities. Of the ten cases of independent religious-education agencies, two or three presented examples of positive rivalry and actual ill-will. The federation in these communities had attempted to secure the formal affiliation of the religious-education agency and the integration of the work of the two. This had been resented; the effort had failed; and the reaction had brought about the strained relationships just described.[9]

All told, then, church federations and councils of religious education, or their full functional equivalents, are organizationally identified in sixteen of the twenty-seven cities, or else are so adjusted that they operate as though they were identified. In two or three cases, the two organizations persist on a definitely antagonistic basis. This leaves eight or nine cases in which relations are casual or negative. In view of the closer adjustments reached in the majority of cases, it is natural to ask in respect to these, whether it might not be to the advantage of the total interdenominational work to unite the two agencies.

Internal Organization

As one of the expressions of its distinctiveness, religious education inclines to an exceptional richness of internal organization. Within the department or autonomous council the practice of the movement dictates that there shall be a general controlling body and divisional committees corresponding to the major divisions of the program. A fully organized department will consequently have its central board and subcommittees for each field covered, such as church schools, week-day religious education, vacation schools, community-training school, etc. A second set of subcommittees will cover the same areas of interest from the standpoint of age-, and sex-adaptation; for example, children's, young people's, and adults' divisions. There will also be committees that supply resources for the work, such as those on finance and publicity. All told, from six to ten divisional

---

[9] For a running account of the relationships between federations and agencies of religious education, see *Church Council News Letter*, v. 1, no. 5, Federal Council of Churches, November, 1928.

committees, in addition to the central body, will demand an aggregate of from seventy-five to one hundred and twenty-five members.   This elaborate committee system carries to the extreme the position habitually in vogue in all areas of federation activities.   It makes no allowance for the fact already noticed that religious education has relatively more professional leaders than any other field.   In consequence, perhaps, of this duplication of functions, the typical performance of committees stands on a lower level than that of committees in most other departments.   The situation is, however, eloquent testimony to the willingness of federations to have religious education preserve its own values and go its own gait if only ultimate unification of organization is secured.

Adequacy of the Solution

Relationship within the federation fold on terms so liberal has proved satisfactory to the religious-education forces in a majority of cases.   Why may it not in all cases?

In addition to the natural disinclination of established interests to lose their identity and their complete independence of action, a set of objective considerations obtrude themselves upon the attention of any one who undertakes to make a concrete answer to such a suggestion.

(1) Many federations are too weak to commend themselves as inclusive movements.   If they were responsible for religious education, they could not guarantee it any better backing, nor perhaps as good, as it now has.   The chapter on finance will show a considerable number of cases of absolute or relative failure with necessary reduction of budgets and work.   Separately organized religious education will be little inclined to affiliate with federations that are financially weak.

(2) On their part, the agencies of religious education are sometimes traditional and non-progressive, and would be so under any auspices.   They are not in line with modern organizational tendencies in their own field, and follow their own national leadership afar off, if at all.   This seems to be true in all cases of active ill-will between federations and councils, and to explain a majority of cases in which relations are merely negative.   It is a question whether federations would do well to include religious educational movements while the latter remain in this mood.

(3) Generally radical differences in tradition and spirit involve actual or potential clashes of personalities.   This is sure to be true when the old-guard of religious education is on the defensive

in behalf of its own prestige and methods, and the federation is aggressive for organizational integration.

(4) Occasionally a divergence of theological views is involved. The federation is too liberal for those in control of the religious-education group.[10]

(5) More than one of the preceding factors are frequently present in particular situations. There have been abrupt, premature, and untactful efforts at affiliation on the part of some federations. These have naturally invited flarebacks and fixed a mood of antipathy.

To induce a reluctant religious-education organization to affiliate with it, a federation might well strengthen itself in other lines. Every increase in prestige and effectiveness makes more natural such combinations as have proved advantageous in the majority of cases.

Temporary Adjustments

It is obviously important strategically that wherever there is a federation but no council, the federation should occupy the field of religious education comprehensively. It should, at the earliest possible moment, undertake a standard community program and affiliate itself with the state and national agencies of religious education.

It is equally pertinent to ask whether it might not be well, in some cases at least, for a council, where no federation exists, to take over certain federation functions and seek recognition by the federation fellowship without breaking its connections with its own national organizations.

If this were done, the present writer would be content to let the situation in each place work itself out, at least until new overhead adjustments should be made. Negotiations to this end are now in process between the Federal Council of Churches and the International Council of Religious Education.

WOMEN'S INTERDENOMINATIONAL ORGANIZATIONS

During the field work of the present investigation, first-hand studies were made of women's departments of church federations, or paralleling women's organizations, in twenty-three cities. The period covered by the investigation was one of high tension and active agitation among these organizations. Conferences of rep-

---

[10] It should be noted on the other hand, that religious-education commissions are sometimes too advanced for the more conservative elements in federation constituencies.

resentatives of local women's interchurch movements were held in 1927 and 1928 in an attempt to develop national expression and leadership for the growing movement, with emphasis upon its distinctiveness and autonomy.   The problem of the relations of women's organizations to the general structure and functions of the Church, both locally and denominationally, are also acute. The situation in the federation movement is different from that in the Church generally, in that this movement has no strong overhead organization to challenge or constrain the woman separatist tendency which is strongly in evidence.   The immediate present is therefore a time of extraordinary interest, in which federation is shown in a most dynamic phase, and exhibiting both the strength and the weakness of a movement that is voluntary in contrast with movements that possess defined ecclesiastical authority.

Antecedents

Obviously, then, as a prelude to any illuminating account of women's interdenominational organizations as related to the federation movement, something must be said regarding the place accorded to, and occupied by, women in the modern church. All organizational issues are probably mere incidents of this large problem.

Within the local church, the earliest functional distinction made was that between clergy and laity; the second was that between men and women.   Differentiation of certain spheres of action as of particular interest to women, and the creation of a set of organizations corresponding to these responsibilities, are among the most widely accepted of ecclesiastical arrangements in the local church, where they have become virtually universal except in the smallest rural churches.

Women's Denominational Organizations

This same tendency to separate women's organizations passed over into denominational affairs at an early date.   Many denominations developed women's boards of missions; and all have recognized both the support and the control of definite parts of the work of the Church as the primary responsibility of women's groups.   Denominations have found it necessary to reintegrate their own agencies, especially in notable reorganization movements during the last fifteen years.   In connection with this process, the re-alignment of hitherto separate women's organ-

izations with the work of the denominational churches as a whole
has constituted one of the most serious and vexing problems.

Women Banded for Moral Reform

Parallel with the development of women's organizations within
the Church, notable movements arose associating Christian
women primarily for the sake of moral reform. These reached
across denominational lines and sought united action in realms
of common interest. The most notable example of such movements is the Women's Christian Temperance Union.

When interchurch coöperation and federation at length came
upon the stage, it was obviously in line with previous tendencies
that there should be a distinctive women's coöperative movement
with appropriate forms of organization as a pioneering and parallel phenomenon. In this field, the first interdenominational
coöperative work was that of foreign and home missions. From
about 1895, but more particularly from 1910 on, interdenominational unions of women in behalf of this cause began to appear
in many cities. At first the two spheres of missionary interest
were usually organized separately. The primary object of both
was united prayer for, and study of, the far-flung extension work
of the Church. Some of these local missionary unions also
adopted bits of local philanthropic service as incidental parts of
their broad program.

As the vision and understanding of the social implication of
Christianity came into the consciousness of the Church, and
especially as specialized fields of social service with new technical methods were developed, it was equally natural that the
interests of women should find coöperative organization in these
new aspects of service which in a sense continued their traditional flair for moral reform. Consequently a second stream
of organization arose.

Alongside the development of city church federations, sometimes as separate parallel movements, sometimes as departments
originating within federations, the organization of women along
these two interchurch lines has steadily proceeded.

Summary of Antecedents of Women's Federated Organizations

Many of the older separate organizations have been drawn
into more or less close alliance with the federations. Of eighteen
women's interchurch federation movements that were studied,
and whose historical evolution was clear, nine had old roots in
the two characteristic movements already described; three orig-

inated under federation auspices, with the objectives including both missionary and social-service interests; while five recently organized, all with inclusive objectives, reveal the reaction of the immediate past from too close identification with the general federations. In brief, the minor trend of the hour is toward a new separatism.

This trend is partly explicable when one considers that women's interests and points of view nowhere found mention in connection with the organization of the Federal Council, nor in any considerable measure figure in the basic organization of the earliest federations. It will probably be agreed that the movement for separate organization, however currently emphasized, is related to, and is ultimately of less significance than, the role and status of women in the general coöperative processes of the Church.

Accordingly, both phases of the situation have been covered by the present investigation and are reported upon in the following section.

Present Relationships

The purpose of the section is thus twofold: first, to give a contemporaneous account of women's coöperative organizations, the roots of which have already been sketched; and to disclose situations and attitudes that bear upon the problem.

The part taken by women in the interchurch movement will be described under the two major classifications already suggested: first, those revealing the status of women within the general movement; and, second, those pertaining to distinctive women's organizations.

Status of Women Within the General Federation Movement

Constitutional provisions for the inclusion of women as representatives of the churches in the governing bodies of the federations have already been set forth in the chapter on structure and organization.[11] Nearly half the federations studied require the central bodies to have women members to the extent of one-fifth to two-fifths of their total. On the other hand, constitutional provision for secondary memberships from non-church organizations, while frequently including such organizations of Christian women as the Y. W. C. A., rarely specify federations of church women. The probable reasons are that as independent

---

[11] P. 83.

organizations, they were rare when most of the constitutions were drawn, and that the traditions of the federation movement are now to include such women's organizations as departments, where possible.

Local Women's Interchurch Organizations

Before discussing the significance of the above facts as indices of the role and status of women in the modern church, the parallel facts concerning specific women's organizations should be presented. Some of these organizations are independent of the federations, others autonomous but allied to them; while still others are fully integrated departments with no autonomous existence. But the actual situation is more complicated than is suggested by these distinctions. When all factors are considered, it appears that nine different situations need to be recognized. These will be briefly enumerated:

(1) Some cities where federations exist have no parallel women's movement whatever. Boston is a case in point. It should be noted, however, that several of the Boston suburbs have strong women's interchurch movements which in certain cases might be affiliated or integrated with local councils of churches or religious education.

(2) Still other cities have only the older forms of interdenominational unions carrying on the traditional programs in behalf of missions, but with no responsibility for, or program of, local community work. Baltimore and Brooklyn at the date of the study represented this phase of development; but in both cities active negotiations looking to some affiliation with the church federation were under way.

(3) No cases of long standing were found in which the two older streams of organized women's interests, namely, that in missions and that in community work and social service, had merged and were going on merely as a women's movement entirely independent of the federations. When women get together, they go still further and become parts of other more inclusive organizations.

(4) In one case, however, that of St. Louis, an older organization of the missionary type and a newer one for the coöperation of church women in social work were going on independent of each other, but both as auxiliaries of the church federation. The degree of identification with the federation was, however, quite unequal.

(5) No current cases were found in which one of the two types of women's organization had affiliated with the federation while the other still remained independent.

(6) In a single case, a women's interchurch organization formerly affiliated with a federation, had broken all recognized connection and was working on parallel lines, with great emphasis upon the fact of independence, but coöperatively in certain projects. The position of this organization seemed somewhat tentative. Whether it represents the beginning of a new separative movement, or rather an extreme reaction that will later be modified, only time can tell.

(7) Seven women's organizations were closely affiliated with church federations in two similar ways: five by the formal recognition of an affiliated relationship, organic independence still being maintained; and two by constitutional affiliation which limits organic independence. In all of these cases, essential administrative autonomy is preserved and there is increasing stress on functional independence. Not only have the terms of affiliation been less explicit in the case of the more recently organized women's organizations, but several of them have experienced an actual loosening of ties without going to the length of entirely breaking away from the affiliated relationship. Thus in the case of a women's department originally organized under federation initiative, a revision of the constitution struck out provisions that amendments had to be acceptable to the executive committee of the council of churches; that a member of the finance committee of the council should be treasurer of the women's department; and that the department should make monthly and annual reports to the federation. The revision, however, still preserved the statement that the purpose of the women's department was "to coöperate with the church federation in carrying on whatever phase of work may be agreed upon after consultation between the executive council of the department and the executive committee of the federation."

(8) Ten federations were carrying on women's departments as organic parts of their organization. Most of these departments have been established constitutionally; but in a few cases only by special compact and enabling action. Chicago, Cleveland, Minneapolis, New York, Oakland, Pittsburgh, Sacramento, San Francisco, Washington and Wichita have women's organizations of this type, providing opportunity for women to administer and support particular bodies of work. All undertake distinctive programs. In the main they represent functional specialization.

In some cases, however, the women's sub-committees largely parallel those of the general federation, and the work attempted in the same general area is not jointly planned or conducted.

(9) Nowhere was a unified city-wide women's interchurch movement found entirely out of touch with the general federation movement, either historically or contemporaneously. In brief, the progress of the women's organization as a unified movement is not separate from those of the general federation. It turns out rather to be a phase of the larger movement.

Twenty-one of the twenty-two cities studied had organized interchurch movements of Protestant women. In seventeen of the twenty-one cases the women's organization was definitely affiliated with the church federation, or constituted an integral part of it. Whatever may be the future, the two elements of the movement are at present very genuinely interrelated.

Modifying Factors

In the development of the situations just summarized, a number of factors have obvious part:

(1) In contrast with commissions and committees, women's departments are like other departments of federations, in that they represent in the main the assimilation of previously independent organizations.[12] In nearly all such cases, marks of the former cleavage remain, and the work is less closely related to the major interests of the federation than that in fields that were never under separate agencies.

(2) The fact that the status of women in the general federation movement, as in the denominational churches both local and national, does not accord them administrative position and responsibility equal to their numbers and activity in church work, tends to occasion separatist tendencies beyond any real functional advantage. The separate movement, in considerable part, is an entirely explicable reflection of feministic psychology.

(3) Federations differ in the degree of independence and initiative accorded to all commissions and standing committees responsible for particular fields of service. Those that encourage initiative and independence in these agencies are giving the women's movement only what they give to all other phases of their work. On the contrary, federations whose commissions are closely supervised by the governing boards have to make exceptions in the case of the women.

(4) A partial explanation of these differences in policy is finan-

---

[12] P. 440.

cial. There are strong practical reasons for decentralizing the financial burden. Accordingly, women's departments that are maintaining expensive programs out of their own resources, are likely to reach an independence which others have not.

(5) This is indirectly an illustration of the difference which the particular nature of the program undertaken makes. Distinctive and non-competitive programs not closely paralleling the work of federations make for independent women's organizations, while overlapping programs raise the problem of coördination.

(6) Federations that have women secretaries tend not to have separate women's organizations. This is true also of federations whose delegated memberships are more largely composed of women than is usual. In brief, when women run the federation itself, they have less motive for separate organization.

INTERDENOMINATIONAL YOUNG PEOPLE'S ORGANIZATIONS

Most large cities have some form of Protestant young people's organization loosely affiliating the denominational Christian Endeavor and other similar societies which have become characteristic of the Church. In some cities, these are largely paper organizations, functioning feebly and discontinuously; in others, they have developed continuous life and institutional stability. Some of these maintain salaried executives and carry on significant promotional and service activities. As the federation movement has developed it has had to consider, and to ask the young people's organizations to consider, the place of such agencies in the integrated Protestant system.

In this case, progress has been less rapid, and adjustments less satisfactory, than in the spheres of women's work or religious education—largely because it involves the exceedingly difficult problem of youth and the Church—itself, in turn, a piece of the problem of youth and the age. At least a rough charting of this problem is necessary to make intelligible the efforts of the federations to include youth organizations.

Youth and the Church

Every individual parish has its version of this problem. It is a cause of heart-searching in every communion. Organizationally speaking, the Church traditionally has attached youth to itself in two ways. Besides the voluntary, self-supporting and largely self-directed agencies of the Christian Endeavor type, religious education undertakes the culture of youth in Sunday-school and mission-study classes. In contrast with the voluntary societies largely representing the initiative of youth itself, these school processes represent what adults think is good for youth.

Under either method, youth is segregated from the operation and control of the central functions of the Church. Young people do not have membership on local church boards, cannot be elected deacons or elders, are not brought into responsible participation in church affairs in proportion to their numbers in church-membership or to the hours which they devote to religious activities. The propriety of this situation the federations merely take for granted.

Modern religious education, however, is making marked effort genuinely to enlist youth in its processes. It is limbering up its methods and making room for initiative and a large measure of self-direction. But it cannot be said that it has yet proposed terms satisfactory to the historic young people's societies. From the standpoint of current religious practice the problem is sensed but not solved.

This is the legacy of the Church to the federations in the field of young people's work. In attacking its interdenominational phases, they start where the Church leaves them and must not be blamed for not moving faster than the world to which they belong.

Adjustments Attempted With Young People's Organizations

The preceding section of this chapter showed that the constitutions of many federations require the election of a quota of women as delegates on any board of directors and executive committees. The representation of young people is never protected in this way. Neither are the young people's societies included in the affiliating devices with which the previous discussion has made the reader familiar. The Church does not seem to think it necessary either to recognize youth as such or to conciliate it. It is presumably supposed to be represented by its elders.

This situation is made all the more conspicuous when the age of committee-members is considered. Young people might be put on committees even though constitutions do not require it. But they are not. Committees are composed overwhelmingly not merely of adults, but of elderly adults.[13]

---

[13] P. 299.

Coöperation Without Combination

The most frequent actual situation in American cities is one in which a rather inchoate type of interdenominational young people's organization coöperates incidentally with a church federation without any systematic adjustment of relationships. The young people's organization conducts interdenominational sessions for the promotion of the traditional type of young people's work. It may, undertake the lay conduct of special religious services, sometimes taking the form of seasonal outdoor preaching in parks and places of resort, sometimes that of bringing religious ministries and entertainment to hospitals and philanthropic institutions. In these cases, the federation may treat the young people's organization as a specialized adjunct doing a part of the common work though without any recognized common plan.

Formal Coöperative Alliances

About half the federations studied maintained commissions or committees on young people's work, the majority of which represented some form of formal coöperative alliance between the federation and the previously existing interdenominational young people's organization. As in the case of all departments, there was great variation in the resulting closeness of relationship. On the one hand were types of affiliation that left the young people's organization self-determining and self-supporting, carrying on virtually the same work which they had carried on independently, but with only a slightly greater degree of common planning in advance. On the other hand were cases in which the federation itself had taken the initiative in developing the young people's department, which it proceeded to give the same general character of semi-independence possessed by the majority of commissions.

As with other departments, the young people's department frequently includes churches of non-federated denomination—thus widening the effective scope of the coöperative movement.

Young People's Divisions in Departments of Religious Education

More federations would show young people's departments but for the fact that a good many of them think it sufficient to develop young people's work as a division of the department of religious education. As was previously indicated, this implies a greater degree of adult initiative and control. Since some of the departments of religious education are themselves exceedingly feeble affairs, the young people's division as a mere fraction of a fraction of the work, remains infinitesimally small. Sometimes, indeed, it exists virtually only on paper. The federation has stuck up a signboard indicating that it has preëmpted the field, and warning others off, but without really occupying it. Only two federations have special paid executives at the head of their young people's departments; and though the aspiration of modern religious education to become an instrument of spontaneous youth movements is good, the present degree of realization leaves much to be desired.

Facilitation of Young People's Community Councils

The real lack of rapport between the self-directed young people's movements and federations, both as under adult and ecclesiastical control, and the present inability of departments of religious education to give satisfactory place to spontaneous youth movements, coupled with the further fact that many important youth movements are non-ecclesiastical, has lead a number of federations to prefer to facilitate young people's religious councils rather than to attempt to tie them up even remotely to the federations.

This is at once a confession of the limitations of the movement and an expression of its genius, in that it has from the beginning professed to be able to work through other agencies as well as under its own banner.

The particular advantage of the broader community basis of young people's organizations is that it can include the Young Men's Christian Association and the Young Women's Christian Association (which themselves do not fit easily into the federative form of ecclesiastical coöperation); also such character-building agencies as the boy and girl scouts and the numerous philanthropic boys' and girls' clubs, either independent or attached to social centers. Recently, the Boston Federation after a careful canvassing of the elements entering into the situation, took the initiative in setting up such a young people's council; and other federations have shared the promotion of such councils with other city-wide agencies.

The young people's council is then both self-determined and non-ecclesiastical in ideals. It is under no obligation to do what the federation wants promoted; and is able to get more vitally at what youth believes to be its own current problems. Actually, however, on the whole such youth movements ultimately rely much upon the existing agencies and can be lead to undertake many of the activities that would be assigned to them if they were departments of federations.

Putting together all the methods by which the affiliation of young people's religious movements have been sought, one cannot say that the results are commensurate with the importance of the problem. The major trend is to some type of systematic affiliation under the church federation movement; but the present bristles with problems, and the future with uncertainty.

AFFILIATION OF OTHER TYPES OF INTERDENOMINATIONAL AGENCIES

Interdenominational men's work is so casually organized in most cities, and such organization as exists is so intermittent in functioning, as not to afford a recognized field for cultivation by federations. In only one case has a federation a commission on men's work. It promotes an annual interdenominational dinner of men's clubs, and tries to develop sentiment in behalf of law enforcement. Potentially, however, men's work constitutes a field for interdenominational organization that would constitute a natural function for church federations.

Interdenominational children's work is either handled as a division of departments of religious education, or through women's organizations in their missionary functioning.

CONCLUSION

The attempt of federations to affiliate other interdenominational organizations displays so many ragged edges of incomplete adjustment that one may easily underestimate its significance. Viewed as a process which, with only twenty years of relatively feeble institutional life behind it, has had to overcome entrenched institutional separateness in so many directions at once, it has really exhibited remarkable progress. The glorious ideal that a federation is an expression of the Catholic unity of the Church, a repairing of the rents in the seamless robe of Christ, has not greatly convinced leaders of older movements that had to be revamped to fit into the scheme of federation hegemony. These leaders have been rather inclined to see in it "just another organization," a presumptuous rival backed by precarious loyalties and slender funds; accordingly, they have yielded ground to it only so far as the logical and practical strength of the federation's position has compelled them to.

It has been shown how far affiliation has been accomplished in its various forms, and with what different groups of agencies. While offering nothing final, the story of evolution up-to-date does, nevertheless, seem to indicate that the group of interdenominational agencies considered—the ministers' unions, councils of religious education, women's interchurch organizations, and (with less certainty) the interdenominational young people's agencies—are essentially assimilable to the characteristic type of loose integration which is the essence of the federative pattern so far. In the large, they have come under the federation scheme of Protestant integration whenever that scheme has been locally developed to normal strength and completeness. In this sense and to this extent, then, the organizational complexity of urban Protestantism is actually relieved by the federation movement.

Many technical and practical problems of adjustment remain; and it is not settled in the case of any agency that there shall be just one typical form of adjustment. It is not a requirement of the federation's genius that there should be.

Chapter XI

PRESENT LIMITS OF FEDERATIVE COÖPERATION

When it comes to the assimilation into a common organization of the non-denominational allies and extensions of the Church, the coöperative movement, so far as its federative form goes, virtually stops short. These agencies constitute a distinct problem. They may be remotely attached to federations by formal membership and sometimes by significant participation. At times they may become slightly and discontinuously involved in the work of federations, at other times profoundly and continuously; but they are never integrated with federations as the interdenominational agencies treated in the last chapter usually are. Just because they are extensions and allies of the Church rather than ecclesiastical elements within it, the agencies now to be considered lie beyond the present limits of coöperative achievement in the sense that coöperation has come to be realized in the strictly interdenominational field.

THE PROBLEM OF RELATIONSHIP WITH ALLIES

The outstanding representatives of the Church's extensions and allies fall into three main types: the Young Men's and Young Women's Christian Association; organizations representing special interests of public morality like the Anti-saloon League and Lord's Day Alliance; and specialized service agencies like the Bible societies. The organizations comprehended within this group all have Protestant roots, if they are not Protestant by constitution. They are voluntary and self-perpetuating lay organizations, not conducted by formally appointed delegates of churches and denominations; and they are, in the main, concerned with special segments of Christian interest outside the round of activities and concerns with which the local parish church is chiefly occupied.

The existence of these agencies in cities adds to the problems of both organizational complexity and of competition. Any general analysis of the larger issues of Protestant coöperation must therefore include them in its survey; but interchurch coöperation of the federative sort centering in a definitely inter-

182

denominational agency has achieved only superficial adjustments
of relationship with them, and has not dared actively to attempt
to make this relationship one of subordination and inclusion as
has been done in the case of the interdenominational agencies.

This is not to say that there has not been continuous consciousness of their part in the problem. Testimony to a sense
of its importance stands out in the national records of the Protestant coöperative movement. The earlier local organizers of
the Federal Council recorded many conferences with the Young
Men's Christian Association, Young Women's Christian Association, Lord's Day Alliance, and social agencies "with a view to
preventing overlapping friction and waste." What they called
the problem of "effective economical and harmonious adjustment" could in their opinion not be solved until the adjustment
of these agencies to the federation idea was secured.

In 1914 the Federal Council established a commission on
Federated Movements which reported in 1915 that it "has one
distinctive field * * * the adjustment of interaction between
the great interdenominational movements of our country like the
Young Men's Christian Association, the Young Women's Christian Association and the Laymen's Missionary Movement." Ten
years later a series of conferences of Allied Christian Agencies
doing Community Work were held, in which representatives of a
still larger group of organizations committed themselves "to
such approaches in field administration as will make it clear that
all plans adopted locally should include the interests of all the
institutions rightly interested, and endeavor to keep the emphasis
on the larger goals of the kingdom."

At present a national "Church Counseling Commission" of the
Young Men's Christian Association is coöperating with the Federal Council in studying the relations of the local associations
to the churches, giving chief attention to smaller cities.

These evidences of continuous recognition of the problem of
churches' extensions and allies as related to the federation movement, have been echoed locally in many utterances. Probably
no ministers' union has ever failed at least annually to discuss
the relation of the churches and the Young Men's Christian
Association, and "the possibilities of closer coöperation between
them." Indeed, the concern of local church federation officials
for a restudy of the total coöperative problem (out of which the
present investigation arose) definitely pointed to relationships
with the Young Men's Christian Association and Young
Women's Christian Association as crucial issues.

In incidental discussions engaged in during the field investigation, it was commonly agreed that the churches are slowly coming around to the broader interpretation of religion as related to "body, mind and spirit" for which the Christian associations have stood, and that the increasing use in churches of recreational methods, organized clubs, and the like are bringing them more and more into fields first explored by these associations. Recent attempts of the Young Men's Christian Association particularly to redefine its functions in terms of the community, make it clear that this agency has come to think of itself as far more than an organization carrying on a program for particular types of men and boys within its own buildings, and to stress more and more its contribution in the total religious life. In view of this expansion of ideals, the opportunity for further complication, and indeed for competition, is increasing. The coöperative movement in its present federative form has not been able to forestall this possibility.

ATTEMPTED SOLUTIONS

This chapter narrates the facts of relationship between the churches as federated and their extensions and allies, as they have been met with in the course of the present investigation. In it the adjustments attempted in harmony with the foregoing analysis are classified, and the conclusion is reached that the actual amalgamation of the federations and their extensions and allies of the churches—though a sound logical possibility—is nowhere conceded to be a live issue of present churchmanship.

RELATIONSHIPS WITH THE Y.M.C.A.

The story of relationships and of particular adjustments between the federations and each major agency is now to be told, beginning with the Young Men's Christian Association.

Facts Bearing on Relationship

The twenty-one cities whose twenty-two federations were covered by the present study reported to the federal census in 1926 a total of 7,760 Protestant churches (of all types) with about 2,785,000 adult members, and annual expenditures of about $186,371,000. The twenty-two federations, of course, had no individual memberships paralleling those of the churches. They were spending only about $360,000. The Young Men's Christian Associations in the same cities (as reported in the 1928 yearbook) consisted of eighty-six organizations (counting branches separately) with 117,256 adult members, and annual expenditures (other than those covered by commercial income) of about $7,400,000. The churches owned property in religious use which had an aggregate value of nearly $1,000,000,000. The Young Men's Christian Association plants were worth more than sixty million dollars, while the federations were virtually propertyless.

Attempted Statement of Relationship

The Young Men's Christian Association regards itself as a Christian movement spiritually within the Church, and primarily as a brotherhood incidentally using institutional features. It repeatedly proclaims itself "the servant and ally" of the Church; an "adjunct" to the Church as well as to the home and the school. In connection with pressure to enter Community Funds, local Young Men's Christian Associations have frequently argued that their affinities are with the churches, which are not included, rather than with the social welfare and charitable agencies, which are. The National Council of the Young Men's Christian Association maintains a department representing "the desire of Association leaders, national, state, and local, to work more effectively with the churches in their service to men and boys." This department has set up a Counseling Commission of the Churches. The opening statement of the 1928 meeting of this body asserted:

> At its beginning * * * it was a problem whether the Young Men's Christian Association Movement could function without more direct ecclesiastical or denominational control. As it has developed, the churches have been content to leave the leadership of the Movement in the hands of Christian laymen who are members in good standing of the evangelical churches with the sympathy and counsel of leading clergymen of all churches.

The formal report of the commission further stated:

> There are indications of a growing sense of obligation in the Brotherhood to serve in counsel or in coöperative enterprise any of the churches which are developing a religious educational program for their men and boys, in city or rural fields.

Current relationships with federations have been generalized by the counseling commission and individualized by local Young Men's Christian Associations. Speaking officially, the national Young Men's Christian Association reports itself—as a by-product of its ordinary functioning—as ready to foster federations "in fields where there is no council or federation of churches with an employed representative." It declares that its leaders and facilities have often been of service to federations, and that Young Men's Christian Association secretaries have sometimes served at the same time as secretaries of local federations. It expresses the desire to work out experimentally with the Federal Council the best methods of furthering united-church programs.

Local Associations take for granted that they and the federations have mutually sympathetic purposes and, in the main, mutually exclusive fields. Conventional expressions of goodwill are naturally frequent. Thus a Young Men's Christian Association financial campaign document will be certain to assure its public that its "relation to the federation of churches is most cordial, and the mutual services rendered are many." But 'many' and 'most' obviously have to be taken relatively in such a connection; and the situation leaves the matter of relationships to be judged by deeds rather than by words. The study discovered no case (except that of Wichita, which received separate comment) in which the Young Men's Christian Association had propounded a clear and adequate definition of the respective places of itself and the federation in the total scheme of Protestant coöperation, nor of its exact relationships with the local federation.

The Church's Reaction

As represented by the federation movement, the Church's attitude toward these approaches of the Young Men's Christian Association expresses a certain wariness toward a friendly but, at the same time, an aggressive agency whose scope and objectives are imperfectly defined. Thus Dr. E. B. Sanford, as the executive head of the federation movement of 1911, reported officially as follows:

> Local federation work almost invariably comes into close relation with the Young Men's Christian Association. The International Committee * * * has expanded its work to such an extent that its support requires expenditures running into hundreds of thousands of dollars. With no thought of criticising this work, my study of the present situation has convinced me that this service has gone so far beyond the original and definite purpose for which the Young Men's Christian Association was first organized that it would be most helpful and possibly avoid very grave dangers if the National Committee of the Young Men's Christian Association could be brought into conference.

More than one federation leader since has been inclined to agree with Dr. Sanford. What they have apprehended in the

Young Men's Christian Association is a vastly enterprising agency that has girdled the world with Christian activities under an opportunistic instinct; but which seems to them to have followed the call of apparent need with inadequate regard to any rigorous theory of a proper sphere and function relative to the other agencies of the Church. Ecclesiastical observers have repeatedly commented on this characteristic.

There have been, moreover, within the Young Men's Christian Association movement itself, voices that counseled a greater degree of specialization and the acceptance of specific objectives more exactly expressing the original purpose of the organization. For example, the expert Report of the Survey Commission on the Young Men's Christian Association of the City of New York in 1926 declared: [1]

> In considering future purpose it is the opinion of your Commission that the primary objective of the Y.M.C.A. of the City of New York should be to provide what is necessary in order to adjust the young man between the ages of sixteen and thirty to his city environment with a view to developing a balanced personality animated by a keen sense of social responsibility. Stated more briefly, it should be "personal guidance." The work of the Association should be organized with the aim toward producing a balanced personal program for each young man. * * * It should also offer the more important services needed by the young man which are not elsewhere available in the city on a basis which compares favorably with that which the Association is prepared to offer. Your Commission deems the suggestion that personal guidance be made the controlling principle of the Association's program in the immediate future, the most significant development of the survey; and desires to lay special stress upon it as at once an outstanding need of the City and the primary opportunity of the Association.

But such a judgment represents a minority opinion—or at least an unusual limitation upon practice. As already indicated, the more general tendency is for the Association to define itself as a broad agency of Christian evangelization and education primarily concerned with men and boys, but finding in the needs of each community whatever type of program its opportunities and resources seem to make appropriate. It is with this latter sort of Young Men's Christian Associations that federations, either actually or potentially, have to do in the main.

---

[1] Pp. 5 and 6.

Actual Relationships

The "Y" as an Initiator of Federations

The fact that many Young Men's Christian Associations thus broadly define their functions has enabled them to play important parts in the establishment of local church federations.[2] No other type of community organization except the Ministers' Union has had so much to do with the origin and early development of these agencies. So well established is this role of the Association that the Federal Council's extension committee (in harmony with the attitude of the Y's counselling commission as previously stated) agreed upon a deliberate policy of experimentation for 1929-30, in which it was proposed to seek Young Men's Christian Association leadership in the establishment of new federations in ten smaller cities. The record of the past, as well as these present relationships, are of genuine testimony to the large-mindedness and adaptability of the Young Men's Christian Association and to the willingness of the churches to profit by it even though they may question some of its practical implications.

Organizational Membership

The customary provision in the constitutions of federations for organizational membership on the part of the non-ecclesiastical Christian agencies was set forth at length in Chapter V. This affiliating device has been extended to the Young Men's Christian Association more frequently than to any other agency. Beyond this, the Association's officers characteristically receive *ex officio* standing on governing boards and executive committees.[3] It perhaps needs to be noted that no such provision of organizational membership is ordinarily made for agencies that federations expect to assimilate. That is to say, remote attachment of the sort habitually provided for the Young Men's Christian Association is a virtual testimony to the sense of the impossibility of securing more intimate integration.

Y.M.C.A. Coöperation With Federations

As already indicated, the general willingness of the Young Men's Christian Association to help to found federations doubtless assumes that the two agencies have, in the main, a mutually exclusive field, and that their helpfulness to each other will be essentially incidental. And this is what one actually finds. In

[2] P. 42.
[3] Pp. 80 and 84.

the bulk of their activities, each proceeds with its own tasks, and no question arises either of active coöperation or of competition. The lack of departments of federation work for men and boys, for example, indicates a tacit recognition that the Young Men's Christian Association is already functioning as an interchurch agency in these fields. Such departments, which formerly existed in certain federations, have all but disappeared.

Frequent exchange of services between Young Men's Christian Associations and federations mark the lowest level of positive coöperative relationships. Young Men's Christian Associations furnish office headquarters and committee rooms to federations. They frequently contribute clerical assistance to federation enterprises, and render them technical services through the presence of professional experts on federation committees. They contribute promotional ability to federation campaigns. Federations, in turn, vitally assist Young Men's Christian Associations with their major financial drives, and serve as a continuous guarantee of their value to the whole body of churches. The total of services exchanged reaches an impressive number.[4]

Like denominations, however, Young Men's Christian Associations and federations also discover that sometimes there are services to the community which they can do together better than they can separately. Of the 204 standard activities of federations, the one most frequently undertaken coöperatively by the two agencies was found to be visitation evangelism. Ranking next in frequency were: assistance in Young Men's Christian Association finances; father's and son's activities; shop and factory meetings; and interchurch athletics. The Young Men's Christian Association is the direct beneficiary of the first activity, while the second is likely to be so interpreted as to constitute a bid for Young Men's Christian Association support. The third and fourth, on the contrary, are characteristic Young Men's Christian Association activities which federations have only occasionally entered upon. Less frequent coöperative activities of federations and Young Men's Christian Associations include: broadcasting services; community training schools; conferences; normal classes and speakers' bureaus in religious education; Americanization classes; work for foreign students; employment bureaus; and missionary education. Some

---

[4] In many smaller cities Association secretaries have served as volunteer federation executives; but in such instances the federation program has been very meager, consisting chiefly of such activities as could be conducted without expenditure for paid personnel other than part-time stenographic service, and not comparable with the work done by the federations studied in these volumes as defined on p. 108.

of these items also have greater traditional affinity for the Church, others for the Young Men's Christian Association.[5]

This considerable list of actual coöperative activities does not mean, however, that federations habitually coöperate with Young Men's Christian Associations at any point in their characteristic programs. Coöperation between the two agencies remains exceptional. One accordingly has to ask: Why does it take place at the points listed rather than at others; and why, when it does take place, is it only occasional at best?

While one familiar with the experience and resources of the Young Men's Christian Association could show definite aptness at each point of reported coöperation, just as many equally apt ones that are not taken advantage of could easily be picked out. The actual selection appears, therefore, to be largely accidental, depending upon the presence or absence in the particular time and circumstances of some of the special conditions found to govern the coöperation of denominations.[6] The agencies were pushed into coöperation by external circumstances; they had to work together to win just then. There is at least no recognized policy, no settled presumption of habitual coöperation, on any given point.

In other words, what figures externally as coöperation is a reflection of the fact that the fields of the two agencies overlap, and that no one can tell where the responsibility of one ends and that of the other begins. Being of good will, they meet such situations with coöperative devices. But the existence of these devices may often but thinly veil essentially competitive situations and not a little conflict of purposes. Thus coöperation may coincide with the feeling on the part of either agency that it would be better if the other would surrender the entire responsibility to it. In this way, a feeling of dissatisfaction and restlessness may accompany behaviour that is externally fraternal. Indeed, established reputation for national leadership in coöperative movements may not prevent a man asserting that the federation in his own city was misborn, has always been misrepresentative, and will probably have to smash completely before a genuine start in local coöperation can be made. This view is not inherently inconsistent. At least, it helps to explain actual cases of conflict.

In a considerable number of the coöperative activities, the

---

[5] The administrative combination of the Wichita Federation and the Young Men's Christian Association involved other mutual activities such as a joint publication.

[6] P. 122.

Young Men's Christian Association and the Young Women's Christian Association both figure along with federations: and each of these three agencies may privately consider the other two superfluous.

Competition of Y.M.C.A. and Federations

Since their respective spheres are not well differentiated, and since it is often an open question which organization is primarily responsible for a given activity in a given community, it is inevitable that attitudes of the kind indicated should result at times in definite competition.

At the start of the investigation it was the intention to classify the common activities of the two agencies as either coöperative or competitive. It was soon found that both moods may be associated, and generally are, with the selfsame activity. One agency may feel hampered, at a disadvantage, and compelled to work fragmentarily because the other is in partial possession of activities that it would like to control. This is to be recognized as a state of incipient conflict, even though the situation is borne with Christian resignation or good humor. It can hardly avoid settling into fixed antagonism if one organization continues to feel that the other has infringed upon a field naturally belonging to it.

Active competition, in turn, is sometimes cruder in its expression, sometimes more refined. It is capable of taking the form of very elaborate consultation with another agency with a view to compelling it to choose one horn of a dilemma, both of which are damaging. It may, on the other hand, and in a few cases apparently did, reflect a violent and admitted clash of personalities and prerogatives.

The main areas of active friction, as sensed during the investigation, were four: (1) the status of the agencies as the representatives of Protestantism in its approach to the public; (2) finances; (3) decentralized community work in various districts of the city; (4) religious education.

Case evidence could be deduced on each of these topics; but it will be sufficient to generalize regarding the conflict situations which they express.

(1) Federations are likely to feel that the formal summoning of the Protestant forces to action in any general community interest, that the role of spokesman in moral issues, and that the providing of a general community hearing for representative Christian messages of great moment, are inherent ecclesiastical functions essential to the idea of a central official agency of the

united Protestant churches; and consequently that its prerogatives are infringed when such functions are undertaken by the Young Men's Christian Association except in phases technically concerned with men and boys. But Young Men's Christian Associations have often been performing some part of these functions before federations have appeared in their communities, have already mustered the Protestant forces and brought forward the commanding voices. Now, it is no easy thing to surrender institutional prestige when it is once secured. The Association may accordingly strive to control or share the control, say, of religious broadcasting; it may continue to bring Christian leaders of national reputation to the communities under its own auspices. The federations feel that these are the essential phases of the extra-parochial, central ministry of the Church; and natural functions of an ecclesiastical agency rather than of a voluntary one.

(2) Pressed by the difficulty of financing their organizations by appeal to a common constituency along with the Young Men's Christian Association which gets a very much larger response, a good many federation secretaries carry about a feeling that there is injustice in the situation. They doubt whether the budgets are at all in proportion to the value of the services of the two organizations. Whether warranted or not, this feeling colors the relationships of the two agencies. It should probably be set down as unavoidable in the relationships of an older and stronger but narrower institution with a younger and weaker but more inclusive one, especially when there are no objective means of determining their present relative values in the community, or the ultimately best distribution of function and support.

(3) The federation's primary function is to unite local churches for coöperative activity. So long as the Young Men's Christian Association deals with individuals—especially individuals drawn into its own institutions—it can scarcely conflict with this function. But in recent years, and in the larger cities, many Young Men's Christian Associations have decentralized their work. They have erected district buildings, or created district offices, from which they are undertaking community work in various parts of their cities. This has not only set them to operating within the territory of a large number of individual churches, but has made possible a new policy in which the Association adopts the church as such as its unit of service. A group approach, for example, is made to all its boys. The cluster of neighborhood churches is organized around the Young

Men's Christian Association as a center, and coöperative functions are undertaken in the spheres of education or recreation, such as training classes for church workers, interchurch athletic leagues, etc. To develop such activities, Church-Christian Association Councils composed of delegates from "affiliated" churches have sometimes been set up. In a few cases the community work of the Young Men's Christian Association has been enlarged to include women and girls. Such a plan for "serving every member of the family" makes the Young Men's Christian Association's neighborhood program exactly as inclusive as if it were jointly undertaken by the churches themselves.

In such attempts at organization of the local churches for coöperation activity, federations can hardly avoid seeing an invasion of a field that is most naturally theirs, whether or not they have strength to cultivate it at present. In the study accordingly, were found several instances of irritation and perplexity focusing upon this point.

(4) The recent disposition of the Young Men's Christian Association to define itself as a religious-education movement,[7] has raised important questions as to its relationship to the organized educational work of the churches, and especially to comprehensive schemes of community religious education as undertaken interdenominationally.[8] Association secretaries have frequently rendered valued service to the churches in this connection; but it may be questioned whether the majority of them are adequately in touch with the expanding program of religious education under church auspices, or understand its pedagogic basis and implications. This program distinctly includes the expressional and group activities of men and boys such as the Young Men's Christian Associations have specialized in. A consequent fresh need of articulation between the work of the churches and of the Association has resulted. Specific recognition of the Association as having a stake in the religious-education work of the federation was frequently found during the investigation. The special relationship of the boys' work to week-day religious education has, for example, brought about occasional agreements looking toward the over-multiplication of programs to the confusion of parishes and homes. But granted —as federations tacitly assume—that the Church is committed, by its basic conceptions and entire history, to teaching, organizing and maintaining pastoral and parochial responsibility for constituencies that represent complete cross sections of humanity,

---

[7] Bartlett, Hogan & Boyd, *The Y. M. C. A. Executive Secretary.*
[8] Pp. 368 ff.

it is inconceivable that she should give over to a specialized agency fundamental control of any segment of that work. Now the adjustment of religious-education agencies themselves to the larger vision and authority of the Church is still very incomplete, and presents many sore points. The Bible Schools and the youth's organizations are being reintegrated with it at the very moment when their distinctive problems and technique are most keenly recognized. The Young Men's Christian Association can scarcely hope to escape a still more drastic re-examination of its functions if it desires to serve the Church in this field.

Administrative Unification

The most definite and adequate test of systematic administrative relationships between a local federation of churches and the Y.M.C.A. movement was made in Wichita. Here, the executive secretary of the federation, after seven years of service in that capacity, became also general secretary of the Young Men's Christian Association.

The experiment was confined to this employment of a joint executive. One practical advantage was that the arrangement released sufficient funds to make possible the employment of a full-time religious-education director for the federation. The Young Women's Christian Association was also associated in the publication of a common house-organ, and infrequent joint staff conferences were held, the secretaries of all three bodies attending. Practically, however, the general secretaryship of the Young Men's Christian Association and the administrative secretaryship of the federation were two distinct functions, temporarily and accidentally united in one individual. No effort was made to fuse programs or merge staff procedures as between the two organizations. "Probably," wrote the secretary, "there was a sharper differentiation of function at the conclusion of the experiment than at its inception."

The Wichita experiment continued for two years, and terminated because the Young Men's Christian Association was under the necessity of raising a large capital fund, which no joint executive could hope successfully to accomplish while serving another organization. The local verdict upon the experiment stressed the following points:

> (1) The community work of the Young Men's Christian Association is essentially an undenominational function of the Church, and the Association should be increasingly coöperative with the churches.

(2) Economies in administration are made possible by joint leadership.

(3) Freedom from ecclesiastical control as enjoyed by the Young Men's Christian Association is a distinct advantage to the churches as well as to the Association and is not lightly to be abandoned. The joint secretaryship proved something of a liability at this point.

(4) The churches cannot fairly establish a more intimate relationship with the Young Men's Christian Association than with the Young Women's Christian Association.

(5) The Christian Associations, with their extensive capital equipment and relatively large budgets, are able to command gifts toward operating expenses, deficit funds and special purposes, many times as large as the gifts available from the same individuals for the work of interchurch organizations. Whether this is due to the relatively recent organization of local ecclesiastical coöperation, the sense of lay proprietorship in the undenominational enterprises, or to other factors, is not plain. What is unmistakably plain is that even individuals who proclaim the Church to be the primary agency, potentially capable of taking over the entire work of the Christian Associations, at this stage of the development of coöperative Protestantism are willing to give to the Christian Associations up to ten times the amount which their most generous consideration makes available for church federation purposes.

Probably the ratio between the gross budgets of federations and Christian Associations would be a misleading index as to their relative importance in the life of the community.

(6) Owing to the necessity of utilizing every foot of floor space at maximum income, the new administration of the Young Men's Christian Association found it impossible to provide the federation with adequate quarters. The federation was consequently compelled to move into an office building.

In general, this experiment in a city of more than 100,000 population, chiefly Protestant, seems to confirm the wide-spread feeling that the status of the Young Men's Christian Association as an institution is not commensurate with that of the federations. The former is independent of such control, while at the same time it is broadly representative of the Protestant churches. The latter is officially ecclesiastical and representative. At the point of their community programs, the two movements have very important relationships that need adjustment. The experience of Wichita has but given added point to this discovery. The secretary concludes:

> Given a sufficiently self-abnegating attitude on the part of the Association in cities not large enough to employ special federation leadership, organized church coöperation utilizing a Young Men's Christian Association secretary as executive furnishes a promising field for further experimentation.

General Conclusions as to Y.M.C.A. Relationships

So long as the statistically vast and impressive body of ecclesiastical Protestantism existed merely in its divisions and was without any organizational unity, no question of formal relationships could be raised between it and the infinitely smaller but coherent and aggressive lay agencies organized on the voluntary and non-ecclesiastical basis.

The attempt of the Young Men's Christian Association in certain communities to assume the leadership of divided Protestantism has made it acutely conscious of the weakness of division, and of the great difficulty of achieving practical unity. The Association accordingly has needed and has welcomed ecclesiastical federation as a means of strengthening the Protestant cause. It has given this cause heroic assistance, and has sometimes stood by the federation idea when the churches have wearied of it and dropped out.

But in so doing, the Young Men's Christian Association has never redefined its own function in its relation to the original and official ideal of the federation as the central organ of a united church. It has greatly desired to coöperate in establishing and assisting federations; but with no expectation other than to maintain its own complete independence, and with no thought of having its policies and activities wrought out through the mutual counsels of a superior Protestant agency. The occasional election of a federation secretary to membership on a Young Men's Christian Association board of directors constitutes no real exception to this rule. The Young Men's Christian Association has not begun to think of accepting the status of a part whose place is defined for it within the organized Protestant whole.

Unity as achieved by the federations is relatively so new, institutionally so weak, and so lacking both in established authority and functional scope, that they are in no position to compel the well-established non-ecclesiastical agencies to give any significant consideration to the problem of ultimate relationships. The working programs of the two types of agencies manage to get by fairly well with essentially superficial exchange of services and coöperation at minor points. Neither can afford to bring on an open conflict as to prerogatives, and neither desires to do so. The federations, however, frequently feel that there is an irrepressible issue, and think that someone else ought to raise it for them. The Young Men's Christian Associations generally do not concede that there is an issue.

From the standpoint of logical analysis, the situation is not difficult to formulate. As separate entities, the federations are little more than bits of fragile machinery with small resources, no property, and a history of many failures. Is this all that they are? Or are they the tentative forms of a central agency through which, for example, the 7,760 Protestant churches and 2,785,000 adult members of the twenty-one cities represented by the inquiry, intend to exercise a certain collective control of the vast resources and mighty processes of the total group? In the latter case, there would be no impropriety in their expecting in the long run to acquire the function of reviewing and adjudicating concerning the infinitely smaller and specialized work of the Church's non-ecclesiastical allies.

At present, however, the possibility of radical readjustment of relationships involving such functional and organic subordination has no standing as an issue. From the viewpoint of frank discussion, the subject is absolutely taboo in most of the community studies. Coöperation in its federative version has simply not yet come as far as this point.

With no inclination to hustle the progress of evolution, it seems reasonable to ask how long the demand for coördination to match the progress of social differentiation—a demand which rises in all progressive groups—can remain satisfied with instances of merely casual coöperation. The two types of Protestant agencies, the ecclesiastical and the non-ecclesiastical, are not at present functioning as a precise and fully efficient set of common machinery. They can hardly be expected to do so on a purely opportunistic basis. By what means shall they get upon any other basis?

THE FEDERATIONS AND Y.W.C.A.

In its attempt to relate the entire body of organized Protestantism to itself, the federation movement has locally extended to the Young Women's Christian Association the same opportunities for affiliation that it accorded the Young Men's Christian Association. The Young Women's Christian Association is frequently given secondary, if not primary, membership in the federation; and in a number of instances its paid officers have *ex officio* status as members of boards of directors or of executive committees. These essentially formal devices, however, leave the same unsolved problems of relationship that have already been met with in the case of the Young Men's Christian Association.

Since the Young Women's Christian Association is a smaller organization, problems of adjustment are practically less acute. While the sphere of this association is not determined with exactness, it has kept more nearly than the Young Men's Christian Association has, within its self-chosen limits, namely, those of Christian service for young women. Moreover, its character in this sphere is much more clear-cut and distinctive than is that of the Young Men's Christian Association in its sphere. One would be put to it to tell what kind of men make up the Young Men's Christian Association leadership and constituency. But one could hardly go astray with respect to the Young Women's Christian Association. Its present generation of leadership, both paid and voluntary, is consciously allied with the feminist movement. It represents distinctly different attitudes from those found in any Christian association under the control of men, especially one under the control of ministers; and it is scarcely less different from those found in church-women's organizations of the parochial and denominational type. The attitudes reflected are definitely those of independent women in business and industry. This is not to say that leaders of the Young Women's Christian Association are not church-women, but merely to say that they are a highly selective group of church-women. Programs carried on both by the Young Women's Christian Association and the denominational groups will, for example, reveal a definitely different tone in the two organizations. Thus, the Young Women's Christian Association's emphasis on world friendship diverges strikingly from the traditional missionary interest of the church group. Again, in the field of industry, the Young Women's Christian Association has been distinctly originative and prophetic, while church-women as such, have only gingerly undertaken to think in this field at all.

In spite, however, of the rather clear demarcation of fields and emphases, the work of the Young Women's Christian Association touches, and may overlap, that of the federations in certain aspects of community work and religious education. This possibility is potentially the more important because of the unusual strength and aggressiveness of women's church organizations and the growing program of women's departments in the federation. No similar situation exists with respect to the parallel men's departments and the Young Men's Christian Association.

Exchange of Services and Coöperative Activities

Considerable exchange of services of the types illustrated in the case of the Young Men's Christian Association occurs between the Young Women's Christian Association and the federations incidentally. Of coöperative activities, assistance by the federation in Young Women's Christian Association financial campaigns was the one most frequently found. Coöperation in juvenile-court work, in the promotion of international goodwill, in shop or factory meetings, and in mothers' and daughters' events rank next; while visitation evangelism, community training schools, conferences on religious education, Americanization activities, missionary education, and the collection of old clothes for the poor were also found, but were of rare occurrence. Of the approximate eighty standard activities of the average federation, not one is so frequently carried on in coöperation with the Young Women's Christian Association that such a relationship could be thought of as characteristic. For the most part, each agency goes its own way.

Potential Competition

While definitely competitive attitudes or situations were much less frequent than between the federations and the Young Men's Christian Association, the same areas of overlapping interest and of possible conflict of programs exist. Thus the new aggressiveness of women's departments of federations in social service has sometimes brought them to occupy some part of the field commonly covered by the Young Women's Christian Association's International Institutes. Again, the expanded program of religious education under interchurch leadership, particularly in its week-day version and as it undertakes to guide the voluntary activities and expressional phases of youth, brings the church into the field which the Young Women's Christian Association is endeavoring to touch in its Girl Reserve program.

At present, however, these problematical and overlapping areas of service are not extensive enough to raise the issue of relationship with the Young Women's Christian Association separately. Though it could not precede it, its adjustment, it is felt, would be involved in any large-scale re-alignment of the Protestant forces. Some of the problems met might, however, become separately acute if the development of women's departments in church federations continues at its present rate.

RELATIONSHIPS WITH OTHER PROTESTANT AGENCIES

The same general story which has been told for the Young Men's and Young Women's Christian Associations applies to the group of agencies of service and propaganda represented by the Bible societies, the Sabbath-observance associations, and the Anti-saloon League. The specialized function of these agencies prevents any considerable overlapping between them and the federation movement at large. In individual cases, something like regular affiliation occurs. A reform agency may virtually be operated by federation leaders and promoted as though part of the federation's own program; or a federation may correlate the work of a group of reform agencies. Minor exchanges of services are natural and technical relationships common. An occasional federation has temporarily functioned as the local agency of the American Bible Society; but the success of the experiment has not seemed particularly impressive. As is shown in another connection,[9] federations in the large are glad to have specialized reform agencies relieve them of the direct responsibility of urging legislation or compelling law enforcement, and especially of doing detective work in unpopular issues. The fact also that these agencies belong to their own national systems of support and control, makes their closer affiliation with any local movement a matter requiring readjustment of relationships from the top down. If this, at some future time, should become an urgent matter, it would naturally start with the Federal Council. No such sensitiveness over, or desire for, adjustment to federations attaches to this group of agencies. But the ultimate problem of an all-inclusive Protestant planning agency with possible central administration of some sort, logically involves this group also.

CONCLUSION

Considering the Church's non-denominational allies and extensions as a whole, the total impression of the evidence is that they constitute a parallel and related group, but one essentially non-assimilable to the present federation movement. The reasons for this have already been given. They are non-ecclesiastical in form, organized as voluntary associations of interested persons rather than as agencies formally representative of churches. They are characteristically under lay management and control, and often have strong secular affiliations and sympathies. Furthermore, they belong to national systems of their own which

---

[9] Pp. 382 and 383.

demand their loyalty and resist their integration locally with any general Protestant movement. Finally, some of the lay types which they represent are distinct from the characteristic lay types of the denominational churches.

As affected by these agencies, complexity of religious organization, for the most part, reflects a necessary differentiation of function: so that duplication of machinery, though actual, is at a minimum. Conflict between these agencies, while not totally lacking, has no such permanence nor inevitability as that involved in the distribution and rivalry of sectarian churches.

What the situation demands, therefore, is first, a division of function as clear-cut as possible, so as to prevent the minor overlapping of these agencies; and, second, a thorough-going attempt to work out a more inclusive common principle in place of the two principles of organization now operative within Protestantism.

For voluntary Christian effort freely gathering adherents to the support of types of service in which they are interested must obviously remain a possibility in any church order that is Protestant in instinct. Whether such movements might still be included within some ecclesiastically official plan and system of oversight—say some form of united church—would entirely depend upon what type of church was proposed. The voluntary principle could not find adequate lodging in any repressive, nor in any merely tolerant, type. In the light of history, who would dare to commit the future to a merely ecclesiastical church? On the other hand, the ideal of the One Holy Church is not incompatible with freedom and fluidity of organization within which the voluntary principle might have free course and be glorified. Some organ of social control co-extensive with the Protestant group is entirely in line with many, and perhaps the most massive, tendencies of social evolution. Its exact form may well be the result of experimentation and compromise.

A distinct contribution toward the solution of this basic problem would be made if, on the one hand, the Young Men's Christian Association as a Protestant organization, could decide how far it agrees with the conviction so stubbornly held by federation constituents (many of them Young Men's Christian Association constituents as well) that federation is not "just another organization" but rather a manifestation of "the essential oneness of the Christian churches" and the organ of their coöperative purpose. Is this conception of federation to be accorded emotional power, and are Protestants to strive to make it good by giving federations in fact the magnitude and the attributes that go with an adequate incarnation of the ideal?

If, then, on the other hand, the Church could decide whether it is willing to accord permanent place within the organized Christian movement to lay organizations constituted on the voluntary principle, and how much freedom it is willing to allow such movements to express and conduct themselves within the Church, a basis might be laid for the working out of radical adjustments.

Occasional evidence that the first suggestion is thought of was found during the investigation; for example, the grounds of the Wichita experiment, as locally rationalized and phrased in terms of religious piety, included the feeling that "the Young Men's Christian Association as a separate organization must be willing, like John the fore-runner of Christ, more and more to decrease that the Church may go forward." If such a feeling should have general vogue, its implications for organizational relationships might be considerable.

For a reformulation of the permanent place of voluntary organizations within the Church, one may look with obvious propriety to theories of church union now increasingly under discussion.

Chapter XII

FORCES UNIFYING AND ENLARGING THE FEDERATION MOVEMENT

The local federations, as their history has shown, constitute part of a unified national ecclesiastical system of church federation heading up in the Federal Council of the Churches of Christ in America, through which they enter into still wider coöperative relationships—Protestant, interconfessional, and secular. Especially through some of their departments, the local federations also constitute organizational units in other national religious movements and agencies (such as the International Council of Religious Education) that intersphere with the ecclesiastical system of church federation. The purpose of this chapter is to set forth the present major aspects of these unifying and enlarging relationships as they have been discovered in this investigation.

THE NATIONAL SYSTEM OF CHURCH FEDERATIONS

With few exceptions, the local federations are products of a promotional process working from the top down.[1] The national coöperative movements preceding the Federal Council had established subsidiaries in many cities; and the Council's constitution specified that one of its objects was "to assist in the organization of local branches * * * to promote its aims in their communities."

In the earliest phase of Federal Council effort, this objective was taken literally. District secretaries undertook to effect local city organizations on the basis of "rules as laid down in the standard by-laws approved by the Federal Council * * * subject to the Christian law of liberty." While it was reported that the "codes" had first been "argued out" by many state and city federations, the obligation of the local "branches" to be guided by the deliverances of the Federal Council, to use literature approved by it, and to make monthly reports was somewhat urgently stressed.

Three or four years' trial amply demonstrated that this basis

---

[1] P. 49.

was not workable. From 1912 on, without changing the Federal Council constitution, the doctrine became established that "there is no organic relation between the Federal Council and state and local federations, and it can assume no responsibility for the constituency of such federations or the form which they may take." District secretaries were discontinued, and local promotion was committed to a Commission on State and Local Federations. The keynote of the changed policy was struck by the executive secretary of this commission, Dr. Roy B. Guild, as follows:

> Local autonomy is a fundamental principle. Each Council of Churches is a law unto itself. It has no organic relation with other Councils. All fellowship between these Councils, whether local, state or national, is voluntary.[2]

In the recent past, the Federal Council has newly accepted responsibility for promoting a national system of local and state federations. This strengthening of policy was taken primarily under pressure from the local federations themselves. A new general secretaryship has been established in the Council, and a "counseling committee" directly representative of the local federations has been created. The purpose of this latest adjustment is to assure that promotional policy shall proceed equally from the top down and from the bottom up.

PRESENT RELATIONSHIPS WITH THE FEDERAL COUNCIL

The actual local situations growing out of current relationships with the Federal Council are revealed in several ways, which the following pages will discuss.

(1) CONSTITUTIONAL RECOGNITION OF RELATIONSHIPS

Several federations begin their constitutions with a recognition of their formal partnership in the national movement of Protestantism heading up in the Federal Council. The typical formula used is as follows:

> The constitution of the Federal Council * * * is hereby recognized * * * as the basis of this Council of Churches.

Such recognition appearing in earlier constitutions was occasionally dropped in subsequent revisions—thus indicating the growing stress on autonomy. On the contrary, certain other revisions as late as 1924 were retaining the old phraseology and

---

[2] Guild (ed.) *Community Programs For Coöperating Churches* (New York: Association Press), p. v.

declaring it part of their purpose "to promote the aims of the Federal Council in their communities."

(2) NATIONAL RELATIONSHIPS AS REPRESENTED TO LOCAL CONSTITUENCIES

In interpreting the situation to supporters, the autonomy of the local federation is the aspect generally stressed. The Federal Council is represented as an "advisory" body. Under attack for not conforming to some Federal Council pronouncement, local secretaries explain that, while the Council in the large represents Protestant consensus, their organizations are under no obligation to agree with it in detail. More than one secretary has privately explained to the investigators that it is inexpedient to stress the Federal Council's industrial program in his community, or that it is very convenient to be able to prove that the local federation has no organic relation with the Federal Council and no responsibility for the latter's industrial positions.

(3) ASSERTIONS OF AUTONOMY

In the persons of their representatives on the "extension" committee of the Federal Council, the local federations have sometimes voiced a desire to be informed in advance of national administrative plans which it is proposed to promote locally. Thus, the 1929 meeting of this committee requested Federal Council secretaries "to prepare a concise statement of the special features of their work which they would be presenting to local Councils of Churches during the coming year" in order to give the Association of Executive Secretaries of Church Federations a chance to discuss them in its annual meeting. Local federations habitually exercise discretion as to the timeliness and applicability of headquarter's proposals, the degree of coöperation which these proposals deserve, and the seriousness with which they are to be actively promoted.

(4) ACTUAL RELATIONSHIPS VARYING IN DIFFERENT DEPARTMENTS

Local federations are characterized by loose internal structure.[3] Their commissions and departments consequently stand in unequal degrees of dependence on national agencies. Religious education is not locally promoted by the Federal Council to any appreciable extent: nor is comity. Evangelism is stimulated rather than exactly programized. On the other hand, local programs of industrial justice, international goodwill, and

---

[3] See Chapters V and IX.

especially racial relationships are, in the main, the children of
Federal Council promotion, without which many federations
would have no such departments and would give these interests
very inferior stress.

(5) REPRESENTATION IN THE FEDERAL COUNCIL

As vital factors in the total coöperative system, local federations have found important place in the working machinery of
the national organization. In addition to representation on the
special counselling committee on extension, the local and state
federations now have the right to nominate four representatives
on the Administrative Committee of the Federal Council; and
at least five of the commissions of the Federal Council have as
members from two to three secretaries of state and local federations. It has recently been urged that the "large city Councils
of Churches" should also have membership in the Federal Council itself.[4]

RELATIONS WITH STATE COUNCILS OF CHURCHES

The development of state units of organized Protestant
coöperation has lagged. Probably in view of the relatively
small number of such bodies, almost no trace of their recognition is found in the constitutions of local federations. The
Buffalo Council presents an exception: one of the clauses in its
constitution reads: "This Council may be associated with the
State Federation of Churches if one exists."

ACTIVITY IN INITIATING STATE COUNCILS

A few city federations have, however, taken steps to realize
their conviction that state councils ought to exist. Thus, the
secretary of the Rochester Federation recently served as the
organizing secretary for the incipient New York State Council;
and the secretary of the Wichita Federation was active in a
preliminary effort for a Kansas State Council.

DETERMINATION OF RELATIONS OF STATE AND CITY FEDERATIONS

Whenever State Councils have been long in existence, the
necessity for determining the mutual relations between them and
local city federations has been evident. Thus the compact determining the respective spheres of the Massachusetts and the
Boston federations covers four points; territory, finances, legislative and industrial effort, and evangelism and religious educa-

---

[4] P. 210.

tion. An agreement as to comity was also sought but not decided upon. With respect to its capital city, Columbus, the Ohio State Council has solved the problem by administering the local agency directly through its own office.

Pending agreements, unpleasant uncertainties and friction have sometimes arisen. Competitive financial appeals have not always been prevented; and experience increasingly proves the necessity of compacts covering this issue. Most frequently it is felt that a state coöperative agency should not solicit support within a territory covered by a city federation without the latter's consent. On the other hand, in a good many states, both population and wealth are so concentrated that to limit a state agency to such support as it can get outside the large cities is to make its existence forever impossible.

ASSOCIATION OF CHURCH-FEDERATION SECRETARIES

The most self-conscious and aggressive agency in defining the relations of local federations to national and state councils has been the Association of Executive Secretaries of Church Federations.[5]

While the state and local federations are autonomous with reference to each other as well as to the Federal Council, their executives have voluntarily maintained this national association, which for more than a decade has held annual meetings in June. Other sessions of the Association are held in connection with the annual meetings of the executive committee of the Federal Council, and on other convenient occasions. In spite of its discontinuous volunteer leadership, this organization has gradually built up a body of sentiment and precedent that makes it an important factor in the total federated movement. If, as a professional group, it has not attained the status achieved by the national organization of chamber of commerce secretaries, or of community chest executives, it is largely because the number of church federations is relatively small. On the other hand, this very smallness has permitted the association's group-thinking to be unusually effective. It has developed an institutional membership basis, with fees graduated according to the budgets of the federations represented; and has begun to make provision for the participation of paid employees other than executives.

The deliberations of the Association of Executive Secretaries have always received the serious attention of the Federal Council; and a most vital formal link has thus been established

---

[5] P. 205.

between the two types of organization. Obviously the relationship between the secretaries' association and the particular Federal Council secretaries charged with the extension of local and state federations has had to be most intimate; and increasing stress is laid upon frequent attendance at its meetings by the general Federal Council staff.

Besides the mutual counsel directly secured in the annual meeting of executive secretaries, and the common points of view mediated by Federal Council representatives, local federations get a good deal from one another incidentally. Considerable communication keeps going on between them; and exchange of publications enables them to borrow promising ideas and even effective phraseology. A secretary who wants to experiment with radio broadcasting, or who is invited to subject his organization to a survey, is likely to write around and find out the experience of his fellows on these points. The *Church Council News Letter*, published since 1928 by the Federal Council, has supplied a helpful vehicle of intercommunication.

CONCURRENT ACTION OF FEDERATIVE AGENCIES

The reality and direction of the national system of Protestant coöperation now evolving, have largely been the result of processes carried on concurrently by the federative forces whose relationships have now been separately described. At this point, what they have done informally has been more profoundly significant than what was officially initiated by formal action of the denominations coöperating through the Federal Council.

The chief device whereby the unifying processes have been focussed is the general convention of the coöperating forces. Two such conventions have been held, one in Pittsburgh in 1917, and one in Cleveland in 1920. The primary object of both was to "boost" the coöperative movement; but beyond this, each marked a notable stage in the progress of collective thinking and comparison of experiences.

The Pittsburgh congress recorded the existence at that date of thirty-one city federations with salaried executives. It announced as a final objective:

> To assemble, digest, and put into accessible form for use everywhere, a record of the experiences of those who have engaged in coöperative work in their several communities.

This purpose issued in *The Manual of Inter-church Work*, a compilation and revision of the work of eight commissions as discussed by the congress.

The Cleveland "Church and Community Convention" was held under the joint auspices of the Federal Council's Commission on Councils of Churches and the Association of Executive Secretaries of Church Federation. Its report, entitled *Community Programs for Coöperating Churches*,[6] covered the principles and methods of local federation organization and brought down to data a summary of experience in the major departments of their work.

The product of this congress, both emotional and literary, has tended strongly to unify the coöperative movement in practice without imposing upon it an official uniformity.

The most mature and recent effort to rethink the problem of the functional relationships of agencies within a complete national system of Protestant coöperation came to a head in action of the 1928 meeting of the Association of Executive Secretaries of Church Federations, as follows:

Preamble: We believe the time is ripe and the need is urgent for a closer coördination and integration of the activities of the Federal Council, the State Councils of Churches, and the local Councils of Churches.

Based on the experience of a score of years, the respective places of these three types of councils of churches, would seem to be as follows:

1. The Federal Council being set to "express the Catholic unity of the Church" and being composed of the official representatives of its constituent denominations in the United States, is fitted to make pronouncements on many questions that affect those constituencies as a whole, and to institute actions in the name of its entire constituency on matters where the mind of the churches is sufficiently well known.

2. State or regional councils being made up of the representatives of the denominational groups and local councils of churches of a given area, are equipped to deal both in pronouncements and in activities in matters that affect those areas, especially in counties unable to employ executive secretaries.

3. Local (municipal, county) councils, consisting either of organized denominational units, or of local churches, find their field first in community tasks which await coöperative effort of the churches, second in regional tasks which are undertaken by the state councils or other regional agencies, and third in the larger—national or international—tasks which are headed up in the Federal Council.

4. All of these types of Councils should be in communication with each other, and while the autonomy of each in its actions and policies is preserved, the spirit of unity and coöperation requires that general agreement should prevail so far as is consistent with the best interests of the Kingdom of God. Especially should state and local Councils give careful consideration to the positions taken by the Federal Council, and local Councils, the same consideration

---

[6] Association Press, New York, 1920, 253 pp.

to the positions taken by the State Councils so that where possible the same policies may prevail throughout the Federal and State Council constituencies.

5. We commend to State Councils of Churches the plan of having on the governing body not only representatives of the denominational groups within the state, but also representatives of local Councils. We further commend to the Federal Council a consideration of the same principle, that is, of having a governing body composed of both denominational representatives and representative of the State Councils and possibly of the large city Councils of Churches. * * * we are convinced that policies which state and local Council representatives, or state and Federal Council representatives agree upon together are more likely to be carried out effectively than under the present plan.

Problems of the National System from the Local Viewpoint

As the unifying forces of church federation have been engaged in working out a national system, certain outstanding problems have emerged from the viewpoint of the local federations. The first has to do with their representation and practical share in the administration of the central national agency; the second relates to the preservation of local rights when the national agency seeks to operate in the several communities.

REPRESENTATION AND SHARE OF CONTROL IN FEDERAL COUNCIL

The formal representation of autonomous local federations in the Federal Council is difficult because that body is constitutionally an alliance of denominations. As such, it cannot logically admit units of another character. What the federations demand involves a mixed organic basis for the Federal Council, combining a territorial with a denominational system of representation.

The local federations, as has been shown, make no difficulty of illogical systems. Repeatedly they allow organizations that are not churches to hold direct membership in a church federation that supposedly unites the Protestant denominations through ecclesiastical units. But local federations also use secondary affiliating devices,[7] and this is the type of solution at present used by the Federal Council. The association of local federations is permitted to nominate four members to the Administrative Council of the Federal Council. They thus get a back-door admission to power in the ultimate administrative body; while, at the same time, the theoretical basis of representation is not disturbed.

A second phase of the problem of an administrative share in

---

[7] P. 80.

the Federal Council has already been indicated by the action of the association of local federations desiring that administrative plans be communicated to it for discussion before they are carried out in local communities.[8]

NATIONAL PROMOTION IN LOCAL COMMUNITIES

A second group of major problems has to do with the relationships of national and local agencies when the former attempt to execute their projects in local territory.

The general feeling of the local federations is that, in these circumstances, they should always be given a chance to act as the local agents and representatives of the national organization. This feeling is sometimes disregarded in two ways; first, Federal Council secretaries communicate directly with departments of federations rather than with the executive representative, and thus initiate movements that fail to appreciate problems of balance and proportion in the local program. Each department of the Federal Council naturally boosts for itself, and uses the corresponding local agency merely as its means, without much consciousness of its relationship with other phases of the work.

Again, Federal Council secretaries sometimes promote their objects through agencies other than the federations. It is not difficult to point to cases in which a very popular project was given over locally to a rival none too friendly with the federation. Thus, in their eagerness to carry forward their own interests, the representatives of the national agency have sometimes tended to depreciate the position of their permanent local auxiliaries.

It remains an academic question whether a local federation should have veto power to prevent any unacceptable action by the national agency in its community. Technically speaking, it is plain that the denominations nationally coöperating in the Federal Council have given that body power to promote measures officially agreed upon throughout all communities. At the same time, the logic of facts is creating a national system under which the reciprocal rights and duties of the national and of the local agencies require more exact definition.

OTHER MAJOR PROTESTANT ALLIANCES

RELIGIOUS EDUCATION

As has already been indicated, certain departments of local federations stand in dual relationships to national interdenomi-

---

[8] P. 205.

national agencies. Thus, in a number of cases, departments of religious education are officially auxiliary to the International Council of Religious Education. This connection is frequently safeguarded in the compacts by which formally independent local councils of religious education unite themselves to the local federations.

From the standpoint of the interests of the International Council of Religious Education, three things would seem to be required: first, a type of federative organization that allows the department to develop as a permanently acceptable auxiliary of the Council; second, a measure of financial support for the Council from the local federation; and, third, a generally sympathetic regard for the religious-education program as nationally developed. These demands, it is felt, are adequately met in most of the cases in which the local religious-education agencies have been organizationally affiliated with the federation movement.

From the standpoint of continuing relationships between the two interests, the chief local problem is one of proportion. A department of religious education may normally constitute from a fourth to a third of the total work of a federation.[9] But suppose it proves to be the more popular and the more easily financed department, with such possibilities of growth that it might quickly come to absorb more than half of the federation's interest. Obviously, at this point, the organization becomes something other than a typical federation. On the other hand, if the department of religious education is checked in its growth by its federation affiliation, it naturally begins to feel restive and to reopen the problem of independence. As already indicated,[10] the normal solution is for the federation to strengthen itself proportionately in other departments—something not always easy to do rapidly.

WOMEN'S NATIONAL INTERCHURCH ORGANIZATIONS

Very recently the numerous women's interdenominational agencies in local communities have effected a national integration under the National Commission of Protestant Church Women, representing local "women's organized interdenominational groups" as well as the established national federations of women for home and foreign missions. This organization is seeking affiliation with the Federal Council, an arrangement which, when consummated, should help local adjustments.

[9] P. 456.
[10] P. 169.

In this sphere, the chief local problem of dual allegiance is raised by the separatist psychology of the dominant leaders among women in some of the communities. This factor may be expected to lead to different adjustments from city to city.

Other national agencies, like the Home Missions Councils which are already affiliated with the Federal Council, are in occasional direct contact with local city federations. Their activities have in the main, however, related to the rural field.

CONCLUSION

A system of nation-wide Protestant federation is thus in the making. There is interaction in the experiments in local adjustment between interdenominational agencies and the larger movement of integration on the part of national inter-church agencies. In the main, the local federations have gone faster and farther than the national agencies in effecting adjustments; and it is not too much to say that the pressure from the bottom up is one of the chief impulses actuating the integrating movement at the top. On the other hand, the system is strikingly incomplete. Viewed from one standpoint, it reveals much resistance, much stubbornness of separate institutional purpose, much insistence that certain interests are so dear that they must not be brought into organizational constrictions. From the standpoint, however, of progress toward integration, the total result appears to show the unifying forces definitely controlling the larger aspects of the situation. Its acquisition of a central organ of group-purpose and expression—incomplete though the process is—makes it inevitable that the Protestant group should redefine its relationships and attitudes toward other religious bodies, on the one hand, and on the other toward the voluntary welfare agencies and the State. The remainder of the chapter is concerned with this latter process.

INTERCONFESSIONAL COÖPERATION

In the cases of a few federations, constitutional provisions do not limit membership to Protestant bodies.[11] Nevertheless the well-established fact is that there is a much greater permanent sense of social and religious distance on the part of Protestants toward Roman Catholics and Jews than there is between any of the Protestant groups. Now, since the remoter types of Protestants almost never get effectively included in federations, it will

---

[11] P. 90.

not be strange if the other religious communions are never effectively included.

The nearest approach to the successful federation of more than one communion has been that of Protestants and Jews in the Greater Boston organization. Inasmuch as this federation is a friendly association of local churches not constitutionally limited to the Protestant faith, and since it includes both the conservative and liberal wings of Protestantism, there is nothing to exclude individual Jewish churches from membership on equal terms. A number of them have accordingly appointed delegates and make contributions to the agency: but embarrassment over the Christocentric emphasis in union services dominated by the Protestant majority later led to the virtual withdrawal of the Jewish element.

Significance of Coöperation Without Affiliation

Assuming it to be demonstrated that the organizational inclusion of different communions within the same federation is for the present impossible—and must remain so until there is a real shift in the underlying sense of religious distance between them —the federation movement still has possible significance as a means by which the Protestant group may coöperate with the other communions. Efforts to this end have frequently been made. For example, nine of seventeen federations studied, maintained committees to foster friendly relations between Jews and Christians. The results of such efforts, however, have rarely come beyond the occasional stage.

Such systematic and continuous coöperation between communions as exists is virtually limited to a few cases in the fields of religious education and of moral reform. In the former field, the coöperation of Protestants, with Catholics and Jews through the Greater New York Federation, in behalf of week-day religious education, is the best example. In the sphere of moral reform, committees of federations have sometimes worked along for many years with corresponding Roman Catholic committees; while in still other cases, official representatives of all three communions have been associated in non-sectarian movements primarily backed by the Church.

In the main, however, interconfessional coöperation, both in these fields and in all others, has found relatively scant expression. It has been confined, either to mere courteous gestures or else to minor separate projects that were soon over. The following illustrations suggest the nature of occasional coöperation of these two sorts.

OCCASIONAL INTERCONFESSIONAL COÖPERATION

Interconfessional Thanksgiving services have been observed in a number of places. In others, union religious services partaking of the nature of a discussion forum have been undertaken. In the realm of social service, Catholic, Protestant and Jewish agencies have sometimes been brought into coöperation on committees of councils of social agencies. The Detroit Inter-church Athletic League, under federation auspices, arranges competitive games with teams from Catholic churches. Such illustrations might be greatly extended: yet the typical Protestant federation in a typical year is not likely to be carrying on so much as one specific coöperative activity with any other communion.

RELATIONS WITH THE GREEK ORTHODOX CHURCH

While the measurement of constituents' attitudes places the Greek Orthodox Church farther from average Protestant sympathies than are even the Roman Catholic or Jewish churches, a greater willingness to coöperate with it practically than with the others has been shown. This is explained in part by the relative weakness of this communion in many communities. Under such conditions its churches have sometimes welcomed practical Protestant assistance, and have occasionally accepted membership in church federations. The federations, in turn, have looked upon such relationships rather as expressions of good will toward a group of alien antecedents than as a form of ecclesiastical recognition.

CONSTITUENTS' ATTITUDES

The study did not find enough interconfessional coöperation going on to yield statistical data concerning the attitude of federation constituents on this point. But a good many chance revelations of attitude were met with in connection with other data.

Vigorous and more frequent objections were found to even the slight coöperative relations just described. "Evangelical Christianity," asserts one supporter, "has no common grounds with Jews and Catholics." Another writes: "The federation should eliminate every anti-Christian element, such as Jews, Unitarians, and Universalists. Its broadness is its greatest weakness." These latter attitudes are in line with evidence as to the prevailing feeling of social distance between religious bodies. Specific Protestant complaints as to social-service activities of Catholics are voiced through a number of federations, particularly as relating to juvenile dependents and delinquents. The most frequent assertion is that Protestant children are turned over to Catholic charities and sent to Catholic institutions.

Nevertheless, almost as many volunteer opinions supported the inclusion of Jews and Catholics as urged the exclusion of non-evangelical Protestants. The grounds of these opinions varied from indefinite religious toleration to the very definite convictions of some high-church Episcopalians that no ultimate reunion of the churches can be consummated without the inclusion of the Roman communion. But most of the judgments favorable to interconfessional relations were specific. They included somewhat frequent and strong utterances in favor of including Jews and Catholics in a broader system of religious education, and especially in favor of coöperation with them in securing ethical teaching in the public schools.

Two federations were sometimes suggested; one interconfessional, for coöperation in civic and social service: the other strictly evangelical, for spiritual concerns.

DIRECTIONS AND LIMITATIONS OF PRACTICAL INTERCONFESSIONAL EFFORT

Both courteous gestures, and limited project coöperation, have doubtless served to make the interconfessional atmosphere somewhat more friendly; but the total body of federation efforts in this field is so small that its permanent results are hardly appreciable. Too often they are swallowed up in the maelstrom of large general issues with their accompanying passions, such as were exhibited in the recent presidential election.

With respect to friendly relations between Protestants and Jews, the coöperative experiments of the local federation have fallen within a centrally promoted plan of effort under the Federal Council. This circumstance has tended to make them somewhat continuous, and to conserve their results. In expanding the movement so as to include Catholics, it proved necessary to suppress the fact of original Protestant initiative, and ostensibly to start anew with a situation in which individuals from all these confessions figure as co-originators of the goodwill movement. Out of this movement has developed an unofficial independent organization bearing the name, The National Conference of Jews and Christians. Thus, as in so many other cases where significant organized coöperation on the part of main bodies is impossible, the more freely-moving scouting forces which precede the several armies are acting together voluntarily to test out the conditions on which the larger forces may possibly later unite.

Meetings conducted by the National Conference of Jews and Christians have included representatives from cities in which interconfessional experiments had been tried out under federation auspices. Their deliberations consequently may be taken as fairly reflecting a consensus of local federation experience. Summarized, they lead to the following conclusions showing the direction of practical interconfessional effort and its present limitations.

(1) With respect to common worship, as sometimes undertaken in connection with the interconfessional religious celebration of national holidays, the preponderant feeling of these conferences was that the suppression of all features distinctive of any of the three communions left so small a residuum as to be scarcely worth expressing in common. The resulting common worship was not satisfactory emotionally to most of the participants, and had little of the inner glow and uplift believed to be essential to true worship. Even so, interconfessional services were judged sometimes desirable on civic occasions. (2) In the sphere of comity, sensitiveness over proselyting was expressed, but no constructive formulae of coöperation were presented. (3) The largest measure of hopefulness as to interconfessional coöperation was evidenced in the sphere of social service and moral reform. Here it was believed that the communions could go together for a considerable distance, exercising a united influence as a religious group in matters not involving ecclesiastical issues. It was sharply manifest, however, that theological positions may seriously affect ideals of social policy; as in the Roman Catholic attitude toward birth-control. Again, sharp criticism was directed against forms of ostensible social service that were suspected of being disguised attempts to undermine the loyalty of beneficiaries of other faiths. (4) Finally, in the realm of religious education, it was felt that the three communions might exert large influence in the direction of greater stress on religion in all educational processes. On the other hand, vigorous protests were raised against what were believed to be efforts to saddle a system of church education on the nation, contrary to its historical genius.

Analyzing the conditions under which interconfessional coöperation, even of the existing occasional sort, is believed possible, the conclusions seem warranted: (1) that such coöperation must be essentially limited to efforts to secure common objects which if reached, would be separately enjoyed. Thus, in the realm of religious education the ultimate result sought is three large systems of week-day instruction under the separate communions all equally tolerated by the state, and not in any sense combined into a single system of religious education. (2) Agreement as to morals, as a basic condition of coöperation, is possible only within conventional realms. The communions may on occasion get together in defence of accepted positions. They can hardly function coöperatively in support of advanced ones.

It is nevertheless a real advance to have explored even the limited possibilities of interconfessional coöperation, both concrete and theoretical. The effort of the federated Protestant forces in this direction constitutes a genuine enlargement of the coöperative expression of religion in America.

Secular Alliances

The magnitude of the federation movement is not fairly set forth without final mention of enlarging areas in which it comes into contact, and makes working alliances in behalf of the Protestant churches, with secular agencies.

With respect to the great group of voluntary agencies of social welfare, in which so much of the constructive idealism and effort of our generation are focusing, the federative movement in Protestantism constitutes an important reinforcement. The linking-up of a national system of Protestant coöperation with the integrating movements of social welfare expressed in community chests and councils of social agencies, adds new power and resource to civilization in meeting its social responsibilities. The distinctly significant character of these alliances is demonstrated in the discussion of social service.[12]

It is equally clear that the evolution of a national system of church federations initiates a new era in the relationships of organized Protestantism with the American state. As an agency voicing collective Protestant sentiment, it increasingly focuses the power of a largely unified body of opinion upon political action, both legislative and administrative. As an auxiliary of the state in social-welfare activities (notably in the courts and public institutions), and as an adjunct to the system of public education, the coöperative movement is thus forging between the churches and the government new structural ties which have high significance for civilization.

It is thus not too much to say that this movement which on the ecclesiastical side finds its final significance in being a poten-

---

[12] P. 394.

tial movement toward church unity, finds still vaster significance among the ultimate integrating forces of American civilization.

ALLIANCES WITH VOLUNTARY SOCIAL AGENCIES

As related to the field of modern social-welfare activities, coöperative social service by church federations is a late adventure in a densely occupied area. In the larger American cities, it confronts hundreds of already established social agencies—in the largest cities, thousands of them. Many of these agencies are privately supported; others are publicly supported and carry the weight and authority of government. All together, they present a range and variety within which no single body of work can make a conspicuous showing.

Among the private agencies, those supported by the various Protestant denominations and their non-denominational allies and extensions like the Young Men's and Young Women's Christian Associations, are themselves outstanding.[13] But they are, so far, very slightly unified by the coöperative movement.

Within this overgrown realm of social organization, highly significant federating movements have gone on parallel with the relatively meagre ones within the Church. These are represented by various Councils of Social Agencies which seek to promote mutual planning, common standards, and some measure of voluntarily accepted criticism and control. On the financial side, the federation idea is aggressively represented by the Community Chest movement. This movement attempts the correlation of financial appeals to the public and exercises a large control of programs and activities through the approval or disapproval of the budgets of the several agencies.

Into this realm of active evolution, the relatively feeble church federation movement has had somehow to insert itself. It has had a certain advantage in more or less genuinely representing the total body of Protestants. Its problems have been to find whether it had any place at all; to place itself, according to its historical affinities, along with the denominational philanthropies and Protestant reform agencies; finally, to discover larger fields of profitable service. In the large, the most profitable ones have been discovered in the various forms of coöperation with existing non-sectarian social agencies; especially agencies of two sorts; first, those that themselves represent federations of social agencies; and, second, individual social agencies that can use voluntary social workers recruited by the Church.

---

[13] P. 19.

Increasing Recognition by Social Agencies

A most practical test of the success of social service under federation auspices is, accordingly, the extent to which it has won the recognition and approval of the standard-making social agencies.

Federations maintaining social work generally are held eligible to membership in local councils of social agencies. In Minneapolis, for example, the federation was invited into charter membership in the group chosen to operate a new building to house the entire social work of the whole city.

A few federations only—of which Detroit, Indianapolis and St. Louis are examples—receive financial support from local community chests, for some part of their social work. (There is no question but that the work of many more is quite as worthy as a good deal of other work that gets such support.) In these cases, the Chests have sometimes forced important revisions of federations plans and methods. Other federations have not desired the aid of Community Chests, feeling that the resulting complications would cost more than the aid would be worth.

Because they solicit the public for financial aid, federations sometimes find themselves among the social agencies under the scrutiny of endorsement committees of Chambers of Commerce or similar organizations. No case was found in which endorsement was withheld.

The rôle of religion itself as a vital factor in the rehabilitation of social failures and misfits is also increasingly recognized in recent years. This tendency has compelled the social agencies to face more thoughtfully than before the position of the agencies of organized religion in the social field. As regards church federations, this has resulted, in virtually every city studied, in a two-sided development of feeling; first, of a desire by the social agencies for reinforcement by the Church; second, of a distinctly critical attitude on their part. Their criticism has tended to focus upon two points; (1) the alleged failure of the religious agencies to comprehend how numerous and difficult are the factors involved in social case-work, and how great the need of the expert coöperation of many agencies through technically exact processes operated by especially trained persons—in brief their failure to recognize social work as a profession, like medicine or education, in the requirements that it imposes upon its practitioners. (2) The technical organization of the federation's own social work and the training of its workers have generally been held to be deficient when judged by current social-work standards.

Both the recognition of the religious point of view and the criticism of the federation's standard may be regarded as gains compared with the previous ignoring of religious movements by social agencies. They indicate the increasing vitality of the alliance between the religious and the secular forces.

PROBLEMS GROWING OUT OF SECULAR ALLIANCES

Acute problems are implicit in, and can not but come out of, this enlargement of secular alliances. The most comprehensive of them concerns the division of responsibility.

HOW OUGHT RESPONSIBILITY TO BE DIVIDED

The burden of poverty, weakness, delinquency, and kindred evils rests ultimately, of course, upon society as a whole; but is more immediately borne by certain major institutions. Historically speaking, the Church was the first great almsgiver and builder of charitable institutions for western civilization. But secular wealth early assumed part of the responsibility; so that when modern organized charity came to the fore, it was in the main non-ecclesiastical. Meanwhile, from the period of the emergence of the modern nations, poor-relief had become fixed as one of the inescapable major functions of the State; and in recent times the public agencies of charity and correction have vastly advanced, not merely in range and variety, but in the acquisition of a humane and scientific spirit. Present-day civilization, then, fields these three groups of institutions—the Church, the private social agencies, and the State—engaged in the same general humanitarian task: but it has made no final decision as to the division of responsibility among them. It is in the face of this uncertainty that the federation movement comes, attempting to unite the Protestant forces for the performance of their share of the task. But what is their share, or anybody's share? A first approach to an answer is likely to be found in a breaking up of this too general problem into separate subordinate questions.

ECCLESIASTICAL VS. PRIVATE NON-SECTARIAN SOCIAL AGENCIES

First, how should responsibility for social welfare be divided between the agencies of the Church and the private non-sectarian social agencies?

In attempting social service in behalf of coöperating Protestantism, the federations have actually had much to do with the voluntary social agencies. These agencies represent secular idealism. They constitute an extensive and powerful group that determines social policies in very important phases of civilization. Indeed, it is scarcely too much to say that in communities where social need is most acute, it is the social agencies and the police that preserve the social order itself.

The social agencies and the Church's philanthropic activities are in general pointed to the same ends, and in much the same way. But the agencies are not attached to any ecclesiastical roots.

With respect to the Roman Catholic and Jewish faiths, the problem of relationships with non-sectarian agencies is pretty definitely settled. Both of these faiths regard extensive philanthropic work under ecclesiastical control as an inherent and permanent function of the Church. Wherever they are normally strong, both tend to develop essentially rounded systems of ecclesiastical welfare work, paralleling the work of the social agencies.

This leaves the group of voluntary non-sectarian agencies Protestant in three senses. First, they have not been deserted deliberately and systematically by Protestant sentiment; second, they deal primarily (but by no means exclusively) with Protestant clients; and, third, they are in the main supported by Protestant money. On the other hand, they are not technically Protestant; nor are they interested in ecclesiastical Protestant ends as such; nor are they willing to compromise in any measure their non-sectarian independence or their purpose and competency to minister to the needs of the entire community.

Firmly maintaining this position, the non-sectarian agencies, nevertheless, have sometimes quite definitely voiced the desire to be accepted as substantially the representatives of Protestantism, both in their specific functions through their coördinating movements as expressed in Councils of Social Welfare, and as the training agencies for the volunteer social workers recruited by the Church. Matching this attitude, a few federations accept non-sectarian agencies directly into membership along with churches as appropriate units of the Protestant group.[14]

This, however, is a rather exceptional solution. The issue remains whether the voluntary agencies can become generally acceptable organizations of Protestantism while maintaining their essentially non-sectarian character; and whether the philanthropic responsibility of the Protestant public can in considerable measure at least be exercised through them. No actual suggestion has been observed to displace the present denomina-

[14] P. 81.

tional philanthropies wholesale. The practical issue concerns rather the attitudes of Protestants toward the non-sectarian agencies and Protestant policy for the future as it faces the possible creation of new agencies. Should Protestantism regard both the denominational and the non-sectarian philanthropies alike as the instruments through which its impulse to help the needy is to operate? Should it incline in the future to extend or to restrain the development of ecclesiastical organizations in the social-work field? Would it, or would it not, be better for the Church to leave the primary burden of social welfare to non-church agencies, assuming a secondary and ancillary role for herself? A genuine alternative is apparently presented to Protestant churchmanship. Shall it trust increasingly to the idealism functioning outside the Church, expressing the common sentiment of men of good will, both inside and outside of it; or shall it permanently divide these forces into the ecclesiastical and non-ecclesiastical camps, each maintaining a separate and, in part, a duplicatory system?

At present decision between these alternatives tends to show a regional variation within the nation. In New England, for example, there is a strong tendency to leave to non-sectarian agencies many types of social service undertaken by the Church elsewhere. On the other hand, in parts of the country where Protestant denominations of foreign origins are particularly strong, and where civil government in the field of social welfare is unprogressive, the Church tends to undertake more extensive and varied forms of social service under its own banner.[15] But obviously, advice as to federation policy cannot be given until a decision as to the Protestant attitude toward non-sectarian social agencies has been reached in a given community.

PRIVATE WELFARE AGENCIES VS. THE STATE

A second and parallel issue concerns the division of responsibility for social welfare between the entire group of voluntary agencies, both ecclesiastical and non-ecclesiastical, on the one hand, and the agencies of government.

Though relatively meagre, the social-service work of federations is deeply involved in the problem of relationships with the State; because, as has been shown, federations not infrequently function in connection with public institutions.[16] Their workers

---

[15] This regional distinction is well illustrated in the author's surveys of Springfield, Mass., and St. Louis. See *The St. Louis Church Survey*, chapter ix, and the *Springfield Church Survey*, chapter xi.

[16] P. 402.

then come under the partial control of governmental officials. Some of the workers are even clothed with public authority; and, in rare cases, the State bears part of the cost of their services.

Beyond this lies the still more urgent problem of the increasingly overlapping spheres of Church and State in social work. Historically speaking, it is the State in the main that is the aggressor, crowding into fields which the Church once controlled. As representing the Protestant church as a body, it is the federations that most directly feel the onus of this situation.

The situation is one to which different elements within Protestantism react in different ways. In most areas of service, the status quo is accepted by most Protestants as essentially right. The State, for example, assumes major responsibility for dealing administratively with poverty and crime. But in more novel fields of service, certain types of Protestants somewhat definitely suspect the widening functions of the State as a possible invasion of the ecclesiastical province. While the instincts of the average Protestant are slow to feel any current issue with the State, it is a question whether he is not potentially just as capable as a member of any other religious group of asserting the superior rights of the Church in opposition to the State in such a matter, for example, as the voluntary group organization of youth which the Catholic Church has had to face in Italy under the Fascisti regime.

At least, the issue of the proper division of responsibility remains potentially important. It presents essentially the same alternative as that found in the case of the social agencies. The Church might feel that, under proper conditions, it could increasingly surrender large areas of primary responsibility to the State. The Church might focus upon borderland cases, that is to say, upon persons in difficulty and need, before they become paupers or criminals. This would set apart prevention as the Church's primary sphere of action. Beyond this it could still assist the State in fields which the State has made its own.

If this view were taken, federation policy with respect to social service would be very different from what it would be if the Church must insist upon doing for "her own" virtually everything that the State does for the community in general.

Decision on this point is likely to be reached only in the light of a previous question, namely, what is necessary to render social service Christian?

"CHRISTIAN" SOCIAL SERVICE

The grounds on which the substitution of the State or the social agencies for the Church in the realm of social service are opposed, are ordinarily stated as follows: that the State is secular; that the nature of effective social work requires it to have some peculiar inwardly Christian power and motivation; that at vital points it ought to be consciously religious.

This makes the problem one of the secularity of certain agencies. What constitutes secularity? It may be argued that whether the State is secular or not in any given function depends upon the spirit that animates it in that function. Radical Protestantism would be willing to say the same thing of the Church.[17]

Such a standpoint naturally leads to the further position that religious and spiritual motivation and specific Christian quality and service are not limited to the Church as their instrument. Such values might be found both in the Church and the State. There might then be concurrent organization and functioning by both institutions in the same sphere; while it might be left to experiment to determine what function is most essential to each, and what is the best division of responsibility between the two.

One of the logical courses has already been indicated, namely, that the Church could get Christian spirit and motive into fuller action if it attempted less social welfare under its own banner and operated more as the helper and constructive critic of other institutions. Specifically, how far could coöperative Church agencies like federations render non-sectarian and public-welfare service "Christian" by coöperating with it in a subordinate capacity?

THE DIGNITY OF THE ANCILLARY RÔLE

One may incline to believe that the Church should concede larger areas of responsibility through the State and the non-sectarian agencies, and still hold that the Church is greatly needed in the social field. One might acknowledge that welfare agencies may function Christianly outside the Church, and nevertheless be convinced that it is well to utilize so acknowledged an expert in some phases of social service as the Church is.

The practical question in any given social field would be: In what capacity should the Church act just at this point? How should it function in this specific area? Now if attaching a Protestant court-worker to the staff of a juvenile court, or sup-

---

[17] For a commentary upon the similar difficulty of maintaining any objective distinction between "Christian" and secular education, see Leonard's *Survey of Higher Education For the United Lutheran Church in America*, Volume III, p. 217.

plying a chaplain to a charitable institution, enables these agencies to function more Christianly, the same principle might be carried a good deal further both as related to voluntary social institutions and to the State.

But the degree of satisfaction that federations can find in such a policy will depend upon the dignity they attach to the ancillary rôle, in contrast with the more independent one. It will greatly affect decision as to the division of responsibility between forces working in the social-service field, if the Church is content to make social service Christian, and does not also demand that it be ecclesiastical.

POLITICAL ACTION

But the secular alliances of the coöperating churches lead them beyond the realm of philanthropy. Almost invariably they invade that of politics. The crucial issue is: What kinds and degrees of explicitly political action are necessary to realize the Church's concern for moral and human welfare?

As commonly interpreted by federations, this concern sooner or later involves the attempt in some form to focus Protestant group-sentiment upon the conduct of government. It involves political action in the sense that organized pressure in behalf of Christian ideals is brought upon the political processes or personalities of city, state, or nation. Such pressure may take the form of organized action by groups of citizens expressed, for example, in voting; or may express itself through one or more permanent agencies of agitation or reform.

As the evidence shows, federations may and do act directly in such matters as representatives of the coöperating churches. But they make more habitual use of specializing agencies of reform; agencies not officially Protestant, but having strongly Protestant antecedents.

Current relationships with reform agencies present several peculiar features. Many of the agencies continue to maintain strong sentimental ties with the Church. When the tests of loyalty and approval arise, they may be more strongly favored by churchmen than agencies working in the Church's own name.[18] At the same time, they are not ecclesiastically governed, and would be entirely unwilling to accept the limitations involved in becoming technical representatives of the churches.

Again, such agencies are nearly always under acute criticism from a minority within the Church. The most frequent charges against them are that they are dogmatic and non-progressive, that they depend on propaganda rather than on education, and

---

[18] P. 382.

that they are sometimes attempts to impose the Puritan mores upon the nation in the name of religion; and in all these aspects, when they are roundly challenged by certain elements of Protestant opinion.[19]

The problem at this point finds itself on two levels; first, how available are the existing reform agencies as virtual representatives of the coöperating churches? Second, what, if anything, must the coöperating churches do at points where the present agencies are not suitable representatives, or beyond the fields which the present agencies cover? Bearing upon the availability of the reform agencies to represent the coöperating churches, one senses a suspicion that these agencies are inclined to use church federations when it is to their advantage, and to disassociate themselves from church alliances at other times. Should the federations be willing to play the cat's-paw for such independent agencies, however pious their antecedents? Will it not be appropriate for federations to be somewhat coy in their turn, and to keep the reform agencies guessing as to whether they will get Church support in a given issue or not? On the other hand, should the Church wish to hide behind the skirts of the reform agencies when it can more bravely, and perhaps just as effectively, act in its own capacity?

It may be questioned, however, whether the political efforts of federations and reform agencies alike do not lack in scope and imagination. Assuming that it is legitimate for voluntary organizations of citizens to consider and criticize the actions of government and to propose such policies as they believe in, and recognizing the Church as such an organization with special concern for social morality and welfare, the Church may legitimately work along with such agencies. But why should the Church be content to be identified merely with a few and highly traditional phases of reform? Might it not equally well be concerned with broader programs of municipal administration, with taxation and with public schools, instead of with a too-limited range of noble experiments.

The churches, then, are uneasy and uncertain whither their secular contacts and alliances are leading them; they are undecided as to where they ought to lead. But this state of mind only serves the more to illuminate the massive fact that the integration of Protestant forces inevitably involves the redefinition of relationships in the very largest social spheres. It revives issues forgotten so long as sectarian division made the group negligible, and compels age-long controversies to be faced afresh.

---

[19] P. 247.

Chapter XIII

CURRENTS AND EDDIES OF FEDERATION THINKING

The official formulations of major federation ideas and the traditional forms which these ideas have taken in the minds of the great mass of constituents, have been set forth concretely and at length in previous chapters. Official thinking takes form in constitutions and platforms, in authoritative expositions and promotional arguments, and occasionally in the findings of conventions that attempt to register and integrate the results of federation experience. From these sources one learns what federation purports to be, its announced objectives, and its form and structure. The scope of the federation movement and its grounds of inclusion and exclusion are indicated and rationalized. The authority of the movement is stressed as essentially one of voluntary agreement. The principle of representativeness is put forth in an extreme form. Working unity is affirmed on the one hand, while on the other any necessary implication of organic unity is denied. Thinking in this aspect is embedded in the history, structure, and on-going processes of the federation movement with which the report up to this point has been mainly concerned.

The unofficial federation tradition has also been traced in the casual utterances and volunteer correspondence of constituents, in the recognitions which they accord the federation movement, in the values they ascribe to it and the loyalties they aver. A strong majority agrees on all these points. The burden of its consciousness goes somewhat like this:

> The federation is a good movement which we ought to back. It is our agency which we will support. In it we satisfy our fraternal feelings and testify to our conviction of the essential unity of the Church. By it we avoid duplication and waste, and through it we achieve greater efficiency.

Such formulas and such informal agreements represent the zone of established federation thinking. They express the static phase of the Church's intellectual and emotional reaction to the coöperative movement.

Moreover, and on the whole, official formulas and established agreements are what characterize the situation as respects federation thinking. This is a consequence of the necessary terms on which the federation system has had to insert itself within the competitive ecclesiastical scheme. It could do so only by curbing its critical faculties, by suppressing the consciousness, and the discussion, of differences. The more suspicious supporters have been lulled by such a formula as: "Come along and let us work together. Our respective rights will be well safeguarded, and no ultimate question of faith will be raised." Accordingly, the rank and file rest easy in the conviction that federations represent no distinctive position on debatable issues. The existence of federations implies no challenge to, and no change in, any one's deeper view of the Christian life, belief, or organization. It is the inaction of federations in these spheres that has permitted them to exist. Their avoidance of definite official positions on as many points as possible makes them acceptable. And this inevitably gives intellectual tone and character to the movement.

Contrasting with official formulations and dominant tradition there are, however, minor and more dynamic reactions to the same phenomena. The evolution of federations has been paralleled by, and expressed in, currents and eddies of critical thinking. Thinking in this phase is recorded unofficially in the same incidental sources that have shown the major trends. These sources present also marginal elements of data, mere waifs of dissenting individual opinion; but opinion aggressively searching and challenging. At this other extreme come also the more clearly defined and penetrating appreciations of the federations. Official thinking, too, furnishes its more dynamic phases. These record the stages by which leaders and representatives have reached decisions on actual issues through processes of discussion; they reveal the bases of official action as laid bare through controversy. These eddies and currents in federation thinking, whether official or unofficial, afford some of the most illuminating and exhilarating approaches to the movement. They furnish the theme of the present chapter.

UNOFFICIAL THINKING

The objective data which the preceding chapters have presented, relative to the organization and work of church federations, do not all look in one single direction. It is not strange, therefore, if the body of thinking which parallels and relates to the movement and the operation of federations is not completely harmonious. One who is not expecting identical views need not be surprised, for example, to find a relatively small group of constituent's judgments relating to social service yielding opinions as conflicting as the following:

(1) World peace, international relations, law observance and industrial relations, are the "crucial tests of our Christian civilization." In advocating these interests the Council of Churches performs "a truly prophetic service to the city."

(2) The federation does not seem to function in relation to civic, national or international questions. It does not mobilize the social conscience of the churches. Perhaps the social conscience is too feeble and uncertain.

(3) "In all my relations with the social service committee, since the organization of the federation, every recommendation of the committee has been vetoed by the 'higher ups' (within the organization) except one, that on pornographic literature. The position taken has always been that 'it is not the province of the federation.' I am sure that it should be."

(4) Adequate consultation with constituents in advance is very important: "Cannot see that Dr. Cadman (nationally) or Dr. Price (locally) has any right to claim that they represent the churches of the country on internationalism, pacificism or prohibition. When, where, and by whom were they ever authorized to take the position they have assumed?"

(5) "Social-service activities should be carried on entirely by other agencies."

In contrast with such a wide scale of conflicting views, a genuine consolidation of the sentiments of a strong Protestant majority is perhaps to be anticipated only with respect to the more conventional and less aggressive phases of collective thinking.

The present chapter accordingly undertakes to illustrate something of the range and variety of this thinking with special reference to its focal points and its major directions.

SOURCES OF DATA

A fortunate circumstance made it possible for the data to include a representative cross section of federation thinking covering unfavorable verdicts and critical diagnoses as well as favorable ones. As previously indicated, questionnaires with opportunity for supplemental expression of opinion were sent to the entire mailing lists of the federations. As shown in Chapter VI, on Membership and Participation, federations habitually communicate their more general plans to the entire body of Protestant clergy; their Sunday-school proposals to all superintendents and leaders, etc. The constituencies thus canvassed for expressions of opinion were therefore representative, not merely of denominations belonging to federations, but of the entire Protestant body. Opportunity to comment was thus afforded to a good many who deliberately denied active allegiance and who may have been actually opposed to the agencies upon which they were passing judgment.

Furthermore, it was of course possible for one and the same person to be both friend and critic. Such a person often expressed both his minds, pointing out shortcomings in connection with verdicts favorable on the whole.

Many hundreds of opinions from these various sources were studied in the belief that the body of data was essentially representative of the more important content and variety of federation thinking, though not, of course, of its statistical distribution.

MINOR ISSUES CHIEFLY EXPRESSIVE OF CONSTITUENTS' MOODS

First to be considered are a varied group of practical but essentially minor issues in which the judgments of the constituent minority reveal a range of moods rather than any balanced and systematic exercise of their critical judgments.

Opposition Without Explanation

Some constituents are simply opposed to the federation; they are just against it without qualification or explanation. Thus, the questionnaire gives a Methodist minister opportunity to deliver himself as follows:

> I have little use for the Federation and none whatever for the Council of Churches of Christ in America.

A Methodist Sunday-school superintendent reacts on certain items of the social-service efforts of a local federation as follows:

> *Internationalism:* dangerous; have no sympathy with pacificism or socialistic tendency. *Race Relations:* Evangelical Christianity has no common ground with Jews and Catholics. *Church and Industry:* The Federal Council a most dangerous source of information controlled largely by socialistic tendencies.

Somewhat similarly a Presbyterian layman of Baltimore puts himself on record thus:

I strongly disapprove of telling the government how it should be run, the recent naval bill in particular. I am opposed to internationalism and pacificism as represented by some members of the community.

Superfluous and Burdensome

In very rare instances someone deliberately asserts that the denominational way of doing things is better than the coöperative way:

> The Kingdom of God would be better off if each denomination would do its work separately without wasting time on federation.

Somewhat more frequently opinion charges federation with being burdensome additional machinery; as this from a Presbyterian layman:

> I have not, nor can I support the local or Federal Council of Churches. The need for such organizations does not exist. Indeed each denomination now has in itself so much of an overhead of the same character that the real effort of the individual church and minister is buried so deep that they are rarely engaged seriously with the purpose to which they were dedicated.

In similar vein a Methodist minister writes:

> Pressure of local and denominational work too frequently hinders coöperation. A half dozen outside causes is enough in one year for a small church. Our denomination already has that many.

Another similar utterance comes from a secretary of a national reform organization which also gets its support from local churches:

> The individual churches can best attend to their own local needs. Too much machinery is dangerous; takes people away from work to run the machine.

LOCAL OR INCIDENTAL GROUNDS OF CRITICISM

FEDERATION LOCALLY UNACCEPTABLE

Contrasting with these general grounds of opposition are fairly numerous answers which merely assert that federation is not locally acceptable. One such judgment reads:

> So far as W—— is concerned, federation is not necessary and sentiment would not be conducive to a successful federation. Coöperation without federation is best here.

Except for this last, all the above grounds of opposition appear to lie against the federation movement as such and not merely against its actual administration as a concrete organization.

CRITICISM OF FEDERATION PRACTICE

A larger body of incidental criticism aims at one or another of the practices of federation rather than at the basic idea. Thus the charge appears with some frequency that federations fail to establish adequate contact with their constituents. "Less machinery and more personal contact is needed." "Establish more real relations with individual churches." Such expressions tend to come from the smaller and more remote churches which as a matter of fact are found difficult of intimate cultivation.[1] A more bitter version of the same charge holds that "the federation caters to the big down-town churches and the big churchmen and neglects the humbler members of the brotherhood."

A somewhat unusual complaint is that the federation claims credit for the work of others. A Methodist layman, holding numerous committee positions in his own denomination, expresses this feeling as follows:

> Council should never take credit for results of activities in individual churches unless these activities were actually promoted by the officers or committees of the Council. This causes resentment on the part of pastors and raises a resistance to the appeal for support of the Council.

Inasmuch as it is the genius of the federation movement to attempt to gather up total Protestant work under a common point of view and to regard it as all part of a single whole of which the federation itself is the chief exponent, this criticism raises exceedingly basic problems. Here is a point with respect to which federations need constantly to be on their guard.

Particularly bitter criticism sometimes arises from the failure of the federation to take the same point of view as the constituent in matters about which he feels deeply. Here is a typical example which could doubtless be duplicated in numerous cases:

> I am against any organization that takes the name of the Church and is supposed to stand for better citizenship, etc., and then opposes a man like Billy Sunday and his efforts.

Still another incidental criticism has primary reference to state federations, namely, that their proposals frequently are of

---

[1] P. 94.

remote character and are not related to local problems. They invite all the churches to take approved positions in general, but do not show how taking the position implies doing anything specific in the church's own community. This criticism may or may not imply a narrowly parochial point of view.

APPROVAL CONDITIONED UPON LEADERSHIP

Criticisms of another type fix upon the quality of local leadership as a ground for at least a discriminating attitude toward the federation movement. The wisdom of federation proposals, one constituent notes:

> Depends not a little on the wisdom of men in control at the time. Have to make a reservation as regards the ability and wisdom of the federation's local representative.

As another puts it:

> A great deal depends upon the local personnel of the Council. If I had confidence in their judgment as individuals, I would feel strongly obliged to support the Council.

Still another constituent says:

> There is personal element to be considered. For example, I have confidence in Dr. —— but would not care to coöperate in everything the Federal Council allows to come out.

CAUTIONARY COUNSELS

A great quantity of merely restrictive comment which is essentially temperamental in origin probably deserves but little attention. Federations are told:

> To stick to matters in which Protestant denominations are in substantial agreement; to limit themselves to their present activities, or to cut them down in number; not to ask the impossible; to concentrate upon evangelistic work with individuals; not to spend so much money.

These and plenty of other "go slow" signs are thickly scattered along all the main highways of federation practice.

Perhaps the most valid of them is the one that cautions against the danger of attempting too many things. This feeling is voiced in the following opinions:

> I feel that we are overorganized. It is not possible to give intelligent support to so many branches of work and most of the work done by the laity is futile.
>
> Many of your proposals are not feasible, or too large to accomplish satisfactorily at present. Do something big first, in a big

way; then add others. To attempt too much is to spell failure in many.

Fear there is danger of 'scattering' and losing influence. We get too much mail from the Federation office. Care should be exercised to avoid ground already covered, e.g., retreat this fall.

RESULTS NOT WORTH THE EFFORT

A few critics end by saying that their local federation at least is not worth the time, cost, or effort put upon it. The following utterance illustrates the changes rung upon this theme:

> I believe in evangelism but not coöperative, as I do not believe it accomplishes results in accordance with energy expended.

The foregoing somewhat extensive quotations have been offered from the supplementary schedules and correspondence of constituents of more than twenty federations, in order that, so far as possible, the reader may hear the more critical members of the rank and file speaking with their own voices. No attempt to count the frequency of any particular attitude has been made and no weighting or evaluation of any attitude has been offered.

MAJOR SENSITIVE POINTS

Another group of frequently recurring judgments relates to issues inherently more fundamental, and attacks them in a more penetrating way. It indicates exceptionally sensitive points within the movement, points at which serious difficulties are met with in experience or felt in basic theory.

AUTHORITY

The issue of authority presents such a point. More constituents took occasion to file caveats in behalf of the right of individual judgment as against a federation decision or policy than on any other issue. This may have been due in part to the form of questions proposed for statistical answer.[2] Widespread fear of authority and concern lest a federated movement should conceal a tendency to an over-lordship of the churches, however, lies apparently very close to the surface of feeling with regard to the movement. Of this sensitiveness, reservations of rights and constitutional provision for the easy dissolution of federation ties have already given warning. Characteristic expressions in this vein follow:

> I regard any position of the federation as worthy of respectful consideration, but I reserve the right to determine my position for myself in accordance with my own judgment.

---

[2] P. 69.

The proposal by the federation would be treated the same as a proposal by our own fellowship. I would form my own judgment and act accordingly. If personal judgment is to surrender to group dictator, where is the gain?

Would reserve the right of individual judgment on specific proposals. My denomination does not determine my attitude. I support federation or Council policies on general confidence in them and dissent only if specific proposals seem unwise.

Would coöperate except where the decision or action conflicted with my moral judgment. Would not, for instance, coöperate in patriotic meetings or 'Services of Intercession' in time of war, even if sponsored by federation.

Instead of questioning the authority of the federation as a general principle, certain constituents attempted to discriminate among different spheres of operation. They desired to ascribe responsibility and consequent authority to the federation in certain spheres, while reserving them in the main to the denominational churches. This echoes the formula of the historic documents to the effect that federation should undertake "what the churches can best do together rather than in separation."[3] Constituents, however, were not very successful in indicating what specific spheres of action could properly become the province of the federations under this principle. Examples of this type of thought follow:

I look upon the federation as a body competent to pass upon certain matters, and when it expresses a judgment I accept it as the findings of a specialist.

Certain functions of the general character should have an authorized and organized clearing house such as the federation.

Another constituent warns:

The federation must be careful to choose only the very essential things to advocate or it will lose influence.

Discriminating statements of this general point of view which assigns the federation the very important role of expert, come from two Massachusetts ministers:

Every question is put in such a way that I am glad of a *clearing house* that attempts to settle so many highly important matters. And although as a pastor I cannot comply with every request and my church may not always be interested, yet I regard the work of the federation as very stimulating and suggestive. It furnishes common objectives.

I feel a sense of security against unwise or overlapping effort in denominational propaganda. I believe that a busy pastor can

---

[3] P. 121.

very safely rely on the judgment of the Council in debated cases, thus having an expert at hand to help him determine his own course. Out of the things advocated there is an opportunity to choose that which affects his work.

The authority of federation as the organ and voice of Protestantism is thus checked and balanced by caveats and limitations at many points.

INCLUSIVENESS

Still another group of constituents chiefly values or fears federation as an instance or an omen of interconfessional inclusiveness, of the recognition and fellowship of religious people beyond the bounds of the traditionally evangelical family with which the movement is historically associated.

Direct complaints on account of their exclusion elsewhere occasionally come from constituents belonging to non-orthodox denominations who may be included in particular federations or may have become constituents through the extension of memberships in some of the various ways explained in Chapter VI.[4]

An appreciable number of constituents belonging to traditional evangelical bodies voice their aspiration for a more inclusive fellowship, as in the following:

> Should take in more denominations and creeds or faiths, such as Catholics and Jews. Should work toward combination or unification of as many Protestant denominations as possible. Should combine the many small denominational churches in small towns into one large Protestant church. Should do away with the evangelism of Jews.
>
> Believe all people should coöperate, Catholics, Jews and otherwise.
>
> All churches, including the Catholic and Mormon, are doing good and I will coöperate with all.
>
> Should admit liberal churches upon same conditions as other churches.
>
> Amendment of by-laws or articles of association so as to allow all Christian denominations to become members.
>
> Admit certain denominations now outside of Council.
>
> Recognize Unitarians and Universalists.
>
> Coöperate with and admit to its membership all God-fearing denominations.

A person of Jewish faith was somehow included in the constituency list of the Rochester Federation. Her questionnaire elicited the following very interesting reply and challenge:

---

[4] P. 90.

Being a Jewess, why not call into coöperation the rabbis? If Christ (as you claim, I believe) was crucified by Jews (which I do not believe) would an apology by one for such offense (based on our doubt, of course) start an era of actual peace between Christianized world and older beliefs? I hereby present such an apology, for I embrace all.

Naturally the attitudes of those who value the federation as a symbol of inclusive religious fellowship are counterbalanced by those who desire to keep it as a symbol of rigorous orthodoxy. Expressions of this position are illustrated in the following quotations:

Though I have checked your items under evangelism, I am very doubtful as to whether I could coöperate with your plan herein. If I am rightly informed, you recognize as evangelical churches or denominations that are, according to my belief, neither evangelical nor Christian, and many whose teaching I strongly oppose. If this is so, I could not endorse your religious program.

Considering that I am what is generally known as a Fundamentalist, I approve almost all the work of the Federation except where religious opinion might not agree.

The church federation should be the exponent of United Protestantism, evangelical, evangelistic, uncompromising on essentials, definitely and solely Christian and courageous in proclaiming that fact. No liberalism, no modernism, puritanical.

Will always coöperate with any movement or group of Christians who ever magnify the Lordship and atonement of Jesus Christ as central in all our efforts.

My replies are predicated on the assumption that all teachings are in compliance with what is understood as orthodox Christianity, and not on purely 'social uplift' to the exclusion of salvation through the atonement of Christ on the cross.

I am strongly in favor of the Federation but would mention one danger: that of leaning away from the evangelical faith towards *'modernism'* for the sake of offending none. The heart of the people is evangelical.

Will coöperate as far as the Federation will refrain from modernism and the teaching of evolution. President Charles Smith of the Atheist Association in a circular letter of July 25 says: 'The time for dodging is past. Evolution is atheistic. It bankrupts the Bible. Failure to take that stand is treason to truth.' Why have our churches been so slow in finding this out?

The main body of sentiment naturally falls between the two extremes just illustrated; but there is enough narration to keep the issue sensitive in both directions at once.

REPRESENTATIVENESS

Many answers indicate the feeling of constituents that representativeness is an urgent issue. The variety in which this general viewpoint is expressed is suggested in the following examples:

The federation now seems to me not sufficiently responsive to local church desires.

Believe that the Council should reflect the best judgment of the churches of the city; that it should have better chance to get this judgment. It is in no case a governing body but a counseling body.

Would carry out the above (i.e. corporate) when the Federation work becomes the corporate expression of the Protestant churches, but not this half-way support of about half the group.

Am doubtful as to just how much is accomplished by church federation. A mere handful run the business and dictate the policy. Little interest on the part of masses.

Some questions should be referred back to the churches in a vote or referendum before federation speaks.

I feel that all such work should be taken up with each individual church and let them have a say in how it ought to be done.

We should coöperate in all those projects on which we have carefully been consulted in advance and where the decision is a synthesis of opinion rather than a majority decision.

I feel that the Council of Churches should recommend and then submit important matters to its constituency for approval, after which action should be taken. But I am not in favor of the Council deciding important matters without the proper approval of the denominations.

Action taken by denominational representatives without coercion should be considered authoritative unless violating some denominational law. Action taken by some officer and then crammed through the Council by an appeal for personal vindication, as has been done a time or so, would not receive my support, even though the action in itself was comparatively harmless.

ACTUAL MISREPRESENTATION OF THE CHURCH IS RARELY CHARGED

Even at most, criticism is mainly to the effect that federations should be careful to make themselves representative. Only a few times does the charge appear that they have actually misrepresented the churches in specific issues. This is, however, the opinion of an Episcopal minister of Boston:

The great bulk of the activities conducted in the last few years by national and local federations is, in my opinion, a waste of time and money, and has on several occasions misrepresented the Church in the eyes of the public.

Even this critic does not specify just what these occasions were.

FEDERATIONS MUST NOT OUTSTRIP THE CHURCHES

Relative to representativeness, the most frequent ground of criticism is not that the Church should not do what the federations are attempting in its behalf. It is rather that the federations, just because they are professedly representatives, must not go beyond that to which their constituents agree.

That federations by their very nature cannot lead the main body of Protestant conviction is suggested in the following opinion:

> Federation is chiefly criticized for its advanced position in international, industrial and legislative matters. I wish . . . it might have influence in these activities. However, . . . its chief value is in being *a united movement*. Therefore the functions of advanced leadership cannot be so well assumed by it. (Congregational minister—Boston)

A Southern Methodist minister in Baltimore expresses himself in similar vein:

> The federation of churches is not a reform movement, nor a pioneer, but an expression of collective achievements. The object is to state and make effective this collective achievement.

That federations are sometimes not truly representative seems to be the view of a Boston layman (Congregational):

> I do not think the federation has any mandate to speak for the churches in matters of this kind. As to some of them the attitude of the churches is undoubtedly favorable; as to others, the churches probably have no real opinions one way or the other; as to still others the sentiment of the Church is sharply divided if not actively adverse. The federation ought not to assume to act for the churches in these matters unless some kind of method is devised to make sure that it represents the real opinions of the churches and not those of a few individuals.

Another slant on the question appears in the response of another Congregational layman who seems to believe that the trouble is that the layman is not adequately represented:

> I suggest the study of proposed legislation by other than ministers.

CONSTRUCTIVE CRITICISM

Constructive suggestions emerging from the body of criticism take two general directions. First, it is sometimes implied that the frequency of the federation's attempt at representative utterance, especially on social issues, might be reduced. The federation may assume to speak for the churches on sufficiently rare occasions—"Act in emergencies. Don't be a nuisance," writes a Methodist minister.

The other suggestion—voiced in several previously quoted opinions—is that federations should systematically seek to discover what the constituents actually think before venturing to speak for them—a method obviously harder to carry out than to propose, but perhaps holding the germ of a real solution. This view is implied by two other ministers in the following quotations:

> My only serious criticism of the federation is its tendency to claim a representative position even when no effort has been made to learn the minds of its constituency. A board of directors with members from each denomination is not necessarily a representative group.

> I value the federation's advice and argument to me and my church but question its right to speak for us before it has received our formal resolutions. I wish there might be a voice of united Protestantism. Perhaps federations could arrange for some adequate form of expression, but it must avoid arrogating to itself the right to speak.

A variant upon this suggestion is that federations might limit themselves to the study of debatable problems and announce the results of their study to their constituents without taking sides. Thus another Congregational minister writes:

> I question somewhat the wisdom of the federation doing more than to study thoroughly and state the results of study, and believe that it might well do in some instances as the League of Women Voters does, namely, to offer its platform to both sides.

An even more cautious view was presented to the Philadelphia Commission on International Relations by a distinguished professor, as follows:

> In view of honest differences of opinion in the fields of politics, sociology, economics, morals and ethics, it should be the policy of the federation to facilitate the presentation of all interpretations of the gospel of Christ, to endorse none.

The commission, however, disagreed and decided that its function was to enunciate principles and to indicate "the application of principles in specific instances as need may arise." This, as has already been noted, fairly reflects the average official attitude of federations as over against the hesitancy of a minority on the inside.

SIGNIFICANCE FOR CHURCH UNITY

In great part the sensitiveness of constituents was not directed toward federations as separate entities either good or bad, but rather to their symbolic significances, the hopes or fears which they arouse. Thus, the suspicion was frequently voiced that federation is a step towards unity of the Church. This viewpoint is often expressed obliquely: for example, a request for one's judgment of the federation brings the answer, "I strongly favor Christian unity." More often, however, it is set forth straightforwardly, as when the federated movement is directly characterized as a step towards uniting the various churches of the world into more harmonious activity; or "a step toward the consolidation of the Protestant churches"; "Protestantism will have to unite some day. Why not now?" The sentimental verdict that "the Council is the best method known to the Protestant churches to "answer the Lord's prayer 'that they may all be one'" recurs in the documents like a refrain. "The churches should all work together as one body 'even as Christ and the Father are one.'" Penetrating still further into the religious basis of the idea, a constituent affirms, "There should be but one Protestant church organization, as 'we have but one Christ and Saviour.'" Considering the prevalence of this mood, it is not strange when an occasional constituent breaks into the fervor of prayer and invokes divine blessing on the federation as a movement for Christian unity.

A Sunday-school teacher thinks that federation will help youth to grow up more tolerant than their parents, and in that way bring about unity. An original and suggestive response reads: "I look upon the federation as the upper house in the law-making body of the Church and possibly as the true Christian church nucleus." A more typical statement is, "I regard the Council of Churches as an important step toward an ultimate union of all the evangelical denominations and support it accordingly."

Other constituents hope that federation will at least "reduce the sects to a few leading types."

Still other replies draw distinctions between ecclesiastical and *spiritual* unity, advocating "unity not in name but in principle"; or wanting essential unity, unity of work without involving denomination or theological issues. Most of the attempted distinctions are, however, rather indefinite.

Within this chorus of praise, whether absolute or qualified, an occasional discordant note is heard. Thus, a constituent asserts: "The Council is an agency promoting unity, but not union." A good many others warn their federations not to let it appear that they are unity movements or that they have any necessary trend in that direction. This is, of course, the only officially correct position.[5]

---

[5] P. 88.

A Common Organ for Protestantism

A vigorous and varied set of constituents' utterances stress the need and value of some common organization and voice of united Protestantism, and register more than ordinary appreciation of their federations from this standpoint. Shadings of thought which point in this common direction are evidenced by the following examples:

> The Federation of Churches is one of the biggest steps of progress the Protestant churches have made, and I think we should give it our loyal support.
>
> I have always favored the coöperation of all Protestant churches and feel that now that the federation is our representative, it should be supported in all ways by all the churches.
>
> Recognizing that the Council is composed of the same human stuff that goes to make up the Church, I would attribute to the Council one of the best interpreters of coöperative Christianity, allowing room for mistakes due to the human element. The proposals which the Council would advocate certainly would find moral backing.
>
> In the light of the experience of seven years of coöperative contact, I regard the Council of Churches thoroughly adequate to speak and act for Wichita Protestantism.
>
> I believe strongly that group spirit, and a feeling of group responsibility, is the next step forward in spiritual evolution. Lack of this spirit is one of the great handicaps of the Protestant churches today.
>
> Would not compromise for sake of council but feel that it is best known system of coöperative work.
>
> Believe Councils of Churches such as we have here are of very great benefit to Protestantism and the community. We sometimes *speak as one* and are heard.
>
> The Council is the only means for coöperation of the various denominations. Coöperation and mutual endeavor are needed; therefore it is necessary and wise to support the Council.
>
> The Church Federation is the corporate organization for united Christian service in our cities and nation.

As already noted in connection with the exhibition of more critical opinions, the study has no direct evidence of the frequency of any of the views quoted above. Answers to questionnaires presented in other connections show statistically how constituents' sentiments are distributed on stated questions.[6]

Official Thinking

In contrast with official thinking as fixed in constitutions and authoritative expositions or conventionalized in sales talk, its

---

[6] P. 134.

more dynamic phase is marked by occasional wrestlings with novel issues by representative individuals or groups. Not infrequently they have left records of the stages and processes of the thinking and the final grounds of decision and action.

One expects representative leaders and committees normally to be borne along upon the established tides of corporate thinking until it is challenged or resisted by criticism. Often such criticism arises with, or is shared by, some portion of their own membership. This breaks up the old complacency and compels them to find a new way out. Thus, one comes upon thought in the making but still utilizing official group processes.

UNEQUAL DISTRIBUTION OF DYNAMIC THINKING

At this point one also comes upon the fact of the uneven distribution of the data.

The major departments of federation have not had anything like equal intensity or originality of thought put upon them. Some have presented few intellectual problems, others many. Thus, the intellectual basis of evangelism is essentially traditional; that of religious education is technical; while that of comity is a set of generalizations from practice; leaving social service with no commonly accepted intellectual basis of thought.

(1) Coöperative evangelism in the federations proceeds on the basis of a vague common tradition assumed to be universally accepted. But vital discussion of possible differences in the basic conception of the nature and content of the Gospel message is completely inhibited. This would be called unkind criticism of a brother's theology, something which by common consent is utterly taboo. Indeed it is not believed possible to discuss theology frankly and at the same time to keep the peace necessary for a working unity. This condition compels the federation movement to get along without any adequate and illuminating statement of the grounds of its religious fellowship. Critics have been quick to pounce upon this weakness. For example, the argument of the United Lutheran Church (as publicly set forth to justify its refusal to become an organic member of the Federal Council) asserts that Protestants cannot reach any significant union merely as Protestants, but only as confessors. The policy of the federation movement in meeting this criticism has generally been to ignore it; or else to trust to the formula that federative coöperation is for service only and that it does not raise questions of theology or policy. No one can tell whether the consequences of limiting discussion of these points have been to limit following more or less than free discussion would have

done. Logically, however, an undefined and uncriticized religious tradition can hardly be an adequate basis for a final working synthesis of the Protestant cause.

(2) Religious education within the federations has taken over from the general field of religious education the tendencies of psychological and pedagogical thinking which have so radically transformed that realm. Within itself it has had controversy in plenty; but this has taken place outside the federation's realm. While no final agreement has been reached (because its dominant mood of thinking is not dogmatic), religious education has made a well-considered approach to its problems through philosophy, has achieved precise techniques through partially scientific experimentation, and has developed considerable capacity for self-criticism. In short,—no special thanks to the federation movement as such—religious education is dominated by an intellectual attitude entirely different from that which dominates evangelism.

(3) As is shown in the separately published report,[7] federation thinking in the realm of comity exhibits a steady development of an important body of principles and procedures which, though still weak on the more positive side of a theory of churchmanship, go far toward furnishing a working basis for this essentially practical phase of the coöperative movement. The thinking out of these conclusions has involved frequent reconsideration and formulation of the significance of results wrought out in inexperience. On the whole, the most nearly adequate accomplishments of indigenous thinking within the federation movement itself are to be found in this field.

Social Service in Federation Thinking

(4) Federation thinking in the sphere of social service is less uniform and more inconclusive than in any other; while, at the same time, it presents a much larger bulk of records and declarations of the processes and results of thinking. Here, in brief, is the ultra-dynamic phase of the movement.

Social-service thinking centers on a large general issue, namely, that of the social implications of Christianity. It concerns the insertion under the impulse of partially novel moral ideals of a united church as an augmented force in a world of conflict. The massing of divided Protestantism inevitably constitutes a new challenge to some of the established orders of civilization. It tempts the Church to a new courage and attack, and at the same

---

[7] *Church Comity,* pp. 16 f. and 78 f.

time stiffens the resistance of whoever constitutes the opposition. Coöperating Protestantism thus finds itself playing a new role in which it is confronted by an intellectual counter-challenge questioning whether it is observing the proper sphere of the Church in the pursuit of its newly discovered objectives.

Here, then, one finds the hottest of the current discussions and the most vigorous contesting of debatable issues.

The Social Gospel

An accepted tradition, a common technical formulation of standards, a set of working generalizations, and a comprehensive formulation of social philosophy are all lacking in the realm of social service. Nevertheless, the exigencies of the practical conduct of social work have compelled federations to give more than occasional expression to certain central ideas assumed to be of general validity.[8] As a matter of fact, what is called social service as it exists today constitutes a marked addition to what would have been the federation's activities if it had gathered up the coöperative interests of the churches of forty or fifty years ago. So substantial a fact could scarcely avoid creating some change in the Church's thinking. For merely expository reasons, it has been virtually necessary to label the contrast between the conventional individualistic view of religion and the newly emphasized social implications of the Gospel, and to attempt to harmonize the two. The most distinctive of these attempts attaches itself to the concept of the "social gospel." This has involved a broadened vision of the function of the Church in the world, an extension of the catalogue of matters with which the Church is immediately concerned, and a reconsideration of the ways in which the Church is to express its mission externally. Thus, summarizing its progress in social service up to that date, one of the older documents of the Pittsburgh Church Federation asserts:

> There has been a marked increase in sense of social obligation on the part of religious forces, and just as marked an increase in appreciation of religion as a social force on the part of religious workers. One of the things over which we should be particularly thankful is the unquestionable growth of a realization on all sides that personal evangelism and social service are mutually dependent on each other, that no social service is enduringly vigorous which does not root in evangelism, and that no evangelism fully arrives which does not fruit in social service.

[8] Although many of the federations at one time or another have circulated the "Social Creed" promulgated by the Federal Council, or others prepared by the various denominational bodies, it is very rarely that these or any other organized doctrines of social relationships are actually appealed to.

QUALIFICATIONS AND LIMITATIONS OF SOCIAL SERVICE

Except for the rather unconclusive outcome up to date, the germinal idea of the social gospel has taken the normal course. It has been refined and tested by controversy, and maintains currency only with qualifications. The most frequent discriminations that have actually emerged in connection with this idea in federation thinking have next to be presented.

The Sacred vs. the Secular

The more indefinite and traditional types of mind naturally fall back upon the immemorial distinction between the sacred and the secular. Social service is not the concern of religion—as understood, for example, by a Boston Episcopal layman who wrote:

> Interchurch movements are like internationalism—evidences of losing loyalty to one's own faith or country respectively. The churches should concentrate on religion, on spreading the Word of God, or holding and interesting their own members. They should not meddle in secular affairs whether political, industrial or international. What is wrong with the Protestant Church? Too little religion and too much interference in affairs that are none of its business.

Not the Church's Business

Official thinking of the federations, on the contrary, seems never to have denied outright the responsibility of religion for social service. But it has frequently tallied with the attempt to exclude some phase of social service as not the business of the Church. Thus, under the caption, "The Church Federation and Political Action," the Protestantism of a northwestern city was made to declare:

> The Federation will never act except upon measures which involve a clear principle of moral or religious welfare; and only when it can express the practically unanimous opinion of the churches.
>
> In the interest of the American principle of "the separation of the Church from the State," it is not the function of the Church Federation to initiate or engage in political action.
>
> Political action is interpreted as including the initiation and passage of legislation, the nomination and election of candidates for office and the correction of abuses or mal-administration.
>
> Religion, through the agency of the Church, should provide those inner resources which energize men to act on the highest levels of citizenship.
>
> The Church states the great principles, laws, precepts, such as the Ten Commandments, the Golden Rule, the Law of Love,

the Law of Forgiveness, etc. But the application and the method of application is the right of every individual. The individual intelligence and conscience should guide. The principle of "religious freedom" is violated whenever the Church controls or dictates political action.

A similar note is struck by a report of the Commission on the Social Order in an Eastern city:

> We have given careful consideration to the question, 'how should this Commission function?' Shall we plan to be a militant body, attacking directly specific evils; or shall we endeavor so to set forth the principles of the Gospel in their bearing upon social conditions that we shall stimulate the members of our churches to right action? We prefer the latter course.

Numerous practical warnings from constituents tend to reinforce this position.[9]

For example, an individual version of this same distinction comes from Baltimore:

> Am opposed to the Church taking an active part, either from the pulpit or otherwise, in politics. Churchmen as individuals and associations (non-denominational) should do so. Back legislative programs provided the pulpit is not used and churchmen, not the Church, take initiative.

That a definite reminiscence of historically conflicting doctrines sometimes furnishes the framework of such thought appears in the following criticism from a Lutheran minister:

> I believe the churches should not interfere with the tasks of governmental authorities on the basis of any reform plan (after Calvin's example), but rather see that their own household is in order, that the redemption in Christ is preached and that Christians vote for Christians.

The Church's Business—but a Very Secondary One

A distinction between primary and major duties and secondary and minor ones as relating to social service is attempted in the following resolution passed by the Directors of the Greater Boston Federation of Churches in 1928:

> The function of the Greater Boston Federation of Churches is to promote fellowship and coöperative activities among the churches of its constituency, and to cultivate and register the convictions of the Christian conscience upon matters that involve the moral and spiritual welfare of the community, the nation and the world.
>
> The main purpose of the Greater Boston Federation of Churches

---

[9] See p. 417.

is to increase fellowship and coöperation between the churches. This is a field so great that it would require all our time and resources. Occasionally the Federation should consider questions in other fields, but these should only be presented at a time of urgency where the facts are known to the board of directors, the issue clear-cut, and a pronouncement by the Federation would be of some influence.

The Church's Business—but Only in One Aspect

A further discrimination attempts to preëmpt for the Church a particular phase of the social-service field.

The Social Service Committee of the Indianapolis Federation, for example, developed its 1926 program under the following declaration:

> The Committee conceives its mission to be primarily of a spiritual character, and that its effort should be with souls, minds and morals. In addition to this, it believes it should seek to link together the churches and social-welfare activities for mutual understanding and coöperation.
>
> The Committee believes and will act upon the foundation that the Church has as distinct a service to render the community as does a hospital or a clinic or a court, and that the purpose of the Committee is to make the soul service of the Church available to men, women and children in distress as well as those in normal condition.
>
> As to the program for this year, the Committee recommends the securing of a representative of the churches who shall labor in the courts with persons for whom such spiritual service may be given, and at the same time to organize volunteer workers in the churches who may be willing to be Big Brothers and Big Sisters, and in general to act as liaison officer between all organizations and agencies interested in better social conditions in the city.

Here is insistence upon a distinctive function which is presumed to keep a federation to fairly definable areas of social work and to prevent it from entering upon others.

Concrete Attempts to Apply Principles to Issues

Such attempted limitations of federation's responsibility in principle are, of course, mainly by-products of actual controversies. A long series of records of discussions and decisions shows that federations frankly mingle expediency and principle in the course of their efforts of self-criticism in the sphere of social service. Most of the discriminations noted above actually originated in internal disagreements.

A thoroughly typical instance is presented by the joint meeting in 1927 of the directors of the Massachusetts State and Greater

Boston federations to discuss the role of such organizations in the social field. In opening the meeting the secretary of the Boston Federation set the issues forth as follows:

We have a very important question to consider, namely, shall the church, and in particular a Federation of Churches, take part in the political or economic or social issues of the day, and in what way shall it take part? Let me try to clear the ground just a bit before the discussion is joined.

(a) The church can and should preach righteousness, for example, the Ten Commandments and other Christian virtues, as temperance, the tender care of little children or the aged, justice and kindness toward the poor, the prisoner, the alien.

(b) The church should rarely, if ever, enter the field of partisan politics; that is, siding with Republican or Democrat as such, or with Jones against Smith, by name. It should, however, stand for the right principle where there are clear moral issues involved.

(c) The difficulty arises when it is a question of method rather than example. Is a state pension for the aged necessarily the most Christian way to care for the aged? Or again, the child has a right to an education as well as to the safeguarding of its health and morals; is the church justified in advocating compulsory schooling up to any definite age; or a system of playgrounds that will promote juvenile health and happiness? These issues might be presented in such an extreme form that the church would wisely refrain from putting itself on record. It seems to me it is largely a case of proportion. If it appears that, beyond a reasonable doubt, a measure is really necessary to promote a person's well-being, his happiness and education not only for his own sake, but for the sake of society, then the church ought to feel free to befriend such a measure or to oppose any measure to the contrary. For myself, I am committed to the social interpretation of the gospel. 'No man liveth to himself.' No man can be saved all by himself, and our Supreme Teacher and Exemplar certainly 'went about doing good' and teaching a practical Christianity. He healed the sick. He fed the hungry. He rebuked the Pharisees who were more concerned with ritual than with deeds of mercy. The Church of Christ when awake to the full implication of His message has always erected three symbols of its faith: the church, the school and the hospital. In other words, it recognizes that Christianity deals with the whole man—spirit, mind and body. In the specialization of modern life, secular agencies have mostly taken over the provision and maintenance of school and hospital and of the various agencies we designate as philanthropic. The church inspires and trains the workers in the fields of education and charity. But I believe the church should do more than inspire by sermon and service. It should come out into the open and let it be known where it stands with reference to economic and social matters when any important Christian principles are involved. Of course, where church people are themselves divided in opinion, definite action should be limited to such cases where there is a very substantial majority on one side. It might be left to the wisdom and courtesy of the Board to decide just what this majority should be as each case arises.

Commenting from its own angle upon this discussion, the Massachusetts Federation reported to its constituents as follows:

> From the beginning, the question how far the Federation could go, in legislation and the expression of opinion, has been debated within our own Committee. When this question was raised again this year, a special joint-meeting was held of our Committee and the directors of the Greater Boston Federation. Discussion again led to the conclusion that, while the greatest caution should be observed, the policy followed is justified. The Federation has never acted except upon measures which involve a clear principle or moral or social welfare; and only when it can express the practically unanimous opinion of the churches.

Re-examining a similar issue of its own, the Chicago Federation centered its discussion upon the principle of representativeness. Recalling the fact that it was the representative of fourteen Evangelical Protestant denominations, it asked:

> How far may a federation presume to speak for the combined constituency? The federation faces the challenge of various advocates of efforts to advance the civic and moral welfare of the people, urging that it is the duty of the federation to recognize the opportunity of its members to exert a positive influence for such movements in the realm of Christian citizenship. These movements are not always limited to the immediate moral issue and may involve political and governmental processes; but they vitally affect moral interests in their settlement. How far shall the trustees of the Federation venture to voice their convictions regarding such questions?

The subsequent discussion of this issue by the constituency brought forth a proposal of a further limiting principle, namely: That a position in such controversial matters should not be adopted by the Federation without reference to the constituent bodies through their representatives and without giving opportunity for different sides of the question to be heard. The argument for this position was formally expressed as follows:

> It is better rarely to represent without doubt all the churches than to put forward the pretence to represent them on innumerable matters involving opinions, appeals and protests. The latter course leads to a lessening of dignity, discredits the force of all our acts and discourages the participation of those who can conceive the functions of the Federation as too important to be carelessly exercised.[10]

---

[10] *Chicago Church Federation Bulletin,* March and April, 1921.

The foregoing quotations have had to do with general principles limiting federation responsibility. In nearly all federations, controversy, through the years, has served also to evoke attempted distinctions on specific points. Thus relative to political candidates and policies, the organ of the Baltimore Federation recently said:

> No church, nor anybody connected with any church organization, has a right to try to dictate how a church-member shall vote. Not even the overwhelming Protestant sentiment in favor of prohibition justifies anybody in saying that every church-member must vote for dry candidates. That is an individual matter for each man's own conscience. But the churches do have the right to say that every church-member ought, as a religious duty, to exercise his franchise at every election.[11]

Relative to the criticism of public officials by federations, the Pittsburgh Federation early set forth its distinctive functions as a "religious organization."

> As such it has a definite field with established boundaries. It is not ours to do the work for which civil officials are paid; it is ours to expose the things working against morality and human welfare which may result from these officials failing to do their duty. This is the reason for what we have done and for what we have not done. For the same reason we shall continue doing similar things till these evils are removed.[12]

Acute Controversy

A movement characteristically lacking in the intellectual urge or the capacity for rationalizing its behavior, may nevertheless be clubbed into defensive thinking through acute controversies thrust upon it from without relative to some of its positions. Such thinking may be genuinely clarifying and the product of a series of controversies may add significantly to the movement's total body of thinking. Extensive data in the files of the federation point to this conclusion. But it is in the nature of controversy to become prolonged and verbose, while at the same time and by its very genius it cannot be explained but only presented. The present report accordingly has to omit the detail of such illuminating exchanges as those between the Pittsburgh Federation and Mr. Samuel Harden Church, through the Carnegie Magazine, over law enforcement; between Secretary E. Talmadge Root and the Massachusetts Daughters of the Revolution (who blacklisted Mr. Root as a dangerous pacifist); or between the

---

[11] *The Coöperator* (Baltimore Church Federation, November 1, 1926), extract from editorial, "Shall the Church Vote Continue Negligible?"
[12] Extract from *Bulletin No. 3*, June, 1915.

Baltimore Federation and H. L. Mencken. This latter controversy started over the relation of Mr. Mencken's philosophy to
his attitude toward the Church, but was turned by Mr. Mencken's
counter-attack into a spirited dissertation on "well-heeled and
mainly elderly men and women, all of them eager to do good by
force." All these controversies were, in Mr. Mencken's phrase,
instructive. They showed that people with a sense of a rightful
stake in the Church, a sense of responsibility for the nation or
a sense of personal integrity, sometimes react with exceeding
violence against what federations assert or undertake in behalf
of united Protestantism and in the attempt to apply the Gospel
to all the relations of life.

The nature of the phenomena which this chapter has set forth
and the form in which they were available for comparison do
not permit one to arrive at rigidly accurate deductions at the
end of the study. To represent the currents and eddies of federation thinking as bearing one on to a single set of necessary conclusions would be most presumptuous.

All that the above review shows is the actual terms in which
casual thinking goes on, the points to which it is chiefly directed
and the range of variation and alternatives which it actually
presents.

Chapter XIV

ORGANIZATIONAL CHARACTERISTICS OF THE FEDERATIONS

The general report has thus far treated objectively the more obvious aspects of federations as organizations, has set forth their actual practices as going concerns, and revealed the operation of more or less distinct and recurrent factors. It is now the purpose to give a brief account of what the author believes to be the more important of these factors. Some of them have to do primarily with federation functions; others with attitudes that determine which functions are undertaken and which pervade their performance; still others are related to the organizational means used to carry out what federations undertake.

This chapter accordingly treats, first, the functional characteristics of federations; second, their psychological characteristics; and, third, the characteristics of the typical agencies by means of which federations do their work as organizations. It omits any further characterization of the idealized vision of federation, which at the outset of the study was identified as one of the phenomena of the movement, but which is little altered by modifications of organizational characteristics, and in turn appears not to affect them separately.

FUNCTIONAL CHARACTERISTICS

LIMITATION TO COÖPERATIVE SERVICE

The federation movement has to do with practical coöperation, not with the joint promulgation of a common faith, nor the establishment of an all-inclusive order of church life. This is probably its most far-reaching single characteristic. In the greater part of its ministry to the world, the Church proceeds from some assumed basis of united conviction and belief. This common basis finds most frequent expression in various official formulations, such as creeds and platforms.

Following this analogy, one might naturally look for some comprehensive formulation of Christian ideals of supernatural and human relationships as a basis for church federation. One finds, on the contrary, a movement that centers upon service and tries to avoid all theological or ecclesiastical implications.

This is insisted upon in varied phraseology: federation is "a fellowship in service in spite of theological differences"; "the pathway to larger unity lies through the fields of common action, not of theological discussion." What is thus proposed is association related to one phase of the Church's life; with the assumption that the unresolved differences confessed at other points are not so extensive or of such a nature as to make coöperation in service impossible.

COÖPERATIVE SERVICE LIMITED TO "LINES AGREED UPON"

In the federation movement Protestant coöperation is narrowly limited to matters concerning which it is expressly agreed to coöperate.[1] Beyond these its scope and authority do not run. All other activities are reserved to the local churches and denominations. These are preserved intact in all the fullness of their distinctiveness and prerogatives. The churches are more than a little touchy as to their reserved rights.[2] Regularity of denominational procedure in the initiation of any coöperative activity, and denominational profit in carrying it on, are practical tests of all proposals. "What can best be done in common" invariably means what will not hurt the denominations. With the ecclesiastical leadership of the movement one finds almost no generous ignoring of consequences for the sake of the common end sought. Only women and young people somewhat inadvertently rise to such heights.[3]

ACTUAL SCOPE OPPORTUNISTICALLY DETERMINED

The federation movement is characteristically opportunistic. One finds no explicit account in advance of what is to be done in common. No clear-cut field of responsibility is assigned to the federation as such. No comprehensive definitions of functions exist. Specific functions vary enormously from city to city.[4] The program as a whole is entirely experimental and opportunistic. Coöperative work is simply carried on up to the point at which somebody challenges its wisdom or authority. These challenges fluctuate greatly from time to time and place to place. Moreover, even after the denominations agree to assign a given function to a federation, they frequently prove to be Indian givers and take back what they once granted. The federation has to worm its way into nooks and crannies not yet

---

[1] Chapter VII.
[2] P. 77.
[3] P. 436.
[4] Pp. 108 and 109.

preëmpted nor later discovered by the denominations. At no point has it free course to run and be glorified.

GRADUAL EMERGENCE OF CONVENTIONAL AREAS OF ACTIVITY

Nevertheless, as the body of the investigation has shown, usage is gradually blocking out a central field of service within which functions may cover the more conventional areas of activity. But what is actually open to any federation, even in this field, is by no means invariable, or universally conceded.[5]

PROGRAM RAGGED AND UNBALANCED

A second result of opportunistic policy is that the federations are conducting an unbalanced program. This will be entirely evident to any one who reviews the list of specific activities,[6] and who notes their fragmentary and highly peculiar response to the manifold logical possibilities of the situation. The impression is still further heightened when one compares, for example, the social service of any federation with a complete inventory of the social-welfare concerns of its city, or with any theoretical statement of a comprehensive social-work program.[7]

Actual federation programs follow from the particular historic antecedents of the movement, from the institutional feebleness and opportunistic mood of these organizations, from their limitation to the ecclesiastical point of view. They have caught into situations as best they could. They have followed the easier way, always with a leaning toward the most familiar and traditional types of work. The result is no well-proportioned scheme of service "fitly framed together." It is a thing of accident and compromise. And this, which is true of the aggregate service of the entire body of federations, is immeasurably more true of the average work of the single organization.[8]

NATURAL HISTORY OF FEDERATION FUNCTIONS

The characteristics just outlined determine the typical course of evolution through which federation functions are finally determined. Starting with a small group of activities so common as to be accepted as traditional,[9] the range of functions is enlarged in two ways; by imitation, and by piecemeal response to concrete issues.

Imitation is a mere generalized term for the fact that federa-

---

[5] Pp. 111 ff.
[6] Chapter VII and Appendix III.
[7] P. 423.
[8] P. 108.
[9] P. 106.

tions actually borrow from one another. One's success with a novel activity suggests its possible spread to others.[10] If the denominations let it be tried in new places and it succeeds practically, it tends to become an established feature of the enlarged program.

THINKING RELATED TO PARTICULAR ISSUES

The range of federation functions is further extended by the spontaneous reactions of the movement when confronted by some instant need. The characteristic attack is upon particular issues by means of piecemeal thinking. Confronted by one actual problem after another, the impulse to limit the scope of the federation's responsibility repeatedly falls down. The appeal of each specific situation rouses a very strong demand for a coöperative attempt to do something about it.[11] Thus, to visualize any outstanding social need is almost equivalent to recognizing it as a sphere of the collective duty of Christians.

Similar reactions in favor of some organized response to a social challenge occur in situations in which the method of direct service is not applicable; for example, with respect to relationships between America and foreign nations. In these cases the characteristic tendency is to resort to some collective verbal reaction, generally taking the form of a resolution. Thus, starting with the Declaration of Independence and the ideals of the new diplomacy, many federations proceed to elaborate arguments and issue declarations against American intervention in Mexico and Nicaragua.

In social action, then, and generally in spheres not denominationally preëmpted, the mental processes of the coöperative Protestant forces are characteristically quick on the trigger. If their positive impulse happens to outrun the inhibiting forces in a given situation, such action has a chance of remaining permanently annexed to the coöperative field. Even the ecclesiastic can scarcely forbid water, that they should not be baptized on whom the Holy Ghost has already fallen!

TRAITS OF THE GROUP MIND

FEAR OF COMMITMENT

In turning now to a consideration of the psychological characteristics of federations, one notes first that the psychology of the official coöperators is that of a mouse dallying with a trap.

---

[10] For means by which suggestion is communicated, see p. 54.
[11] For an illuminating commentary upon this as a general tendency of American religion, see Siegfried, *America Comes of Age*, pp. 34 ff.

They are terribly afraid of getting farther in than they intend. The federation bond is so loose at best, and so easy to undo,[12] that it is difficult at first sight to understand why denominations think it necessary to protect their freedom of action so narrowly. There is a good deal of evidence to suggest that they are afraid of the warm-hearted irresponsibility of their lay constituents—perhaps also of their own better natures. Do their instincts discern in church federation the symbol of a unity that in principle they cannot deny? Do they dread something that may enforce itself upon them by the connivance of their own consciences?

GENIUS OF MOVEMENT NOT PHILOSOPHICAL BUT PRACTICAL

The federation movement reflects the obvious qualities of the American people. Its most naïve and authentic mark is a genius for practical achievement.

Administrators, not philosophers, are the accredited representatives and spokesmen of the federation movement; but they do not personally have to dig into reasons for what they are doing; they are permitted only to gather up the results of ideas already initiated and established in the several churches.

The situation, so to say, calls for a federating of existing notions as well as of existing organizations. True, the movement is subject to qualms and hesitancies foreign to the American business man and his works. Otherwise it runs true to type. Problems get recognition in the order of their historic emergence. Interracial committees, for example, came into being just after the great northward migration of Negroes; peace committees after the World War.[13] Such newly awakened interests are separately propagated among the local federations and independently organized within them—with scant reference to their integration with the total purpose and program.

This characteristic piecemeal attack of the intelligence upon problems as they separately arise in experience, means that the principles involved are either assumed, or else deduced, so to speak, on the spot from shadowy postulates, and for the sake of the limited purposes immediately involved. The evidence definitely stresses the lack of any clear-cut doctrine of the ends in social effort, or of the means of attaining them, or of any other commonly accepted group of integrating ideas. It is safe to say that in not one issue out of a hundred that have

---

[12] Pp. 81 f.
[13] P. 54.

confronted church federations, did any one appeal to a general theory.

In the case of one or two federations, and relative to certain limited aspects of the social field, the accumulated piecemeal thinking of a series of years has begun to yield a body of precedents. Thus the Massachusetts Federation of Churches feels able to point to "a consistent record of ten years" in the advocacy of international peace, which it is perhaps justified in announcing as "an official position." The gradual building up of a system of precedents as related to local church locations and relocations has already been presented in the companion volume entitled *Church Comity*. Such results, however, even in limited areas, are most exceptional. On the contrary, the piecemeal nature of practical thinking, and the improvised philosophy through which decisions are characteristically reached, get continuous stress throughout the record.

In seeking an explanation for the temperamental tendency just noted, one is led to question whether it may not be a sense of the lack of agreement within the Protestant body upon basic philosophical postulates that has led the federations thus to press ahead with various types of service justified by no comprehensive theory. This would constitute a sort of protective device for covering up the fact of intellectual disunion.[14]

SMALL USE OF READY-MADE FORMULAS

Even a movement incapable of generalizing its own thinking might find use for ready-made formulas. This does not hold good in the case of the federations. The Federal Council's "Social Creed," for example, is annually recapitulated in the Labor Sunday Message and has a certain recognition as the expression of the common position of the churches.

But no evidence was found of the slightest effort to use this, or any similar formula, as an intellectual standard. Except for the St. Louis Federation, no case was discovered in which the systematic and repeated use and inculcation of the social creed had formed part of the federation's actual advocacy of social ideals.[15]

---

[14] For evidence that it looks this way to others, see Ross, "How Catholics See Protestants," *The Inquiry*, New York, 1928, p. 19 f.

[15] It ought incidentally to be noted that the social creed itself falls far short of being a comprehensive utterance of the Church's social thinking. It originated with an industrial commission and is distinctly overweighted on the side of industrial interests. It understates Christian thought relative to the family and the state as well as relative to international and interracial issues. An attempt to broaden out and balance up this statement occupied the attention of the Federal Council at its 1928 quadrennial meeting.

GENERALIZATION BY DRAMATIZATION

In no field in which it has to deal with numerous practical issues over long periods, can the mind get along without a synthesis of some sort. The mere accumulation of successive actions or resolutions inevitably tends to refer itself to and to cohere about some implied planetary center. There are, however, genuine alternatives to philosophies or systems of precedents. Men think in pictures as well as in concepts. Instead of rationalizing, it is possible to dramatize, and thus to create the possibility of unity of action as on a stage, or of unity of design as in a picture, without achieving unity of ideas.

Now this in effect is what a good many federations have done. They have substituted dramatization for generalization, and have found the ground of their actions in a work of constructive imagination rather than in a set of intellectual formulations. For this many reverend precedents exist. Indeed this tendency lies very close to the essential genius of Protestantism, if not of Christianity.

Thus a certain federation discerns behind the particular political and moral tensions of its state, a "conflict of two opposing tendencies." On the one hand stands secularism; on the other hand, "the new Puritanism—sane, scientific, restraining self and society for the sake of the life more abundant." On the side of Puritanism thus defined the church federation declares itself an agency "for mobilizing our two thousand churches on each issue, as fountain-heads of public opinion." Only two-fifths of the population of the state, it thinks, is at present ranged on the (Protestant) Church's side. To control results, the Church must win and educate another fifth. To do this it must increase its membership by 50 per cent. This can be accomplished by aggressive united evangelism. On one recent issue, the statement goes on to declare, "Nearly 100 per cent. coöperation was secured from the pastors of the state." Here is visualized a perfectly definite goal to be reached by intelligible means. This federation is looking forward to the good time when, by so mobilizing the augmented ecclesiastical forces of Protestantism, it can dominate in a wide area of public affairs. A good many other federations think after this literally sketchy fashion.

PRACTICAL THINKING NEGATIVE IN TENDENCY

Because thinking is done piecemeal under external pressure and little steadied by the ballast of adequate theory, tendencies of thought are predominantly negative. Thinking chiefly concerns the discovery of limitations.[16] It is defensive rather than constructive.[17] It indicates difficulties and counsels delays. It suggests what not to do. In general it weakens rather than strengthens the impulse to action. This is typically illustrated in resolutions of the board of directors of the Greater Boston Federation taken in successive years. The board first took action as follows:

> The Federation shall not be committed to any important action or opinion in matters chiefly political except by a two-thirds vote of all members of the Board of Directors present at any meeting of the Board in the call of which notice of such proposed action shall have been given to each member of the Board, provided, however, that in no case shall such action be taken by a vote of less than one-third of the entire Board.

During the following year this same federation found it expedient to follow up this resolution with one intended to curb the independent utterances of subcommittees. The resolution read:

> Resolved, that the Directors of the Greater Boston Federation of Churches reaffirm their conviction that it is a proper function of the Federation to voice, through the Board of Directors, the prevailing sentiment of the churches and religious organizations on all matters of public concern; that the Federation should be committed to any comment on such matters only by vote of the Board of Directors; and that it is expedient to take positive action for or against proposed legislation or in comment upon industrial, governmental, racial or international problems only when at least two-thirds of the Board of Directors vote affirmatively upon resolutions referred to the Board by the appropriate committee.

DEFENSIVE THINKING MEETING SPECIFIC ATTACKS

Another form of characteristic negative thinking may be called the defensive or counter-offensive type. This appears frequently in federation records. Certain broad general tendencies of the generation constitute implicit attacks upon conventional moral ideals and assumptions. Federations as such come under acute attacks. The manner and tone of thinking under these circumstances are essentially apologetic. It dares not assume a solid massing of the entire Protestant church behind any recognized and accepted principle.

[16] Pp. 239 and 240.
[17] P. 252.

SUPERFICIAL RESTATEMENTS OF CONVENTIONAL MORALITY

Controversial thinking might conceivably lead to a critical re-examination of the federation's implicit assumptions. What actually results is an occasional superficial restatement of some phase of Christian social morality in the light of modern views and tendencies. Thus, for example, in connection with "Sabbath observance" measures, a number of federations have been led to re-interpret their positions so as to base them on social grounds. They have, for example, connected the maintenance of a weekly day of rest with the eight-hour movement and the Saturday half-holiday. In other cases the problem of the ethics of gambling has been rephrased. Still other issues, whose solution the conventional Christian takes for granted, have also been somewhat inadequately reconsidered in the light of the peremptory challenge of the modern world. But no radical ethical reformulation has been forthcoming.

TENDENCY TO CONCESSION AND COMPROMISE

All movements experience opposition and go forward by means of concession and compromise. The peculiar composition of federations, their history and feebleness, together with the stress on representativeness, all conspire to magnify this characteristic in their case. The federation secretary tries to give to all something of what they want and is ordinarily prepared to concede something to anybody who raises strong objection to what is proposed. Thus, the secretary confesses to "doing a bit of wowsering" to satisfy constituents who clamor for activity in law-enforcement; to backing an evangelistic campaign for which he has no immediate relish because influential churches desire it; or to promoting a Federal Council proposal that he devoutly wishes had never been made. This is the penalty for trying to be all things to all men. It marks the operation of federations as a practical art little guided by rationalized considerations.

ACCUMULATION OF TABOOS

Within a movement thus dominated by concession and compromise, federations whose position is at all precarious tend to build up systems of taboos. These, in many instances, become so numerous as greatly to limit the federation's freedom of activity and development. To the original prohibition of any discussion of theological differences are added whole decalogues of other restrictive commandments. Any practical failure is likely to result in sealing up a whole area of discussion. The federation must not raise issues of industrial justice or racial relationships; it dare not tackle the problem of the relation of women's organizations; it must maintain total silence about the local organization of religious education; to raise any question of relationships with the Young Men's Christian Association is utterly anathema. Still less can church union be talked about openly. Ultimately there is very little which the federation can frankly discuss except accepted routine. The resulting mood cannot be very courageous.

CHARACTERISTIC PRACTICES AND POLICIES

DEPARTMENTALIZATION

A consequence (in part) of fragmentary thinking and the lack of central integrating ideas is the sharply departmentalized machinery of federation practice. Federations divide their work on the basis of segmentation by age and sex which already dominates the organization of local churches and denominations.[18] They further fix the departmental idea by admitting independent organizations which they are unable genuinely to absorb, to a sort of dangling attachment.[19] Finally, they rationalize and routinize this separation of functions in a scheme of committee machinery,[20] according to which each interest is separately staffed and financed.

Now, all this conspires to keep federation thinking departmental. That is to say, thought goes on in the terms of the frequently inefficient machinery of action. It is much easier to accept and handle ideas that do not disturb the existing machinery but can be immediately carried out by its means. Consequently, integrated thinking that cuts across departmental lines and puts like together with like in despite of departmental labels—and that might even require a federation to make itself over—is exceptional and difficult.

UNCRITICAL ACCEPTANCE OF COMMITTEE SYSTEM

Organized Protestant coöperation is firmly wedded to a system of representative committees.[21] Functions, though limited, are minutely apportioned, and responsibility is subdivided among very numerous groups of this sort. All coöperating denominations are supposed to be represented on each committee in due proportion. By what infallible revelation the

---

[18] P. 105.
[19] P. 80.
[20] P. 143.
[21] Chapter XVI.

coöperative movement discovered that it can conduct its business only through such an elaborate system, no objective consideration fully explains. What is in general clear is that vogue of this system reflects the effort to make the movement denominationally acceptable. The voluntary committee, of course, furnishes cheap and inexpert machinery roughly democratic in theory, considerably less so in fact. A few federations minimize the committee system, but they only serve to throw the all but universality of the method into higher relief. The investigation discloses the system's many shortcomings; but the movement in general has never seriously contemplated whether or not there may be some better way of carrying on.

LARGE USE OF UNTRAINED VOLUNTEERS

The committee system means that federations depend upon large numbers of non-professional volunteers. No other departments of federation work employ so many paid professionals as those of religious education and social service. At the same time, none is more likely to rally groups of lay members for unpaid personal work under the federation banner. Religious education traditionally requires armies of Sunday-school leaders, now supplemented by vacation-school and to some extent, by week-day school teachers.[22] Coöperation with social agencies largely furnishes the key to federation social work. Federations that attempt to perform a liaison function between the Church and social agencies, are likely to have to recruit and train large numbers of lay people as visitors, group leaders, entertainers, clerical aids, transportation aids, etc.[23] Evangelism also—though discontinuously—calls for large numbers of lay workers in visitation campaigns.[24] It is characteristic of the movements then, to have large use for lay volunteers.

INEXPERT PROFESSIONALS

In its present form, organized Protestant coöperation is a young movement that has not yet developed a professional leadership of its own with fully elaborated and well-established standards.[25] Its masses of lay volunteers are not led by a continuous body of men especially trained for their work nor with long experience in it. This is equally true of general executives and those who serve in specialized capacities. The typical federation secretary is a minister, occasionally a former

---

[22] Pp. 347 and 350.
[23] P. 394.
[24] P. 335.
[25] Pp. 146 ff. and Chapter XVII.

denominational executive, who occupies his present position more or less accidentally and temporarily and who must cling to his former denominational standing as a minister, particularly with respect to future preferment and retirement pensions. He is essentially an experimenter who must get his training on the job. He dodges here and there among the checks and balances of denominational control to find an opening in which the federation may function. He must necessarily walk delicately, because so few established fields of acknowledged leadership have been permanently committed to him. His functions are not settled by conventions as is the case with the pastor; nor is there a routine of ecclesiastical supervision as would be furnished by a denominational bishop or superintendent. The secretary must write a part for himself to play, a part acceptable to his constituency; and he must attempt to create the character which the part calls for. The existence of a few picked men who have fairly won their spurs must not blind one to the essentially inexpert character of the average professional federation leader.

A SLENDERLY SUPPORTED MOVEMENT

Whether representative of fifty, one hundred, two hundred and fifty, or a thousand churches, a church federation is likely to have only the staff and resources of a single more than average church of the community concerned.[26] Relatively speaking, the coöperative churches put no more than the slenderest resources behind their common agency. The median annual budget is about $13,500. All judgments upon the scope and variety of the coöperative program, as well as with respect to the general effectiveness of the movement, must consider its limited resources. Even such liberty of functioning as is theoretically allowed is thus practically circumscribed. The coöperating forces as yet do not intend to give federations adequate resources with which to carry on in their behalf.

UNSTANDARDIZED METHODS

In glaring contrast to the extraordinary vogue and authority of the committee pattern is the exceeding variety of the subordinate methods used by federations. With respect to staff, finances, facilities, and other practical resources, no single tendency prevails. As compared with the methods of the local church or of the denominations, federation work is experimental

---

[26] Pp. 143 ff. and 448 f.

and unstandardized. It has ventured into uncharted realms and has not yet had time to put the experiences of the various explorers together into a consistent story.

UNEVEN PROMOTION

The activities of any still plastic institutions are naturally modified by the personal emphases or biases of their leaders. The paid leaders of federations vary greatly in the vigor, seriousness, and originality they employ, especially in the more novel and less established aspects of federation work.

As an external promotional agency, the Federal Council also exerts very uneven pressure. If it were not for the activity of certain Federal Council departments, notably those of industrial and interracial relationships, social service in the local federations would represent itself in very different proportions than it actually has. Existing emphasis is quite definitely the result of Federal Council initiative and prodding.[27]

INFLATED PROMOTIONAL CLAIMS

The classic temptations of feeble institutions that cherish high visions is to get vision and reality mixed in public statements. Federations have not infrequently fallen into this error of feeble institutions. They overadvertise. They make inflated promotional statements and overplay their hopes and ambitions when more effective expositions of their actual prospects and achievements would be more honest and convincing.

The foregoing account of the characteristics of federations shows all too conclusively that they are not adequately equipped with steering devices that enable them to fly straight in the prevailing fog, nor with stabilizers sufficient to keep them on even keel under all circumstances. They are fragile and highly experimental devices operated by entirely fallible men.

Many considerations challenge this as a final verdict. These impose a certain obligation to attempt some statement of the grounds of a verdict that shall keep the entire data in view, even though it cannot pretend to stay within the realm of strictly scientific deductions, and must reflect in large measure conclusions that may be peculiar to the investigator.

VERDICT

RELATION OF RESULTS TO RESOURCES

As it appears to the author, the relation of federation resources to results must first be considered. What they have

---

[27] Pp. 386 and 388.

conceived and undertaken is obviously beyond their powers at many points; and further expansion of their functions must wait, in the main, upon the mobilization of stronger forces behind the enterprise.

In considering the work of church federations, the very first necessity is thus to arrive at a reasonable viewpoint. The high-sounding name borne by these agencies tends at the outset to create an inflated expectation with respect to their results. Here are movements professing to lead in the total range of concerns held in common by the Protestant agencies. Yet, as repeatedly noted, the average federation has the financial support and the working force of only a single good-sized church. Whatever a federation does, it does with such relatively limited resources. Magnitude of results is limited by the small average size of the total enterprise; or, considering aggregates, a paid force of 131 workers, with a budget of $360,000 cannot adequately conduct the central and common interests of nearly 8,000 churches with a probable staff of 10,500, an annual budget of $186,000,000, and property worth nearly one billion dollars.[28] As an overhead enterprise this is too small.

Federation work might well be carried on more selectively at certain points; it can hardly become commanding until the movement can enlarge itself all around.

DEPENDABLE LOYALTY OF CONSTITUENTS

A second factor of highest importance in reaching a verdict on the federation is the fact of the dependable loyalty of the central body of the constituents. An important part of the data of the present study was the result of measurement and comparison of the general attitudes of constituents of the several federations.[29] Constituents, as a group, are strongly behind the programs of federations in all departments; but they also show marked ability to discriminate among the several aspects of the programs. Their verdict accordingly cannot be discounted as a mere rubber-stamping of the decisions of officials, the wisdom of which is taken on faith and backed through prejudice. The rank and file know their own preferences and assert them while strongly backing the movement as a whole and in its more significant details.

---

[28] Cf. Chapter XI.
[29] Pp. 135 and 136.

VITALITY HEIGHTENED BY SELECTIVE MORTALITY

All told then, in spite of its frequent institutional feebleness and instability, the current movement of organized Protestant coöperation impresses one as having extraordinary vitality and promise. This is not to close one's eyes to many evidences of failure at many points. The long list of lapsed federations may, however, probably be regarded as reflecting a selective mortality which leaves the survivors the more assured of continuance and strength. Within the major cities which this study has chiefly considered, the federation movement is thoroughly entrenched. Any real doubt which persists has to do with federation in the smaller cities, the states and rural districts. All that is maintained for the present is that it has become part of the established order of the urban church.

A VERSATILE AND UNEXHAUSTED MOVEMENT

What the federation movement will ultimately come to does not yet appear. It is still very much in the making. The author is personally persuaded that the genius of the movement is bound somehow to escape its narrow limits and to fulfill itself in some of the realms of larger promise which the rank and file of the church so stubbornly ascribe to it. In his mind the larger significance of it does not lie in these areas of the coöperative functioning of the churches through specific means and methods which the report has described in laborious detail, but rather in the moral gesture which is thus symbolized.

PRACTICAL VIRTUES GREATLY OUTWEIGH INTELLECTUAL AND MORAL QUALITIES

To complete his verdict upon the federation movement the author, therefore, cannot avoid reiterating what, from this standpoint, he senses as its chief lack: It is not profound enough for the ends which it seeks. Here is a practical achievement of the greatest significance, incarnating one of the supreme impulses of the Church, in the carrying out of which the more admirable intellectual and moral qualities are not sufficiently in evidence. The movement succeeds on practical levels by the utilization of naïve impulses and the avoidance of major difficulties, not primarily because of penetrating thought or high courage and leadership.

The specific complaint lies against the failure of the federation movement to find, and indeed its general avoidance of any attempt to find, a basic philosophical and religious ground-work for itself.

Such an attitude was perhaps excusable at the outset. At its inception, the movement had to rally the dissimilar religious bodies into some kind of a working fellowship. Consequently, there was strong motive for conceiving and announcing itself as concerned exclusively with the church's life and work, and not at all with the more difficult problems of its faith and order. But such an attitude ought to be inconceivable as a permanent policy, and is no longer tenable.

For this conviction the author finds three major reasons. First, as has already been reiterated, the federation movement does not publicly stress and on the whole does not vitally regard the deepest character and values that a large number of its constituents find in it. Even the fragmentary utterances of any group of constituents reveal a larger significance in the movement than its leaders are effectively proclaiming.

In the second place, a changed mood has come over the religious world within recent years. Thinking about coöperation has the advantage of what Dr. Samuel M. Cavert aptly calls "a changed climate." Now issues can be talked about the mention of which formerly would have produced a cataclysm. While the federation movement, governed by old fears, has been bound by the assumption that its larger implications—with respect, for example, to church union—are undiscussable, more daring movements have appeared focussing themselves on such world conferences as those at Lausanne and Jerusalem, and are independently springing up into church-union proposals in numerous mission fields. These have faced and stated mutual differences and measured agreements and disagreements without producing an explosion or setting back practical coöperative measures. Whether or not any theoretical gains have been made, their effort was at least philosophically conceived and acknowledged gains in mutual comprehension and integration of purpose have resulted. Undoubtedly, the practice of coöperation through federations has measurably contributed to the new mood; yet without itself profiting intellectually by it. "Twenty years ago," declares Dr. A. E. Cory, "the Federal Council was the most daring thing on the denominational horizon; but what was daring twenty years ago is not daring now." Should not the federation movement now freely enter into its share of the era of profounder and braver thinking?

Finally, it is not too much to say that the world is achieving a new moral attitude toward conflict situations. According to this newer analysis, conflicting opinions and purposes, say as between nations or between employers and employees, are most dangerous when unacknowledged and unconfronted. So long as they are not mutually faced, the door to their solution is completely shut. Their poison works inwardly. On the contrary, it is precisely through the tension of confronting divergent views together that "new values get their first due attention," and the possibility of agreement including, and thereby modifying disagreement, is created. From this viewpoint, the feeling that basic differences between coöperating religious bodies cannot be faced is an ignoble one—a sort of hiding of one's head in the sand.

The author feels, then, that there is a moral demand, which cannot longer be ignored, for the creating of some common intellectual instrument for rationalizing and synthesizing the federation movement, and for expressing the grounds of its assumed unity, as well as to serve as a basis for testing its practical objectives and policies.

It is permitted to doubt whether an attempted agreement upon some creedal formulation of the common faith or some all-inclusive doctrine of the Church is what is needed. Very likely even these would be better than no means of synthesis at all. But one is not reduced to this alternative. The process of synthesis should start with a generalization of federation's own facts and experiences. Beyond this, the unifying instrument may consist merely of a set of working hypotheses most tentatively combined into a philosophy and subject to continuous criticism and revision. Even so, a function would get performed that a loosely defined coöperative tradition, on the one hand, and improvised piecemeal deductions from particular experiences, on the other, cannot possibly effect. The roughing out of such an instrument is, in the author's view, the most conspicuous need of the federation movement at the present moment.

The author therefore feels compelled to associate himself with a judgment of the movement of Protestant coöperation pronounced a decade ago by Dr. Robert E. Speer:

> There is only one other difficulty of which I would be speaking, and that is this orgy of energism that we are passing through, that bids men everywhere to do something, not to be still and to know; that robs us of the gains, and the absolutely essential gains, only reaped when men sit down deliberately to think out their courses of action before they plunge. We have not taken time enough to put prayer and deep reflection into our plans of Christian activity. I think it was a true criticism that one of our

British friends passed just a few months ago when he was here studying our American contemporary religious movements. "Yes," said he in effect, as he went back, "you are painting a very big picture, but I don't think you are mixing brains enough with your paint." And while it was a rather painful criticism, it was just. We need far more grave study, far more deliberate thought, far more penetrating and intelligent setting of our schemes against great backgrounds, than we have ventured as yet to take time for.[30]

---

[30] Guild (ed.) *Community Programs for Coöperating Churches* (New York: Association Press), Chapter X, p. 216.

Chapter XV

SOME LARGER MEANINGS OF THE CHURCH FEDERATION MOVEMENT

As the previous chapters have shown, the movement of organized Protestant coöperation manifests itself in a great variety of forms. It is entangled in very large relationships. Its participants feel that it is pregnant with profound implications. What one can see of the performance of federations without looking behind the scenes has just been summarized. But no set of phenomena so great and complex could possibly be covered fully by a study of its mere institutional aspects. Moreover, the evidence which the study has produced is conflicting at many points. Here is a movement obviously in unstable equilibrium, presenting alternatives rather than a single clear-cut probability. It is at once more significant than its claims and less so; at once more successful in fact than in form; and still unable completely to fill its forms with vitality.

Long contact with, and reflection upon, closely-related facts inevitably tempts the mind to give itself such a connected account as it can of all the phenomena. This search for explanations and meanings will obviously stay with, and be bound by, the concrete and measurable data so far as the data, as investigated, will carry it forward. Ordinarily one may freely draw upon such previously established knowledge, or other sources of rationality as one thinks one has, in the effort to make the largest sense of the situation.

But he who is presenting the results of objective study of any phenomena stands on a somewhat different footing. He must at this point make a decision. Either he will keep the meanings he thinks he has discovered to himself, or he will announce them on his own responsibility; not as an exhaustive or exclusive version of the truth, but as possibly significant material for criticism. On the whole, it is by this latter method that science goes forward; and it is in this spirit that the author offers the following interpretation of the church federation movement.

THE HISTORIC MOVEMENT

The reality behind any historic movement showing continuity is that some social group is forming or reforming itself, and that its stuff is being strained in the process. The church federations define their limits varyingly, they try to get into the fold those who belong there, and to keep them belonging; try to keep the excluded out, or let them in part way; strive to hold the diversities of the included within bounds, and to allow the total group to be modified only gradually and within limits lest it fall to pieces under the evolutionary stress.

Here, in a word, is a perfectly classic example of the struggle between permanence and change, between order and progress. Federation at every step is challenged either by older divisive instincts or by impulses toward a still more complete integration of the Protestant group, or by both. Certain denominations enter the movement more hesitantly than do others, and tend to keep it slowed down once they are in. Others enter it more quickly, and press forward sooner into its more dynamic phases. Either extreme must be tempered and restrained.

As the outcome of this conflict, the prevailing temper of the group comes to array itself, either temporarily or permanently, on the side of one principle or another. At any given time it tends to reflect either the triumph of order over progress or of progress over order.

ACHIEVEMENT OF A DOMINANT TEMPER

The special version of the basic conflict between order and progress habitually appears in church movements as a conflict between two types of personality, formed in turn partly by native temper and partly by the particular social situations. The conservative, on the one hand, wants to preserve the existing ecclesiastical order—in the present case contemporary denominationalism. He is jealous for its most shadowy values and equities. A stickler for the letter of ecclesiastical legitimacy, he must be satisfied with the complete formal authority of any movement.

The innovator, on the contrary, regards any religious movement, such as church federation, as a process rather than as an organization with a fixed character. As he senses it, the essential spirit of the movement may well be in advance of its authorized leadership. His conscience is clear, therefore, if he represents the constituency as intending what he is sure it will intend when the meaning of its present attitudes has been made clear to itself. This he identifies with what he himself now intends in its behalf.

The genius of religion being what it is, any vital church movement may be expected to exhibit the conflict of these two types.

Labeling them by particular names makes their differences neither greater nor less; but, through the ages, they have been most often identified with the ecclesiastic in contrast with the prophet.

Now the achievement of working unity in the Protestant group through federation is so recent that the dominant tendency is to conserve the dearly-bought gains. In this it only repeats familiar history: Many an allied army has stopped fighting at the end of one great advance because afraid to face the consequences of further victory upon the relations of the allies to one another. The principle of order, rather than that of progress, is, for the moment, definitely uppermost. Church federation means coöperative denominationalism; that is to say, the dominance of the ecclesiastic and as little disturbance as possible of the newly-established status quo.

ACTUAL ECCLESIASTICAL DOMINANCE

That the advantage of the conflict is strongly with the ecclesiastic at present is evidenced in many ways. It is evidenced by the structure of the movement. Conspicuous care is given to the safeguarding of the denominational order in all formal agreements. Constitutions reaffirm the old allegiances and are phrased to show that denominational interests are in no way impaired; they promise that denominational liberty of action shall not be abridged. Churches can get out of the federation movement at any time and find their previous status intact.

Not only is the existing ecclesiastical order safeguarded, but it clearly receives the dominant emphasis. Any purpose to change this order is explicitly denied, according to exposition and sales-talk. Federation merely supplements, and in no way alters, the present status of the churches.[1]

Still again, the veto power of denominationalism vitally determines the scope of federation programs; and their actual development comes only when, and at places where, this power is temporarily or in part broken down.[2]

NUMERICAL PREPONDERANCE OF THE CLERGY ON FEDERATION COMMITTEES

Still further evidence that the ecclesiastic is in the saddle is found in the overwhelming preponderance of clergymen on federation committees, and in provision for the dominance of denominational executives as *ex officio* members.[3] Local churches

---

[1] Chapter IV.
[2] Chapter VII.
[3] Pp. 300 and 308.

are institutionally operated by lay officials; the major denominations require at least an equal number of laymen and of clergymen in their governing assemblies; but the coöperative machinery is in the hands of those who live by ecclesiastical order. Many—perhaps most—of these men genuinely desire working unity of a sort—but whose sort should it be if not their own? No group has done more to bring coöperation to its present point; none will do more to keep it from getting out of hand or from following its own inner urge if this should carry it beyond the safety point as sensed by the official group.

ECCLESIASTICAL ORDER GUARANTEED BY NATIONAL RELATIONSHIPS

Still further, the national relationships of the local federations commit the movement to denominational regularity. The Federal Council is literally interdenominational; most of the local federations are new Protestant entities potentially under their own headway. The units of the Federal Council are the denominations as such, whereas those of the local federations are usually individual churches entering into free covenants of coöperation with one another across denominational lines. Such agencies have to be watched by their denominational leaders lest they kick over the traces in their federated capacity. The situation is made safer, denominationally speaking, because it is headed up in a national system strictly subject to denominational action.

The coöperative movement as a whole, then, is definitely fixed in the clamps of current denominationalism. This is no news; for it was so intended and is so professed. Indeed, the denominations have contrived to strengthen their position through its connection with the federation movement. They are following a probably sound instinct in feeling that if they coöperate a little, Protestant public opinion will be slower in forcing them to a degree of unity for which they are not ready

A REMINISCENTLY PROPHETIC MOVEMENT

The federation movement, however, remains reminiscently prophetic. It includes, for example, one essentially non-conformist sphere. This is the sphere of social service, an original instinct of the movement that has run through it continuously as a wire vibrating to its own peculiar waves. It is the least ecclesiastical of the coöperative interests, and the one least influenced by the denominational viewpoint. It starts with the needs of people and communities. Its mood is to press forward by such means as the occasion demands, disregardful of denominational cautions.

Chiefly by virtue of this element in it, federation—although essentially a middle-of-the-road movement—has been turned a little toward the left wing of Protestant progress. It has consistently tried to preserve balance between extremes; and it is only by virtue of this inner tendency that the movement keeps a certain capacity for finding its own center of gravity. Some federations more than others retain a prophetic impulse not quite brought into captivity to ecclesiastical regularity and the mind of the majority.

Women's organizations and young people's departments especially exhibit a certain independence of the ecclesiastical dominance. Along with radically socially-minded souls, they constitute the non-conformist minority[4] in a movement which is essentially stabilized—haunted only by occasional memories or disturbed by infrequent dreams.

THE EVOLUTIONARY PROCESSES

But even were the federation movement actually progressive and self-critical with completest frankness in vogue, one could not hope to extract its full meaning from observation and analysis merely of its historic moods and conflicts. What underlies the whole range of overt facts? How explain the movement as such?

The study as a whole seems to the writer to make increasingly tenable the hypothesis that the current coöperative movement is due to objective processes of assimilation going on within the historical group roughly identified by the Protestant name. If the Protestant people and churches are working together better than formerly, it is because they feel more kinship for one another. This, in turn, is a reflection of the fact that they are at once mutually producing and absorbing a common culture. The factual evidence bearing upon this conclusion was presented in Chapter II.

The data thus presented emphatically demonstrated the high consistency between actual membership and participation in the federations and the strength or weakness of the sense of barrier or distance between various members of the Protestant groups that habitually coöperate in federations, and between them and persons of other faiths and denominations. The organizational lines and limits observed by the actual agencies almost exactly

---

[4] Pp. 436 and 445.

reflect the actual feelings of large bodies of religious people toward one another.[5]

In general, this series of facts seems to prove that federations are the expression of varying degrees of like-mindedness. The denominations of which, in the main, they are made up do not feel far apart either on theoretical or practical issues. The movement hesitates, however, to include churches that vary even slightly from the central group on historical or psychological grounds, even when they agree substantially in theology. It practically excludes the marginal Protestant groups that are unimpeachably orthodox. It tolerates, and that only occasionally, no more than incidental relations with Jews or Catholics. A federation, then, is an organization that excludes the unlike, includes the like, and associates the like in different degrees and manners according to the actual degrees of their likeness, as established by evolution.

FUTURE EXTENSION OF ORGANIZED COÖPERATION

If this principle explains the past, it is safe to suppose that any future extension of organized coöperation must be conditioned upon the still more compelling sweep of assimilating processes, which shall align together groups now excluded when these have undergone some modification in their culture and consequent change in their feelings. How far such a realignment can be influenced or hastened by deliberate effort, and how fast, only experimentation can determine. The impulse to try either to hasten or to retard the day of more inclusive unity must of course seek independent warrant on moral grounds.

ASSIMILATION THE ESSENCE OF UNITY

Further federation, then, must wait on assimilation. Anyone who is disappointed by this verdict can, however, take comfort in the fact that assimilation has, if not legally the last word, at least the actually determining word in coöperation. So far as assimilation is actually achieved, the substantial grounds of group unity are already laid. Without it, federation is hard to get. With it, federation is hard to prevent. Ecclesiastical action can little more than register the accomplished fact. Whether the unity thus expressed be called federative or organic is of some importance, but in the long run must be regarded as incidental to more fundamental social processes. Sociology then agrees with the long-time insistence of pious people that a spiritual unity must precede any visible unification of the divided Church.

---

[5] P. 27.

Sociology, moreover, supplies a certain suspicion that spiritual unity might not be instantly recognized and welcomed even when it arrived. According to analogy, a lag might be expected between the achievement of common culture and the ability to overcome the inertia of entrenched organizations. Thus the inertia of the established order in the Church might unquestionably retard the visible expression of such unity as exists. In this view, instead of ecclesiasticism having to wait on assimilation as a warrant and ground of unity, assimilation is having to wait on ecclesiasticism. Disunion is so buttressed that no normal play of evolutionary forces can pull it loose.

From the sociological viewpoint, the achievement of like-mindedness and a common religious culture would constitute objective religious unity—unity in no mystical sense and in no attenuated sentimental version such as might say "I love Henry, but I don't like him." Rather it would be the unifying result of a deeply objective social process more profound than any subsequent registering of the fact by the Church.

FEDERATION AS A SYMBOL OF COMMON FEELING AND ASPIRATION

By a profoundly correct instinct, which has repeatedly revealed itself, the rank and file of the federations' constituents have apprehended the fact of inner likeness as the deepest characteristic of the Protestant group, and have allied themselves with federation as a testimony to their essential unity. This is the meaning both of their pronouncements and their attitudes as measured. The data prove how consistently the church federation movement is given more than institutional significance in the minds of adherents and opponents alike.[6] Any or all of its concrete aspects are subordinated to its emotional value as related to fraternal unity. The enormous symbolic meaning thus assigned to the movement is in strange contrast with the very limited practical scope it is permitted to have. Men think of the church federation as they think of the Church itself, as no mere earthly institution. Their judgments of it refuse to be bound by utilitarian results, or to be overinterested in the details of programs. Imagination will not bring itself down to the small proportion of federation resources. Scant attention is paid to the shortcomings of agents. It is as a gesture toward church unity that the federation movement interests men. It is as an emblem that they love it or dread it.

It is not, therefore, a true account of the working of constitu-

---

[6] Cf. Chapter IV.

ents' minds to contrast slight organizational magnitude and
accomplishment with exalted attitudes and ideals, or to treat
the discrepancy between the two as an example of failure. The
constituents' characteristic position treats the situation as a case
of the transcendence of an ideal over the mere objective facts.
In the terms of popular usage, federation is not just another
organization, nor is it an organization that falls short of its
purpose. It is equally a purpose that inherently surpasses any
possible organization it may create. Its importance as a goal is
entirely superior to its importance as an agency.

The stubbornness of this characteristic attitude was not fore-
seen. Only continuous dealing with the evidence has shown how
profoundly the constituency regards the federation as an omen,
the significance of which is largely independent of facts as they
relate to concrete functioning or practical success.

It is then nothing peculiar to them as federations that makes
these organizations behave as they do, but rather the outworking
of deep-seated phenomena of a social group under evolution.

PRACTICAL PROBLEMS

The recognized practical problems of church federation do
scant justice either to the richness of the primal force and quality of the historic movement or to the profundity and dominance
of the evolutionary process. The points at which the movement
feels responsibility and practical concern are properly those at
which it believes that it is able to do something about the situation. At these it sets up rationally defined objectives with the
view to directing its purposeful effort. About these objectives
it thinks within the permitted limits; with respect to them it
organizes, but without much attempt directly to control sentiment or to hasten or retard the assimilation of cultures. In the
main, the movement remains unconscious of the gravitational
forces that hold it in its course.

CONCERN WITH COMPLEXITY AND COMPETITION

In its own consciousness, the federation movement is the outstanding reaction of the Protestant church to the challenge of
overcomplication in its ecclesiastical machinery and of rivalry
among its constituent denominations.[7] It is the Church trying
to remedy these twin ecclesiastical evils. In the majority of
large cities, existing federations have reduced the former by the
coördination of Protestant ecclesiastical agencies and the absorp-
tion of previously independent organizations into the federation

---

[7] Pp. 22 and 23.

scheme. Undoubtedly, too, they have prevented many new organizations that would otherwise have been separately initiated. Not only has the feeling of fraternity and coöperation been substituted for that of competition, but literally thousands of concrete measures all along the line have displaced formerly competitive activities. This is at once the essential feature of the movement and its most obvious achievement.

In some cities, however, it must be confessed that the movement, thus far, has added to the excess of church machinery rather than reduced it. Indeed this is perhaps true at some points in most cities. The denominations have not really submitted their separate activities to coördination nor given over to the federations any significant range of functions. They are rather keeping on with all that they had before and maintaining the federations in addition.[8] A possible remedy for complexity rather than a completed solution is what the data prove. Whether federations have succeeded as well on this point as they should have, must be judged with respect to the relative brevity of their history and the inherent difficulties of their problem. The trend at least is definitely toward coördination and coöperative spirit. Certainly no other movement rivals the federations in their direct and practical attack upon the evils of the divided church.

MORE ULTIMATE PROBLEMS

Historic momentum, underlying evolution and purposeful effort have coöperated to bring the federation movement to its present status and phase; but have left it struggling with ultimate problems common to social organizations, problems that neither one nor all can fully solve. It is imperative that attention be paid to these problems because, in the conviction of many, only in the light of them can it be determined whether or not federations can serve as the vehicle for a permanent integration of the Church.

AUTHORITY

Take, for example, the problems of authority and of government. Federation practice seems to imply a special version of the Protestant church's attempted solutions of these issues, but one not very clearly defined. Somewhat equivocal traits are evidenced in the federation movement. As is commonly recognized, Protestantism is neither consistently authoritarian nor consistently scientific. While tolerating science and while pos-

---

[8] Pp. 121 ff.

sibly capable of ultimately achieving a scientific position, its traditional appeal is still to authority. The scientist does not really belong within the ecclesiastical scene anywhere. This, as has been shown, leaves the contest between unity and variety to be personalized in two types, both authoritarian, namely, the ecclesiastic and the prophet.

ECCLESIASTICAL AUTHORITARIANISM

The ecclesiastic's source of authority—however varyingly he may define it—is a common tradition. Positions assumed to be held more or less generally by the Church are accepted uncritically as working postulates. As has been noted, denominational variations tend to be ignored. These variations are chiefly significant of criticisms of authoritative dogmas. The investigator watched federation officials dodging such issues time and again. Virtue is made of the avoidance of controversy. But this deprives the movement of its chief means of protest against ecclesiastical authoritarianism. It is impossible to over-emphasize the impoverishing results of this characteristic position upon federation as a religious movement.

PROPHETIC AUTHORITARIANISM

Equally authoritarian logic following a different line is seen in the efforts of the more prophetic elements of federation thought to establish their own relatively novel positions.

The source of authority to which they appeal is the Gospel. This appeal is implicit in the terms "social gospel" and in such slogans as "the practical implications of Christianity"; as well as the frequent definition of social service as "an attempt to apply the teachings of Christ to the relations of life." [9] It is tacitly assumed that rules for the Christian's social conduct may be derived straight from the New Testament and fitted to particular modern cases. The result is an attempt at authoritative preaching on many issues that actually remain in hot debate by the religious people.

A THIRD POSSIBILITY

Now, recognizing that it is natural, inevitable, and right for the mind to try to tie up its present convictions to the more illuminating sources of the past, the question remains whether one can actually derive a program, or even find step-by-step guidance, in a Testament, new or old. Is it possible to pass from principles to conduct by way of any process of authoritative

---

[9] P. 45.

interpretation? Is there not rather a danger amounting almost to a certainty that, in connection with such an effort, masses of traditional philosophy or ethics will be read back into the sources? Can one slightly rearrange and extend old patterns of thought and match them with present issues? Finally, were the implications of the New Testament, even if perfectly implied, meant to be all-inclusive?

SIGNIFICANCE OF POSITION WITH RESPECT TO AUTHORITY

The outstanding importance of the position of church federations with respect to authority lies in their strong disposition to use power whenever and so far as they can get it. This is evidenced in the prevalence of committees on political action and moral reform; in the stress on legislation and law-enforcement, strongly backed as it is by constituencies. The rank and file of federation supporters are very solidly behind their efforts to put Protestant pressure upon the agents of government in behalf of social morality, measures of this type being favored by more than four-fifths of the constituents replying to questionnaires.[10] What is popularly spoken of as law-enforcement shows an especially high ratio of approval. This, with concomitant political agitation, appears to be in line with deep instincts of American Protestants. One has to raise the question whether a good many ecclesiastical leaders are not examples of the will-to-power. What else is the meaning of the attempt to force the State, by pressure of consolidated Protestant opinion, to use its physical force to restrain the evil and establish the good?

Now, it will make a real difference in the practice of federations—say as to law-enforcement or measures in connection with an industrial strike—whether one assumes that the matter may be settled by appeal to some type of authority; or whether it must be held altogether open for further testing by experience; or whether one may at least adopt a tentative plan of action subject to revision. In the latter case, trustworthy clues to action may be found in proved relationships between tentative hypotheses and provisional judgments (some of the best of which may well be received from the past) and bodies of fact studied by the most objective means available—always with the aid of the most vital insights of a sensitive ethical intelligence. Results thus reached may be trusted to assert themselves in the strength of their own vigor, and permitted to make such sense of the situation as they can without reference to any external

---

[10] P. 418.

authority. Which of these positions will the federation movement finally incarnate in its actions? Obviously the decision will affect the degree of hopefulness and confidence with which different minds can regard it.

REGULATIVE DEVICES: REPRESENTATIVE DEMOCRACY

What one is really observing in the study of the government of federations is a social group using a regulating device whereby its internal conflicts are provided with methods of adjustment. The Protestant church had large part in discovering for western civilization the typical means for this purpose, namely, representative democracy. This it has transferred to the use of the federation movement uncritically as something to be taken for granted.

Now, on general principles, it is a fair question whether an important reapplication of any traditional instrument should be made without a re-investigation of the meaning and applicability of the instrument. For, in the thought of many of the Christian communions, a succession of apostolically ordained authorities, by appointment of Christ himself, constitutes an essential if not the predominant element in giving validity to any action of the Church. Certainly such a fact challenges reconsideration of the theory of representativeness when the instrument virtually rejects other ecclesiastical alternatives and becomes the weapon of a powerful movement.

For the federation movement, if successful, will put reality and force behind the working philosophy that the consensus of Protestant opinion, ascertained through the forms of representative interchurch government, is right. This will be accepted and acted upon by millions of people.[11] Such a possibility renders it most necessary to observe wherein the representative character of church federations is presumed to consist.

REPRESENTATIVENESS

The vast emphasis which the federation movement puts upon representativeness, together with the recorded sensitiveness of its constituents on this point, indicates its crucial nature. There is obviously a two-fold problem. Federations have to ask how they are to secure formal representativeness through some system of delegated responsibility on the part of the bodies that ultimately coöperate. But a still more important question faces them beyond the purely mechanical processes of democracy, namely, how actually to create common sentiment.

---

[11] P. 66.

The formal aspect of the matter was thoroughly explored in the data of the present study.[12] The coöperating entities are churches and denominations. They seek to read representative character into what they do by making the number of representatives strictly proportionate to the numerical strength of the denominations or other bodies represented. The appointed delegates are presumed to display the particular characteristics of their respective bodies for whose special interests they stand. The formal structure of the federation movement is based on this principle; by virtue of it, the federation assumes to have become the organ of Protestantism.

But even when the resulting system of delegates and committees has acquired the organizational virtues of valid parliamentary procedure and good committee performance, when it has drawn forth the loyalty of an institutional constituency, only a preliminary type of representativeness has been attained. These conditions amount to little more than a very important framework of behavior through which more vital processes may be worked out. When these vital processes are in temporary confusion and conflict, the whole mechanical arrangement is debased into mere grinding of parliamentary wheels.

The positive and inner reality of the representative processes is reached only when the group of formal delegates have coöperatively achieved a body of agreement superior to the mere alternating compromises such as the adjustment of their partisan positions demands. In all the more effective federations, the legally designated machinery of delegates and committeemen sometimes actually rises to something of this super-representativeness. The time comes when it is not in any particular sense Methodist or Presbyterian sentiment that a Methodist or Presbyterian delegate expresses. It is, rather, common sentiment held in behalf of Protestantism as a whole. From this viewpoint, it is only in an inferior sense that representation constitutes a device for sampling the divergent viewpoints of constituency, and for testing the range and force of differences. Beyond this, and chiefly, it becomes an example of the integration of thought and feeling that would be reached by the entire group if all its members could be subjected to the same experience their representatives have had. The representatives vicariously achieve for the larger group what the group in its entirety has not yet had opportunity to achieve.[13] The representatives become a coöperative collection of minds seeking to reach common understanding and

---

[12] Pp. 76 ff.
[13] *Church Comity*, p. 180.

wise practical conclusions without the suppression of divergencies. Piety very naturally identifies so vital a process with the operation of the divine leadership within the Church.

From the more liberal interpretation of this general viewpoint a great freedom pervades the situation. No longer is there any obligation, on the one hand, narrowly to reflect partisan interests; nor, on the other hand, is there any obligation entirely to agree. What the group possesses in common is first of all a controlling inner spirit and, secondly, a method, namely, discussion. Discussion becomes an educational process and leads to more or less complete consolidation of conviction upon any point or issue. Maximum agreement is likely to be reached in the more traditional spheres, minimum agreement in the more debatable ones: but the fact of disagreement does not tend to disrupt the unity of the organization. It remains continuously a forum for divergent views as well as a means of securing the convergence of attitude and sentiment.

This leads on to a still more advanced version of representativeness. Not only is there ample room left for minorities, no matter whether they are reactionary or advanced, but there is deliberate desire to facilitate the expression of minority views as part of the understanding of the total situation. The existence of extremes is accepted as natural and permanent. The extremes, of course, cannot be representative in the statistical sense; but each is authentically representative within its place as a factor in the total situation. The genuine prophet will not be pleased to be representative, and it is a singular misinterpretation of his genius to think that he would be.

Now, federation policy will be one thing if it assumes that decisions are representative when they merely reflect the mechanical combinations or compromises of views of different constituencies. It will be a very different thing if it relies on a synthesis of views beyond the power of formal representation. It will be still different if it is desired to get dissent expressed as well as assent. Different minds will react to the federation according to the version of representativeness that it vitally adheres to. Coöperating Protestantism must first decide what sort of representativeness it seeks for its coöperative agency. It can then pass judgment on its own existing policies as the present study cannot do.

SUMMARY

Obviously, if the fullness of reality could be expressed, it would disclose the federation movement as a resultant of innumerable individual drives and decisions on the part of many persons and groups. Disregarding these as minor accidents, and abstracting what has seemed to constitute a permanent core of the phenomena, the author has tried in this chapter to present the movement as starting with the stuff of contemporary denominationalism, endowed with capacity for evolution, equipped with a certain dominant disposition, with ability to rationalize its own processes and partly to direct them by setting up authority and elaborating a set of regulatory machinery. The working out of results by the system of factors tends to "explain" the character of the present institution as the investigation has disclosed it in detail. What federations do, grows out of the fact that they are entities of this sort, pointed in a given direction by external forces and discharging in the same general direction by the urge of their internal energies, with deliberate control playing a very minor role in determining their fortunes.

THE CONDITIONAL OUTCOME

From such a viewpoint the federation movement appears as one whose outcome is distinctly conditional. It may be false prophet, or forerunner, or Messiah. Who can be sure which?

On the whole, the present movement—so far at least as Protestantism is concerned—seems too general, too substantial and too profound for the first of these three roles. If it is really the product of deep evolutionary forces, it cannot itself be a false prophet though one might easily read into the message more than is rightfully there.

From the writer's standpoint, as voiced particularly toward the end of Chapter XIV, it is, however, very much within possibility that the federation movement may nearly have reached its peak, that it may have come close to the end of its course as a narrowly coöperative agency limited to the fields of the Church's "life and work" and ignoring those of its "faith and order." Perhaps it has reached the limit of its growth with its present depth of soil. Very likely it must now become much more than it is, or else much less.

Constant subjection to unnatural inhibitions, the weight of narrow and suspicious denominational control, the continuous thwarting of vital impulses by the ecclesiastical hand upon the machinery, might well render the best of movements permanently powerless to incarnate the profounder meanings implicit in it.

Even this need not spell the movement's failure: rather it might constitute a role of exceeding glory if it genuinely prepared the way within the Church for some more authentic movement of integration.

As the author senses it then, it is not impossible that the federation movement may be shunted to a side track to make way for a more virile and popular, a more fearless and affirmative movement advancing in the same direction but going much faster. Outdistanced and outmoded, federation may then taper off into a respectable maturity and fulfill a useful place during an indefinite future, but by no means realize the deepest desires of its present adherents nor satisfy the better natures of the conservatives themselves. Should this be the lot of the movement, it is as certain as anything can be that these hopes would press on to fulfill themselves in some other and more vital way, borne forward by forces neither of their creating nor subject to their withholding.

PART II

THE TECHNICAL REPORT

This, the second major division of the report, concerns the more technical processes involved in the conduct of federations. An account of many of these processes will be of interest to any thoughtful reader. They are reported in detail, however, particularly for the benefit of paid leaders and other responsible workers in federations. The technical report raises many of the outstanding problems with which such persons have to do. In it federations are compared on significant points. At certain other points the work as the investigator understood it is evaluated, and suggestions are made that may help toward improved practices.

The technical report begins with the human elements in the federation situation, specifically its paid leaders and the unpaid representatives of the churches who make up its officers and committees. Next, the major departments of federation work are described one after another. The material means by which the work is accomplished, namely, its finances and facilities, are then considered. Finally, the promotional means by which federations create and cultivate the public and their more intimate constituencies are discussed.

Chapter XVI

THE COMMITTEE SYSTEM

The general report has already set forth the characteristic scheme of internal organization under which federations operate.[1] The most outstanding feature of this scheme is the committee system.

Though in general the federation movement follows the tradition of representative government for voluntary social agencies, it has at this point gone further and magnified the rôle of committees. It has spun them out into an elaborate network, made all the more complicated because the principle of denominational representation, though constitutionally required in only a minority of cases, is actually followed in the composition of a great majority of them.

The essential machinery includes: the virtually ubiquitous central governing committee, termed a board of directors or executive committee; a system of standing committees representing the major departments or aspects of the federation's work; and minor and temporary committees.

The present chapter describes the more permanent parts of this machinery as they were found in the study of federations from city to city. In it, certain pertinent problems are raised and the author has ventured to offer certain practical suggestions.

BOARDS OF DIRECTORS AND EQUIVALENT ORGANIZATIONS

Turning now to particular committees, one naturally starts with boards of directors as representing the broadest and most general delegation of administrative authority.[2]

One should notice in passing that it is possible for a federation to be its own board of directors. Its membership already consists of representative delegates. It convenes at least annually, and sometimes three times a year. In these gatherings a federation may undertake to make its major decisions in town-meeting fashion, entrusting only their execution to agents with limited authority. A few federations tend somewhat strongly in this direction. The rule is, however, to set up a rather large representative body of directors to conduct the affairs of the organization.

---

[1] Chapter V.
[2] Pp. 85 and 140.

The constitutional phraseology in which the delegation of authority to boards of directors is set forth varies greatly, but tends to fall under three somewhat general formulas; the formula of *ad interim* responsibility, under which the directors are "to act for the federation between meetings"; the formula of general oversight, permitting them "to exercise general supervision over its affairs"; or the formula of plenary authority, which gives them "full control over all policies and activities." It is not generally possible, however, to trace in these verbal differences the specific degrees of authority it is intended to delegate.

Real differences get definite expression in the particular powers conferred upon directors. Thus, in the New York and the Brooklyn federations, they appoint the officers of the organizations. This fact gives point to the phraseology of the Brooklyn constitution which reads: "The management of the federation is vested in the directors." Such strong concentration of authority is in extreme contrast with the town-meeting tendency previously noted.

The more typical responsibilities of directors, as usually enumerated, include the appointment of committees and commissions, and of executive secretaries and other paid officers.

Fourteen boards of directors (or functionally equivalent organizations bearing other names) were intensively studied from the standpoint of their composition, the characteristics of their memberships, and their methods of operation; with results that are now to be presented.

SIZE AND FREQUENCY OF MEETINGS

The aggregate membership of the fourteen boards was 714 persons. Membership varied from 29 to 124, with a median membership of 44. In theory the boards, with one exception, met either monthly, bi-monthly or quarterly; but meetings were commonly omitted during the summer; so that the actual number of meetings per year were most frequently either ten, or five, or four. Only about one-fourth of the federations fixed the number of meetings in their constitutions.

COMPOSITION OF BOARDS

As determined by their constitutions, boards of directors characteristically involve five types of members: the officers of federations; the chairmen of all standing committees and commissions; certain members at large; representatives of denominational or non-ecclesiastical Protestant agencies *ex officio*; and denominational delegates.

Upon this point twenty-one federations were studied. Two-thirds of them drew upon at least three of these five sources of members. *Ex officio* members appeared in twelve cases out of twenty-one; while denominational representation was constitutionally required in only three cases.

This was something of a surprise, in view of the strong insistence of constitutions upon proportionate denominational representation in the make-up of the federations themselves. In two of the cases, the constitution declared that proper denominational distribution shall be regarded in the selection of members at large; and even when not required, their actual choice is likely to be made with this point in view. When directors are listed, they almost always appear under a denominational classification.

The size of the directing body was usually specified by the constitution only as regards the number of delegates at large; though the number of officers, and of *ex officio* representatives also, is likely to be indirectly fixed. The size of the other elements may vary from time to time.

Four constitutions required that a due proportion of directors at large be lay persons; and one required a specific number of women. About three-fourths of the time the president of the federation was *ex officio* chairman of the directors. Otherwise, the body elected its own chairman.

<h3 style="text-align:center">CHARACTERISTICS</h3>

The actual age of committee members was not recorded in any case. Careful estimates on this point were made, however, by executive secretaries in twelve federations. The returns were grouped in five-year periods with forty, forty-five, fifty, fifty-five, etc., as the mid-points. In all but three federations, the median age of directors most nearly approximated fifty years; while in two it was forty-five years; and in one, fifty-five. Only one federation had any appreciable group of directors as young as thirty-five; and only one had as many as one-fourth of its directors as young as forty.

Fifty-two out of every hundred committeemen were ministers; thirteen were representatives of other professions, including the non-ordained employees of the church; 23 per cent. were engaged in business or industry; 9 per cent. were house-wives; and 3 per cent. were from all other occupations. Since the governing boards of local churches are composed of laymen, the extreme clerical dominance on federation boards is noteworthy.[3]

[3] While the social status of directors was not investigated, an amazing sidelight is accidentally thrown upon it by a study of the resident directors in a

Half the members of boards of directors did not belong to any other federation committee. But 30 per cent. belonged to one other committee, 12 per cent. to two others, and 8 per cent. to more than two. This considerable integration with other functional committees was partly due to the fact that from a fourth to a third of the directors came on the board by being first made subcommittee chairmen. The result is as intended; namely, a high degree of concentration, both of the total control of the work and of its detail, in the same committee members.

Familiarity with, and continuity of interest in, federation work was less completely secured. About a third of the directors had served on federation committees two or three years. Nearly a fifth, however, had served one year or less; and an additional fourth either four or five years. Seventy-two per cent. of all directors had thus had not more than five years of federation experience. On the contrary, there was an old-guard, numbering about one-fourth of the group, that had served eight years or more. This was the conservative leaven in the rather transient mass of general membership.

ATTENDANCE

The actual attendance on meetings of the fourteen boards of directors ranges from 26 to 44 per cent. of possible attendance, with a median of 35 per cent. Modal attendance was slightly higher.

For the group as a whole, the most frequent situation was one in which a member attended only a fifth of the meetings held. More than two-thirds attended less than half the meetings—this included 20 per cent. who never attended at all.

In hunting for an explanation of this showing, it was found that neither frequency of meetings nor the size of the committee corresponded at all closely with the ratio of attendance. There was, on the other hand, a distinct correlation between the attendance and the composition of the committee. The possibility of such a result is shown in the tabulation on page 295 of attendance ratios for the different elements in eight boards of directors.

As one might have expected, those responsible as officers make the best attendance showing, while members at large, representing no specific responsibility or interest, stand lowest.

---

single federation. Here it was found that forty-six out of fifty were drawn from a single area where the wealth of the city is concentrated. All denominations had picked their representatives independently, and all had agreed with the federation in going to the same area for all classes of members. Undoubtedly, the reason was that persons of leadership caliber were thus actually concentrated in that particular city.

Classes of Directors	Per Cent. of Actual to Possible Attendance
Officers of Federations	46
Chairmen of Committees	40
Ex Officio Members	39
Denominational Delegates	31
Members at Large	27

A comparison in detail of the records of the eight boards showed that their attendance was largely accounted for by the fact that some one or more elements of the committee exceeded or fell below the average performance of its class. Thus in Indianapolis and Baltimore, which ranked highest from the standpoint of attendance, members at large attend considerably better than was true elsewhere. Committee chairmen in Indianapolis also attended better than was usual, as did officers in Baltimore. Oakland and Chicago stood at the foot of the list. The reason, in the case of the former, was that the board of directors includes *ex officio* a large number of non-resident ecclesiastical officials whose primary associations were with San Francisco. As members of the San Francisco board of directors these very individuals helped the federation of that city to a relatively high attendance-rank. But in the case of Oakland, they pulled down the record. In the case of Chicago, the poor attendance-record was largely due to denominational lay representatives, of which this federation has a very disproportionate large number.

The particular composition of the board of directors thus tends to explain its attendance record. But back of this lie obvious differences in general loyalty and in the degree to which the sense of responsibility has been cultivated in committee memberships. The investigator feels certain that he can trace the effect of these factors in the cases of certain federations at either end of the ranking scale. Thus, the poorest attendance-record found in any board of directors was that of a federation that dismissed its secretary within a few months after the study.

Such, in general, is the body of voluntary workers to which federations commit the primary responsibility for directing their affairs.

EXECUTIVE COMMITTEE

About half the federations, particularly those with large boards of directors, make a secondary delegation of administrative responsibility to executive committees. In reality these committees fall into two quite distinct types. One type merely acts for the directors in emergency. Such committees actually average only one meeting a year. Their existence simply makes it unnecessary to call special sessions of the directors.

The second type tends to meet at intervals alternating with the meetings of directors. It is chiefly found in federations whose directors meet four or five times a year. The executive committee then meets during the odd months, giving the organization the equivalent of a monthly administrative session except for the summer months.

Executive committees are generally composed of the permanent officers of the federation, plus a group of members at large. Their occupational composition corresponds closely to that of boards of directors. Their average size is slightly more than one-fourth the size of boards of directors, and their average attendance is decidedly better.

COMPARISON OF STANDING COMMITTEES

The committees that administer the major functions of federations are separately described in the discussion of these functions in other parts of this report.[4] A summary comparison of these committees point by point, with boards of directors, will serve, however, to throw into relief the general characteristics of the committee-group as a whole, and its place in the federation enterprise. The means for such comparison is supplied in summary Tables XXI-XXIV.

On the basis of the showing of these tables the more important aspects of the committee situation may be briefly generalized.

TABLE XXI—MEETINGS AND ATTENDANCE OF VARIOUS FEDERATION COMMITTEES

TYPE OF COMMITTEE	AVERAGE No. MEMBERS	No. OF MEETINGS PER YEAR	AVERAGE PER CENT. ATTENDANCE	PER CENT. MEMBERS ATTENDING Less than Half of Meetings	Never
Directors	44	4, 5 or 10	35	67	20
Executive	12	1, 4 or 5	50	55	20
Executive Women's Dept.	24	8 or 10	53	58	10
Comity	17	4 or 5	38	*	30
Religious Education	26	1, 5 or 9	28	70	36
Social Service	16	†	29	53	38
Finance	16	†	36	65	28

* Not calculated.
† No common tendency.

NUMBER OF MEMBERS

Because the board of directors is most inclusive in responsibility, and most acutely dependent upon its representative character, it naturally has the largest average membership. It is equally natural that the executive committee, as essentially a

[4] P. 141.

subcommittee of the directors, should have the smallest average membership.

It is also natural that the executive committees of the women's departments and of commissions on religious education should be relatively large, because, within their own spheres, they carry responsibilities parallel to those of boards of directors. Committees that are strictly limited to the carrying out of the work of special departments of interest under policies determined by superior bodies, are smaller. It is apparently a mere coincidence that three out of the four types coming under this category should average either sixteen or seventeen members each.

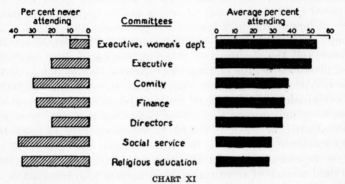

CHART XI

Comparative attendance of members of specified types of Church Federation committees

FREQUENCY OF MEETING

Committees whose executive functions cover the total area of federation interest, or semi-independent departments, tend to meet at stated intervals, either monthly, bi-monthly, or quarterly; but with summer sessions omitted. Comity committees generally meet on call; but there is ordinarily enough business to convene them four or five times a year. Committees in charge of other single fields of interest generally meet less frequently and at irregular intervals. Moreover, they rather easily fall into inactivity. Thus, five out of eleven finance committees reported no meetings during the year preceding the study. Certain federations were notorious on account of the virtual collapse of the committee system.

ATTENDANCE

Committees responsible for single interests (other than comity) show a poorer attendance-record than committees administering departments or the work of federations as a whole. Probably it is the larger and more substantial interest that calls forth the greater loyalty as measured by participation. In the most frequent situation, the ratio of actual possible attendance is only about a third. At best, less than half the members of a committee are present as much as half of the time, and in most cases the proportion is about a third. From 10 to 38 per cent. never come at all. Women's departments make the best showing in point of attendance, probably because the great majority of members are not gainfully employed and can command more leisure.

COMPONENT ELEMENTS

The simplest way to make up a committee is to find the required number of competent people and to appoint them members at large. But with most federation committees, much more complicated requirements actually control the situation. All officers and the chairmen of standing committees are likely to find places on boards of directors. Nomination of delegates by denominations is sometimes required on these boards, and also on commissions of religious education, and on comity committees. This seemingly means that where delegated authority is highly concentrated, or when it relates to spheres concerned with the very existence of churches, the denominations are insistent upon direct representation. In the case of religious education, the national scheme of constituting local units is also involved.

The elements generally entering into the composition of each type of committee are indicated by stars in Table XXII.

TABLE XXII—COMPOSITION OF VARIOUS FEDERATION COMMITTEES

TYPE OF COMMITTEE	Federation Officers	Chairmen Standing Committees	Denominational Delegates	Representatives Of Other Protestant Movements Ex Officio	Members At Large	Denominational Executives Ex Officio
Directors	*	*	*	*	*	*
Executive	*			[*]	*	
Comity			*		[*]	*
Religious Education			*		*	
Social Service				[*]	*	
Finance					*	

(Note: Elements characteristic of a given committee are starred; elements less frequent, though still characteristic, are bracketed.)

AGE, SEX, AND RACE

The characteristics of federation committee members with respect to age, sex, race, and occupation are shown in Table XXIII. The preponderance of ministers in committee membership (shown in the next paragraph) has obvious bearing upon the characteristic age of committeemen. It is known that the city minister scarcely achieves eminence before fifty: this tends

TABLE XXIII—CHARACTERISTICS OF MEMBERS OF VARIOUS
FEDERATION COMMITTEES

TYPE OF COMMITTEE	AGGRE- GATE MEMBER SHIP*	NO. OF NEGROES	MEDIAN AGE	PER CENT. WOMEN	PER CENT. DISTRIBUTION BY OCCUPATION				
					Minis- try	Busi- ness and Indus- try	Profes- sions (other)	House- wives	All Other
Directors.....	714	8	50	13	52	23	13	9	3
Executive....	107	0	50	1	51	26	13	9	1
Executive Women's Department	200	2	50	100	0	1	7	91	1
Comity......	318	1	55	1	72	16	10	0	2
Religious Education..	310	6	50	17	46	11	31	8	4
Social Service.....	626	54	50	18	46	12	30	11	1
Finance......	175	0	55	2	21	57	19	2	1

* Membership of committees included in the comparison.

to explain the strongly modal place of this age-group in committees. Another factor that helps to determine is probably ability to command one's own time. This is more often achieved by successful people in middle life than by younger people of equal capacity.

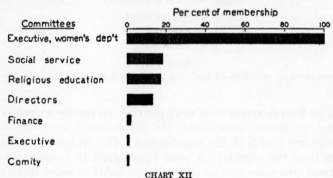

CHART XII

Women members on specified types of Church Federation committees

The relatively small place of women on federation committees reflects the complexion of the situation as a whole.[5] Aside from their own departments, women are given greatest representation in the fields of religious education and social service. The very

[5] P. 445.

few Negro committeemen reflect a lack of efficient participation of the Negro denominations in the federation movement, even though they are fully eligible to membership, and are nominally members. Nearly all the Negro members are found in committees on interracial relationships.

OCCUPATION

The ministry furnishes an absolute majority of all committee members, other than those of finance committees and women's departments. The proportion of ministers ranges from 21 per

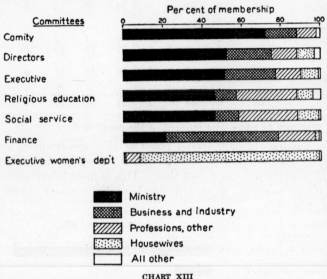

CHART XIII

Occupation of members of specified types of Church Federation committees

cent. on finance committees to 72 per cent. on comity committees. Except on finance committees, the business-man element never exceeds one-fourth of the membership. The professional group, other than the ministry, is most emphasized in committees on religious education and social work—probably because these two fields have developed their own types of trained leadership.

DURATION OF COMMITTEE SERVICE

Considering the combined membership of committees, more than half the members are found to have had not more than three years' experience in such positions. Boards of directors naturally get a higher proportion of members with long experience. More than a fourth of their memberships consist of "old timers." Religious education and women's department members represent the briefest average experience—owing in part to the relative newness of many of these departments.

TABLE XXIV—DISTRIBUTION OF MEMBERS OF VARIOUS FEDERATION COMMITTEES, BY YEARS OF COMMITTEE MEMBERSHIP AND BY NUMBER OF OTHER FEDERATION COMMITTEES IN WHICH MEMBERSHIP IS HELD

Type of Committee	Per Cent. Serving Specified Number of Years				Per Cent. Serving Specified Number of other Committees			
	1	2-3	4-5	Over 5	0	1	2	Over 2
Directors	17	35	20	28	50	30	12	8
Executive	42	15	26	17	..	..	..	*
Executive Women's Department	32	59	6	3	92	(8%—1 or over)		
Comity	27	34	25	14	54	21	17	8
Religious Education	20	37	41	2	91	4	4	1
Social Service	33	37	16	14	70	20	8	2
Finance	15	40	30	15	52	20	18	10

* Not calculated.

RELATION TO THE FEDERATION ENTERPRISE AS A WHOLE

Table XXIV shows that committees responsible for single interests (especially those representing the semi-independent subsidiaries) have almost no relationship with other departments of federations. This is particularly true of religious education and women's departments. On the other hand, half or more of the members of boards of directors, and of comity and finance committees belong to other federation committees. Virtually a fourth of the members of comity committees have belonged to at least two other committees, and are thus carrying many-sided responsibilities within the organization.

Conduct of Committees

The method used to discover how committees are actually conducted was primarily that of direct observation. This was possible, however, on only a limited number of occasions when committees were in session during the brief period of field work in any given federation. A generalization based upon relatively so small a sampling must consequently be understood to be a loose one, in which the comparison of committees of different types can be only secondary.

TIME, PLACE, AND DURATION

About two-thirds of the committees met at noon, except for a very occasional case of evening meetings; the rest met late in the afternoon. Those holding noon meetings invariably did so in connection with a meal. This was true of only one committee meeting in the evening. The meal was usually served in a private dining-room attached to the cafeteria of a Young Men's or Young Women's Christian Association. These organizations commonly provide such facilities for their own committees and make them available to other Protestant agencies.[6] Otherwise the meeting was likely to be in a private room in connection with club or restaurant, or very infrequently in the main dining-room. Meetings not held in connection with meals commonly occupied a committee room in the office building in which the federation had its quarters, or in a near-by church. Occasionally, the federation maintained its own committee room; but a good many committees had to crowd uncomfortably into the limited space furnished the federation officers for their regular work.[7]

With nearly two-thirds of the committees, the average duration of the meeting was from one and a quarter to one and a half hours. Extremes ranged from forty-five minutes to three hours, each represented by a single case.

PREPARATION

Excepting for a few subcommittees, a docket of business was prepared in advance. About three-fifths of the time such preparation was in the hands of the paid executive exclusively, while in the other two-fifths he was accustomed to confer with the chairman. In a few cases, the chairman himself took the initiative. Regular consultation with other members of the committees in the preparation of the docket was very infrequently reported.

NOTICE OF MEETINGS

It was customary to mail a notice of a committee meeting to every member, and frequently to enclose a postal card on which he might reply as to his expected attendance. In about one-third of the committees, the notice contained no indication of the particular business to be transacted. In another third, some at least of the items of the docket were regularly mentioned; while in the remainder the usage varied from time to time. This showing was modified by the habit of some federations of giving last-minute reminders of meetings over the telephone. In urging attendance by this method, the nature of the business to be considered was frequently stressed.

[6] P. 151.
[7] P. 467.

Copies of the docket, when not sent out in advance, were rarely furnished to members at the meeting. Generally it remained a mere order of business in the hands of the chairman. Some data bearing on particular business, however, was occasionally reported in at least one-third of the committees studied, though this was a regular practice in only a single case.

FORMS IN WHICH BUSINESS IS PRESENTED

In nearly two-thirds of the cases, routine business was habitually presented in the form of specific proposals on which the committee was asked to take action. But in a somewhat larger proportion of cases, at least a part of the business came up for preliminary discussion without formulation for action. This condition was notably more frequent with subcommittees. It is in these committees that the first attack on problems is often made. Here the analysis of the problem in the raw takes place before the data is worked over into "units of transaction," as it is in the case of the major committees.

In about two-thirds of the cases studied, reports of officers and subcommittees were habitually rendered in oral form. Treasurers generally reported in writing; executive secretaries did so in a minority of cases. It was most unusual, however, for copies of these reports to be multiplied so as to supply each member; and they were almost never sent out in advance. Certain data in typed or printed form was, however, frequently put before workers at the time of the meeting. Religious-education committees in particular seemed addicted to the circulation of printed material.

THE RÔLE OF THE CHAIRMAN

The means of studying the chairman in action was a rough rating-scale on which the investigators noted their impressions on such matters as his independence, his interest in thoroughgoing discussion, his fair play toward minority opinion, his recognition of the representative rôle of certain members with respect to particular elements in the constituency, his competency in summarizing the discussion, and his aptness in stating the nature of the agreements reached. Only one or two chairmen in fifteen impressed the observer as seriously deficient on one or more of these points, the rating usually falling between 70 and 90 per cent. on a scale of one hundred. No real objective validity is claimed for these ratings. The method merely assured a uniform approach to the phenomena under observation.

COMMITTEE DECISIONS

The investigator's impression of the adequacy of committee processes and the genuineness of the agreements reached in the committee's sessions was also registered by means of a similar device. The points considered were: whether the decision was reached without coercion, whether there was actual consent, or whether a silent minority was left disagreeing. Only about one committee in fifteen was noted as flagrantly deficient on these points. The observers rated the deliberative quality of the total group of meetings as from 70 to 90 per cent. genuine.

MINUTES

All the committees studied kept regular minutes; and almost all recorded the names of members present, but rarely those of absentees. Two-thirds of the committees, however, kept minutes in skeleton only: votes were recorded, but not the course or content of the discussions. One-third of the committees claimed to record the processes of discussion either usually or frequently. By about one-third of the committees, documents elucidating the minutes were frequently attached. In only about one-seventh of the cases were minutes sent out to members after each meeting.

CONCLUSIONS AS TO COMMITTEES

By what standard shall the foregoing record of committee performance be judged?

This report does not pretend to set up objective criteria. It is greatly impressed by certain recent important but tentative studies of committee functions and processes, but does not feel that sufficient scientific authority attaches to their preliminary conclusions to warrant their adoption for systematic use as norms.

The formal standard of perfection—that every committee member should be present and participate in every meeting—is, of course, too naïve for practical consideration.

But almost equally futile is the position that interprets the committee exclusively in terms of the deliberative group which sometimes it conspicuously is not.[8] First of all, this position tends to make humanity more completely rational than it is, or perhaps ought to be. The committee meeting is not an exercise of pure social intelligence, and not all of its valuable product is to be looked for in terms of its decisions. The fact that so many committees meet around a table at meal-time suggests the value

---

[8] P. 294.

of informal social contacts in creating the mood of friendliness and the capacity for agreement.

A few committees conspicuously exhibited the leader-follower pattern of social grouping. They were not associations of colleagues. The chairman nominated the other members of the committee. In three or four cases he financed, largely out of his own pocket, the federation activity assigned to his committee. Other committees existed primarily to educate the members. Marginal members on still others not infrequently did no more than rubber stamp the conclusions of executives and working minorities. Whatever may be set forth in constitutions, groupings of this type may have practical justification; and they were sometimes definitely in mind when the federations set up their committee systems.

It is manifestly unfair, therefore, to judge the entire round of federation committee work as though it started out to be essentially a matter of deliberative action.

In a large proportion of committees the members who possess the greatest representative significance are available for committee work only at the cost of short-circuiting committee processes. They sit with their watches in their hands, and must be taken on these terms or not at all. The practical application of any theory of committees has to start with such conditions as these.

No real good can come from teasing out the practice of deliberation in matters that from all practical standpoints can really be settled by shorter methods. Reflecting upon his own experiences, the author can recall many occasions when a committee decision was not talked out to his satisfaction. He very much doubts, however, whether to have talked it out would generally have been worth while. His loyalty and coöperative attitude in the enterprise concerned was not appreciably diminished by the fact that the debate was cut off before the committee was entirely exhausted.

To say this is, of course, not to doubt the ideal of the representative committee as an organ of creative thinking for a social group. The author reaffirms his conviction that it may not be altogether wrong to surround the process "with a sort of mystical halo. Assuming the Christian conception that the divine will sometimes take possession of the human will, no circumstance could be more favorable for the realization of this high transaction than that a competent representative body, using the best practical techniques, shall have possessed itself as completely as possible of the fraternal spirit in the effort to reach wise and right decisions concerning the Church."[9]

But the time to attempt to make good so exalted an ideal is not when the committee actually assembles to conduct its business. One must go back to the conception of the particular committee, its constitution and composition, its specific function and inherent limitations. The more mongrel the elements of which it is composed, the greater the necessity of creating the practical conditions of place, time, and continuity, which alone can make their spiritual fusion possible. In brief, if committee transactions are to represent vital integrations of collective thought and will, if committee decisions are to reflect creative achievement, a fair chance for these results must be provided both in the set-up and the circumstances of the committee group. The extraneous and merely adventitious values, such a formal representativeness or financial ability, are a poor exchange for the fundamental and inherent values of the committee process at its best. But many federations have thrown away these values in advance because they have devised their committee systems with other considerations in mind.

PRACTICAL CONSIDERATIONS

In the interests of more ideal, as well as of more efficient, committees the following suggestions are ventured, as legitimately growing out of the study.

(1) Federations should label the separate classes that have to be recognized in the make-up of committees. Merely honorary members should be so designated and not called vice-presidents. Advisory members should likewise be so designated. It will perhaps be going too far to label any one a rubber-stamp member, or to admit that any one is selected for financial reasons alone; but so far as possible, each class should know what is really expected of it in the way of committee service.

(2) The attendance and participation of the members of each class should be separately recorded and interpreted. This would enable future investigators to tell what proportion of committee-men who are expected to attend, actually do so.

(3) Committees should devise a definite schedule of meetings which may utilize all types of memberships at least part of the time. Advisors should be brought in when they can really function, in their expert capacities, and the other marginal members should be drawn upon on suitable occasions.

---

[9] *Church Comity*, p. 180.

(4) A federation should adopt a sliding standard of satisfactory committee performance beginning with a reasonable advance upon its present level. If 35 per cent. of possible attendance represents the present average, the standard might be raised to 45 for the following year, and the practical limits of improved performance be determined by experiment.

The most promising line of experiment would appear to be that of intensive cultivation of committee members. The total constituents of federations, including all with whom they have any specific contact by direct or regular cultivation through publicity, constitute an exceedingly small fraction of the total Protestant body which the federation purports to represent. It ought not to be too much, then, to attempt aggressive educational contact at least with the entire body of committee members.

MORE GENERAL SUGGESTIONS

As a means of making the foregoing suggestions practical, the writer again suggests a reduction in the total committee machinery of federations which he believes to be now too extensive for the body of services they are actively performing. As a result, wider areas of responsibility would be left in the hands of boards of directors, and there would need to be fewer departments. Evangelism, comity, religious education, and social service are so well established as probably to constitute an irreducible minimum; but numerous newer interests departmentalized in the Federal Council need not necessarily be represented by separate committees in each and every federation.

Such a suggestion undoubtedly implies also the entrusting of larger responsibility to secretaries and other professional employees. In the world of American politics generally, the deliberative branch of government has sunk relatively in popular esteem, while the executive has gained in favor. Similarly, it is a question whether the average committee performance in federations does not suggest somewhat diminished confidence in the committee scheme as a whole. To the ultimate constituent, the federation must largely be personalized in its executive leadership. The secretary becomes the delegate of all the churches in a more vital sense than is true of numerous poorly attended and little integrated committees which cannot really function in their representative capacity because they function so little in any capacity. Is it really maintaining the representative principle to continue such committees?

In giving this counsel, there is no purpose to advocate a change in the vital balance of the federation machinery. Such committee machinery as is left should be worked most faithfully; and might, in the long run, win back some of the ground apparently lost by the over-grown committee system. Perhaps the greatest single need is the development of a larger group of competent lay amateurs.

Certain men, long experienced in coöperation, have already become the equals of the professional federation secretaries, the denominational executives, or the leading ministers who so largely dominate the situation at present. This rather occasional type is nevertheless one of the most significant factors in the situation. No secretary can do anything better for his organization than to find and develop more men of this sort who will outstay the transient breed of executives, become the custodians of funded experience, and incarnate the continuous and ripened loyalties of the Protestant group.

Chapter XVII

THE PAID STAFF

Chapter IX of the general report has already enumerated and classified the paid workers of twenty-one church federations covered by the investigation, and has indicated their general relation to the federation machinery.

The present chapter reports the results of a vocational study of this employed personnel, including both the central administrative staff and the special professional leadership of the more important departments.

SIZE OF STAFF

The size of a federation's paid staff naturally reflects the relative magnitude of its operations and the size of its budgets. Workers are very unevenly distributed among the twenty-one federations as is shown by Table XXV.

TABLE XXV—SIZE OF PAID STAFF IN 21 FEDERATIONS

No. of Paid Workers	No. of Federations Employing
1	3
2	1
3-4	7
5-6	4
7-8	2
9-10	1
More than 10	3

It will be noted that a third of the twenty-one federations studied had three or four workers, and that more than a half had from three to six workers. On the other hand, more than half had not more than four. The one-worker federations ordinarily employ part-time clerical assistance not shown in the accounting. The typical staff of three or four workers consists of an executive secretary, a clerical worker, a religious educational or social worker, or both. The larger staffs simply add more department executives, other social and religious workers, other clerical assistants, and rarely assistant general executives.

CHARACTERISTICS OF WORKERS

The vocational characteristics of workers of each class have next to be considered. The points included under this category

309

cover their preparation, experience, remuneration and general community standing; also an analysis and measurement of their respective duties.

EXECUTIVE SECRETARIES

More than anyone else the executive secretaries are the men who make or break federations, and whom federations make or break. It is correspondingly important to know what manner of persons they are.

With respect to age, two-thirds of the executive secretaries fall within the fifteen years between forty-five and sixty. This, the dominant group, is in turn about equally divided among the three five-year periods, 45-49, 50-54, and 55-59. Three secretaries were in the earlier sixties, and five were under forty-five. Most of the unordained secretaries fell in the lower age-group.

Of the ordained secretaries, two-thirds had served from twenty to thirty years in the ministry, or in other forms of professional religious work, before coming into their present offices; while an additional fifth had had from twelve to fifteen years of similar experience. The group thus corresponds rather closely in experience to ministers who hold the more conspicuous city churches.[1]

None of the women executive secretaries were college graduates, and three of the men were not. But all the ordained secretaries had taken a full theological seminary course, and three had attained the Ph.D. degree. Two others had engaged in postgraduate work for a considerable period, and one non-college man was a graduate of a professional school of religious education. The education of the clerical portion of the secretarial group thus closely corresponds to the tradition of the city ministry.

Two non-ordained secretaries, and one ordained, were to be credited with considerable business experience, the results of which are not a little apparent as factors in their present success.

Three of the twenty-one secretaries included in the investigation on this item, had served more than one federation in this capacity; while two more had served federations in other capacities. Three brought to the position previous experience as denominational secretaries. Four were attached to the Young Men's Christian Association during the World War; and three others had been employed in the Interchurch World Movement, or in coöperative community programs of similar types.

Thus, all told, more than half the secretarial group under investigation had professionally engaged in other phases of Prot-

---

[1] Douglass, *1000 City Churches*, p. 215 f.

estant coöperative effort before embarking upon their careers as secretaries. In most cases, however, these other services were rather brief episodes rather than adequate preliminary experiences.

At the date of the field study, the longest period of service in the secretaryship had been twenty-four years, and the shortest less than one year. On this point, however, the secretarial group shows no common tendency. Thus, five secretaries have been in their present positions from two to five years, six either six or seven years, and five from nine to twelve years. This accounts for about three-fourths of the group. But even this ragged showing indicates a considerably longer average tenure than is achieved by city ministers as a group.

Male secretaries giving full time exclusively to their federation received salaries of from three thousand to seven thousand dollars. In three-fifths of the cases the salary was from five to six thousand dollars. With a single exception (that of the Massachusetts State Federation), the small salaries were in small cities. The larger salaries generally reflected longer tenure of office as well. In general, salaries closely correspond to what would be paid a city minister whose church budget matched that of the federation. About two thousand dollars is the typical salary of the full-time woman secretary.[2]

In addition to salary, a considerable number of secretaries received allowances for the up-keep of automobiles. In the case of two or three of the lowest-pay men, this amounts to an appreciable addition to income. Other perquisites of the secretaries' office are found chiefly in honoraria received for supplying city pulpits. These were alleged to reach considerable sums in certain cases. Some secretaries turn all such receipts back into the federation treasury, and those who fail to do so were sometimes criticized.

The executive secretary of a federation usually got one month's vacation annually, though exceptional cases occur of six weeks' or two months' vacations.

With almost no exception, the ordained secretaries had reached enough eminence to receive the degree of Doctor of Divinity. A few were deeply involved in the professional, civic, and cultural life of their community, and in the larger interests of their denomination; that is to say, they belonged to large numbers of

---

[2] The above showing applies also to secretaries who occupy two offices; as for example, the secretary of the Washington Federation, who is also a representative of the Federal Council; and the secretary of the Wichita Federation, who was also chief executive of the local Young Men's Christian Association at the time of the study.

clubs, to the boards of directors of educational institutions, and to numerous civic committees. This, however, is, in general, the privilege of men who have remained a long time in their positions.

The Executive Secretary at Work

As active administrative head of a federation, the executive secretary is concerned with his organization's activities. The description of these activities in previous sections has revealed much of their method. It remains, however, to study the executive secretary directly on the job. This is made possible by exact records of a week's work kept by ten different secretaries. Their vocational experiences undoubtedly reflect pretty accurately those of the profession as a whole.

The executive secretary puts in a long work-week. All but one of the ten were on duty seven days in the week, the Sunday work-period ranging from seven to three and a half hours. The work generally consisted in making an address in some church, some time spent in the preparation of the address, travel in going and coming, and sociability incidentally required of a visiting minister. Only one secretary took an entire day off during his recorded week, though most of them reduced their hours on Saturday.

The executive secretary puts in a work-day of moderate length. The average hours per week for the group was 55.5, or about eight hours a day on a seven-day basis. The shortest work-week was forty-seven and three-quarters hours; the longest, sixty-seven and a half hours: but more than two-thirds of the cases varied less than four hours from the average. Unpublished investigations by the author show that city ministers, as a group, habitually work considerably longer hours. The fact that the secretary operates from an office where most of his fellow-workers follow the routine of the commercial work-day, probably operates to reduce his time on duty: whereas the minister is always on call for pastoral services.

The combined week's work of the ten secretaries was divided among the main types of duties as shown in the list on page 313.

While no individual's week was spent in exactly this manner, this division of combined duty-time serves roughly to generalize the typical secretarial week. Nearly twenty-three hours may be expected to go to administrative routine, including about nine and a half hours of personal interviews (either face to face or by telephone); eight and one-third hours in formal committee meetings, or informal group conferences; and five hours to correspondence, the preparation of publicity material, the planning and general supervision of the work.

Type of Duty	Per Cent. Distribution
Total	100
Administration	41
Meetings	26
Clerical routine	14
Travel	8
Technical processes	6
Pastoral relations	3
Study and research	1
Conduct of public worship	½
Janitorial	½

Often no sharp distinction can be drawn between what is classified as administration and what as clerical routine. The latter is credited with nearly eight hours a week on the average. Thus, a secretary may personally handle the mail and work on records and accounts; he may write letters, file documents, and do miscellaneous work of a clerical nature which an assistant would do in another case. Secretaries naturally do more work of these sorts when they have only limited assistance. In the large, however, the amount of time so spent appears to depend primarily upon the man's idiosyncracies and the closeness with which he attends to details, especially those of a financial sort. Because the two are thus so closely related, it is fair to add the secretary's clerical work to the administrative block of time, and to think of him as ordinarily spending thirty hours a week, or 55 per cent. of his time, in administration from within the office.

A large quarter of the secretary's time, averaging some fourteen hours a week, is spent in attending meetings outside the office. During more than four-fifths of this period his role is an active one. He is presiding over the meeting, making an address, or exercising some remoter type of supervision. Less than one-fifth of the time is he merely a passive participant, present because his office requires that he show himself on such occasions.

Adding about four and a half hours for travel per week (largely necessitated by attendance on committees and other meetings), all but about 10 per cent. of the secretary's time is accounted for. He gives very little time to what are classified as technical processes; that is to say, to such things as supervisors of religious education, social workers, and other staff specialists are chiefly employed in. If no such specialists are employed, work of this nature must go to volunteers; for the executive secretary does not do it. Only occasionally he teaches a class, meets with a club, or conducts technical training processes for workers. In connection with the appropriate committees, it is his job to see that other people do these things. However, the secretary's typical week does not escape some slight hint of pastoral responsibility. Some individual case of need or sorrow must be dealt with; he must counsel and comfort some fellow mortal, often a brother minister or one of his staff associates. In the main, however, here is a man whose work is cut out for him. The bulk of it consists of interviews, committees, and meetings in endless reiteration, but involving the rather varied interests and program of the average federation and the many problems of its practical conduct.

Summarizing the case of the executive secretary as the investigation found him: here is a group of well-trained, experienced, industrious, versatile, and somewhat adequately paid men. They are primarily administrators dealing with people and organizations. They were not trained for, and most of their experience has not been in, the particular job they now hold. Their pay hardly suggests that they are heading up the combined Protestant enterprise of their community. They are not protected from the distractions of petty detail, as the heads of corresponding industries would be. They find little time to reflect upon the principles and issues that underlie their work. They are generally not philosophers or scholars, and could not have got their jobs if they had been. To cap the situation, they are directing highly experimental and often financially unstable enterprises. They are much harassed by budgetary worries. They are ever trying to steer between the right and the left wings of Protestantism, ecclesiastically and theologically. They dodge in and out trying to avoid the sore spots of denominational pride and assertiveness. The writer has received innumerable kindnesses, and has been accorded highly valued confidences, from this brotherhood; and he honestly credits it with very much of the success of the federation movement. Most cases of failure, he thinks, were not due to the secretary but to the essential difficulties of the situation. Contrast, for example, the federation secretary's lot with that of the denominational secretary backed as the latter is by strong traditional loyalties, a disciplined body of supporters, and more or less authoritative budgets. The federation secretary's situation is one that calls for supermen; and the Protestant church possesses no such body of leaders anywhere.

ASSISTANT AND DEPARTMENTAL SECRETARIES

Of workers of this group, only the directors of religious education are numerous enough to reveal separate group-characteristics. These accordingly are considered separately.[3]

About the other assistants, only rough generalizations can be made.

Male assistant secretaries, and religious-work directors, are almost always ministers in full professional standing; but average considerably younger than executive secretaries. Their experience has been less and their tenure is briefer.

The few social-service directors are laymen trained as educators. In one or two cases these came up from the ranks in social work in spite of limited scholastic education.

The few women assistant secretaries present two types; first, the highly-educated college woman who has fallen into religious work as a career; and second, the aggressive local church worker who has lifted herself into a paid position in the federation by reason of conspicuous service as a volunteer. One woman assistant secretary had formerly served as the executive of a small federation. Full-time women assistants are likely to receive $1,800 or $2,000 salaries; male assistants and religious-work secretaries, from $3,250 to $4,000. Both are likely to get a month's vacation. Obviously, federations can have discovered no fixed source of supply for these few positions and the workers fall into no single type.

WOMEN'S ASSISTANTS AND OFFICE SECRETARIES

Between the executive secretary and other department executives on the one hand, and the group of purely clerical workers on the other, falls a group of women administrative assistants, occasionally called assistant secretaries, but more often office secretaries. In form, their duties are chiefly clerical; but they involve considerable responsibility and initiative.

Work-records were kept by fifteen representatives of this group, thirteen of whom were employed for full-time, and two for part-time.

Vocational Characteristics

Half the group were between thirty and forty years of age, the extremes running from twenty years to as high as fifty years. About half had enjoyed two or more years of college education. This number included an occasional girl of unusually good social

[3] P. 317.

connections who from idealistic motives had deliberately entered federation work as a career. The great majority of such workers, however, had worked up from the ranks of general clerical workers by reason of their executive ability. A few had been notably active in local churches or in denominational work, and had perhaps commended themselves on these accounts. Most, however, had no unusual experience in church work. Their apprenticeships were those of the business world and their reputations had been made in, rather than outside, the office.

No common tendency as to length of business experience, or duration of time in federation employ, was shown by various groups. Salaries of $1,600 or $1,800 were definitely modal; but the range varied from as low as $1,000 for inexperienced office secretaries in small federations, to as high as $2,000. The more responsible members of the group customarily get a month's vacation.

Duration and Variety of Work

The average full-time workers of this group were on duty forty-three and three-quarters hours during the sample week for which a record was kept. Sunday work was reported in only two cases, one involving work on records, and the other general planning and study. In all but four cases, a Saturday half-holiday was taken. The actual daily average on the basis of a five-and-a-half-day week, was thus just under eight hours a day. This indicates a slight amount of overtime work.

The duties of the full-time workers were typically divided as follows:

Type of Duty	Per Cent. of Time
Clerical	64
Administration	26
Information and accommodation	3
Attendance of meetings	3
Pastoral, janitorial and miscellaneous	4

The secretarial and clerical duties of these positions naturally cover a wide variety of functions, including stenographic work, the keeping of records and accounts, filing, and miscellaneous office work. The mediating character of these positions, vocationally speaking, is particularly evidenced by the fact that administrative duties take over one-fourth of the time. Interviews consume about half of this block of time. The office secretary is the federation's first point of responsible contact with those who have business with it. People come in to see her on matters they do not think it necessary to bring to the executive secretary. Office secretaries attend committees, conduct considerable correspondence over their own signatures, and occasionally supervise other workers in minor administrative capacities. The few women workers who classify as assistant secretaries, actually spend approximately half of their time upon administration, while in their cases, stenographic work falls to a very small fraction of duty-time. In two or three other cases, an office secretary specializes in the preparation of publicity material, or in the department of finance.

The group as a whole, thus bears a very significant share in the responsibilities of federation administration, in contrast with the purely routine duties of strictly clerical workers. More than one executive secretary owes a good measure of his success to the tact and intelligence of a woman assistant.

GENERAL AND DEPARTMENTAL CLERICAL WORKERS

This group includes a few bookkeepers, switchboard operators, and filing clerks, as well as general stenographic and clerical workers. They may be employed in the general federation office, or in the departmental offices such as those of religious education. Most frequently the age of such workers is under thirty. Only one of those studied had a college degree. The majority had found employment in business before coming into federation service. The average length of federation employment was not over two years. Salaries range from $850 to $1,800 per year; $1,200 and $1,500 salaries being rather more frequent. The rate of pay obviously reflects the prevailing standards in a given city, and tends to increase with the size of the city; but the fact that the salary of over a third of this group was $1,000 or less, points to rather low rates of pay on the part of certain federations.

In nearly all federations, the clerical force was on a seven-hour-a-day schedule, with a Saturday half-holiday. The tabulation of a limited number of work-schedules indicates an average of two hours a week overtime. When more accurate measurements are sought, it is found that the workers break up into such small groups, according to particular types of work they are engaged in, that no typical distribution of time for any single group can be arrived at.

PAID WORKERS IN RELIGIOUS EDUCATION

Religious education employs relatively more paid professionals than any other department of federation work. Of the twenty-one federations intensively studied with respect to this department, nine employed paid workers. All but two of these employed more than one worker, the aggregate number totaling twenty-four exclusively and continuously employed. No enumeration was made of workers rendering part-time services, or working seasonally, as, for example, in the capacity of week-day school teachers or vacation-school superintendents. Since practically all of the federations maintain committees on religious education carrying on organized activities, the twelve cases where specialists were not employed left these functions to be administered by the general executive and staff of the federation.

The twenty-four workers noted above classified by positions as follows:

```
Directors of councils or departments of religious education............. 8
Directors or supervisors of weekday education......................... 4
Supervisors and secretaries of divisions.............................. 6
Secretarial and stenographic workers................................. 6
```

Fifteen of the twenty-four workers were women; two directors, seven supervisors, and six stenographers.

Vocational Characteristics of Directors of Religious Education

Measured by median age, directors of religious education averaged twelve years younger than executive secretaries. The group included a few workers still in their twenties. All are college graduates, and all male directors were graduates of theological seminaries as well. One woman director had spent two years at a theological seminary. One had specialized in religious education at her university. More than a third of the group all told has pursued advance work in religious education. The group had thus enjoyed much more definite professional preparation than was true of executive secretaries.

All but one of the male directors were ordained and had had experience in the ministry, generally for rather brief periods. The exceptional case was that of a man who came up through professional employment in old-line Sunday School Association work. Salaries of male directors who give full time, and work exclusively for a single federation, were from $3,000 to $4,600; those of women, from $2,100 to $3,000. Vacations of one month were customary.

While directors of religious education sometimes have important denominational and professional connections, most of them do not get any such general community recognition as falls to the executive secretary. Few of them have contributed to the scholarship of religious education. In brief, theirs is the common lot of departmental administrators: they do not get the full advantage either of executive position or of professional specialization.

Assistant executives in departments of religious education, and directors or supervisors of divisions of work such as week-day education, vacation schools or leadership training, together with supervisors of greater departments, are generally women and are rarely ordained. They thus lack the basic ministerial training that characterizes the director's profession as a whole. On the other hand, they have generally had specific professional training for their work. The exceptions were persons who had come up from the ranks of voluntary teachers in vacation schools or week-day religious classes. Salaries of from $1,800 to $2,500 were characteristic for the women of this group; only for the few men did they go as high as $3,500.

The Workers at Work

Twelve full-time workers in religious education, and two part-time workers, each furnished an itemized record of what was done during hours spent on duty for a week. Five of the twelve full-time workers reporting were women, including one director, three supervisors, and one stenographer.

The full-time workers were on duty an average of fifty-six hours each for the week. Their duty-time ranged from forty-four and one half to eighty and one half hours. The group, however, divides sharply according to sex. The short-hour group included all the women and one man, while all other male directors and supervisors were in the long-hour group. Sunday work was involved in eleven out of the twelve cases, the exception being that of the stenographic worker. From five to six hours was the average time reported for Sunday work. Five out of the eleven Sunday workers were compensated by a day off during the week; the other six worked seven days. The duties of the long-hour workers very frequently required night work as well as Sunday work. The work of principals on religious-education staffs thus characteristically corresponds to that of executive secretaries as to total hours per week. But they have less frequent Sunday work. In both these respects their work contrasts with that of clerical workers in federation offices.

Kinds of Duties

Omitting the single secretarial worker from consideration, the records of the thirteen remaining cases show what sorts of duties are carried on by religious-education workers in federations.

Because directors and supervisors are both primarily administrators, the two groups are first discussed as one, and the divergent characteristics of each are later commented upon.

Five general kinds of duties account for most of the time spent by these workers.

First, from eighteen to twenty hours on the average goes to strictly administrative work. What the federation is carrying on is essentially a system of educational activities, looking to the improvement of methods, primarily in church schools which are individually administered by unpaid volunteers, and in the training of such volunteers. In making the arrangements, and giving direction to the necessary processes, the director or supervisor in his administrative capacity has to confer with individuals. If these conferences are put end to end they occupy from seven to eight hours of the week's time. Next, the worker has to attend committee meetings, to an average total of from four to five hours. His correspondence will take perhaps two hours, and he will give about three hours to the planning of his work.

Second, the religious-education worker must supervise and exemplify some of the actual educational processes, primarily those of instruction. Concretely speaking, he must go into the school and show how to operate it, and into the classroom and actually conduct a class. This direct participation in educational processes, including the necessary study in preparation, will take ten or twelve hours all told.

Third, the religious-education worker has to keep certain school records and reports, and to handle certain supplies and materials primarily relating to the curriculum and to the apparatus of study. Since few workers have secretarial assistance, work of this type, including the keeping of accounts, filing, and other detail, will aggregate about ten hours a week.

Fourth, in his supervisory capacity the religious-education worker has to go from place to place to attend committee meetings, to visit schools, and to hold individual conferences. Travel accounts for about seven hours of the week on the average. (Commuting from the worker's home to his office or place of duty is not counted as duty time.)

Fifth, the religious-education worker has to attend a good many meetings, which he does not conduct and for which he is not directly responsible, either to present his cause or to show support of some wider interest of the federation or of the coöperating churches. About half the workers who attended such meetings did so to make addresses, while three attended conventions in a delegate's capacity during the week accounted for. The time spent in this way will aggregate from five to six hours a week.

A very small fraction of time, aggregating less than an hour a week on the average, goes to study and research outside of the planning of the particular job. This includes professional reading. Less than half the workers studied, report anything under this head, so that their actual average approximates two hours. Perhaps this was the "off" week for the larger half.

Seventh, very scattering activities, taking on the average about 1 per cent. of the time, include the conduct of public services (generally by a director who is also an ordained minister); such chance pastoral ministries as fall to a worker when someone in trouble confides in him; and miscellaneous service functions. The greater part of the work in each case falls to the general office staff or to other specialists.

Directors vs. Supervisors

In spite of the general similarity of their work, a fairly clear-cut distinction between directors and supervisors appears. Both hold individual conferences and attend committees with about equal regularity and for equal lengths of time, the difference at this point being merely that between more general and more specialized responsibility. The director, however, is for a greater time in his office, while the supervisor frequents the schools and classrooms. The supervisor ordinarily spends more time upon records and in other clerical operations, this depending upon whether or not the federation directly operates systems of schools as part of its religious-educational processes. Again, travel, which takes about one-quarter of the supervisor's time, demands only about one-tenth of that of the director's; and would probably not take so much except for the fact that in small federations the directors have to do whatever supervision is done.

Directors devote relatively much more time to attending and to addressing meetings. Both directors and supervisors, then, are administrative officers. The majority of directors are supervisors also, but the two groups have the characteristic differences just outlined.

PAID WORKERS IN SOCIAL SERVICE

Of the seven general types of social service carried out by federations, only two habitually employ paid workers; namely, social service in courts and in public institutions.

Only four federations maintain social-service executives, while a fourth has a part-time secretary. Even so small a group represented three types of executives: one is primarily an educator and promoter; a second, a liaison man between the federations and the social agencies of the community; while the duty of the other two is chiefly to administer specialized phases of institutional work under the federation's own auspices. Although their major function is that of court workers, two women workers were also rated by their federations as social-service secretaries, because responsible for the promotion of social-service interests in women's departments. In the main, however, the administrative side of social-service work is carried by the general secretaries of federations in addition to their many other duties.

The four social-service executives had two full-time and two half-time secretarial workers as assistants. These workers were primarily engaged either in clerical routine related to educational and promotional work, or in the keeping of case records, or, where the secretaries under whom they worked were conducting departments under the federation's own auspices, in more general secretarial duties.

Vocational Characteristics

With so small a number of cases to deal with, the social-service executives and their clerical helpers can not be characterized as groups. Chaplains and court workers on the contrary, are more numerous and show certain common characteristics.

Chaplains are usually rated by their federations as religious workers.[4] Since, however, their duties lie in social institutions, they should be regarded vocationally from the standpoint of their fitness in this capacity. They are nearly always ordained ministers. They are generally well-educated and experienced men. Their previous work in parishes is assumed to have prepared them for institutional work without further special training. Occasionally an uneducated man with aptitude for dealing with human misfortune gets into the chaplain's ranks. None of the chaplains reported any special social-service training.

Court workers (of whom ten were reported in addition to the two women secretaries previously mentioned) were generally women. The age of the group varies from thirty-five to fifty-five years. The average salaries approximated $1,500 a year. The two women who rated as social-work secretaries received maximum salaries of $2,400. Most of these workers have benefitted by previous experience in social service. Only one of the

[4] P. 406.

group, however, had received any considerable technical training. Professional workers do not look upon the technical training of the average federation representative in similar work as sufficient. In rare cases, federation workers were trying to overcome this deficiency by taking extension courses. Salaries for full-time chaplains averaged about $2,000; those of the few male court workers about $2,700. Both types of workers frequently supplemented their salaries by preaching in churches.

Hours of Labor

In connection with the investigation, twelve full-time and two half-time social-service workers kept detailed accounts of a week's work. The two half-time workers were on duty seventeen and twenty-one and a half hours respectively. The week's work of the full-time workers ranged from thirty-six and three-quarter to eighty and one half hours, the average being about fifty-six hours. From fifty to sixty hours was strongly modal. With regard to hours of labor, the workers fall into three perfectly clear-cut classes. The short-day workers were all women. The male court workers all worked medium hours. Institutional chaplains or social-service executives all worked long hours. Sunday work appeared in all but two cases; but was compensated for, in the cases of some of the women, by a week-day holiday. The average number of hours on duty on Sunday was six. Night work appeared primarily in connection with chaplaincies, some of which involved evening services. Most of the preparation of addresses and such professional study as was reported also took place at night. Case records were occasionally kept out of office hours; but only very rarely did actual emergency cases arise requiring night work. In the main, then, the long hours were due to the apparent attempt to perform a full round of active duties during an ordinary working day and then to carry on study or preparation for public appearances in addition.

Kinds of Work

For the social-workers' group as a whole well over half the time was spent in duties directly relating to persons in need or trouble, in conferences immediately concerning them, or in travel involved in one of these processes. Case-work activities in turn divide rather evenly between direct efforts to influence the individual concerned and put him into helpful and character-building situations, and those involving technical adjustments, as, for example, with courts and social agencies.

The other block of the workers' time—about 47 per cent. in all—was found to be divided among numerous other types of duties. Twenty-five of these minor duties were distinguished and tabulated. So many fell under the general category of administrative work as to account for about 20 per cent. of the total duty-time. Of separate minor duties, that of attending public meetings for which the worker was in no way personally responsible but which were professionally profitable to him or to the cause, took 5.9 per cent. of the total duty-time. Keeping technical records took 4.9 per cent. of the time. Committee meetings, preparing and making addresses, and planning work, each accounted for between 3 and 4 per cent. of the duty-time. Various forms of clerical work and (on the part of ordained ministers) the conducting of public services constituted the other appreciable elements in the work of the group.

Differentiation from Other Types of Federation Workers

The emphasis on personal case-work, as thus shown, differentiates social-service workers from all other classes of the paid personnel of federations. Except for the handful of pedagogical supervisors in religious-education departments, the duties of all other types of workers are primarily administrative, or else almost purely clerical. The coöperative exercise of the pastoral functions of the Church in behalf of Protestantism thus falls almost entirely to social-service workers.

Variation According to Position

Naturally the distribution of workers' duties as thus generalized differs according to the various types of work. For example, on the basis of the distribution of their duty-time, two types of chaplains appear. One is responsible for public services in his institutions; the other is purely a pastoral worker. But both spend a good deal of time in attendance on public services. This apparently means that the pastoral worker must support organized religion in his institution by his personal presence at services whether he is responsible for their formal conduct or not.

Court workers again fall into two groups, one of which has to share to a considerable extent in the promotional work of the federation, while the other does not. Thus a woman worker spends as much time "telling sob-stories" to local women's organizations from which she receives her support as she does in the courts. This really amounts to raising one's own salary. On the other hand, social-service executives, whose functions are essentially those of liaison officers between the federation and social agencies, naturally have to attend many committee and other meetings.

Still another distinction, relating to both social-work executives and court workers and chaplains, is that between workers whose time is chiefly spent in carrying out technical responsibilities, and those who recruit and direct volunteer workers. Thus a chaplain may spend as much time at the telephone keeping ministers in touch with hospital cases as he does in personal hospital visitation. A court worker may spend more time in inducing individuals to act as "big brothers" or "big sisters" to juvenile delinquents than in the direct handling of delinquents themselves. A social-work executive may be primarily concerned with the training of volunteers, rather than with the administration of any form of direct service.

All told, the field of social service under federation auspices has developed almost nothing of standardized types of professional service. In every department the work is tentative and experimental. A worker going from one position to another bearing the same designation would have little likelihood of finding similar requirements to be met. Standards of professional performance are still almost entirely lacking.

VOCATIONAL PROBLEMS OF THE PAID WORKERS

The vocational problems that such a study of federation staffs inevitably raises are, of course, conditioned by the generally feeble, struggling and unstandardized character of the movement.

Many of them can be solved only as federations multiply in numbers, gather strength, and increase in years.

Within this general setting the familiar issues of the selection and recruiting of workers, their training, management, and pay have to work themselves out. Each of these issues takes on a special complexion to match each major type of worker employed.

Considering paid federation workers as a whole, one has to admit in advance that their numbers, all told, are too small to warrant elaborate special machinery either of selection or of training. The limited magnitude of the problem, on the contrary, keeps the issue of management relatively simple and characteristically personal. The issue of pay falls within the general and somewhat niggardly tradition of the Church: which, however, does not operate more flagrantly with respect to the federations than usual. Federations can be expected to do better by their workers, however, only when churches do better by theirs.

Selection and Recruiting of Workers

Except as the Extension Department of the Federal Council is incidentally available for advice and assistance, the selection of federation secretaries is a matter for the individual organization. Some conscious effort to turn the minds of theological students toward the secretaryship of the profession has been incidentally evidenced by the Federal Council and Association of Federation Secretaries; but the requirement of prolonged experience precludes the immediate employment of seminary graduates. Directors and supervisors of religious education on the contrary, require less experience and may frequently be drawn from the body of religious educators employed by the churches of a city. Social-service workers generally come up through some connection with denominational charities; or, one suspects, they are sometimes employed as themselves objects of charity. This accounts for certain unfortunate cases of inferiority or inefficiency. Employing officers hitherto have shown little sense of the precise technical qualifications demanded by the respective social-service positions.

Training

Except as an exceedingly small minority of theological seminaries has projected a mere ghost of special training for the administrative and supervisory positions in the Church at large, no means exist for educating men directly for the profession of executive secretaries. The Association of Executive Secretaries has repeatedly gone on record as believing that it is necessary to create special provision for such education. A beginning in this direction was made in the fall of 1929 by the inauguration, under the Federal Council Extension Committee, of a traveling lectureship in interchurch coöperation among the theological seminaries. This position was filled by the appointment of Dr. Charles Zahniser, formerly of the Pittsburgh Council of Churches, whose lectures are giving special attention to federation ideals and methods.

So far as religious education is concerned, training in the theory of the administrating of community programs frequently appears in connection with scholastic preparation, but generally as a very minor phase. General educational administration, however, is broadly stressed and the direct adaptation of education to federation needs is more possible than is adaptation in any other field. The training of social-service workers, on the contrary, is technically almost a complete blank—this in spite of the fact that virtually every city now has a professional school for social workers in which many well-trained young people from Christian homes and churches are students.

Management

In view of the autonomous character of the local federations, their executive secretaries are under no system of overhead supervision or management. It is possible to conceive, however, of the body of secretaries setting up its own technical advisorship through its Association, in connection with the Federal Council. Such an agency might provide persons of exceptional experience and ability, not only to meet emergency calls for administrative advice, but to undertake routine inspection in behalf of the total group and to assure the systematic collation of experience, so that all federations might profit by the successes or failures of any.

The direct personal character of the supervision of subordinate membership of the general office staff has already been noted. In this connection the emergence of the woman office secretary as a sometimes unrecognized assistant executive, is noteworthy. Few federations, however, have analyzed the jobs of subordinate workers so that any objective standard of judgment as to their results is possible. Facilities, too, are not always what could be desired.[5]

The supervision of educational workers is part of the tradition of the school; and this aspect of management appears to be most satisfactorily carried out in religious-education departments. Records also are likely to be the most complete and systematic in these departments.

In glaring contrast is the almost complete absence of adequate supervision or records in social-service departments. A few striking exceptions merely prove the rule. In extenuation, one may note that the executive secretary has been trained in the individual parish tradition, which is strongly individualistic. He has no deep-seated instinct for staff management. This leaves him at outs with one of the strongest tendencies of modern social work, and explains much of the critical attitude of the social workers toward such work undertaken by federations.

Pay

With respect to ordained ministers (who make up the large majority of male federation workers), the most acute problem

---

[5] P. 466.

relating to remuneration is that of retirement pensions. The leading denominations have now generally provided somewhat adequate retirement allowances for their respective ministries; but until recently the benefits of these funds were in most cases not available to ministers in interdenominational service. Several leading denominations now are ready to regard federation workers as temporarily loaned to the common cause, and to leave their equities in pension funds unimpaired. This is entirely justifiable so long as the profession has so few numbers and their tenure is so brief. In the long run, the federation movement itself must presumably face the problem of remuneration, and of current salaries, in the light of total provision during the worker's professional life-time.

As professional opportunity for women emerges in connection with the federation movement, the problem of remuneration equally arises for them. Except for deaconesses in a few communions, the Church has reached no reasonable solution for workers of this type. Probably the federation movement is too feeble to be expected to lead off in this connection.

All told, then, no very definite or impressive evolutionary trends can as yet be discerned with respect to vocational problems of federations. This area remains particularly tentative and unilluminated.

Chapter XVIII

EVANGELISM

Beginning with this chapter the major departments of federation work are reported upon one after another.[1]

As defined by federation usage and adopted for the purposes of this chapter, evangelism covers the regular ministries of the Church through its customary worship and preaching, and the general advocacy of the central Christian ideals; also organized methods of recruiting individuals for church-membership, and specialized ministries to people classified according to their special needs. Every federation studied was maintaining a commission or committee on evangelism, or religious work, or an equivalent. This is only what one would expect in view of the primary emphasis of the Church, and the announced objectives of the coöperative movement. Occasional activities logically falling within these categories, are sometimes assigned to other departments. That is to say, as in all subdivisions of work, there are borderland areas that may profitably be discussed or programized under more than one head.

SCOPE AND MAGNITUDE

What departments of evangelism specifically do, and the relative frequency with which the more characteristic evangelistic activities occur in the federations studied, are shown in detail in Appendix III.[2]

As shown by this comparison, the conduct of interdenominational Lenten services is the most frequent single item. About two-thirds of the federations also operate campaigns of home-visitation evangelism.

Somewhat less than half make regular use of radio facilities for preaching and religious worship. Considerably less than a fourth carry on specialized phases of evangelism for people in particular circumstances, or for particular age-, or sex-groups. Combining all evangelistic activities reported by one or more of the twenty-six federations studied, an aggregate list of twenty-eight items results.

---

[1] Comity was covered by a companion volume of this report under the title *Church Comity: A Study of Coöperative Church Extension in American Cities.*
[2] P. 490.

The average federation chose eleven out of these twenty-eight. This measures the typical program. Ranking the federations and dividing them into four groups according to standing, those in the group at the top of the list are found to be carrying on an average of fifteen evangelistic activities, while the one at the bottom of the list carries on not more than six, with a minimum of two. The two smallest cities studied show the most limited evangelistic programs. Large federations naturally tend to have broad evangelistic activities. Certain small federations, however, specialize in evangelism and show unusually extensive programs in this field. At the other extreme, are a few large federations whose evangelistic programs are abnormally weak. Some of these have been reduced to a smaller range of activities than formerly by reason of the withdrawal of coöperation by denominations or important individual churches. Thus, the characteristic Lenten and Good Friday interdenominational services may even be lacking.

Among the more infrequent evangelistic activities are pastors' retreats, institutes for training personal workers, shop and factory meetings, outdoor and street preaching, and the systematic circulation of the Scriptures in printed form.

CONTINUOUS ACTIVITIES

Beyond these indications of scope and emphasis, it is desirable to analyze more carefully the undertakings of federations under the banner of evangelism. The succeeding paragraphs accordingly describe the major items of the program as previously listed, beginning with continuous activities.

COÖPERATIVE DISCUSSION OF PLANS

Most denominations maintain city-wide commissions or committees on evangelism. The chairmen of these committees are ordinarily members of the federation's committee, so that the several denominational plans are discussed together and, so far as possible, brought into effective relations. Often, however, not even this minimum ideal is reached, and the federation's influence upon the total mass of evangelistic effort as finally carried out through the separate churches is distinctly occasional and not very obvious.

BROADCASTING OF SERVICES

In contrast with the mere coöperative discussion of plans that are to be executed entirely under denominational auspices, stands the group of evangelistic activities undertaken directly

by federations in behalf of the coöperating churches. Of these
activities, the most frequent is the broadcasting of religious
services, either daily or on Sundays. In Philadelphia, for example, by the courtesy of two department stores that maintain
broadcasting stations, the federation conducts five noonday radio
services per week and a Sunday-afternoon service. The daily
services are specifically designed to bring comfort and cheer to
sick, disabled, or troubled people. They consist of nonsectarian
addresses and prayer, supplemented twice a week by musical
services. The daily speaker invites requests for prayer to be
sent by letter to the federation office. These requests are individually replied to by mail with assurances of sympathy. They
are referred weekly to the members of the Committee on Evangelism which, at its monthly meeting, devotes a regular session
of prayer to these requests. An inspection of the correspondence
conveying these requests discovers very impressive testimony
as to the value of this ministry of religious comfort via the air.

The Sunday-afternoon service follows the conventional order
of the Church with full musical accompaniment. The total
broadcasting of the last year included 286 services with 219
different speakers. In selecting the speakers, the federation
keeps a suitable denominational distribution in mind. For the
Sunday service men of more eminent reputation are naturally
chosen.

Thus in the more typical cases of radio evangelism, the federation attempts to put on the air both the pulpit's message and
its more personal and intimate pastoral ministry. Exceptional
cases may emphasize only one of these aspects to the virtual
exclusion of the other. For example, radio services stressing
the pastoral note are represented by the afternoon Good Cheer
Hour of the Massachusetts State Federation, and especially by
its Midnight Ministry for sleepless people. At both these periods,
comforting messages of Scripture are broadcast, together with
poetical selections radiating cheerfulness and courage. The brief
accompanying addresses are given only secondary stress.

The most outstanding example of specialization upon great
preaching is the group of national radio services conducted by
the Greater New York Federation and sponsored by the Federal
Council.

As explained by the promoters of this enterprise, certain outstanding radio personalities have been identified in the realm
of religion by the verdict of popular approval on the part of
the American public. This approval has been accorded them
quite irrespective of particular denomination or of theological

tendencies as consciously defined. The great corporation that lends its facilities to these national radio services is merely desirous of giving the public what it wants. The corporation, on its part, makes certain technical requirements as to the quality of the services and as to their administration. The supporting musical features have to be of a quality commensurate with national radio standards. The announcers and operators have to be paid at the regular scale and the facilities have to be used the year around. Accordingly each of the three main preachers has come to have a summer understudy.

Such requirements have made these national services very expensive. Their total annual cost is approximately $83,000. It is provided for by the organization of small committees of wealthy men who underwrite the "hours" of the three chief speakers. Broadcasting thus escapes being a direct charge upon the general treasury of the Greater New York Federation.

INSTITUTIONAL CHAPLAINCIES

A second most characteristic and frequent form of continuous evangelism conducted by federations is found in the regular ministries of chaplains in penal and charitable institutions. Such chaplains are maintained by eight federations. Their work sometimes consists primarily in the conducting of formal religious services, while in others it is chiefly pastoral visitation among the inmates of institutions.[3]

When paid chaplains are not employed, federations sometimes organize systems of services in charitable institutions, assigning responsibility from week to week to individual ministers and churches drawn from their coöperating denominations. Sometimes the minister takes his choir with him to such services. Otherwise, the federation provides the musicians. Using this plan, the Toledo Federation, for example, furnishes 900 services annually to the jails, hospitals and old-people's homes of its community.

An infrequent type of continuous evangelistic service attaches itself to industrial plants rather than to charitable institutions. What are commonly called factory meetings are held at the noon-hour in such plants as are willing to coöperate. Thus the St. Louis Federation conducted 729 such services in 1928. They were distributed among eighteen factories and had an aggregate attendance of 4,500 workers. It takes much time and great

---

[3] While evangelistic in purpose, the chaplain's work is most frequently rated as a form of social work. Accordingly, it is described more at length on p. 406.

persistence to arrange for so many hundreds of occasions for each of which a volunteer preacher and musicians must be recruited. Careful track must be kept of engagements to prevent failures. Emergencies must be met and constant supervision given to assure the efficiency and quality of this form of service.

The forms of evangelism so far described go on week after week, supplementing the ordinary preaching of the separate churches.

RECURRENT EVANGELISTIC ACTIVITIES

In contrast with the continuous evangelistic activities are discontinuous ones that recur seasonally. The most important of these naturally revolve about the anniversaries and celebrations of the Christian year and of the nation. Thus the following Sundays or other special occasions are recognized by one or another federation; "Go to Church Sunday" at the opening of the year; Labor Sunday; Armistice Sunday; Thanksgiving; Christmas; New Year; the first week of the year, as a Week of Prayer; Lincoln's Birthday; Pentecost; Children's Day; Fourth of July.

LENT AND HOLY WEEK

The most widely-recognized item in the list is the culminating celebration of the anniversary of Easter. This is nearly always preceded by the special recognition of the Lenten season and the celebration of Good Friday. The particular method employed is usually a series of interdenominational noonday services in down-town churches or theatres, often accompanied by similar services at district centres throughout the city.

When the entire Lenten period, or a considerable portion of it, is covered by such special services, local ministers are usually employed as speakers, perhaps with a few outsiders to attract additional attention. When, on the contrary, the services are concentrated within Holy Week, the federation generally imports a preacher of national reputation and tries to give him a distinguished hearing. It is increasingly customary for business men's associations to prolong the noon-hour period at this season so that their employees can attend services. Stores are often closed on the afternoon of Good Friday. In a number of cases, the mayor of the city has issued a proclamation suggesting the cessation of business during some part of that day.

The result is often a very marked general and civic recognition of this great anniversary of the Church.

The expenses of the Lenten services are generally met by plate collections in the various meetings. When theatres are used as places of meetings, they are generally donated. An unhappy note has been introduced into the situation by the tendency of the federations to bid against one another for the services of the few superlatively popular preachers of the nation. This has tended to run up the scale of remuneration to heights that have sometimes been criticized.

Several other problems have developed with respect to the Lenten services. One concerns the desirability of centering them in down-town locations in contrast with scattering them through the residential districts of the city. Down-town services draw more largely on the business and other employed classes, and are more widely representative. Nevertheless, the total attendance represents only a fraction of the combined church constituency. Ministers of churches in residential areas sometimes feel that it detracts from the dignity of their churches and breaks up the religious habits of their congregations to have the crowning celebration of the Christian year taken to a remote central location. Consequently some federations attempt to maintain both central and district services.

But even this is no solution for certain wings and tendencies within the Protestant denominations. Some of them are unable to approach the culminating experiences of Christian worship rewardingly, except through the use of their own distinctive forms. To meet such situations, various types of worship are sometimes provided for by separate services under denominational auspices, all of which, however, are fostered and given publicity by the federation as expressions of a common celebration.

When the celebration is thus both decentralized and denominationalized, it becomes possible for all Christian communions to lend it a measure of common support. The Roman Catholic authorities have sometimes coöperated with federations in promoting the more general public recognition of Holy Week or Good Friday, and in circulating publicity matter in behalf of separate denominational services.

A good many federations vary their methods from year to year.

SUMMER EVANGELISM

Next to Lenten services the most highly developed group of recurrent activities relates to the summer season. They include street preaching, sometimes at church doors, sometimes at various points of public congregation. In the latter case, speaking is frequently done from automobiles. Thus the Greater New York Federation operates a notable outdoor pulpit in connection with the Marble Collegiate Church. The total open-air work of this federation covers sixty different centres and uses over two hundred speakers annually. In Brooklyn, twenty-one speakers with an equal number of musicians are employed in services conducted from automobiles in many parts of the city, notably at Coney Island. Boston conducts outdoor services from "The Little Church on Wheels" on Tremont Street, as well as on the famous Common. These services employ three volunteer preachers each Sunday and four each Tuesday, a total of 134 for the season with accompanying singers and instrumentalists. St. Louis has maintained extensive summer services for sixteen years. During the last reported year they were attended by 43,000 people.

While religious in purpose and evangelistic in form, the fact that some of the above-mentioned services do not follow conventional indoor church methods, and that they are intended to serve people of particular social classes, lead certain federations to classify them as social service rather than as evangelism. Obviously, this represents an overlapping of departments.

SEASONAL PASTORAL MINISTRIES

Another aspect of coöperative seasonal evangelism is the exercise of ministerial offices by the federation staff. There is a surprisingly general exodus of the professional ministers of religion during the vacation period. Whole areas of cities accordingly find themselves temporarily without an available body of clergy to officiate at weddings or funerals, to visit the sick, or to meet other daily emergencies. To meet this situation, the federation staff is held in readiness to perform such functions in behalf of the total Protestant body.

OCCASIONAL ACTIVITIES

EVANGELISTIC CAMPAIGNS

Besides the stated forms of coöperative evangelism, whether continuous or recurrent, more occasional and intensive methods are employed during limited periods. The most important of these is the interdenominational evangelistic campaign.

The period covered by the study was particularly marked by numerous campaigns of "simultaneous visitation evangelism" intended to cover entire cities or extensive urban districts with series of house-to-house calls in behalf of the Church. Following a systematic canvass to discover unchurched people, these calls are usually made by teams of laymen going about two by two. They are intended to carry a direct religious message and an invitation to become connected with some church. Visitation evangelism thus contrasts strikingly with the more familiar type based upon public meetings.

Though essentially an old method, which has been operated occasionally by federations for a long time, visitation evangelism as recently developed has special technical marks: (1) It is highly organized and follows a precise method of preparation of recruiting and training workers, of collecting "prospect lists," of conducting the calls, and of reporting back results. These processes are accompanied and backed by carefully devised and aggressive methods of publicity. A technical literature expounding the method as thus professionalized, has begun to appear.[4]

(2) A corps of skilled professional leaders has emerged to direct the evangelism of the new type. Paid canvassers are frequently employed to discover the religious status of the population to be visited. Substituting for the older professional evangelist, these organizers undertake the entire charge of visitation campaigns; or, when the administration remains in local hands, they may be called in at a strategic moment to "put the business over." In either case, stress falls upon expert capacity; and the professional spirit is pronounced.

(3) The simultaneous activity of large groups of lay volunteers creates a movement of impressive magnitude. The joint investment of time, money, and effort exemplifies a large scale of coöperation on the part of the Protestant group.

(4) Prolonged preparation, and a definite period for application following the intensive period of evangelistic cultivation, tend to integrate the fruits of the simultaneous method with the on-going life of the Church. In these more extended evangelistic programs, it is attempted to include all phases of religious interest, and to tie up personal religious commitment with the on-going cultural processes of the Church.

Two-thirds of the federations studied had made somewhat recent use of the methods of visitation evangelism. The aggregate results were believed to be very great; but differences in the length of periods covered, as well as in methods of reporting results, make a statistical compilation of results impossible.

---

[4] See Kernahan, *Visitation Evangelism*.

A varying typical example is the coöperative campaign of 160 churches under the Greater New York Federation in 1928, resulting in over 10,000 "decisions for the Christian life and church membership." Twenty per cent. of these represented the reclaiming of lapsed members. The cost of this campaign, including all overhead expenses, was about $15,000.

Advocates of visitation evangelism regard it as a genuine Messianic device; "Greater than the Apostle Paul, greater than John Wesley or George Whitfield, greater than Dwight L. Moody, greater than all of them together is the lay evangelist, going with a team-mate into the homes of the people in the name of the Master." The method may, of course, be operated apart from federation auspices; but a study of cases shows how essential to success is discipline and coöperation, established loyalty, and the habit of team-play, of which the federations are far more representative than any temporary movement can be. Even so, great difficulties are often met in the financing of campaigns of visitation evangelism, in securing sufficient coöperation, and in pushing lay participants to the point of actual results. The numbers reached are often sadly small relative to the vast population of areas it is attempted to cover.

In view of somewhat disillusioning experiences along these lines, federations are becoming somewhat wary of accepting direct charge of visitation evangelistic campaigns with their accompanying financial responsibilities.

It is thus possible that, in the long run, the permanent contribution of this method will be to the technique and leadership of regular federation work. For the method is essentially applicable year after year, at least in some part of any great city. If evangelistic secretaries, as expertly trained as the temporary professionals, could be kept permanently on a federation staff, there is no reason why a city should not be continuously gone over, by taking various areas in rotation. The results might well equal those now secured, and the incidental costs could in the main be met by the churches immediately benefited.

All that would be necessary would be for the churches to transfer to the federation budget for the employment of a regular staff-member the sums they now pay for outside leadership.

EXTRA-PAROCHIAL MINISTRY

Another characteristic form of occasional coöperative evangelism is that which brings to a city Christian leaders of exceptional power and reputation, and secures a hearing for them. Such a function is performed at least occasionally by almost all the federations.

Two distinctive phenomena of our age conspire to make this method possible and inevitable. In the first place, a few leaders have achieved virtually interdenominational standing as ministers at large. Their reputation is so great that the cost of bringing them to a city can easily be met by the audiences that wish to hear them. Many of these leaders regard it as a handicap to have to deliver their messages under sectarian auspices. They desire and expect an interdenominational hearing.

In the second place, certain other leaders with great messages in specialized fields are set apart to the office of nation-wide advocacy and propaganda in which they are supported by various organized agencies. Such speakers are easily available for federation occasions. With the expenditure of relatively little money, federations are thus able to provide an extra parochial ministry in behalf of common Protestantism. This function is frequently carried out in coöperation with other local agencies such as the Young Men's Christian Association.

To this same general category belongs the function of bringing great teachers of religious education who go from city to city delivering courses of lectures on biblical or more general religious themes.

One is not surprised that a federation sometimes finds difficulty in performing this function. What it supposes to be a great religious message sometimes seems to part of its supporters to be stupid conservatism, dangerous radicalism, or concealed propaganda.

Still another type of religious activity commonly classified as evangelistic is represented by the religious celebration of historic events, believed to be of great moment for the Church. Thus, the three-hundredth anniversary of the Protestant reformation, and the tenth anniversary of the Adoption of the Eighteenth Amendment, were widely celebrated under federation auspices.

CONCOMITANT ACTIVITIES

Along with such specific major activities as have been enumerated, goes on a set of varied processes for promoting the general interests of religion. These include occasional conferences on evangelism, ministers' and laymen's retreats for the promotion of the devotional life, constant advocacy of religion in the regular publications of the federation and in its newspaper publicity, the circulation of the Scriptures, and the very frequent religious addresses made by staff-members throughout the year.

ANNUAL COÖPERATIVE PROGRAMS

A good many federations undertake to weave together the various evangelistic activities into community-wide programs covering an entire year. Thus, for 1927–8, the Minneapolis Church Federation proposed first a "stir-up Sunday" early in the fall, and an intensive evangelistic period running from January 1 through Easter. The further details of the plan are suggested by the following schedule: January was to be given over to devotional Bible reading and the institution of a "fellowship of prayer." Five thousand copies of a penny edition of the Gospels were circulated in this connection. During the first two weeks of February, public evangelistic meetings were to be held. For the first week, these were to be group meetings in the several districts of the city; and for the second, city-wide meetings at the down-town centre. Both series of meetings were held and addressed by religious leaders of national reputation.

The second half of February was scheduled as a period of personal evangelistic work on the part of volunteers, and for the holding of catechetical classes in individual churches. Reports from about half of the churches received at the end of this period showed that seventy classes were operated with an attendance of above 2,000. Finally came the celebration of Holy Week with services in three down-town theatres, and an additional observance of Good Friday. During the period of the program, house-to-house evangelistic visitations were set up in a number of localities and carried out by neighboring churches.

Authorization for this inclusive plan was sought in separate action by the ministers' organizations of the several denominations. Five of the larger ones formally agreed to adopt a plan and limited approval was received from others. At the end of the year the federation undertook to gather data showing results of the total effort; but the response was meagre, especially as to the degree to which individual churches entered into the several phases of the program. Relatively little of the projected city-wide house-to-house canvass had been carried out. On the other hand, a very considerable degree of unanimity had presided over the evangelistic efforts of the Protestant body. This is a very typical illustration of the method and the limitations of unified evangelism under federation auspices.

SUMMARY OF ACTIVITIES

Summarizing the work of coöperative evangelism as carried on by federations, one notes, first, that it has centered upon the radio as the most recent means for proclaiming the Gospel and Christian ideals. The use of this device is beyond the resources of the average church, and the agencies operating regular stations are strongly desirous of dealing with some agency of united Protestantism rather than with the competitive claims of denominations and churches. In most cities the federation has been recognized as the natural organization to handle the matter in behalf of Protestantism.

Again, coöperative evangelism has concentrated upon the annual and seasonal events and observances that are recognized by all bodies of Christians in common, and in connection with which it is easy to strike a united religious note, irrespective of denominational differences.

Third, coöperative evangelism finds a place at those seasons in which the separate work of the local churches lets down, and in behalf of those special classes which the churches, as parochially organized, find it difficult to reach.

All told, then, the program of coöperative evangelism is complementary to that of the denomination and parochial churches in that it stresses only the common elements and, on the whole, uses different means and times for its activities. This has not prevented the rise of somewhat numerous problems.

VERDICT OF CONSTITUENTS

A preceding section of the report has shown the degree to which constituents approve or disapprove each of the major elements of the coöperative program.[5] Evangelism is a little less favorably regarded than is the federation program as a whole. It is ranked below comity, religious education, and social service. On the other hand, it gets no such active opposition as do certain phases of these other functions. That is to say, it tends to receive general approval as a set of activities of secondary importance. This verdict should be noted. It is based upon actual programs, not upon the general ideal of evangelistic ministry.

A total of 12,107 judgments were registered by constituents relative to particular evangelistic activities.[6] The per cent. of constituents rating certain items of the evangelistic program as

---

[5] See Chapter VIII.
[6] For form of questionnaire by means of which judgments were registered, see p. 127.

unimportant or improper for federations to undertake is shown at the left of Table XXVI, and the per cent. rating them as highly important at the right.

TABLE XXVI—RANKING OF ITEMS OF EVANGELISM PROGRAMS ACCORDING TO CONSTITUENTS' JUDGMENTS REGARDING APPROPRIATENESS AND IMPORTANCE, IN 17 FEDERATIONS

Item	Per Cent. Unfavorable Judgments*	Item	Per Cent. Highly Favorable Judgments†
Student work	2.5	Student work	91.3
Surveys and statistics	7.7	Surveys and statistics	72.0
Evangelistic conferences	8.1	Interdenominational Holy Week services	70.2
Central lenten services	8.6	Evangelistic Conference	70.1
Union Thanksgiving Services	9.2	Central Lenten services	69.8
Inspirational speakers	9.5	Coöperative evangelistic planning	69.5
Interdenominational Holy Week services	9.6	Neighborhood Holy Week services	69.2
Annual religious retreats	10.1	Visitation evangelistic campaign	68.8
Neighborhood Holy Week services	10.6	Inspirational speakers	68.4
Coöperative evangelistic planning with seasonal emphasis	11.3	Union Thanksgiving services	67.7
Broadcasting	11.6	Annual religious retreats	64.5
Visitation evangelism campaigns	11.9	Street preaching	62.2
Street preaching	12.2	Broadcasting	62.1
Easter sunrise services	24.6	Easter sunrise services	42.3

* Positions 1–3.
† Position 5.

As already suggested, constituents' judgments vary less widely than they do relative to religious education or social service.[7] Of activities that occur in one-fourth or more of the federations studied, or that may be regarded as characteristic of the larger federations, interdenominational Holy Week and Lenten services are the most favorably regarded, while street preaching and broadcasting find least favor. While the judgments are undoubtedly affected by the fact that the respective functions are better performed in some federations than in others, the verdict on the whole must probably be taken as indicating what types of evangelistic activities constituencies recognize as suitable, or as not suitable, to be carried on by coöperative effort.

CHARACTERISTICS OF FEDERATION EVANGELISM

In the light of the foregoing analysis and verdict, the significant characteristics of the federation activity in the field of evangelism are easily discovered. The following stand out as important:

[7] Pp. 134 ff.

(1) Relative to the total bulk of Protestant evangelistic effort, the work of federations is chiefly coördinative. The chief role as evangelistic agents is left to local churches and to the denominations.

(2) Federation evangelism concerns itself almost exclusively with methods and concrete processes.

(3) This means that it almost always avoids the problem of content, either as related to common worship or the common Christian message.

(4) This omission must be recognized as made for policy's sake. It leaves out of account some of the deepest implications of the effort to associate different bodies of•Christians in a united church movement. Thus it is attempted to ignore the difference between those who regard worship in a prescribed way as a means of securing a divine grace bestowed through sacraments and those who regard all forms as immaterial. The former view necessarily puts stress upon the Church and the validity of the ministry in mediating this experience. It hinges the efficacy of the Christian message upon the ecclesiastical means. The latter view minimizes all these things.

(5) The characteristic stress upon union in method while issues of content are ignored, leaves extremists on both sides necessarily unsatisfied. Theological criticism of federations thus largely focuses upon the field of evangelism.

(6) Whether or not the validity of the ministry employed in evangelism is stressed, it is carried on chiefly by the ordained specialists of the Church. The clerical character of this interest thus sets it apart from all other phases of federation work.

(7) Even as relates to method, federation evangelism has never faced such radical and ultimate problems as those of fewer and better preachers and possible substitution of central pulpits, and the general use of broadcasting for the parochial organization of preaching.

PROBLEMS

The verdict of the federation's supporters gives additional point to certain problems emerging from the previous consideration of the facts: While in all of the major spheres of federation activity there is incomplete coöperation on the part of certain Protestant communions, the discrepancy is particularly flagrant and damaging in the sphere of coöperative evangelism. The Protestant body as a whole finds it easier to rally for common effort in the more specialized and technical fields of religious education or social service than in the central field of proclaiming the Christian gospel.

Consequently it is with larger gaps in the ranks than usual that coöperative evangelism faces its secondary problems, namely, the degree to which a federation should attempt to carry on under its own auspices a set of evangelistic activities in behalf of the entire body of coöperating churches, in contrast with acting merely as a suggesting or coördinating agency for measures actively carried out separately by the several churches and denominations; and the conditions under which either method should be conducted.

It seems fairly demonstrated that constituents desire and approve a limited evangelistic program, under direct federation control, combining and supplementing that of the several denominations. This is most in evidence at three points: first, in occasional joint evangelistic campaigns which directly solicit recruits for individual congregations and do not involve interdenominational meetings; second, in the fields of radio preaching and institutional chaplaincies, in both of which the situation is controlled by secular administrators who strongly insist upon a unified non-sectarian Protestant effort, and who will not lend their facilities for coöperative sectarian purposes; and third, in national or civic anniversaries, in the observance of which union meetings were already the rule even before the organization of the federations. Some of these occasions have been partially occupied by denominational ministries, and difficulties have frequently arisen in substituting the federation for more limited auspices. On the whole, however, the value and appropriateness of federation activity in the common behalf is little challenged.

When, however, it comes to substituting interdenominational public services for parochial or denominational services on those occasions which celebrate the climactic events and experiences of the Christian faith (such as Holy Week), a profound and delicate issue arises. Here the feelings of a 'strong minority of Protestants demand services carried out in their own way and in their own place. Denominations and individuals are attached to particular modes and rituals, and feel a lack of vitality and validity in unfamiliar methods of worship. Attempts to create a synthetic form of service combining elements from all services, are likely to fail to satisfy anyone. A primary test of a highly religious occasion is certainly that of making its participants feel access to God and fellowship with one another. Forms that fail to inspire these feelings are properly challengeable. It is a real question whether any appreciable progress is being made in reaching a more satisfactory emotional response through interdenominational services.

On the other hand, it may be urged that the symbolic significance of common worship is heightened just in proportion as the occasion celebrated has high significance, and that the power of the Church's testimony to the world depends upon its capacity to master common forms of religious expression. Objectively speaking, it seems clear that something of general and generic value is achieved for the community in the common celebration of Holy Week and Good Friday. Having summoned the world to mark these occasions, something seems lacking when the religious agencies themselves cannot engage in a common celebration. People have learned to be helped by the forms they use, and have modified them time and again under sufficient impulse. They can learn to be helped by other forms; and may find in the very problem of common worship a motive for modifying their exclusive ones. One would like to see in the interdenominational Lenten services a really creative experience and the development of a vital and truly Catholic art of united worship that goes beyond the mere preservation of forms dear and familiar to the separate coöperating sects.

A PRACTICAL SUGGESTION

A single practical suggestion grows out of the greater willingness of youth than of age to minimize or ignore deficiencies in ritual and ceremony for what it thinks to be a profounder core of common experience. Why not let youth experiment with interdenominational worship in behalf of the Protestant group? Such a task would deliver young people's departments from being employed—as now in numerous federations—at mere busy work; and would set them to an effort to solve one of the capital problems of the Church. They should not be without help in their experiments. Does not youth, however, offer the most hopeful laboratory for determining how far conscientious denominational loyalties, or permanent temperamental differences, are compatible with the use of common occasions and more or less synthesized or else interchangeable forms?

Chapter XIX

RELIGIOUS EDUCATION

Since religious education is obviously one of the most characteristic and important functions of the Church, it naturally occupies a corresponding place in the church federation. This is evidenced by the fact that twenty of the twenty-two federations covered intensively by the present study were found maintaining major departments, either councils of religious education, or standing commissions, or committees, in this field. The Boston Federation was the only one not functioning at all under the label "religious education."

SCOPE AND MAGNITUDE

The particular activities characteristically carried on by departments of religious education in church federations are listed in the appendix.[1] As it turns out, the most common single function is the relatively subordinate one of training of vacation-school workers. Next come the conduct of training schools for church workers, and the general improvement of methods of religious education. Associated with these obviously central functions is the attempt to represent the community in its relations with the wider movement of religious education as auxiliary to state councils and the International Council of Religious Education. Beyond these very general activities, the working program becomes varied. No other single method is in effect in as many as half the federations. Certain service-functions, like the maintenance of reference libraries or of speakers' bureaus, are moderately characteristic; but the direct promotion of vacation schools, for example, is reported by only eleven out of twenty-one federations, and the direct conduct of week-day instruction by less than one-fifth of them.

Twenty-nine federations, whose programs of religious education were analyzed by means of a standard check-list of activities,[2] yielded a total of twenty-five fairly distinguishable functions carried on by at least two or more. Of these twenty-five functions the average federation was carrying on eleven; the broadest

[1] P. 491.
[2] P. 108.

345

program included from fourteen to eighteen, while the narrowest shrank to three or fewer. According to these measurements, the typical program of religious education has greater scope and magnitude, and is functionally more varied, than the typical comity program of church federation; but falls slightly below the typical program of evangelism, and is much less varied than the broad group of activities comprehended under the term social service.[3]

CAUSES OF VARIATION IN SCOPE AND MAGNITUDE

Unlike other major interests, the scope and magnitude of programs of religious education do not closely correspond to the size of the city in which the federation is located. Several of the most extensive programs are found in cities of less than 200,000 population, and especially where week-day instruction has been developed to a high degree. On the other hand, federations in several large cities have but thin religious-education programs, because the community is not yet unified with respect to this interest, or because major responsibility has been concentrated in other hands.

Only nine out of twenty-one federations maintaining departments of religious education employ a professional departmental staff of one or more workers. In all the rest the operation of the department falls to voluntary committees and the general employed officers of the federation.

The above measures of scope and magnitude show that religious education, on the whole, occupies a relatively large but very fluctuating place within the federation movement as at present developed; but also that the degree to which the agencies are unified varies greatly from city to city.

The foregoing section of the chapter has shown what characteristics, and what general agencies, are used in the performance of particular functions of religious education by federations. Each of the more recognized fields of operation is now briefly to be characterized.

THE CHURCH SCHOOL

The church school is the primary agency of religious education of the local church. It is ordinarily operated by unpaid, nonprofessional workers. Its promotion, improvement, and larger supervision are recognized functions of the denominations. Very little contact with church schools directly is allowed to federations; but both the older Sunday-school movement and the

---

[3] P. 113.

coöperative activities of federations have much to do with church-school workers.

Addressing themselves, then, primarily to church-school workers, federations advocate first of all improved standards of religious education. The authority for setting up formal standards is primarily denominational, and the expression of the standard itself may bear denominational color; but the standards are really worked out coöperatively on the national basis, and are most effectively represented in given communities by inter-denominational agencies. Relatively few denominations in most cities maintain fully developed supervisory agencies of religious education; and for the rest the federation is the most available source of authoritative general ideals. These ideals are propagated by systems of regular institutes and conventions, which in turn represent a hold-over of method from the older traditional Sunday-school movement.

The federations' most characteristic means of communicating ideals is to maintain a bureau of information and advice in religious education. Here a competent religious educator, presumed to be equipped with expert knowledge of theory, methods, and materials, is available to the entire Protestant community. One can ask about any phase of the church-school program—worship, instruction, organization, administration, finance and collateral relationships and interests. Nowhere else, in most cities, can the individual church-school worker go for advice with respect to particular problems.

Again each group of church-school workers is systematically organized for the discussion of common problems. Hence the superintendents', department superintendents', and secretaries' conferences, and the teachers' unions of the several grades. Much time, therefore, is spent in setting up these agencies and seeing that they operate continuously.

In relatively few federations is systematic visitation of local church schools undertaken. In New York City, however, members of the professional staff visit four different churches per Sunday on the average during the active season, covering in all more than 200 a year. The status of these visitors is merely that of friendly observers, but much technical advice is given and the results are systematically followed up so that visitation tends to become unconfessed supervision.

As a means to the general promotion of educational interests, federations systematically bring to their cities national leaders in the respective divisions of the field; and, in general, act as intermediaries between local interests and the overhead agencies promoting church schools. In this connection one of their clerical duties is that of collecting and tabulating the annual Sunday-school statistics of their respective cities.

Because it is so largely taken care of by denominations, or because older agencies of religious education still preëmpt the field, the federations as a group have made no such original contribution to the church school as they have in more novel and less firmly established aspects of the work. On the whole, the federation touches the individual school less directly than might be expected. Its more striking services are to be found in other directions.

Vacation Bible Schools

The movement to use the summer vacation period for the religious education of children arose independently in Protestant circles and only gradually found its way into the main stream of organized religious education. Its rapid spread during the last twenty years is probably accounted for by the variety of motives by which it appeals. The movement has been tossed about upon many cross currents. Its story is complicated. It must, however, be told because the most frequent single activity of federations in the entire realm of religious education has to do with vacation schools.

In its original version, the vacation school was partly philanthropic, partly religious, but very little educational. It was an attempt to make profitable use of the leisure time of children in the congested area of cities, to take them off the street, to furnish opportunity for supervised play, incidentally to give them summer outings, to give them the benefit of Protestant influences, to recruit the regular Sunday schools, to give a minimum of religious education to child populations believed to be virtually without any. Great interest was taken in counting the great proportion of children from foreign and non-Protestant homes who could be induced to attend schools of this sort.

As the vacation-school movement caught on throughout the country, especially in smaller cities and village communities, it was valued primarily as a means of extending the all-too-brief time ordinarily available for religious education in the Sunday school. It rapidly became established as a fairly frequent activity of average churches for their ordinary children. The age-range, however, was narrowly limited, the great mass of children attracted falling between the limits of six and twelve years of age.

The present movement varies greatly from community to community according to the motive that is uppermost and the auspices under which it is conducted. In many cities it passed largely into the hands of the denominations, which then proceeded to federate it as they had their other educational functions. In other cities, particularly the smaller ones, federations took up the movement directly, or took it over from earlier independent associations. Meanwhile the movement has evolved more or less accepted methods, has produced an expository literature, sets of textbooks, and apparatus. Finally, it has developed some capacity for self-criticism, especially at the top. Thus Mr. Thomas S. Evans, director of vacation church schools of the International Council of Religious Education, wrote rather sweepingly in his 1928 annual report:

> At present, the general run of vacation schools have not attained, except to a very limited degree, their educational possibilities. There is over the country no accurate understanding of their objectives, and the great majority of teachers have not caught their spirit.

Still more pointedly the director of the Metropolitan Federation of Vacation Schools of New York speaks of numerous schools as so poorly disciplined and so lacking in religious motive that they "had better not have been held." With such a history and such characteristics, the vacation-school movement has passed over into the work of federations and as such has now to be considered.

VACATION SCHOOLS AS A FEDERATION ACTIVITY

In normally developed departments of religious education, a special division for vacation schools is commonly organized under a committee and director. The director, however, commonly divides his time with other interests, or else serves only seasonally. In the latter case he is usually a pastor on vacation.

The logical functions of a division of vacation schools are aptly summarized in the following statement of the Baltimore Federation.

> To provide for the joint promotion of vacation schools throughout the city; to provide a common training school for workers in these schools; to secure general promotional literature; to make available sample copies of the various courses offered by publishing houses; to help discover, train and place workers; to conduct a common supply store; to act as a center from which information, advice and help may be secured.

In comparison with this full-blown version of the functions of a vacation-school division, less complete stages must be recognized. On the lowest level certain federations facilitate systems of vacation schools, but can scarcely be said to promote them systematically. The most they do is to inquire into the plans of local churches and denominations, to act informally as go-betweens for schools and teachers desiring positions, and at the end of the season to compose a report covering the entire work of vacation schools in the community.

In contrast with the stage of mere facilitation, nearly half the federations promote a community system of vacation schools and more or less effectively correlate the various agencies that work in the field. This involves the adoption of specific goals or objectives; the attempt to get the official standards accepted in the training of workers; a setting-up conference at the beginning of the vacation-school term; together with the administrative handling of all general interests. The International Council of Religious Education assumes that the work in each community will be unified at least to this extent.

What the maximum program adds is a more active supervision of the work of local schools and the direct operation of certain schools under the federation's own auspices. These may be conducted for demonstration purposes in the effort to work out some of the problems of religious education, or as philanthropic schools in the congested sections of cities, or as interdenominational schools for groups of neighborhood churches. This maximum program involving a larger proportion of direct operation and supervision is likely to be found in the smaller cities. Here the cost of the entire community project is sometimes consolidated and administered through a central budget.

ORGANIZATION

Whatever the rôle of the federation with respect to them, the vacation school is presumed to be a departmentalized and graded organization with at least four teachers (kindergarten, primary, junior and intermediate). Its session is supposed to cover a minimum of sixty hours distributed over five weeks, and is generally held in daily periods of five and a half hours. In practice, however, the schools vary exceedingly, both in the number of teachers and the length of sessions. Many held under the auspices of local churches do not last more than two weeks. One of the bitterest complaints of those who are trying to give the movement real educational significance is that the time is too short to get results.

FACILITIES AND COSTS

Vacation schools commonly meet in churches and use the facilities already provided for Sunday schools. The majority of teachers are volunteers. The value of these facilities and this unpaid service is never accounted for in reckoning costs. Hence no real financial accounting is possible. The most significant variant in cost is the proportion of paid teachers. Usually this does not exceed one paid to every two unpaid; but in a few cases the proportion is about fifty to fifty, while in New York there are two paid teachers to one unpaid. The volunteer teachers are obviously easier to find when they merely have to teach children of their own respectable congregations. Paid teachers are more necessary for mission schools in congested foreign sections where even Sunday-school teachers have to be imported. Such schools also generally require more supervision. The expense of a system of vacation schools consequently varies primarily according to the degree to which the work is carried on for the under-privileged elements in the community.

CURRICULUM

The standard curriculum includes worship, Bible instruction, music, and expressional activities chiefly furnished by handcraft and supervised play. Freedom from academic tradition permits vital educational experiment. Occasional excellent efforts were discovered to derive the content of the curriculum from life-situations experienced by pupils, and to lead the group experience out into purposeful service. But these are high lights within a rather commonplace type of low-grade education whose bulk is quite disproportionate to its general educational quality.

QUANTITATIVE MEASUREMENT

Systems of Protestant vacation schools of the sort described exist in the majority of large cities; but no agency compiles statistics by cities. Moreover, jurisdiction is so mixed, and the degrees of promotion and supervision vary so greatly, from city to city that it is impossible to isolate a particular body of work and to present it as the exclusive functioning of church federations in this field. The most that one can do is to observe a fairly definite correspondence between the size of the system and the size of the city. Cities of from 75,000 to 150,000 population show an average of ten to twelve vacation schools with from 1,000 to 1,500 pupils; cities of from 350,000 to 500,000, an average of fifty or sixty schools with from 3,000 to 5,000 pupils. Chicago and New York have 225 and 275 schools, respectively, with

22,000 and 25,000 pupils. The number of teachers ranges from about a hundred in the smaller systems to 3,400 reported by Chicago. All told, then, the promotion, correlation, and standardization of vacation-school systems is fairly well established as a coöperative function of Protestantism in the larger cities, and in this sense is characteristic of about half of the federations.

WEEK-DAY CHURCH SCHOOLS

A second phase of religious education commonly organized as a division of the work with its own committee and directors is that of week-day church schools. Thirteen of the twenty-one federations studied were carrying on systems of instruction of this type, but under radically different conditions and to variable extent.

Like the vacation schools, the week-day schools originated outside the organized movement of religious education in its older form. For the most part, they were undertaken through voluntary groups. Sometimes they were initiated by professional educators rather than by the churches. Separate organizations for their conduct next began to be formed, such as the week-day religious association in Rochester, and a similar non-denominational Protestant committee in Toledo. In New York City, the movement was largely indebted to Protestant teachers in the public-school system. The current theory of religious education was quick to see that week-day instruction would add greatly to the scope and genuinely educational character of the movement; and efforts soon began to get the independent movement regularized within the main machinery of organized religious education. The motives underlying this effort were self-evident. If, as in a great majority of instances, week-day religious instruction involved excusing of pupils from public schools during some part of the school session, public authorities naturally demanded to deal with the most representative and authoritative agencies possible. If religious classes were held after school, it was still difficult to finance them on any comprehensive scale; and it was necessary to educate the sentiment of the supporting Protestant constituency. Most of the independent movements, therefore, somewhat naturally came under the care of a federation or Council of Religious Education. If truth were told, some of them were met more than half way by federations that had been kept out of the older fields of religious education by existing organizations and were anxious to break into the game at some point. For such federations, week-day religious education often afforded easy opportunity.

At the same time, however, contrary motives were operating which tended to keep the week-day school movement relatively distinct within the larger movements. Not all the Protestant denominations belonged to federations. This was reason for organizing week-day education in such manner that communions that so desired could coöperate in this function and not in others. This possibility was safeguarded by giving week-day education a certain administrative separateness. Thus the constitutional provision of the Wichita Council with reference to week-day schools reads:

> The commission is to have full autonomy and churches represented in a commission are not required to share farther in the activities of the Council by reason of their relation to the commission.

Still again, week-day religious education shows strong decentralizing tendencies which made it natural to administer it with local independence. Certain districts of most cities have generally taken the lead in these movements, particularly higher class residential areas and the polite suburbs. Consequently, even when it required a central organization to arrange with the school authorities for the setting up of week-day classes, their support and immediate administration has been found largely in the districts immediately concerned.

Two tendencies, then, have been at work. The first to bring the week-day schools under the central control of federations and still to keep them administratively distinct; the other to centralize responsibility and at the same time to decentralize it. No final equilibrium has been reached for the movement as a whole.

ORGANIZATIONAL ASPECTS

As already noted, week-day religious education brings school children into classes maintained by the churches either during, or at the close of, the daily school session. In the main, it draws pupils from grades two to six, though the theory generally assumes that the entire elementary group is concerned. In but few instances are any high-school pupils included, and then in relatively small numbers.[4]

Four types of week-day school systems were met with in the investigation:

(1) The coöperative promotion of denominational parochial

---

[4] The occasional giving of high-school credit for Sunday-school courses in biblical history or literature is not here regarded as a part of week-day education.

schools. This simply means that a group of individual churches maintains separate classes, each primarily for its own children. The coöperative element in the situation is that they are induced to do so as a result of joint planning; and the promotion of the idea that secular education needs such supplementing is undertaken by a common agency. Administration, control, and finance are all parochial; and the instruction given in any particular school bears the distinctive coloring of its denomination. The New York City system is essentially of this sort, though the federation's division of week-day schools exercises a definitely standardizing influence over the total system. Protestants, Catholics, and Jews cordially coöperate in its support. This system is more likely to be employed for after-school classes than for released school-time, public-school authorities not taking very kindly to the notion that religious education that remains so distinctly under sectarian auspices is worth fostering.

(2) In contrast with the parochial type of week-day education is the interdenominational type. Under systems of this sort, Protestant children of all denominations go from a given public school to a neighboring church where they are taught from an interdenominational standpoint. Within a system jointly supported or administered by a federation or council of religious education representing a wide variety of faiths, instruction is generalized so as to be acceptable to the entire coöperating group. Under such conditions, children of the non-coöperating denominations are found in attendance about in proportion to the size of the denomination. This is true even of children of non-evangelical and irregular Protestant bodies.

(3) The third system is mixed. Most of the classes will be of the interdenominational type; but certain major denominations, most frequently the Episcopal and Lutheran though occasionally the Christian Science, will be found operating parochially alongside and within the same system. In matters of release-time, supervision, and reports to the school authorities, they will deal through the central federation office and staff. In matters of support, local administration, and type of teaching, they will operate independently.

(4) A fourth type of week-day religious education is found in schools operated directly by federations, in order to meet certain philanthropic and educational needs that do not naturally fall to groups of neighborhood churches as, for example, in homes for dependent and delinquent children, or in central demonstration schools, or in experimental schools in communities of different

type seeking to work out peculiar institutional and administrative problems.

Organization and administration vary somewhat according to which of the above described systems is in vogue in the given community. In case of parochial after-school classes, the denomination is, of course, the ultimate authority. The public school may coöperate, as it does in New York City, by commending the idea of supplemental religious education, permitting surveys of the religious affiliation of pupils within the public school and furnishing escort for pupils at the end of the school session from the schools to the churches; but the public-school authorities bear no official responsibility.

More teachers are necessary to operate the parochial system, because the classes must come all at once at a fixed time. A higher proportion of volunteer teachers is used, and educational qualifications are less rigorously insisted upon. A good many public-school teachers are secured, however, for these after-school sessions. The average daily session is somewhat longer than under the release-time system, averaging from one and a half to two hours per pupil; but the yearly session is likely to be short. The best parochial systems aim to give from sixty to seventy hours a year of religious instruction to the individual pupil, which adds at least 50 per cent. to the instruction given in the Sunday school.

Under the release-time system, children whose parents formally request it are sent from schools to religious classes by grades, generally for one hour once a week. In some cases the release-time is limited to the last period of the school-day. Increasingly, however, the tendency is to release classes at all hours throughout the week so that the religious instructor may be employed continuously. Salaries in these cases are about $1,500 per year. The holding of the religious classes is commonly announced in the public schools, and the pupils enroll there. School boards make regulations necessary to assure that the quality of the work is educationally equal to that done in the schools. It is assumed that the qualifications for teachers shall be maintained and that the administration of instruction and the teaching processes are of equal value. The right of supervision is implied, but is ordinarily exercised only through the approval of the general plan, the teacher's list, and the curriculum, together with a regular reporting to the public authorities of the attendance and conduct of pupils. The public-school system reserves the right to discontinue the release-time if results are not satisfactory. In some cases a good deal of prodding up has been necessary; but in most the supervision of the public schools is exceedingly nominal.

The body of experience that has gone to determine the internal conduct, curriculum, and general characteristics of the day schools has been drawn from all systems, and is receiving standardized interpretation by state councils of religious education and by the International Council. Teaching methods more nearly approximate those of the public schools than those of the Sunday school, particularly in the use of tests and examinations. All systems have to depend upon church facilities, such as are designed and provided for the brief Sunday-school session. These facilities are notoriously not generally suited for everyday use. Very often they merit the verdict, "gloomy and dirty." Depending as they must upon the local church for janitorial service, the week-day schools are confronted by very uneven conditions. The federations are, however, gradually requiring or directly providing a minimum of special educational equipment, and are learning how to make the best of plants not designed for serious school use.

Under the purely parochial system, the costs of week-day religious education fall primarily upon the individual churches. The direct additional expenditures on this account in New York run from $500 to $550 per church on an average. The cost of the interdenominational system, if centralized, may be included in the general budget of the federation or council of religious education. If decentralized, it may be raised in the localities whose churches coöperate in maintaining the work. Only a few federations substantially cover their cities geographically, and even they are educating only a relatively small proportion of the Protestant school constitutency. Most financial systems are accordingly mixed. Philanthropic and demonstration schools commonly have to be financed from funds secured outside of regular budget. Wichita attempts to collect a small charge from its churches for each pupil coming from their respective congregations. Only a few cities have even attempted to figure out the actual total cost of week-day religious instruction in the community. In New York City it amounts annually to more than $45,000, only $22,000 of which, however, passes through the church federation treasury.

No agency compiles comparable statistics for week-day religious education by cities; and in view of the varying systems in operation, it is impossible to isolate a particular body of work and account for it as falling directly to the church federations as such. In general, the federations promote a much larger body of work than they conduct; and have important relations to the entire week-day religious instruction of their communities, even though they do not claim it as their own. The actual number of children concerned is beyond 8,500 in New York and Brooklyn; over 6,000 in Toledo, with one of the most inclusive systems of all, which serves thirty-nine of the forty-four elementary schools of the city; 4,400 in Wichita; and approximately 2,500 each in Minneapolis and Youngstown. But obviously the ratio between pupils in the week-day school and the Protestant school-constituency varies even more widely than do the bare enrollments. In a number of cities the movement is showing very rapid growth. It is obviously still in its infancy, and has not discovered its final forms or characteristics.

PROBLEMS

Certain problems are inherent in the experiment of week-day religious education under whatever auspices undertaken. The federations are constantly meeting these problems. First, there are the legal problems involving the right or administrative discretion of a public institution like a school to recognize and coöperate with the Church in an important field. This problem is being increasingly met by legislation and favorable court decisions. Federations have sometimes played an important part in carrying up the issue for a decision in the higher courts, as recently in New York City.

Behind the legal problem lies a more general problem of public policy. Does the Church seriously desire to institute a system of ecclesiastical week-day education to supplement the public schools? Does it wish to enter into the necessary relationship for adjusting the two systems one to another? A prime factor in this problem is, of course, the varying attitudes of the great confessional groups into which the religious population is divided. Catholics, for example, stand for religious education, but their preference is for the separate parochial school. Where parochial schools are strongly established, Catholic authorities, therefore, are sometimes found in more or less outspoken opposition to the release of school-time because actually taken advantage of primarily by Protestants. Jews, too, when they are so small a minority in a community that they cannot profitably use release-time for their own children, have sometimes called it a discrimination in favor of another faith.

In the main, however, the professed theories of all the great religious divisions have tended to unite them in support of week-day religious instruction. Thus in New York City, a very important interconfessional committee directly representing the ecclesiastical authorities of the Catholic, Jewish, and Protestant groups is working most harmoniously in support of the movement. No successful example exists, however, of a school in which Protestant, Catholic, and Jewish children are combined under a single system of religious teaching. In view of deep-seated feeling of religious distance, none could be expected.

Within the group roughly classified as Protestant, the working out of lesser differences has already been indicated. Denominations not coöperating in federations may either operate parochially under a mixed system, or may send their children to the interdenominational school.

The profoundest practical issue confronting week-day religious instruction is that of appreciating its necessary magnitude if it is to be educationally effective and of establishing its genuinely educational character in the minds of its ultimate supporters. The disposition to value the week-day school as a recruiting agency for the Sunday school, or to make it work as a disguised evangelism, is a serious handicap. The result is a mongrel institution which does not willingly admit that educational standards apply to it. What is needed is a conception of education and of evangelism under which the two mutually interpenetrate. The substitution of a professionally trained teacher for lay volunteers or clergymen in the week-day schools, together with their public-school supervision, is helping to remedy the situation.

The crux of the matter is likely to be found in the distinctly practical realm of finance. A real educational process will involve more money for plant, facilities, teachers, supervision, and the scientific weighing of results than the Church is willing to grant.

Some of the deepest theoretical problems of all education are acutely emphasized by the week-day school, for example, that of the relationship between voluntary interest and initiative, and instruction and guidance. Does religious education include the young people's societies, the Boy and Girl Scouts, and the various character-forming activities of childhood and youth which the Church fosters? If so, what divisions of thinking and program are necessary on either side? How is religion to be taught? By the presentation of scriptural material to pupils under instruction, or by the stimulation of the spontaneous activities of the group?

Is religion to be taught chiefly in separate terms, or primarily in relation to the content of the public-school studies? Is moral character developed by the same means that inculcates religion, or by another and distinct set of processes? These are exceedingly deep waters to be ventured upon by a popular movement which is in danger of becoming something of a fad. Only in the rare instances of federations closely related to the educational departments of great universities is anything really being done to answer these fundamental questions.

All told, then, the field of week-day religious education opens up an area of immense scope and enormous profundity, requiring resources and understanding very disproportionate to those that are now being spent upon them. Nevertheless, the variant and relatively feeble ventures of federations into this realm constitute a highly interesting phase of the religious-education program.

LEADERSHIP TRAINING

Another major aspect of the current religious-education program of church federations is that of leadership training. This, too, is commonly organized under a special subcommittee, frequently with a professional director.

The old Sunday-school associations had well-developed methods of leadership training that reflected relatively low academic requirements. As the standards of religious education have risen, the number of prospective leaders who could qualify educationally has been reduced, and the supply of persons competent to teach them has become even more limited. Under these circumstances, the machinery of leadership training has naturally had to be coöperatively devised and administered. Community training schools of religious-education leadership are accordingly found highly characteristic of federation programs in this field.

AUSPICES AND LOCATION

In view of the small numbers involved, leadership training in such schools has commonly begun with a single central school, and this continues to be sufficient in the smaller cities. The school is apt to be held in a down-town Young Men's or Young Women's Christian Association building, or in a centrally located church blessed with a modern religious-education plant; but this does not suffice for the largest cities. Here the central school is likely to be supplemented by district schools in various parts of the city. The central school may then limit itself to the most advanced instruction. As an alternative there may be a unified system of district schools without any central school.

The district schools are primarily maintained and operated by groups of neighboring churches (ranging from four to eleven in number in typical instances). The function of the federation in these instances is to promote, approve, and perhaps to supervise the work done, rather than to administer it. In cities that have rival overhead organizations of religious education, a Sunday-school association or independent council will be found carrying on one set of district training schools while the federation carries on a different set.

ORGANIZATION AND INSTITUTIONAL CHARACTERISTICS

As standardized by the International Council of Religious Education, the standard unit of instruction in the religious training schools consists of twelve weekly class-sessions; and the more advanced schools conduct two such semester periods per year. Non-standard schools are sometimes as short as six weeks. Systems that include both central and district schools, sometimes offer terms of unequal length. Thus Rochester, in 1928–1929, had a twenty-four-week central school and two district schools, one of twenty and one of ten weeks. The daily session usually includes two periods of instruction, either both in the evening or one in the late afternoon and one in the evening. A brief daily assembly and worship period is also characteristic.

DIVISIONAL COMMITTEES

A study of eight divisional committees for week-day religious education showed an aggregate of 103 members. The committees were either relatively very small (five to ten members) or relatively large (fifteen to thirty-six members). No committee met more than six times a year, and there was no general tendency as to the number of meetings. Only 10 per cent. of the members were women, which was a much smaller proportion than in general committees of religious education, and about one-third professional educators. Only one committee contained any significant proportion of laymen representing the rank and file of Sunday-school workers. The small committees got about twice as high attendance, relatively speaking, as the large ones; but in both types one-third the members never attended, and another third attended not more than one meeting a year.

TEACHERS AND PUPILS

The teaching staff of the training schools is commonly drawn from ministers who have specialized in religious education, or from professors in the higher educational institutions of the communities. These are supplemented by professional religious educators. The dean is commonly a local educator of reputation. Sometimes there is a separate business manager. Otherwise, the business control falls to the executive officers of the federation. Teachers are paid by the hour at very nominal rates.

The schools are keyed to the capacity of the more promising Sunday-school workers, not too greatly in advance of the rank and file. Some of them come from exceedingly humble churches; and the school must admit such pupils as the churches send. For the advance courses, however, two years of college work and an elementary school certificate of religious education are usually required for admission.

CURRICULUM

As standardized by the International Council of Religious Education, the training-school curriculum must consist of three elements, namely, required courses in religious pedagogy and subject matter; required courses in graded methods; and elective courses dealing with special phases either of content or method, such as worship, missions, recreation, school administration, etc.

The actual number of courses offered at a given time ranges greatly from city to city, from five in a small city like Youngstown to ten or twelve in Minneapolis and Rochester, and sixteen in St. Louis. Chicago lists a total of sixty-five courses which are offered in the three-year cycle.

The individual pupil is presumed to have completed the course when he has taken six required and three elective units, each involving not less than ten fifty-minute periods of instruction accompanied by the study of assigned texts and the preparation of assigned topics. On the completion of such a course, the certificate of the International Council of Religious Education is awarded. The larger denominations also award their own standard leadership diplomas. Federations often give additional certificates for more advanced and specialized work. In about half-a-dozen cases, work receiving university credit is offered by arrangements with local institutions, notably in New York with Columbia University.

The ramifications of organized religion in a great city require numerous types of trained leadership, each of which demands specialized training. The Chicago Council of Religious Education has identified nine such groups, including parents, social workers whose work has a religious side, advanced students of religious education, denominational and interdenominational executives, as well as Sunday-school officers and teachers, pastors, and directors of religious education in local churches. Occasional differentiations elsewhere include school administration in connection with leadership training, and groups of courses in social service or recreational leadership. Such specialized courses frequently involve the coöperation of other agencies like women's departments, the Young Men's Christian Association, and the Scout movements. The training-school curriculum may also include special courses for the preparation of week-day and vacation-school teachers. In addition to advanced courses counting for university degrees, a few federations are beginning to enter the field of adult education and to offer courses of a broadly cultural type in the field of religion.

Still other specialization is found in occasional demonstration classes or experimental projects set up in connection with the more advanced and originative phases of religious training.

All told, the leadership-training courses of the federations and affiliated councils of religious education constitute a conspicuous venture in adult education, and one of real moment for the re-establishment of the Church as a cultural agency in the larger cities.

So much of the work, however, where promoted by federations, is locally maintained and supported, or falls under mixed offices, that it is not possible to segregate any particular body of work as belonging exclusively to the federation. Enrollment statistics are imperfectly supplied; but some indication of the magnitude of the leadership-training enterprise may be judged by the following figures for selected cities for the last reported year.

City	Training-school Enrollment
Youngstown	114
Minneapolis	249
Wichita	269
Detroit	446
Chicago	1208
New York	1729

Of course, the ratio of pupils to total Protestant population is much greater in some of the smaller cities than in any of the larger ones.

GRADING AND AGE-ADAPTATION

Through whatever types of schools, and under whatever auspices it is conducted, religious education naturally has to make special adaptations of its organization and methods to particular age-groups. This is most familiarly evidenced in the age-grading of the Sunday school into infants', children's, youths', and adult divisions. Federation organization reflecting such grouping is well-developed in the larger federations. Efforts to improve the church-school divisions will be assigned to special children's, young people's, or adults' departments, sometimes under special professional supervision. Week-day schools inherently demand a graded adaptation because virtually confined to pupils of primary and junior age. Young people's departments, however, furnish the most pronounced illustration of organization along graded lines. They are frequently in large measure self-directed, and sometimes attempt to relate themselves to the separately organized activities of Young People's Unions and Leagues.[5] The story of the special standards and activities of these divisions is too long for the present report to attempt.

OVERLAPPING OF FIELDS

The field of religious education overlaps other departments of federation activity at a good many points. Thus religious-education methods are used by a number of social-service departments for inmates of prisons and philanthropic institutions. The Brooklyn Federation, for example, gives Bible instruction twice a week to children in the Detention Home for the Society for the Prevention of Cruelty to Children. Chicago conducts several Sunday schools in penal institutions.

Again, on the side of recreation, religious education overlaps the field of organized athletics, sometimes as conducted by independent interchurch leagues, or under Young Men's or Young Women's Christian Association auspices. The introduction of missionary and social-service topics into training-school systems, and the inclusion of social content into graded projects, increase the contacts of the two fields. Evangelism in home and Sunday school, and comity in the establishment of Sunday and week-day schools, illustrate overlapping in still other directions.

COMMITTEES AND COMMITTEE PERFORMANCE

A study of the committees, commissions, or boards ultimately responsible for the conduct of religious education in twelve federations revealed a total of 310 members. Their composition, characteristics, and record have already been compared with those of committees of other departments in Chapter XVI. In size and composition, these governing bodies naturally reflect

---

[5] Pp. 176 ff.

the varying theories and auspices under which the work of religious education is done.

Three quite distinct types of governing bodies occur:

(1) Federations or affiliated councils of religious education, when they conform to the International Council theory of representation, have large governing bodies consisting of from forty to seventy-five members, part of whom are formally designated by the coöperating denominations and part appointed at large. Probably because denominational appointments absorb most of the persons prominently identified with religious education in any community, these furnish a strong majority of the total committee membership.

(2) Federations whose religious-educational work did not originate in independent councils of religious education tend to have much smaller governing bodies, sometimes composed entirely of members at large and following the pattern of representation that governs the other commissions of the particular federation concerned. The characteristic membership of this type of governing body is from five to ten.

(3) An intermediate and smaller group of governing bodies of from twenty to thirty members does not seem to reflect any particular antecedents or theory of composition. The Rochester Federation presents a variant. Its council of religious education is composed of the chairman of all educational subcommittees, and has neither denominational representatives nor members at large.

Occupationally classified, almost exactly half the members of the education committees are ministers, while 30 per cent. belong to other professional classes, chiefly educational. A large proportion, both of the ministers and of the educators on committees, is made of persons already denomination officials, especially in religious-educational capacities, or else are the paid executives of character-building agencies like the Young Men's and Young Women's Christian Association, the Scouts, and similar children's or youths' organizations. Surprisingly little place is left for representation by the rank and file of Sunday-school workers in local churches.

A very notable phenomenon is that members of religious-education committees rarely belong to other federation committees. This is in sharp contrast with other major departments or work which used many of the same people on several committees.[6]

_____
[6] P. 301.

But this showing may be somewhat influenced by the fact that religious-education departments in a number of federations are of very recent origin.

The aggregate annual attendance on the ten committees which met during the year previous to the study was only 28 per cent. of the possible attendance. This was the most unfavorable record found in any of the committees compared. Attendance was naturally greatly affected by the size of the committee and the frequency of its meetings. The typical large committee met sometimes monthly, sometimes bi-monthly. In the former case, attendance approximated the average; in the latter, it rose as high as 30 to 40 per cent. of the possible attendance. The smaller commissions tended to meet but once a year, in which case attendance reached 40 to 50 per cent. In the larger committees, 40 per cent. of the members never attended at all, while from two-thirds to three-fifths were present not more than half that time. In the Greater New York Federation, for example, the tendency was for a member of the Council of Religious Education to attend three out of nine meetings or else not at all. Even when committees met only once a year, more than half their members never attended. When the large governing bodies were supplemented by small executive or administrative committees, these committees showed a much better ratio of attendance.

The above showing calls attention again to the fact that the theory of representation by means of large committees that have frequent meetings does not work out practically in terms of attendance and participation in current business. On the other hand, small committees that meet infrequently do not get good attendance, and manifestly can have little relation to current business.

WHAT CONSTITUENTS THINK OF RELIGIOUS EDUCATION

In response to a questionnaire asking an expression of judgments on specific items of religious-education programs as carried on by their respective federations, the constituents of fifteen federations returned an aggregate of 20,371 judgments. Seventy-three per cent. pronounced the total program "highly important." [7]

The following table shows the varying degrees in which each of fifteen aspects of religious education was criticised and was favored.

---

[7] For form of questionnaire and comparison with more general judgments, see p. 134.

TABLE XXVII—RANKING OF ITEMS OF RELIGIOUS EDUCA-
TION PROGRAMS ACCORDING TO CONSTITUENTS' JUDG-
MENTS REGARDING APPROPRIATENESS AND IMPOR-
TANCE, IN 15 FEDERATIONS

Activities	Per Cent. Unfavorable Judgments	Activities	Per Cent. Favorable Judgments
Coöperation with state councils of religious education..	3.1	Promotion of week-day schools	87.5
Promotion of week-day schools	3.5	Training teachers for week-day schools	86.7
Training teachers for week-day schools	3.6	Conducting leadership-training schools	85.0
Clearing house for denominational plans	4.2	Clearing house for denominational plans	82.9
Conducting leadership-training schools	4.3	Training for vacation-school teachers	80.6
Training for vacation-school teachers	5.0	Promotion of vacation church schools	80.1
Promotion of vacation church schools	5.9	Coöperation with state council of religious education..	78.1
Promotion of graded departmental interests	6.2	Conducting Sunday schools philanthropic institutions..	74.1
Promotion of home and parental religious education..	6.3	Conducting local and district conferences of religious education	72.0
Conducting local and district conferences of religious education	6.5	Promotion of graded departmental interests	69.9
Conducting Sunday schools philanthropic institutions..	8.8	Maintenance of young people's departments	69.5
Maintenance of young people's departments	10.1	Promotion of home and parental religious education..	68.1
Maintenance of library of religious education	10.9	Maintenance of library of religious education	63.9
Promotion of general conferences on religious education	11.9	Thirteen other activities occurring in only one or two federations	61.2
Thirteen other activities occurring in only one or two federations	13.1	Promotion of general conferences on religious education	60.4

In general, the most highly regarded functions related to the
week-day schools, in both the aspect of promotion and that of
technical training; and also to leadership training. Vacation-
school activities rank next. The smallest amount of criticism
had to do with coöperative relations with state councils of religious education; but (as shown by the position of this item in
the second column) this was commonly regarded as a secondary
rather than a primary function. At the bottom of the ranking
scale came functions that federations actually made secondary
in practice, along with obviously minor service-functions. The
very exceptional functions, on the whole, are not strongly favored
by the constituents of the few federations that have undertaken
them.

CHARACTERISTICS OF ORGANIZATION AS BEARING ON RELATIONSHIPS

In addition to characteristics stressed in its history, six aspects of religious education through church federations complicate the problem of assimilating this group of activities to the work of federations in general.

A STANDARDIZED FIELD

Religious education inherits something of the stereotyped habits of the older Sunday-school movement. It stresses the tendency of secular education to accept formulations and to work through precise routine. In no other field has the federation movement brought forth anything so clear-cut or definite. Traditional ideas preside over coöperative programs of evangelism; but this phase of federation work has no such precise technique as education has. Social service, on the contrary, is chaotic both as to ideals and technique. But though the majority of federations fall far short of it, the outlines of a standard community program of religious education are clear. They are explicitly worded in the constitutions of the stronger departments or affiliated Councils of Religious Education, are reflected in the departmentalization of state and national agencies, and are popularly recognized in all educational circles and national agencies.

HIGH DEGREE OF DEVELOPMENT

The realm of religious education is characterized by a high degree of theoretical and technical development, as well as by standardized organization. It commands elaborate ecclesiastical and scholastic machinery. It supplies a conspicuous department to many colleges and theological seminaries. It has created an elaborate scholarship, includes many schools of thought, has a voluminous literature, maintains extensive organs of publicity. Study, deliberate experimentation, and criticism are more generally accepted as methods in this field, and are far more generally used than they are in any other within which federations function. These, which may be termed in general academic characteristics, tend to carry over and are highly distinctive of religious education in its coöperative phase.

DUAL AFFILIATIONS

Religious-education departments also stand in a special set of relationships to overhead organizations, state and national. As phases of the federation movement, they are related through it to the alliance of denominations in the Federal Council, and to the larger movement of the inclusive church coöperation. But they are sentimentally related and often formally—as by provisions in the by-laws—to the State and the International Councils that head up the general movement. In affiliating with federations, previously independent agencies have commonly reserved the right to continue such special organizational and financial responsibility to these overhead agencies.

PROFESSIONAL LEADERSHIP

To a greater degree than is true of any other department, religious education within federations is administered by paid professionals. No other federation leaders, as a group, had received a specialized education for their work. In no other field is the minute specialization of professional functions carried so far as in this connection with the broader educational programs. And in none are so many volunteer leaders professionally trained.

COÖPERATING DENOMINATIONS

Somewhat more, and somewhat different denominations habitually coöperate in the field of religious education than in the federation movement at large.[8] So far as denominations belonging to the United States are concerned, the Federal Council of the Churches of Christ and the International Council of Religious Education represent essentially the same group. All the exceptions are very small denominations. Four of these belong to the Federal Council and not to the International Council, while seven belong to the latter and not to the former. A comparison of those not included by both organizations shows that the International Council of Religious Education is a trifle more able to appeal to denominations whose origins and customs are foreign or that represent erratic tendencies. Local participation in religious education is also somewhat broader than is participation in general federation functions, and along similar lines.

All these general aspects of religious education tend to explain why it is so often separately organized and maintains distinctiveness within the federation scheme.

To conserve the peculiar religious educational values thought to be imperiled by combination with another movement, federations have made extraordinary concessions in the matter of auspices and program.

---

[8] P. 99.

SEPARATE BASIC ORGANIZATION

The tendency to perpetuate the historic separateness of religious education, and to maintain the distinctiveness of its departments, has in some cases been allowed to go so far that the ultimate component units—local churches or denominations—are annually brought into play in the election of governing bodies for these departments. This, however, is not generally true. In the majority of cases synthesis and representativeness are achieved once for all in the election of the governing body of the federation, which then proceeds to constitute the religious-education commission or departmental committee just as it does others. But many of the largest programs of religious education going on formally under federation auspices are actually operated under separately delegated bodies which are just as ultimate in their origins as are the federation delegations themselves. A mixed system, represented, for example, by the St. Louis Federation, divides authority between the delegates of local churches and the governing body of the federation.[9]

PROBLEMS OF RELIGIOUS EDUCATION

The more general problems of religious education fall outside the scope of this report, which is confined to matters pertaining distinctly to federations. More particular problems have already been raised in connection with each type of educational activity discussed in the body of the chapter. Certain large problems of relationship, however, remain.

Federation leadership in religious education is challenged at a number of points, particularly by the larger denominations and churches. As judged by their behavior, these constituents are not at all sure whether a rounded system of community religious education is one of the things that can best be done in common by the Protestant churches. The denominations want to set up their own departments of religious education and to train their own lay workers in schools that preserve the denominational emphasis. They often prefer to conduct their own systems of vacation schools, as well as to keep exclusive contacts with their ordinary church schools. Only week-day education must obviously be done coöperatively, if at all, and that largely on account of the attitude of public-school officials.

---

[9] As is shown in the discussion of units of association, there are two types of federation. In one the organizational unit is the individual church; in the other the denominational unit as locally organized. These same distinctions appear in the composition of departments of religious education; but do not seem to represent practical differences in operation.

Somewhat similarly, strong churches, which can afford highly paid religious educational experts of their own, sometimes think that they can do better to keep all training and administration within their own hands.

These issues may be considered either from the standpoint of the denominations or of the federations. If the former will consult their own experience, they will realize that denominational departments of religious education have had a very checkered history. They, too, have as frequently had funds and workers withdrawn as added. A good many federations can show a far more consistent and continuous ability to handle the situation coöperatively than the separate denominations can show within their own realms. Something of the same thing is true of religious educational experiments within local churches. A large number of them have been very far from satisfactory, and the field is one of many ups and downs.

The weaker denominations, on the other hand, must find adequate leadership in religious education in the federations if at all. Federations cannot furnish this without the support of the stronger denominations. Again, a real community system of religious education must be carried out on three levels; namely, the high-school, the college, and the professional. Courses of sufficient quality to command college and university recognition and credit can rarely be carried out by denominations working alone, and the assurance of the highest professional standards in community systems of religious education seems almost necessarily bound up with their coöperative support and administration. Whether such considerations will generally outweigh the denominational and parochial viewpoint remains to be seen.

Chapter XX

SOCIAL SERVICE

Unlike the other major departments of federation work, social service does not constitute a single unified field. As is shown in Chapter VII, it includes a varied group of activities representing phenomena of very different sorts, whose relationships are not always close. In treating the matter in this comprehensive fashion, the report, however, follows established federation usage. The official formulation of the movement's program in 1920 classified as social service everything that the present chapter does, except international relations; for example, it included local political issues.[1] The Federal Councils' latest compendium accords even broader scope to what it calls "the social work of the churches."[2] It seems logical, therefore, to make the term cover, in the present connection, all examples of collective action by the coöperating churches with respect to the economic, industrial, and political problems of society, as well as the social status of individuals and the relationships of social groups.[3]

MAGNITUDE AND IMPORTANCE

No scales exist with which it is possible to weigh exactly the different divisions of the work of federations. The departments do not ordinarily have exclusive staffs; their finances are not completely separated; their fields often overlap. Several indications of relative emphasis upon social service are, however, at hand.

(1) It is one of the four major fields of federation activity, sharing this rank with evangelism, comity, and religious education.[4]

(2) Though the magnitude of the social-service program varies greatly from city to city, it furnishes, all told, more than one-

---

[1] Published under the title, "Community Programs for Coöperating Churches," Chapter IV.

[2] Johnson (ed.) *The Social Work of the Churches* (New York: Federal Council of Churches, 1930).

[3] Similar logic is seen, for example, in the reorganized "department of social service" of the Minneapolis Federation. It includes three divisions, labeled respectively: civic (local community); interracial; and world-relations.

[4] Pp. 112 ff.

third of the items in the combined federation program.[5]

(3) In formal communications with the churches, social-service interests get, for example, about half the annual total in Pittsburgh and nearly half in Detroit. In the federation organs, social service, though presented in very different aspects, gets more space in Chicago and Pittsburgh than any other topic. In Chicago it figures primarily as a series of reports of successful ministries in lines popular with the churches; in Pittsburgh, on the contrary, it is characterized by the continuous and militant advocacy of somewhat unpopular measures of social reform.

(4) Social service employs more paid workers than any other single field of federation service, religious education being a very close second.[6]

(5) When its practice requires such paid workers, it is relatively costly; when limited to propaganda, it is generally an inexpensive function.[7]

Social service, then, is deeply rooted in the current programs and purposes of the church federations. It is very adequately emphasized when compared with the other interests of organized Protestantism. On the other hand, the social-service field itself is so varied that no single phase of it covers any very large fraction of the total work of the average federation. Such a combination of total magnitude with even greater scope warrants a somewhat extended report on this topic.

MACHINERY

The field of social service as just defined is not commonly administered as a unit. Its actual subdivision is most easily shown by a consideration of the machinery through which its activities are carried out. The twenty-nine federations included in the investigation had a total of eighty committees engaged in various phases of social service. A classification and ranking according to the number of federations maintaining committees of each type is given on the page opposite.

This enumeration groups together committees of like function irrespective of a considerable variation in nomenclature. It does not include, however, various subcommittees, nor committees on social service falling wholly within woman's departments.[8] Occasional missionary, rural, and recreational committees are also

---

[5] P. 105.
[6] Pp. 146 and 147.
[7] P. 457.
[8] For a separate discussion of social service under women's departments, see p. 438.

omitted, although they have strongly marked social service aspects. Even without these, however, the numeration suggests the broad scope and variety of work undertaken by federations in the general field. The average is four committees on social service per federation. No federation is without some organized machinery in this field.

Type of Service	Number of Federations Maintaining Listed Committees
Social Service (undifferentiated)	19
International Goodwill	18
Interracial Relations	13
Political Action, Legislation, Law Enforcement	12
Industrial Relations	6
Court, Hospital or similar institutional work	5
Moral Reform	2
Sabbath Observance	2
Temperance	1
"Better understanding between Jews and Christians"	1
"Better homes"	1
Protestant relief	1
Immigration	1
Coffee club	1
Community funds	1

The present chapter undertakes to catalogue and describe the concrete forms of social work that federations maintain through such machinery, to illustrate them by typical examples, to analyze the major tendencies exhibited under each characteristic form, and to show something of attitudes of constituents with respect to each. The order of presentation of the material follows the analysis of the social-service program in Chapter VII.[9] The first general division relates to social-service preaching; the second to social-service practice.

PROCLAMATION AND ADVOCACY OF SOCIAL IDEALS AND MEASURES

ADVOCACY OF SOCIAL IDEALS AND VALUES

Discussions of the basis of social service in systematic thinking in Chapter XIII made necessary some indication of the forms in which such a theoretical basis has been expressed and declared by federations. When, therefore, one comes to consider the advocacy of social ideals and values as a distinct type of activity, little is left to add descriptively to the scanty facts already presented. Besides occasional homilies on Christian social responsibility, and the still more occasional circulation of some ready-made form of social doctrine, there is nothing characteristic to

[9] Pp. 113 ff.

record except the sponsoring now and then of addresses by well-known exponents of Christian social philosophy. Among these, Sherwood Eddy and Reinhold Niebuhr seem to have secured the most frequent hearing in the recent past. Nothing like the formal declaration in which so many federations set forth their doctrines of comity is to be found in the sphere of social service.[10] The Pittsburgh and Massachusetts State Federations are exceptions in this respect.

The little advocacy that takes these forms is, however, apparently enough for the constituents of federations. Among many hundreds of responses of a questionnaire as to their attitudes toward social-service programs, only two persons uttered any demand for more along this line. A Detroit religious educator, a woman, writes, "Why does evangelism control all of the six Lenten weeks? Give industrial relations, etc., a chance." A minister suggested, "Present the social gospel during the special Lenten program." No one else even indirectly mentioned the issue.

Moreover, what little systematic advocacy of social ideals exists is not highly valued by constituencies. Those responding to a formal questionnaire rate no other social-service activity so low as this—though a strong majority regard even it as at least somewhat important.[11]

In no pressing sense then, do federations systematically advocate social ideals; and their constituents do not expect them to do so. Presumably constituents feel that they can get a sufficiently comprehensive social gospel from their own churches.

In passing judgment on the showing, one must of course admit that piecemeal evangelism is still evangelism, and that the federations may be guilty of no neglect of recognized duty when they deal almost exclusively with specific, rather than with generalized social issues.

ATTEMPTS TO INFLUENCE THE ACTION OF GOVERNMENTS

The Church is much more instant in season and out of season in the advocacy of moral ideals than it is of more strictly social ones. In the furtherance of this end, the chief means used by church federations in behalf of the coöperating churches is that of bringing the Protestant influence to bear upon the conduct of government—this sometimes involving organized political action.

---

[10] Douglass, *Church Comity*, pp. 19 ff.
[11] P. 418.

Since the Church commands and uses so many other moral resources, it is rather more than strange that this one should so dominate its collective efforts. The general absence of non-political coöperative endeavor in this field is unusually noteworthy. To be sure, occasional voices call for it—sometimes demanding that a federation organize a Christian boycott, for example, against unclean plays, or "of our daily newspapers for opposing prohibition or giving it only lukewarm support. We could make them behave. Now they think we do not care." But no instance was found in which measures of this type were adopted, or in which there was a serious attempt or leadership in carrying them out. When federations sound the slogan, "the promotion of moral and social welfare," they almost always mean to try to influence the action of government.

Such attempts encounter two very different typical situations. When the processes of the State in behalf of moral and social welfare are established, institutionalized and professionalized, as in the case of courts, hospitals and homes, it is a very simple matter for church federations to bring pressure upon public agencies for improved facilities, better administration, or even in behalf of moral ideas.

But there are large areas in which the duty of the State is not predetermined, at least not to the satisfaction of many of its citizens. What and how much the State should do in behalf of the general welfare, and how it should do it in these realms, is still much in debate. Such matters are not being settled in general terms, but rather through conflicts over specific issues, one at a time. And many of these issues force themselves into the arena of political controversy.

Planes of Social Action Involving Government

It becomes highly important, therefore, to distinguish the planes and levels upon which social action involving government is undertaken by federations. At least three are to be distinguished.

The first is political only incidentally and not of direct intent; the second is permissibly and, in the main, safely political; while the third involves the deliberate acceptance of political conflict. Needless to say, specific actions pass somewhat insensibly from one to another of these phases; but the existence of distinctive types of action of each level is abundantly clear.

Federation action in behalf of social morality that is only incidentally political, originates in the undisputed fact that it is the Church's business to preach social morality. The federation takes for granted a certain assumed body of common sentiment in this realm and professes merely to gather up and pass on to churches and ministers information concerning the reforms which the churches commonly hold as important. This passing on may take the form of a circularization of the ministers individually, of bringing measures to the attention of ministers' associations for formal action, or of maintaining speaker's bureaus for the presentation of issues before church bodies.

As is indicated in the section on social thinking,[12] these processes involve very little real overhauling of conventional moral conceptions. Generally discussion is piecemeal with reference to somewhat specific issues almost always involving government. Since, however, no organized action is immediately contemplated or sought, the political character of such activities are largely incidental. One must consider, however, that the maintenance of this type of "between-campaign" discussion is largely for the sake of being able quickly to mobilize forces when issues are actively joined.

So far as these politically non-committal activities of federations can be segregated, they appear to have more than average support from constituents. Federation secretaries are under constant pressure to "do something" from supporters who have not thought out the political involvements incidental to the use of any practical means for gaining the ends sought.

Federation action consciously involving government is commonly regarded as permissible where it can get itself taken as non-partisan action. Occasional community improvement issues come under this category. Thus public appropriations or an issue of bonds for schools, hospitals, and other improvements are not obviously political in the sportsman's sense. They are among the things that federations may safely support. The effort of federations to steer clear of the political implications in these activities is evidenced by the names of the committees to which the responsibilities for such questions are referred. They are often called "civic activity," or "public welfare," committees in order to distinguish them from those occupying the confessed field of political action or of law enforcement.

Again, federation action that involves no particular political purpose, though confessedly political in form, is commonly accepted as permissible. Thus, church federations very generally

---

[12] P. 423.

urge upon their constituents periodically the duty of voting, without attempting to indicate how the vote should be exercised. How difficult it is to maintain the attempted distinction between form and purpose is evidenced by a specific case. A resolution had been passed by the directors of the Detroit Council of Churches reading as follows:

> The Board of Directors of The Detroit Council of Churches recognizing the critical significance of the present situation in which an almost unprecedented responsibility rests upon every conscientious citizen to register his convictions in the coming election, asks the churches to assume their share in this common responsibility of an orderly and law-abiding government.
> And with the deepest sense of the far-reaching results which will flow from this election, the Directors urge every church to use every legitimate influence in order that every member qualified to vote shall make that vote a contribution to a city government which will enforce the law.

This action was immediately interpreted by the Detroit press as favoring a particular party and candidate, and the Council of Churches was criticized for taking sides in a political contest.

It was charged in effect that a special appeal to church people to vote *at a given time* must almost always result in stimulating a vote *in a certain way*.

The Council denied such intent, and justified its action because the forms of non-partisanship were preserved. Most federation leaders would probably maintain that such action was correct. A call for a Day of Prayer just before an election has been known to be very effective in getting results. A more systematic method of reaching a similar end is to check lists of registered voters against church-membership lists, as was done by the Massachusetts Federation. The majority of church-members were not registered.

Returns from constituents include rather numerous expressions of the desire to receive suggestions and guidance from their church leaders both as regards political measures and candidates when the issues involved are presumed to be moral. Unbiased information is especially demanded. The unusual difficulty of supplying such information is also sometimes sensed; and this function remains in debate.

Still again, even though they involve political action, the support by the churches of traditional policies with which organized religion has been associated for many years has come to be accepted, and is generally conceded as proper in many places. Support of the prohibitory law is the outstanding example. Most federations in recent years have repeatedly acted in one or another way in defense of this law and in the furtherance of its aggressive administration, though at the cost of probably increasing criticism.

Coöperative action on numerous other issues involving public morality is habitually expected of the churches; but criticism of such action by a majority of constituents is also habitual. An outstanding discovery of the investigation is that reaction to this criticism has tended to close up the ranks of federation support in these matters. Constituents favor confessed political action almost as frequently and as much as they do the non-political advocacy of reform measures; and both stand high in the scale of favorable regard.[13]

Pitfalls and Attempted Safeguards

The attempt of church federations to act in behalf of united Protestantism in matters involving the state, nevertheless brings them into a realm of great difficulty in which the attempted rationalizations of their conduct are vigorously challenged. The oft-quoted maxim is that the Church should keep out of the field of politics. But this, as has been shown, is less and less possible as matters of moral concern are found to be at the same time actually in the grip of political processes. The working theory of most federations has therefore come to be this: that while they cannot avoid entering in any field clearly related to the Church's responsibility for moral and human welfare, they must be sure, before acting, that they have substantially consolidated their own constituents in the support of any position that may be adopted.[14]

In addition to federations that occupy merely incidental or permissive positions in social and moral issues involving government, there are many that maintain committees that directly proclaim the purpose of bringing the collective action of the Protestant churches to bear upon the activities of the State. When this is true, they are likely to have to deal controversially with public officials either in their legislative or their administrative functions. More than half the federations studied had been willing to accept this role, and were playing it for better or for worse.

[13] P. 418.
[14] Chapter XIII.

Legislation

Eighteen out of twenty-seven federations studied, definitely promote legislation believed to be in the interests of moral and social welfare, and try to prevent contrary legislation.

In this realm, however, it is not very often the federations that are the actual originators of specific measures. Most cities have a variety of highly specialized agencies for the promotion of specific reforms or other social progress in specific fields. The Anti-Saloon League and Sabbath Observance Associations are well known cases in point.

Legislative committees of such organizations frequently get bills introduced into legislative bodies. The organizations then proceed to agitate in favor of the bill, or against opposing legislation. A wide range of local reform or religious organizations, ministerial bodies, and other groups of like-minded citizens are expected to line up and bring combined pressure upon public sentiment. Certain types of reform legislature draw a wider religious backing than almost any other effort—Catholic and Jewish agencies often becoming associated with Protestant and non-sectarian ones in their behalf. There is, on the other hand, the danger that professional agitators representing narrow viewpoints may attempt to use the mobilized moral sentiment of the churches when it has not actually registered in behalf of the specific issue they are promoting.

The crucial point comes when the governing body of the church federation is asked to endorse a specific legislative measure, or a principle so clearly covered by such a measure that the backing of the Federation is definitely implied. Thus, in 1927, the Massachusetts Federation of Churches passed a resolution promising "the continued hearty support of our churches in maintaining and enforcing the laws against gambling." On the strength of this action, the chairman of the legislation and moral-welfare commissions of the federation addressed letters to all members of the Massachusetts House of Representatives protesting against the passage of the Senate Bill No. 58 legalizing prize-whist when the net proceeds of the game were to go to charity.

Petitions of citizens may also be circulated in behalf of the proposed legislation. Federation representatives may appear at legislative hearings in their behalf. Meanwhile, the federations' organs of publicity keep the discussion of these measures before their constituents and lead to the development of public opinion in indirect ways.

Lists of legislative issues backed by various federations under the principle that the Church is concerned in moral and social welfare have become exceedingly varied. Thus, the Boston Federation in 1927 and 1928 endorsed the "State Padlock Bill"; the Department of Health Bill safeguarding milk supply; and the Boston Police Department Bill relative to liquor nuisances. It endorsed in principle, bills providing for the payment of wages to prisoners and for raising of the legal school-age. It opposed a bill for referendum on the Eighteenth Amendment and the Volstead Act.

While state legislatures afford the most direct field for federation activity, the mobilizing of public sentiment to petition or communicate with legislators with respect to national legislation is sometimes practised. Some of the most fruitful efforts, on the other hand, relate to local legislation; as, for example, that in Pittsburgh establishing the morals court, in the advocacy of which the church federation had primary leadership.

Complexities and Difficulties

The varieties of attitude and conviction on the part of federations and their constituents which are involved in the promotion of public welfare through legislation, interestingly reveal the difficulties and complexities of this attempted functioning. A commission with a reputation for independent action had its policy defined by its chairman as follows: "This commission functions in matters political which are at the same time clearly moral issues in which there can be no two opinions among Christian people." But just what are these matters? Another federation passed a formal resolution to the effect that the prohibitory law "settled matters." The churches agree upon it and there can be no question of the right of a federation to voice their sentiment without any fresh action by, or reference to, the constituent bodies.

Experience proves, however, the necessity of frequent reconsideration of basic assumptions, and of re-statements of the application of the principle of the Church's concern in moral and social welfare, and of the consequent duty of federations to act for collective Protestantism.

The Referendum as a Method

The method of referring controversial matters to representative sections of the constituency before action is taken, was illustrated in 1927 by the Massachusetts State Federation which circulated a ballot in the following form to its delegates and committee members in advance of the annual meeting:

THE ANNUAL MEETING OF THE MASSACHUSETTS FEDERA-
TION OF CHURCHES, NOVEMBER 21, 1927

Special Ballot to Ascertain Views of Members on Debated Issues

	I Approve	Oppose	Am Undecided
1. Statement of Bishop Gore: "The condition of society requires reforms so thorough as to amount to a revolution by peaceful means"	—	—	—
2. The bill to give Jury Service to Women...	—	—	—
3. Bill to abolish Death Penalty	—	—	—
4. Adhesion of the U. S. to the Permanent Court of International Justice	—	—	—
5. Membership of the U. S. in the League of Nations	—	—	—

Of the issues thus voted upon, the adhesion of the United States to the World Court and the membership of the United States in the League of Nations was approved by so large a majority as to assure the Executive Committee "of the real sentiment of the official representative of our constituent bodies." The committee consequently put the federation on record as favoring these measures.

Jury service for women, and the abolition of the death penalty, were approved by about two-thirds of those responding. The resulting action was as follows: "Though a clear majority supported the vote, the federation, as always when there is not practical unanimity, recommended to the churches the careful study of both issues," in order that it might take future action in case a consolidation of favorable opinion should result.

Returns from constituents show that the attempt of federations to represent the churches for or against legislation, though given average support, is considerably less popular than is either general agitation for moral reform or attempts to bring pressure upon the administration of law when once it is made. Enforcement, not legislation, is the major concern of the churches.[15]

Among the occasional state legislators who replied to constituents' questionnaires was one who pointed out certain problems involved in the attempt of federations to represent the churches. He said:

Do not think the questionaire results represent the opinion of the majority of the church-members, as shown by the small per cent. of answers received last year (1927) at Lynn. Further, I do not feel that it should presume to act on political questions like jury duty, wages to prisoners, and other questions of debata-

---

[15] P. 418.

ble position to many of its members. You should not claim to represent so many thousand members when in fact you do not know the opinion of two per cent. I favored wages to prisoners, but only after sitting on the committee and hearing, not organizations, but officials in touch with both sides of the question. I found that few committees considered representative votes with much favor. They do not usually cover the membership.

Obviously these judgments raise the whole issue of lobbying by representative organizations, including questions both of expediency and of honesty.

Law Enforcement

After legislation is passed, the federation may bring pressure upon the administrators of government in the effort to get laws effectively enforced. It is presumably a basic principle of democracy that it is the right of organized groups of citizens to watch and criticize the action of their public servants; and the major part of politics consists in the exercise of such functions, primarily on grounds of partisanship or economic self-interest. Numerous expert and non-partisan agencies, such as public-school associations and municipal leagues, have also been developed to exercise such criticism more technically. It is a fair presumption that a similar function might properly be performed by a representative church body in behalf of organized religious sentiment.

Spheres of the Church's Special Concern

The spheres of the Church's concern for the administration of government are naturally those most directly involving morals. Outstanding examples are the prohibitory law, and legislation against gambling, sexual immorality, vicious plays, movies, books, etc. Most federations sooner or later come to attempt to influence the actions of public authorities in one or more of these realms.

Methods and Their Theoretical Justifications

The effective influencing of the administrators of government in the fields of public morals is, however, so difficult and expensive, and it so frequently involves highly unpopular measures such as the use of detectives in establishing the existence of maladministration, that the majority of federations are coming to work with, or through, specialized agencies of law enforcement. This policy is expressed in a Brooklyn Federation report as follows:

The Moral Reform Commission does not attempt to set up another organization. It works through Moral Reform agencies already in existence. It encourages those that are conscientiously attempting to make an enforced law. It "jacks up" those inclined to be lax. It keeps the ministers and churches informed and arouses public opinion and enables those in authority to know what the church people want.

Just about half the federations investigated were operating under similar policies. In not a few cases, these specialized agencies are the direct outcome of federation initiative and they sometimes actually function as subsidiaries. Sometimes the federation leaders are known as the chief forces in them. Both organizations get their backing from a common constituency. This is the case, for example, in Philadelphia, Baltimore, Washington and Pittsburgh. By this method, the federation avoids the difficulty of attempting to act in behalf of united Protestantism in highly controversial matters in which differences of opinion as to method easily arise.

A number of federations have taken the position that the public backing of officials who are performing their duties faithfully is just as important as the condemnation of those who are not. Accordingly, the endorsement of certain administrative policies has been tendered; and there are sometimes extended conferences between federation officials and public servants as to the carrying out of these policies.

Problems and Outcomes

In large measure, the problem of the representative authority of the federation pertains to the field of law enforcement as well as that of legislation. The same warnings against entering politics, of mixing Church and State, as have already been well illustrated are somewhat vocal in this field.[16] And, besides the question of the general propriety of this function and the wisdom of positions taken by federations on specific issues, there is that of emphasis. On the whole, the effort of federations in behalf of law enforcement has proved somewhat disillusioning to those who have it to do; and the tendency to undertake whatever is done through an independent organization appears to be increasing. At the same time, it is very strongly supported by the judgment of constituents so far as reported; and far more prodding of federations to take stronger action occurs in this field than in any other.

---

[16] Chapter XIII.

Since the promotion of moral and social welfare, whether through legislation or through administration, is largely undertaken in coöperation with other agencies, the results of the efforts of the federations as such are scarcely traceable. Both the responsibility and the credit are diffused. The mobilized sentiment of the Church, however, is frequently recognized as an important, if not determinative, factor in securing results. And the few federations that have particularly stressed services in this field have got a good many achievements to their credit.

SOCIAL ATTITUDES INCLUDING LARGER GROUP RELATIONSHIPS

Attention now turns from the effort to urge righteousness upon others to the appeal of the federations primarily to their own Christian constituencies. The members of the churches, it is felt, must take personal attitudes and reach individual positions upon very broad and inclusive social issues, such as the justice of the present economic order, race relationships, and world politics.

Industrial Relationships

The earliest of these major issues to be erected into a separate object of the Church's organized concern was that of industrial relationships. Both the Federal Council and the leading denominations developed departmental bureaus for the promotion of this interest, and the city federations early began to fix upon it as a proper field for promotion.

The means employed have included the general education of sentiment on industrial matters; the study of specific areas of industrial conflict, and infrequently, direct intervention in industrial disputes.

The means of educating public sentiment chiefly employed have been the holding of meetings for the consideration and advocacy of industrial justice, exemplified by the annual Old South lectures of the Boston Federation, or such large-scale union Labor Sunday services as that which packed the Oakland Civic Auditorium in 1928; promotion of conscience on industrial issues on the part of the entire constituency, chiefly through the circulation to the churches of the Federal Council's annual Labor Sunday message, and the organized celebration of that occasion; and an occasional elaborate series of conferences and addresses under the initiative of the Federal Council's Commission on Social Service. Seven out of twenty-nine federations reported such conferences. An "Industrial Week" in Boston was carried out through 200 meetings at centers throughout the greater city with an aggregate attendance of 25,000. Finally, a very few federations have recently attempted to maintain monthly discussion groups, including leading representatives of labor, management, and the public, together with students of industrial matters, in order to keep the minds and viewpoints of the several groups tempered together with reference to possible service in times of local crisis. Such an attempt of the Detroit Council of Churches under the leadership of Reinhold Niebuhr was apparently regarded by him as only a partial success.

Competent and significant studies by federations of specific industrial issues have not been numerous, obviously because few of them command the requisite scholarship and the means of utilization. Of studies undertaken for the educating of public opinion with respect to issues not in the acute-conflict stage, the Chicago Federation's investigation of the occupations of Protestant church-members (following a similar Pittsburgh study), and that of the milk situation in the great Chicago area, are good examples. Of studies of actual industrial conflict, the one made by the Federal Council's research department, under the auspices of the Pittsburgh Federation, of the coal-strike situation in the Pittsburgh district is the most recent. Some attempt to guide public sentiment on any special industrial disturbance would be likely, but by no means inevitable, judging from past events. Many somewhat superficial studies of the merits of particular pieces of social legislation are made by social-service committees or commissions in the exercise of their routine responsibilities.

Efforts on the part of federations at direct intervention or mediation in cases of industrial strikes appear to be less frequent than formerly. They are, indeed, so rare in recent years as scarcely to be claimed as typical social service. But several federations still declare their willingness to act as industrial mediators. The Pittsburgh Federation entered practically into the recent coal strike by raising relief funds for unemployed coal miners over a considerable period. Other federations also aided this fund.

Relative Weakness and Outside Stimulation of Industrial Interest

The phases of industrial issues that federations touch are relatively few. The most aggressive leaders in this field are paid specialists, and their promotional efforts do not really reflect wide popular interest. They are not able to bring the federations to any great extent into first-hand contacts with particular industrial facts (a few visits to factories constitute no real exception); and, save for temporary special studies, do not appear to have much first-hand contact themselves. Very few persons actively and responsibly related either to labor or to management are brought into active participation on industrial committees. (The occasional coöperation of influential industrial labor leaders in intensive "labor-week" conferences, though important, is definitely exceptional.)

But for the constant stimulus of the Federal Council and the celebration of Labor Sunday, it is doubtful whether industry would get any stated recognition from organized Protestantism even of the formal sort, save in cases (fewer than the fingers of one hand) where federation secretaries are personally committed to this interest.[17]

All told, federation activity in the sphere of industrial relations scarcely gives one an impression of its great vitality or practical weight.

Interracial Relationships

The problem of contacts between racial populations did not force itself into general Protestant consciousness till the great northward migration of Negroes during and after the World War. The Church's most articulate response to this movement was a systematic effort of the federations to educate Christian sentiment governing relations between the older population and such immigrant groups.

Interracial commissions in connection with local federations have been most actively promoted by the Federal Council. Indeed, in no other phase of social service are the activities of local federations as largely identified with the presence on the field of a Federal Council secretary and his immediate activity in connection with local programs. The wide-spread interest thus aroused, though genuine, can scarcely be said to have been spontaneous.

A Typical Interracial Commission

The history of the emergence of organizations for interracial harmony and a fairly characteristic development of method, is illustrated by the Chicago Church Federation. The Chicago Federation's commission on interracial relations developed in 1923 following the report of the Chicago Race Commission which had been appointed in consequence of the riots of 1919. An interracial committee of the women's department was organ-

---

[17] Chapter XII.

ized in consequence of the Eaglemere meeting promoted by the Federal Council in 1927.

The theory of the commission as set forth in an initial declaration on "Function, Program and Policy" is that its sphere was primarily that of establishing ecclesiastical contacts. It was to concern itself with church coöperation and mutual helpfulness. It was not to undertake the administration of any reform effort; but was to assist reform agencies, or help to create new ones should that be necessary. In the main it was to be a "vehicle for arousing public opinion."

As it has turned out, the commission ordinarily holds two meetings a year. Apart from certain routine business, it has found itself concerned largely with specific problems of contacts along the frontier of racial relationships. Negroes have felt discriminated against in attending meetings in public places even under federation auspices. They have suffered adverse newspaper publicity. The Negro members have been somewhat inclined to use the commission to call attention to, and to ask redress for, such wrongs. Very little has been heard of church coöperation. The commission has, however, had definite value as a shock-absorber, and in process of time has come to stress the organizing of occasions for contact between religious groups of the two races, such as young people's societies, women's meetings, and the like. In such meetings, the two races have made each other aware of their respective sides of the problem of living together in the same communities, of attending the same schools, and of mingling in business and industry.

The most important stated means of advancing a good understanding between races has been the observance of the Sunday nearest Lincoln's birthday with sermons on interracial justice, and so far as possible by an exchange of pulpits between Negro and white pastors arranged by the commission. On these occasions, Negro lay speakers have been used to supplement the ministers. The racial problems are at the same season presented to the union ministers' meeting.

The women's department conducts study courses in interracial goodwill. The commission has been in touch with the social investigations of local Negro conditions by universities. It has also organized occasions for the public recognition of Negro talent, as for example, through the Harmon Awards. Increasingly the duty of inspiring admiration for the achievements of handicapped groups is appealing to federation efforts.

Other Methods and Conditioning Factors

Less characteristic forms of interracial coöperation found in groups of federations are stated coöperation with the Negro Urban League; agitation for better public institutions or social agencies for Negroes; and the encouragement of federations of Negro churches.[18]

Generally speaking, the development of organized interracial interests through federation varies with the size of the city, the proportions of its Negro population, and the acuteness of inter-racial conflict. It also varies with the capacity of the Negro community to coöperate on equal terms with the white. For example, the concentration of Negro talent in Howard University and other institutions of Washington, has aided the federation of that city to organize an exceptionally strong interracial group that has sponsored a scholarly investigation of housing conditions. At the other extreme come small cities whose inter-racial service consists of the periodic adjudication of quarrels within the one or two little Negro churches, and the occasional payment of the expenses of sickness for their pastors.

Constituents' Attitudes

As is shown in Table XXVIII,[19] interracial service is among the less popular phases of federation work. Familiar warnings against racial intermixture are awakened even by transactions so formal as the exchange of pulpits between white and Negro ministers, and "discretion" is urged by constituents. On the other hand, occasional expressions of special interest in the cause of interracial justice and practical Christian readjustments stand out in the evidence.

International Relationships

Both before the entrance of the United States into the World War, and insistently after the Armistice, the question of the Church's responsibility for world peace was raised. Stated briefly, this meant the direction of Christian sentiment relative to international relationships primarily as conducted by, or affected by, the acts of government.

Since the issues involved were national or international rather than local, and since they required a very wide cultivation of the minds of the Church's constituents, movements in the interest of peace very naturally came to be conducted in behalf of organ-

---

[18] For a discussion of the place of Negro churches in the federation movement itself, see p. 91.
[19] P. 418.

ized Protestantism by the Federal Council. The majority of the city federations have actively backed the proposal of the Federal Council, and have relayed them along to the individual churches; thus giving social service in this phase a greater uniformity than it has in any other.

Methods

Four methods have in general been common to the federation peace movement: namely, the observance of Armistice Sunday as the annual Peace Day; educational propaganda; agitation and mobilization of sentiment relative to specific international issues; and friendship projects, especially for children.

Getting peace into the calendar of the Christian year as an interest worthy of perpetual celebrations may well prove a great permanent achievement if backed by educational processes adequate to keep the observance vital rather than formal.

Educational propaganda accordingly has been the more continuous concern of the federation's efforts for international goodwill. This has most often taken the form of systematic courses of lectures upon, or studies of, international problems; or of the discussion of specific issues in the press or by competent authorities. Demonstrating the first, the Detroit Council of Churches coöperated in 1928 with the local Women's Council for Education in International Relations in presenting a series of noon-luncheon lectures on world peace at a leading hotel. Illustrating the second method, the Boston Federation held a conference on Mexico at the Twentieth Century Club with a professor of Petroleum Geology to explain the relation of American capital to Mexican oil.

Another frequent means of education has been the holding of public receptions and hearings for visiting foreign celebrities who come to America in behalf of international goodwill. Such tours are frequently arranged by the national peace agencies and are facilitated from city to city by the federations.

A more characteristically home-grown method is a return to the old declamatory contests. A series of such contests in the interests of world-peace has been presented by the Ohio Council of Churches and held under the auspices of local federations.

Propaganda and Taking Sides in Controversy

These methods are often so obviously those of deliberate propaganda, in the sense of being the organized presentation of one side rather than the other of mooted questions, that some federations have taken pains to guard against the danger of unfairness by stressing the mood of inquiry in the approach to international issues.

Upon certain specific issues, however, federations have definitely assumed the responsibility for taking sides, for sharing the attempt to mobilize sentiment on the part of Protestant church-members throughout the nation, and for getting it formally expressed. The most notable of illustrations of such recent activities were the securing through the churches of resolutions and protests to Congress against the "big navy policy," and petitions in behalf of the Briand proposal for the renunciation of war as an instrument of national policy.

When the former issue became urgent, the Massachusetts and Boston federations appealed to 2,000 ministers to secure instant action by their churches. The response was such that Senator Walsh told their deputations he had been getting one-third of all the mail that came to his floor in the Senate Building. The Detroit Federation similarly organized action by the churches of that city and by 1,000 more throughout Michigan. The Federal Council appealed to the 150,000 Protestant churches of the United States in circular petitions to the President and Senate in behalf of the Briand proposal; and a secretary of the Foreign Policy Association credits these churches with a very large measure of the influence that caused the United States to expand this scope of the proposal and make it its own.

It was nothing short of a stroke of genius that conceived of an exchange of dolls between the school children of the United States and Japan, as a means of developing friendship between the two nations. The idea largely carried out locally by the federations "took" beyond all anticipation, and was so far from being exhausted that a like project with Mexico was carried out on a much larger scale.

More baldly practical has been the emergency aid rendered to several foreign nations since the World War through funds gathered largely in the churches under federation initiation. Of these, the China Famine Relief fund is the most recent.

Constituents' Attitudes and Organized Criticism

An exploration of the attitudes of federation constituents toward the several elements of their programs shows that there is more dissent from efforts in the field of international relations than in any other characteristic social-service activity.[20] Numerous illustrations of criticism and of opposition have already been

[20] P. 418.

given.[21] This, naturally enough, is a reflection of the fact that they have so largely been inspired and guided as to method by national, rather than local, agencies. In a good many communities a good many supporters of federations are simply not up to some of the positions taken in this realm.

In consequence of such activities as have been noted, charges of disloyalty have sometimes been made against the local leaders of certain federations. Speakers whom they have employed in educational propaganda have been individually denounced. Newspaper controversy has followed; and there have sometimes been meetings of protest, and counter-resolutions by "patriotic" organizations.

It does not fully meet the issues that such local conflicts raise to observe how speedily some of the positions denounced as disloyal were adopted by government itself, and got the formal adherence of almost the entire civilized world. What has most impressed the present writer is that these conflicts seem most frequently to flare up in cities where the military or naval establishments furnish a considerable part of the trade or industry of the community, and where international policies directly affect the pockets of considerable numbers of people.

SOCIAL-WELFARE ACTIVITIES

NON-INSTITUTIONAL SOCIAL SERVICE DIRECTLY UNDER FEDERATION AUSPICES

The discussion now turns from the various forms and fields of advocacy of social ideals to the effort to practice them under federation leadership. Most of the specific social ministries performed by federations are in connection with philanthropic or penal institutions, or else are the activities of other agencies in which federations only coöperate. There is, however, a relatively small realm of service that is under direct federation auspices, and at the same time not institutionalized.

The most frequent activity of this sort is social case-work. Four or five federations—usually through or in coöperation with women's departments—undertake work of this kind with "problem" girls; two or three with families, and one with old people.

Obviously, just before a delinquent falls into the hands of the law, or an unfortunate family has to call for charitable aid, there is a period during which they are slipping and struggling. Such marginal cases would seem to afford a peculiarly valid field for the Church and its ministry of sympathy and aid; and work

---

[21] Chapter XIII.

of this type is regarded with favor where it exists. Only one other type of service received higher approval from constituents. Yet there is little spontaneous demand for it. The effort of a few federations to maintain family-case-work conferences for ministers has not spread rapidly; and suggestions to this end have received but qualified approval. The prevailing tendency seems to be to leave actual case-work to individual churches and special agencies, and to trust to the minister's pastoral experience to get it done well.

NEIGHBORHOOD AND COMMUNITY WORK

Many individual churches, as well as social settlements and centers, have made large use of informal social ministries of an educational and recreational nature voluntarily participated in by neighborhood and community groups. The more familiar forms include boys' and girls' clubs, youth organizations and activities, mothers' clubs, neighborhood gatherings, and local movements for community betterment. The parishes and denominations that originated work of this kind do not often surrender it to federations; and it is not highly thought of by constituents in the rare instances in which federations undertake it—probably because it is believed to be under the wrong auspices.

Such cases of neighborhood and community work as were found in the investigation had three characteristics: (1) They occurred in the smaller cities where denominational organization is not so strong as in the larger ones. (2) They appeared as by-products of institutional work that had managed to escape institutional auspices. Certain clubs and centers of the Brooklyn City Mission Society (an agency administratively unified with the church federation) are of this sort. (3) They were undertaken by women's departments, which appear less subservient to parochial and denominational control than the federations as such are, and which occasionally push ahead coöperatively in some localities, as in Philadelphia. Here a group of twelve interdenominational mothers' clubs had been established. While not intended to be exclusively for poorer communities, the majority were actually in the less favored neighborhoods of the city. They were simple fellowships, with child welfare and development as their common interest. Their present programs especially stress the problem of the pre-school child. They also undertook to develop the sense of responsibility for local community welfare in the neighborhood group. The fostering of these clubs constituted one of the major functions of the social-service secretary of the federation; but they were not rated highly among the federation functions by the constituency in general.

MISCELLANEOUS SERVICES

A considerable number of very scattering services not otherwise classifiable take place directly under federation auspices. The most frequent of these is charity to the poor in their homes in the form of Christmas or Thanksgiving baskets or "treats." Next in frequency is the incidental finding of employment for applicants. Of all federations studied, Brooklyn alone has expanded this service into a regular general employment bureau for Protestants. In 1927 this bureau received 835 applicants and found employment for 38 per cent. of them—mainly in permanent positions.[22]

The maintenance of summer camps, of a room-registry for strangers seeking transient homes, and the operation of a "Coffee Club" as a place of wholesome resort for men, are among the other miscellaneous items undertaken by single federations.

Constituents regard such activities—where they occur—with moderate favor, and there are occasional demands for the further development of the employment service.

The institutionalized character, and rather conventional flavor, of much of the social work of federations has already been made apparent. The fact that direct service—especially of an unusual and original character—does not furnish a longer list, seems to imply that federations have little inclination—or perhaps not enough power—to develop far beyond the present range of their programs. Of course, no record was available of the number of suggestions turned down without action in the course of years.

PARTICIPATION IN VOLUNTARY SOCIAL AND REFORM ORGANIZATIONS

One of the outstanding aspects of the social service of federations is participation in voluntary social and reform organizations. The forms of coöperation with voluntary social agencies that occur in at least one-fourth of the federation programs are listed in the appendix.[23]

The federation attempts to represent the churches to the organized social agencies, and the agencies to the churches. Specifically the federation coöperates with, and ordinarily has membership in, the Council of Social Agencies where one exists. It backs the Red Cross and the Near East Relief in their min-

---

[22] The Los Angeles Federation also maintains an extensive employment service for women.

[23] P. 491.

istries to need, especially in foreign lands. Of less frequent coöperative activities, those of providing chaplains in Boy Scout Camps, and the clearance of cases through the Social Service Exchange, occur often enough to merit notice. Scattering examples of coöperation with many special types of agencies are found, such as in community-health or social-hygiene campaigns, movements for recreational facilities, etc.

METHODS OF COÖPERATION

The ways in which social agencies function naturally determine the ways in which church federations find opportunity to coöperate with them. First of all, those that exist primarily for the administration of social service, serve their own clients in approved technical ways. They feed the poor, clothe the naked, and minister to the sick. Second, they conduct educational campaigns to prevent social evils from arising, as for example, in the interest of health, recreation, or safety. Third, in order to function in the way first named, they appeal to the public for funds. Fourth, in case their object is primarily reform, they undertake the leadership of public sentiment, which may involve organized political action.

Church federations are in the best position to coöperate with social agencies on the second and third of the points just enumerated. They help to get hearings before the Protestant public.[24]

Another characteristic way in which the federations coöperate with the social agencies is in the direct support of financial appeals through the churches, especially the community-wide appeals of federated social agencies.

Federations serve less frequently by recruiting workers for social agencies, sometimes for short-time service as in financial canvasses; but also for permanent positions, as for example, those of volunteer visitors for family case-work.

SYSTEMATIC ORGANIZATION FOR COÖPERATION

Perhaps the most systematic example of organized measures for such coöperation is found in Rochester. Here the federation asked the social agencies to designate forms of service in which the members of churches could render voluntary assistance. As the result of the replies, the following list covering eight types of service was compiled:

1. Friendly visitors, volunteer probation officers, investigators and assistants, Big Brothers, Big Sisters.

---

[24] Federations of course may also assist local governments in their social-welfare campaigns.

2. Leaders and teachers in Social Settlements. Boy and Girl Scout troops, including gymnastics, plain sewing, cooking, fancy work, handicraft, music, English to foreigners, and special classes for backward children.
3. Entertainers, library workers, leaders and story tellers in homes and hospitals.
4. Clerical workers and aides in hospitals and clinics.
5. Flower Mission. Distribution of flowers in hospitals and institutions.
6. Sewing at home or in church groups—plain, layettes and sterile dressings.
7. Decorating for holiday seasons.
8. Automobile service for hospitals, dispensaries and social agencies.

Twenty-four agencies were included in the scope of this voluntary work. The forms of service desired and the list of agencies were included in a printed leaflet issued by the federation. In coöperation with the Woman's Council, a pledge card was also attached on which the volunteer was asked to indicate the type of service and the amount of time she was willing to give.

Again, all agencies need reliable and representative people of good intellectual capacity who will steadily participate as members of administrative or functional committees. Occasionally the federation's secretary becomes technically competent to share in the more fundamental deliberations of social-work councils and, as an experienced financial worker, is almost always valuable in connection with financial campaigns. Occasionally other leaders developed by the coöperating churches, find service in similar committee work.

The average case of federation coöperation with social agencies may be generalized as follows: the federation promotes the agencies' interests in many ways. It is a member of the community council of social agencies paying a small fee toward its support. The paid officials of the federations give time and thought to the interests of the council of social agencies and of the several agencies historically related to the Protestant Church. The Secretary may be a member of important committees.

RELATIVE IMPORTANCE OF FEDERATIONS IN COMMUNITY SOCIAL EFFORT

In this total body of service, the federation is habitually a very minor partner; and appreciation on the part of the social agencies for the services rendered may go hand and hand with a rather critical attitude toward such social work as the federations attempt in their own behalf.[25] It is scarcely too much to say that social agencies generally would like to have the federations function as willing coöperators, and as nothing more.

Certain federations have felt that the rôle of minor partner thus commonly assigned to them—especially by councils of social agencies and Community Chests—was scarcely appropriate in view of the large number of definitely Protestant social agencies, and the major partnership of the Protestant constituency in the support of the total body of community philanthropic work. Accordingly, occasional discussions have been had of joint financing of admittedly Protestant agencies only, under federation auspices, or of the merging of the federation's own financial appeal with that of such agencies as the Y.M.C.A. and the Y.W.C.A. in opposition to Community Chest movements; especially when the latter have been alleged to be controlled by business interests with too little sympathy for religious movements. In no case has this attitude gone beyond the point of discussion.[26]

The main body of federation supporters, however, stand steadily behind the social agencies. Coöperation with Community Chests in particular they view with more than average favor—possibly because it sometimes opens up an easy method of getting financial support for the social work of federations.

RECOGNITION OF THE FEDERATION'S UNIQUE FUNCTION

A few federations have professed to find strength in the limitation of their functions,[27] and are learning to accept gracefully, and to magnify, their rôle as liaison agencies between the churches and the organized social forces of the community. This attitude is expressed in a declaration of the Minneapolis Federation in 1928, as follows:

> In order to define more definitely the relations between the churches and the social agencies the following principles of coöperation were adopted:
> 1. The Federation should validate all projects of the social agencies which require the coöperation of the churches, and which require immediate contact with the churches.
> 2. The churches should recognize that volunteer work in coöperation with the social agencies is a form of Christian community service in which its members should engage with the same consecration as they employ in any other type of church work.
> 3. The churches should list among the personnel of church workers all those who are aiding in social work, such as directors

---

[25] P. 405.
[26] P. 183.
[27] P. 382.

and executives of social agencies, community fund campaign workers, paid social workers, and volunteer workers of any kind, who
are members of the church and its constituency. These activities
should be listed among the annual statistics of the individual
church.

4. The Minneapolis Church Federation should act as a clearing
house through which the individual churches and social agencies
may communicate and coöperate with each other.

5. Social workers should recognize the church as providing essential inspiration and motivation for social work.

6. The social agencies should recognize certain forms of social
service as being legitimate activities of the church.

The recognition of a federation liaison-function by a Community Chest organization as a proper ground of financial
support is shown in the following report of the investigation
committee of such an agency in Indianapolis:

Your committee beg to report that in their opinion the Community Chest may well continue to support the Social Service
Department of the Church Federation upon the following basis:

  *   *   *   *   *   *   *

The social service department, outside of such service as the
executive secretary may give to this department, proposes to
work along the following lines,

First, that of relating the different social agencies of the city
to the churches. This will be accomplished by securing volunteer
workers from the churches who may assist in the social service
work, and placing these volunteers directly under the various social
service agencies for guidance, and also by interpreting the work
of the social agencies of the city to the churches through such
means as addresses, institutes, and appropriate literature.

  *   *   *   *   *   *   *

That in line with their policy the Community Chest consider
a request from the Church Federation for an additional social
worker for the coming year as properly predicated on this report.

As a means of carrying out the obligations involved in Community Chest support under the above plan, the Indianapolis
Federation is attempting to make contact with the Protestant
churches one by one in order to educate them in the viewpoint
of the social agencies and in the Church's parallel opportunity as
a spiritual agency. One layman and one laywoman in each
church are presumed to be secured as a nucleus for the spread of
these ideals and for the recruiting of volunteer service. Women's
departments sometimes carry social service down into the individual church in similar ways. Occasional examples of systematic
training for volunteers in social work are noted in other connections.[28] The parallel effort in some places of social-work

[28] P. 410.

executives to educate the rank and file of their fellow professionals in the possibilities of church coöperation, and occasional
case-work conferences that bring ministers and social workers
together under federation auspices should be noted to complete
the picture.

Constituents' Attitudes

Responses of constituents show just about average support for
coöperation with social agencies.

ADVOCACY AND PROMOTION OF REFORM ORGANIZATIONS

Logically considered, the group of voluntary reform organizations with which federations have coöperative relationships
stands coördinate with the group of social agencies just discussed; and the advocacy and promotion that organizations of
the former type enjoy at the coöperating church's hands—the
publicity they receive, and the mobilization of financial resources in their behalf—appear analogous to similar activities
of federations in behalf of councils of social agencies and Community Chests. There is, however, one basic difference. The
social agencies all have as their main responsibilities great
bodies of voluntarily supported social work; and it is for the
sake of individuals benefited by this work that the churches back
them. The reform agencies, with no exception so far as the
investigation is able to discover, have as their main purpose the
influencing of action by government. It is a striking and mo-
mentous fact—not to say an ominous one—that agencies devoted
to voluntary reform are almost non-existent. The stage and the
movies, however, have made sporadic efforts to purify themselves from within; and with these efforts federations have
occasionally coöperated.[29]

But no organization exists whose primary emphasis, for example, is upon persuading Christians to proper "Sabbath"
observance or to respect for the prohibition law under the mere
sanctions of voluntary group action. Churches of most Protestant denominations have virtually ceased to discipline their own
members on these issues. There is, then, substantially nothing
to record of coöperation with reform organizations except in
efforts, actually if not confessed, to bring influence to bear upon
politicians or officials of the State.

This may be an inevitable consequence of political democracy
—it may even prove to be morally superior when its implications

---

[29] In so doing federations have sometimes appeared to compromise themselves rather than to effect reform.

are all worked out. At least it is the way that Protestantism has chosen.

The subject is therefore more properly treated as a phase of the Church's attempted relations with the State.[30]

CORRELATION OF WORK OF PROTESTANT SOCIAL AGENCIES

The church federation movement has attempted to correlate Protestant effort in numerous fields, such as comity, evangelism, and religious education. Analogy would lead one to expect similar effort in the field of social service. But no such general tendency is in evidence.

In a number of federations, to be sure, social-service commissions consist largely of members of denominational commissions or committees on social service (with the few paid officials in this field). To this extent they function as a sort of correlating center, or clearing house, for denominational social work. Perhaps they would more frequently do so if enough of the denominations maintained regular representatives for this interest in each city.

In the types of social work most frequently carried on through denominational institutions, occasional excellent examples of correlation also occur. Thus in Chicago, with forty-two institutions available for the care of dependent Protestant children (in addition to a child-placing agency) with a total capacity of 4,000, frequent delays were found in the effort to furnish care to the individual child because of the variety of denominational and other limitations and the lack of any central agency for routing the needy case to the available institutions. To meet this situation, the federation's commission on public institutions instituted and secured the organization of a joint-service bureau for Protestant and non-sectarian child-caring agencies. Sixteen institutions coöperate in the financing of the bureau, and most of the forty-three agencies accept cases referred to them. About 500 Protestant children are placed annually through this agency. While not touching the large body of dependent Protestant children who are directly placed in institutions by court action, this correlating machinery is well established, and its very large permanent value has won cordial recognition.

The Detroit Federation maintains a less definite "Federation of Protestant Child-caring Agencies," which brings together the professional workers in this field for conference, but without attempting any permanent agency of joint action.

---

[30] P. 375.

In Pittsburgh, the court work is definitely divided between the church federation and the Y.M.C.A., the former taking the women's and girls' cases and the latter those of boys and young men. All told, however, these constitute exceptional cases.

CONFLICT OR COMPETITION OF PROTESTANT AGENCIES

In certain lines of social activities, church federations are not the only agencies that have undertaken ministries in behalf of Protestant churches collectively. Situations calling for adjustment among the agencies are not infrequent. Thus in Boston, the Evangelistic Association carries on hospital work parallel with that of the church federation, thus creating what is recognized as a regrettable duplication of work.

Again, as between federations and the individual denominations, those not belonging to the federation are frequently found maintaining Protestant social workers side by side with federation representatives who purport to be laboring in behalf of united Protestantism. The infelicity of this situation was occasionally pointed out by constituents. It simply reflects the incomplete scope of the federated movement which is in evidence at every point of its work. Pittsburgh presents a contrary example (though even this is not a completely inclusive one). Its social work in the courts for women and girls definitely correlates that of six Protestant denominations that maintain paid workers. But it is imperfectly correlated with its own separately financed department of colored work. Occasionally the separately supported workers are brought together in a sort of coöperative council. Examples of this from Chicago and Washington are presented in the section concerning hospital work.

All told, however, the situation revealed by the St. Louis Survey is still typical of most American cities. The Protestant Children's Homes do not constitute a Protestant system for the care of dependent children. They have conflicting and overlapping policies. Children sometimes cannot be received although the institutions are not filled to their capacities. Neither do the Protestant old people's homes constitute a system. They are generally limited to receiving people of some particular sect or denomination. Some institutions will therefore have vacancies while others have waiting lists; and those that have vacancies cannot take the people on the waiting lists. In other words, the institutions, because of their administrative and sectarian narrowness, cannot as a group take care of the Protestant aged as a group.[31]

In brief, the effective correlation of Protestant agencies has scarcely begun. Although such efforts as exist find average favor with constituents, a really shocking lack of sensitiveness on the whole issue characterizes the situation.

The prevailing tendency is to leave it to the councils of social agencies to include the Protestant agencies and to work out the adjustments necessary to prevent duplication and waste as part of the effort to clear up the whole social-agency field. The federations meanwhile, through the practice of comity, undertake to prevent the same evils in the strictly ecclesiastical field.

CREATION OF NEW INTERDENOMINATIONAL SOCIAL AGENCIES

Except in the rarest cases, federations have not started new social agencies in behalf of the coöperating churches. Examples of such exceptions are the (proposed) Detroit Protestant Hospital, the old people's waiting home of the women's auxiliary of the Greater New York Federation, and an occasional rescue home or neighborhood center. For these cases as a group, more than average approval was received from constituents; but coöperative activities in this realm are very rarely called for. A single questionnaire urges "A home or school for our Protestant boys and girls such as the Catholics have." Meanwhile the creation of new denominational agencies goes on continuously—and their entrenchment behind vested interests makes any functional unification of Protestant institutional effort more and more difficult and remote.

From the author's standpoint, on the whole, the federations probably need not feel apologetic because they find their social-work role so largely that of coöperators in processes carried on by others. This situation is a legitimate result of their late entrance into a crowded field. At the same time, the fact that they have exerted relatively so little influence in the correlation of distinctly Protestant social work, and have so generally been unable fully to correlate their own work with that of closely related agencies of Protestant origin, leaves something to be explained and much to be desired.

---

[31] P. 427.

Chapter XXI

SOCIAL SERVICE (CONTINUED)

COÖPERATION WITH PUBLIC AGENCIES AND INSTITUTIONS

The modern State is by far the greatest single social agency of civilization. For this reason it is natural enough that a large chapter in the story of coöperative Protestant enterprises in the realm of social service relates to coöperation with public agencies of correction or philanthropy.

The State recognizes religion as a force for human welfare and continuously employs it; for example, in requiring persons under legal probation to attend church or Sunday school. The State's attempt to employ religion institutionally, however, always meets difficulty and embarrassment on account of the conflicting religions of its citizens. Administratively, the three major religions—Protestant, Catholic and Jewish—are habitually recognized; but the State is particularly embarrassed by the fifty-seven varieties of Protestants with which it cannot possibly deal separately. Public agencies are accordingly greatly relieved when some single organization arises representing the unity of Protestants in relation to the beneficiaries of the State's charity and oversight. This circumstance makes relatively large and unchallenged place for coöperation with public agencies in the current social-work programs of church federations.

In dealing with childhood and youth, the modern State is slowly learning to avoid the crude method of institutional confinement. It is trying to deal more personally and informally with both juvenile dependency and delinquency, regarding them as products of complex situations of social maladjustment that need radical treatment in order that individuals who threaten to become public charges may go back into society with a fair chance of maintaining normal character. The State, therefore, finds a home for the neglected child and frees the incipient delinquent under the control of a probation officer, in order to assure itself that the combined resources of home, school, church, and expert friendliness will be focussed upon the case long enough to work a remedy. Or else, when no overt violation of the law is found, the State may resign such responsibility to private agencies of helpfulness and goodwill.

COURT WORK

These are the general conditions under which the work of church federations in courts is undertaken, chiefly for juvenile cases. Courts dealing with children and youth differ from city to city. There is no one standard pattern. Whatever the court's peculiarities, however, the federation can ordinarily enter its processes at one or more of the following points:

(1) During actual court procedure, the court worker may become familiar with the record of each Protestant case.

(2) Either before or after the hearing, she may talk sympathetically with members of the family who have come into court in perplexity and sorrow and often embarrassed by material need.

(3) Finally, she may frequently advise the court of what she is in a position to do to assist the case. What the judge wants more than anything else is a feasible plan with an average chance of success. If the religious worker can contribute to such a plan in a fair proportion of Protestant cases, she has gone far towards justifying her position.

Court decisions are not reached instantaneously. During the delay, while the case is investigated and studied, the person before the court may be put in a place of temporary confinement —a receiving or detention home. One of the problems of the federation is to see that a standard receiving home with carefully devised methods is available for Protestant children.

The court worker follows her cases into the public detention home. In Chicago, the girls' detention home, for example, has a daily average population of thirty-five girls, two-thirds of whom are Negroes, the personnel fluctuating greatly from day to day.

The court worker will hold simple religious services, or conduct religious occasions, chiefly as a means of gaining the confidence of the girls in the crisis during which the case is unsettled, and of giving immediate sympathy and counsel:

(5) Meanwhile, the worker uses strong measures to bring quick action on the part of some local church. The pastor of the individual or his family is urged to call at the home at once, and to bring the pastoral resources of the church to bear in the emergency. Regardless of how the case may turn out legally, the aim is to get the church to assume responsibility for the social or moral problems revealed by the court action. Most federations have not enough resources to enable them to follow up the action of the churches in this connection; and when they

have laid the responsibility on the church to which the case naturally belongs, their responsibility ceases.

If, as the outcome of the hearing, the State enters upon a period of custodial care either of a dependent child or of a delinquent on probation, it maintains its own agents who have the primary responsibility for the case. A religious agency might coöperate with these agents for a prolonged period; or it might, on occasion, be itself designated as a custodian with continuous responsibility. For when a case gets beyond the court, the problem, obviously, does not end. The next step is to see that the right social agency assumes responsibility. Except in unusual cases, federations do not take this step. The Pittsburgh Federation, through its women's department, presents a unique example of a religious agency focussing its work upon the technical processes of clearance with other social agencies and the assignment of further responsibility for Protestant cases to denominational workers. Workers of six denominations are included in these processes. The Federation's social-service secretary furnishes each of them with the full case and social-agency record of everyone included in the daily gist of Protestant cases. She also apportions among them Protestants of such denominations as have no representative for case-work. Such a correlating function is clearly in line with the genius of federations wherever there are denominational agents for social case-work in considerable numbers.

CONTINUOUS CASE WORK

Most authorities on social-service policy believe, however, that the Church's court work should end where it usually does; namely, with what are essentially pastoral ministries rendered while the court is in session and during the detention period, and with getting the local church on the job as a permanent factor. Social case-work, it is felt, properly falls to specialized agencies. It requires more technical skill and resources than federations actually possess. They should do religious work and stop when that type of work is done. The exceptional cases in which federations carry on continuous case-work responsibility are especially worthy because they thus challenge the preponderant judgment of social workers. Criticism against the emergency material relief sometimes rendered is particularly vigorous. In such an issue, a careful comparison of experience with theory alone can say the last word.

A small number of federations endeavor to train and utilize volunteer members in immediate connection with court work.

In two cases Negro workers are employed to look after Protestants of their race.

Constituents' and Social Workers' Attitudes

Almost 90 per cent. of the constituents who replied to questionnaires rated the work done by federations in the courts as highly important; and there was almost no criticism of it, except as to its poor financial support. It is, among constituents, the most popular of all the social work done by federations.

Executives and social workers, however, raise many questions. Besides the general problem of whether federations are suitable agencies for carrying on this kind of work, and the constant struggle to find satisfactory and adaptable workers, a specific issue relating to court work, that of arranging a temporary receiving or detention home for Protestant cases, has arisen in the experience of federations. Institutions of Protestant antecedents generally exist in sufficient numbers in cities, and federations frequently arrange with one or another of them to care for their cases. But special care and segregation such as diseased girls may need, is not always available; and the lack is severely felt. Again, the attempt to avoid prison or reformatory has called for all kinds of compromises. The one most frequently suggested is that there should be a series of Protestant protectorates—places of brief or of indeterminate confinement, under definite religious auspices. In several instances, federations have been challenged to establish or take over such institutions, but always with the result that, whatever difficulties are involved in custodial care outside institutions, this solution is felt to be better than the proposed return even to temporary institutionalism.

Obviously, the fairly simple and primarily religious and pastoral work of federations, carried out in direct connection with court processes, makes less strenuous demands than does either continuous case work or the maintenance of institutions. The relative desirability of the varying types of court work have therefore to be considered on the score of the federation's ability to handle them adequately, as well as on that of general social policy.

SOCIAL SERVICE IN PUBLIC INSTITUTIONS

The inmates of public institutions constitute in the aggregate a vast population. A small city will segregate a population equal to that of a large village or town; a large city one equal to that of a small city. The Chicago Church Federation enumerates some forty public institutions with which it would be appropriate to coöperate. Their total population is fifty thousand. It is a staggering fact that in relation to the normal population the segregated population is constantly increasing. This is one of the disheartening social phenomena of our times.

RELIGION IN PUBLIC INSTITUTIONS

The State shelters, feeds, clothes, and disciplines its institutional wards, and furnishes them a minimum of cultural and recreational life. Larger institutions frequently also provide formal religious services through regularly appointed chaplains. But no settled social policy governs the matter generally; and the total religious ministry to this type of population under the State's auspices falls very short of that received by normal populations that voluntarily maintain their own churches. In the attempt to remedy this neglect, many individual agencies attempt to render this or that bit of religious service in public institutions, with a frequent consequence of conflict and confusion. It is a great convenience to the State to have some responsible agency of united Protestantism undertake the systematic charge of religious needs of inmates of institutions. Consequently, this turns out to be one of the relatively frequent methods of social service pursued by church federations.

FEDERATION METHODS

In small cities, Protestant work in public institutions is sometimes cared for with reasonable adequacy when a federation organizes and apportions responsibility for voluntary work to the several coöperating churches and religious agencies. This method is in vogue in Wichita, Kansas. At the other extreme comes the example of Chicago, where the county authorities have officially turned over Protestant religious responsibility in some of the great public institutions to the Chicago Church Federation. The federation appoints and maintains chaplains who conduct both formal religious services and pastoral work. The general tendency, however, is for federations to undertake the more limited responsibility of supplementing such formal religious services as is provided by the State with pastoral work for individuals.

HOSPITAL WORK

More federations have undertaken hospital work than any other form of institutional ministry. The work is primarily with individual patients. The workers are almost always ordained ministers. In the majority of cases they devote only part time to the work. The hospital authorities gladly coöperate with these accredited representatives of federations, particularly in indicating Protestant patients to whom their ministries might be acceptable. The social-service departments of hospitals find the coöperation of the religious workers especially valuable in the attempt to meet the personal and domestic problems accompanying sickness. But, in the main, the hospital visitor finds his own cases by informal friendliness in the wards.

The rapid turnover of hospital population compels the work to take on much of a touch-and-go character; but special attention is likely to be given to patients who are doomed to long hospital confinement; also to Protestants who reside outside the city and cannot expect the direct ministries of any local church. When patients have a regular church connection, their pastors are notified. The hospital visitor also communicates many messages to relatives and friends and does many practical errands for patients. So far as possible the patients are influenced in the direction of permanent contacts with the church.

The Pittsburgh Federation experimentally acted as a clearing house of hospital information, all Protestant patients in hospitals being reported to the federation office and the cases then distributed to the denominational headquarters to be referred in turn to the responsibility of local churches. Fifteen hundred cases were handled in three months; but the plan proved too elaborate for the resources of the federation.

Hospital workers frequently attempt to organize groups of volunteers for hospital work, either as pastoral visitors or assistants in musical and other services. In a number of cases this duty is assumed somewhat independently by women's departments.

An interesting variation in hospital work is found in the amount of stress laid upon the celebration of the Communion as a ministry to the sick. The representatives of certain federations are giving much place to this sacrament. Many funerals, and a few weddings, are other incidents of the hospital worker's ministry.

The work is so highly personal that no quantitative standards have emerged. A representative monthly report of a half-time worker specifies seventeen visits to ten different hospitals, involving eighty-five interviews with patients. Six meetings were held, two addresses made, forty-one Bibles and seven hundred and fifty magazines distributed; such distribution of literature is common. The full-time chaplain of a contiguous group of large institutions averages one thousand bedside calls a month, and conducts twenty services. These figures are far apart and no data exist to show what is the actual average.

The work of federations in homes and prisons differs from that in hospitals primarily because the inmates of such institutions are physically able to come together in congregations. Generally, therefore, a relatively larger use is made of formal religious services. Yet even in these institutions, the bulk of the work is still distinctively pastoral. It takes on a sombre quality from the fact that institutional confinement classifies the inmate as a failure in normal life. Consequently, it is easy to accumulate a collection of pathetic and spectacular examples of the result of pastoral contacts. The total impression, however, left by the record of such contacts is that people in institutions are, in the main, like other people, with whom as with the run of humanity commonplace experiences are the rule.

Peculiar interest attaches to work in the great public institutions for the aged poor, many of whom also suffer the disabilities of extreme age. Chicago has gathered a population of five thousand such people in its vast Oak Forest Infirmary. These are ministered to in behalf of the church federation by one full-time and one half-time chaplain.

The annual turnover of inmates in a hospital may reach 200 or 300 per cent. The population of homes and prisons is, however, sufficiently stable to warrant at times the organization of a permanent non-sectarian Protestant church under federation auspices. In this case, the chaplain becomes the pastor of the church. The social-service commissions or special committees in charge of the work may then begin to assume responsibility for the quality of the services. In Chicago they also attempt annual visitation to the institutions in which they are represented.

CORRELATION OF PROTESTANT EFFORT IN PUBLIC INSTITUTIONS

From the standpoint of the correlation of religious effort, the Chicago Federation has made the most conspicuous success. It has gathered up under its auspices, with more or less intimate responsibility, the work of ten chaplains, partly at the expense of its own budget and partly on that of several coöperating denominations. The total cost is nearly $19,000. This method makes it possible for a considerable group of public institutions to deal with Protestantism as a whole, instead of through its many separate denominations; while, at the same time, the denominations that formerly conducted independent work are able to preserve the identity of that work within a larger whole.

More limited correlation is represented by the voluntary organization into a council of different denominational workers in institutions of the same type along with the federation representatives, as in connection with the hospital work in Washington. In the main, however, denominations still very largely undertake their own separate work with public institutions, and the advantages of correlation are rarely realized.

A peculiar situation is created in a number of federations by the preëmption of the field of institutional social work by chaplains of the Protestant Episcopal Church. The "city mission" organizations of this communion have long maintained extensive work of this sort. Sometimes these Episcopal chaplains are recognized, either formally or informally, as representing the combined Protestant forces. Such arrangements might well be multiplied; but it would then become logical for the Episcopal organization to make formal reports to the coöperating bodies through the federation, and on the other hand for the Episcopal denomination to receive credit for the cost of its chaplaincies as a contribution to the federation budget.

Special aspects of institutional social service, occurring only in scattering cases, include regular ministries to ex-service men by four federations, the conduct of systematic recreational events by two, and a single instance of an attack upon the maladministration of public authorities.

Institutional social service is regarded by federation constituents with more than average favor. In certain cities where federations provide only part-time hospital service, considerable demand was expressed for an enlarged, full-time program.

PUBLIC SUPPORT OF CHAPLAINS

The increasing population of public institutions presents a field of great religious need. But the more general problems of the proper conduct of the institutions are equally important. The coöperation of federations in this field opens a way to no small measure of influence for the bettering of administrative conditions. Instead of undertaking the appointment of its own chaplain, the Pittsburgh Federation, for example, organized a movement as the result of which the city council made an appropriation for Protestant services and recreation in the city home. A conference of public officials and chaplains of state institutions, organized by the Massachusetts Federation of Churches, laid bare some of their crying needs (even in that progressive state), and raised many unsolved problems with respect to division of responsibility between the public and the churches in the support of religious ministries in such institutions. This gathering together of chaplains also enabled the group to begin the development of standards of work, something much needed in a virtually uncharted field.

Technical and Marginal Activities

SOCIAL EDUCATION AND RESEARCH

Between the realm of popular propaganda, in its varied forms, in behalf of particular social attitudes or measures, and the general proclamation of a Christian philosophy of social relationships, falls the realm of social education, distinguished by its systematic form and its academic method. Comparatively little education, as thus defined, is carried on by the federations. Four of them maintain courses in social service in their training schools of religious education. Three conduct ministers' casework conferences. Still others give the subject briefer, though still systematic, attention. Rochester, for example, introduces social service as a topic in the annual training institute held by its religious-education department. In the training of volunteers for service in social fields, a good deal is attempted in the aggregate, particularly by women's departments. St. Louis maintains somewhat extensive courses of this sort. These, under professional leadership, are integrated into a promotional plan that includes printed publicity matter, newspaper articles, addresses, circulation of bibliographies and suggestions for study, and neighborhood conferences, as well as class work. Training courses conducted for volunteers by Councils of Social Agencies are sometimes utilized by federations. Special courses in social hygiene or rural life are occasionally mentioned. On the whole, however, even when the Church commands both, the method of propaganda has greatly outrun that of education. This situation is a reflection of the attitudes of federation constituents; they give only average approval to social education, while the various forms of moral propaganda are popular. It is occasionally hinted that constituents should find such social education as they need in their own churches. The desire for an easier way is sometimes also confessed. "Our women," writes one correspondent "are too busy with home duties, business, etc., to take books for reading from reference libraries. Can you not suggest any way which will not necessitate extensive reading outside of the class." Probably this reflects the actual attitude of many others.

In the field of social research, occasional first-hand investigation of industrial or racial situations has already been mentioned.[1] Five federations reported such activities during the year previous to the present study. Broader studies of community conditions have sometimes accompanied coöperative church surveys, especially as related to deteriorating communities. The Pittsburgh Federation has undertaken surveys of several down-town and outlying industrial sections, and has made a competent study of crime in its city. The Survey Department of the Baltimore Federation is primarily an agency of church extension, but has occasionally made comprehensive summaries of social conditions as affecting religious work in certain districts of its city. A few federations have coöperated with professional agencies in research projects; for example, the St. Louis Federation with the "St. Louis Survey" made by the Institute of Social and Religious Research.

Such research as has been attempted is not very highly thought of as a federation activity by constituents.[2]

ENDORSEMENT OF FINANCIAL APPEALS OF SOCIAL AGENCIES

A highly special aspect of social investigation is illustrated by the Chicago Federation which has assumed responsibility for deciding upon the worthiness of appeals to the public for financial aid on the part of non-denominational agencies conducted under religious auspices. The Chamber of Commerce exercises similar functions for secular agencies. Agencies seeking endorsement have to file elaborate schedules of information about their work, together with certificates from competent accountants showing their financial condition. When grounds for approval of an agency are thus established, the federation issues a formal credential authorizing its appeal to the benevolent public. Several other federations exercise similar functions less formally and continuously, sometimes investigating individuals appealing for charity as well as organizations.

These technical services were regarded with more than average favor by constituents of the federations that maintained them.

In the main, however, federations do not ordinarily establish, by their own first-hand investigations, the facts on which they rely in determining their own social actions or in guiding the actions of others.

---

[1] Pp. 385 and 387.
[2] P. 418.

BORDERLAND ACTIVITIES

No absolutely clear-cut line divides social service from the remainder of the service undertaken in behalf of the coöperating churches. The church is first of all a church, and only secondarily a social agency. The primary stress of federations accordingly falls on church concerns. When, however, one undertakes to organize the church life of a racial group felt to be peculiar and handicapped, as in the Mexican interdenominational church in Wichita, its motive may be quite as truly to improve the community status of the group as to organize its religious activities. The methods of such a church are apt to stress social service; but it may or may not be administered by a social-service commission.

The pastoral care of individuals who may be in acute social need constitutes another borderland. Here the paths of the minister and the social worker cross, as in the case of institutional chaplains; and their mutual work may be classified under either the head of pastoral evangelism or of social case-work.

Religious and character education again necessarily present numerous topics in their social aspects. Thus some federations bring social hygiene into their training schools of religious education; others regard its popular promotion as a phase of social service. The Minneapolis Federation conducted its Youth Peace Movement under the department of religious education. Still other federations have undertaken the organization of the community observance of Thanksgiving in services participated in by Protestant, Jews, and Catholics. Naturally, under these circumstances, ordinary religious forms have to be modified and reduced to their common elements. Civic expression of religion, participated in by elements of populations representing diverse religious antecedents are thus social phenomena quite as much as they are religious ones, and might be so classified. Still again, certain athletic and other recreational activities conducted by federations would be included in any community inventory of social-service work.

These examples illustrate the numerous borderlands into which social service has to be traced if it is to be viewed as a whole, but which do not formally figure in the present discussion.

AGENCIES, RESOURCES AND FACILITIES

COMMITTEES

Some account of the agents, resources, and relationships through which social-service programs are operated in this field is necessary. Of the thirty-three committees maintained by twenty-two federations whose literature was studied, forty-three committees in fifteen federations were studied in detail. Their composition, characteristics, and record were compared with those of other federation committees in Chapter XVI.[3] An average federation will have perhaps sixty persons enrolled in the membership of the social-service committees; a large one from seventy-five to a hundred persons.

Women constituted 18 per cent. of the combined membership of social-service committees, but were very unevenly distributed among them. They composed somewhat over half the memberships of international and interracial relations committees, and just half the general social-service committees, but were a decided minority in committees on courts and hospitals, political action, legislation, and law enforcement; also on industrial relations committees.

Of the fifty-four Negroes found in the combined memberships of social-service committees, forty-eight were named upon committees concerned with race relations.

The general grounds upon which committee members are chosen, and the various methods by which they are authoritatively designated, are discussed elsewhere.[4] In the case of social-service committees, it is impossible to tell by virtue of what qualifications selections were made. Negatively, one may say that members are generally not chosen from the natural sources of specialized competency found in the average city. While professional social workers or executives of reform organizations occasionally dominate, and while a somewhat exceptional representation from industrial occupations is found—enough to suggest that industry is recognized as an outstanding realm of social problems—neither professional scholars in the social-work field, nor representatives of organized labor, have any notable place in committee ranks. Both these classes are occasionally included in connection with special projects or issues, but not in routine work. A number of committees also have developed supplemental advisory memberships of social workers who are called on only occasionally. In the main, however, the competency of committeemen must be measured by qualities, or by the interest, they may have evidenced in their local churches.

As previously shown, 30 per cent. of the members of social-service committees belong to other federation committees, and about 10 per cent. to more than one other. The chief variation

---

[3] P. 298.
[4] Ibid.

at this point was furnished by committees on political action, legislation, and law enforcement. Members of committees of this kind proved less related to other departments of federation work than the average. On the other hand, these committees were full of professional specialists of the type that Mr. Mencken denominates "wowsers."

The total result shows less integration with other federation interests on the part of social-service committees than in any other department except that of religious education.

The forty-three committees held 126 meetings during the year preceding the investigation, or somewhat less than three meetings to each committee. The average attendance was five members per meeting, or less than one-third of the average membership; and the total attendance was only 29 per cent. of the possible attendance. Only religious-education committees had so poor a showing. The padding of social-service committee rolls with inactive members is excessive. Needless to say, this cannot make for full effectiveness. Attendance rates, however, varied considerably according to type of committee. With industrial relations committees, they were only 29 per cent., but reached 51 per cent. in committees on political action, legislation, and law enforcement. This difference may reflect the greater popularity of the latter field of activity as measured by the attitudes of constituents,[5] as well as the larger number of salaried officials available for committee service.

COMMITTEE PROCESSES

Few social-service committees meet statedly. On account of their irregularity, notices of meetings are more likely to include indication of the special business on account of which they are called than would be true in the case of committees meeting oftener and at regular times. Rarely, however, is a full docket of proposed business sent out in advance.

In striking contrast with the field of comity, which is dominated by paid denominational executives, the field of social service includes relatively few professionals in the employ of the churches. Furthermore, as has already been seen, relatively few social-work professionals regularly belong to committees. The absence of other professionals tends to leave responsibility in the hands of the federation secretary. Only in rare cases does a social-service committee possess a chairman whose initiative dominates the committee. There are, however, a few such cases,

---

[5] P. 418.

especially in the fields of political action and industrial, international, and interracial relations.

The actual conduct of a meeting naturally depends upon the nature of the committee's responsibilities. Committees that have to determine the duties, meet the problems, and supervise the work of paid social-service workers differ strikingly from those that have to do exclusively with the formulation of opinion and its promotion. In the former case, reports of paid workers are employed in courts or hospitals and constitute important elements of routine business. Only occasionally does new business concern items referred down to the social-service committee by the board of directors. In matters of policy, however, a considerable series of transactions involving both bodies sometimes occurs. In cases where a social-service committee wants to make a representative utterance in behalf of the federation, a reference to the board of directors for final authorization is sometimes required.[6]

In contrast with the practice of comity committees (most of whose business is initiated in the form of definite proposals on the part of some coöperating denomination), almost none of the business of social-service committees originates with denominational sources.

In view, however, of the numerous coöperative relationships of federations in the social-service field, one naturally expects to find a good deal of business originating in the suggestions of other agencies. Thus in committee minutes examined at random, one finds several formal communications from community chest organizations. Less formal requests are usually presented through the executive or other secretaries.

Committees that have to administer specific pieces of social work find frequent need for additional facilities or for financial support; and a great deal of current business revolves around these points. When one considers the wide range of social-service activities, and the great variety of concrete forms which they take, one can see that the above recurrent types of committee transaction take on an almost infinite number of forms.

Certain more general aspects of committee transactions merit comment. As indicated in the previous studies of the frequency of occurrence of the various forms of social service, research and the use of objective data are not greatly stressed. In the examination of committee minutes, only occasional reference is found to such matters. Lists of Protestant agencies doing social work

---

[6] Pp. 261 and 291.

are sometimes compiled and their functions summarized. References are also found to coöperation with universities or the Federal Council in actual social research.

Again, in the stimulation or direction of committee activities, the rôle of experts also appears to be rather limited. The small number of professional social-service workers belonging to committees has already had comment. Occasionally there is a series of talks before committees by social executives, and sometimes there are technical discussions by hospital superintendents, officials of penal institutions and the like. The expert more frequently appears, however, in the rôle of a promoter of some particular interest than in that of a professional advisor in social-service work.

In harmony with the fragmentary character of federation thinking upon social service as previously discovered,[7] the study of current minutes fails to reveal conspicuous cases of the penetrating analysis of general problems. Discussions of committee policy are, however, fairly frequent. Thus a general secretary formulates a committee's problem as follows: "What we want to undertake, what the women can take, and what must wait for further resources." Most of the discussions of committees, however, relate distinctly to problems in hand; and the categories of thought brought to their solution are strongly practical rather than philosophical.

In a field the debatable character of which has been so amply evidenced, one might well anticipate some effort to develop the technique of creative discussion. Undirected controversy strongly tends to fix minds in their mutually opposing positions. It should be possible, however, for people of opposing views to go at least part of the way together. This is the assumed object of committee conferences. Yet almost no trace of effort to guide and improve the quality of their discussion appears.

All told, the study of committee minutes reinforces the warning voiced in Chapter XIII as to the slight part played by conscious theory in the development of social-service plans and programs. The thinking of committees is vital, but not systematic; and the traces of theory that were earlier set forth represent something of very infrequent occurrence.

The characteristics and duties of the more frequent types of paid workers in social service are treated in other connections.[8] They should be considered at this point in order to complete the picture of the agencies through which this work is done.

[7] P. 257.
[8] P. 321.

CONSTITUENTS' VERDICTS

Direct inquiry was made into the reactions of constituents to the current social-work programs of their respective federations, by a method previously explained.[9]

The outstanding results of the test of this were:

(1) That federations differ considerably in the strength of the backing they receive for their social work. The degrees of variation, however, are not proper matters for comparison since the content and scope of the programs vary so greatly. What has been called for short "the social gospel" differs regionally as well as from city to city; Protestantism similarly differs in denominational composition, as it does also in personal leadership. Stress on social service consequently varies. The average response of constituencies is modified by denominational tradition which makes them sometimes more and sometimes less responsive to the passion of prophetic souls. Although the slogan, "the social interpretation of the gospel," has now had vogue in the United States for more than a quarter of a century, and has won distinct place and made progress, it has also proved divisive. At the same time that it was winning adherents, it was establishing many in opposition to it. These considerations are probably sufficient to explain the quite unequal recognition of the obligation of social service by churches of various cities.

(2) In spite of variations, three-fourths of the combined constituencies of the church federations studied asserted that the social-service programs of their federations were appropriate and highly important.

(3) The combined constituency considered as a whole was, however, found making rather sharp discriminations among the various phases of social-service work. This is shown in Table XXVIII, on the next page, which measures distribution of some forty thousand separate judgments with respect to 23 kinds of social-service activity.

It should be noted that two factors enter into the judgments recorded in this table. They concern both the appropriateness and the importance of the several aspects of social-service work. It is possible that a constituent should find a given phase of work thoroughly appropriate but of secondary importance. His answer, however, could register only his resultant decision in the light of both factors. In most instances, however, a consideration of the distribution of judgments makes their grounds fairly obvious.

---

[9] Chapter VIII.

One notes that two types of social service are very much less favorably regarded than any others: first, social evangelism, or the systematic advocacy of social ideals,[10] and second, neighborhood and community work.

TABLE XXVIII—CONSTITUENTS' JUDGMENTS REGARDING APPROPRIATENESS AND IMPORTANCE OF PHASES OF SOCIAL SERVICE, IN 16 FEDERATIONS

PER CENT. DISTRIBUTION

DEPARTMENT OF SERVICE	No. of JUDG-MENTS	Total	Highly Important	Somewhat Important	Permissible But not Important	Questionable	Should Not Undertake
Total	39038	100	72	18	5	3	2
1. Social Evangelism	145	100	42	47	10	0	1
2. Neighborhood and Community Work	184	100	47	26	15	8	4
3. Borderland Activities	1170	100	60	28	8	2	2
4. Community Improvement Movement	1047	100	61	24	10	3	2
5. International Relations	6815	100	64	22	9	3	2
6. Inter-racial Relations	3378	100	65	22	8	3	2
7. Industrial Relations	2084	100	67	22	5	3	3
8. Social Research	848	100	69	23	6	1	1
9. Practical Service Functions	438	100	72	19	5	2	2
10. Coöperation with Social Agencies	2616	100	72	21	5	1	1
11. Social Work Education	1922	100	72	20	5	2	1
12. Social and Moral Legislation	3634	100	73	14	4	5	4
13. Correlation of Protestant Social Agencies	657	100	74	22	2	1	1
14. Technical Service Functions	591	100	75	17	4	3	1
15. Advocacy of Social Morality	1248	100	75	14	6	3	2
16. Political Action	1730	100	77	14	4	3	2
17. Creation of Special Protestant Agencies	259	100	78	14	3	4	1
18. Work in Hospitals and Other Public Institutions	2835	100	78	18	3	1	*
19. Coöperation with Community Funds	740	100	79	13	5	2	1
20. Coöperation in Reform Movements	994	100	82	12	4	2	*
21. Law Enforcement	2456	100	83	11	2	2	2
22. Case Work	357	100	85	13	2	1	0
23. Court and Probation Work	2890	100	88	9	1	1	1

* Less than five-tenths of 1 per cent.

It has already been discovered how little interest the federation movement has taken in the systematic formulation of its

[10] P. 373.

underlying philosophy. The present evidence seems to prove that this attitude definitely reflects an inclination on the part of its constituency to make this matter secondary. Federation leadership, then, rightly interprets the mood of its supporters when it goes ahead with service while paying very little attention to doctrine.

The low ranking also given to item two, neighborhood and community work, may perhaps be explained by the fact that the instances of this work actually presented by church federations are really not very conspicuous. It is more likely, however, that general opinion maintains that work of this sort belongs to individual churches and denominations.

Next to be considered are six activities (items 3 to 8 inclusive) that are rated as highly important by from 60 to 70 per cent. of the constituents who replied. Here again it is instructive to speculate at least as to the explanation of the facts. Thus one can see that such "borderland activities" as do not clearly function in the social-service field (item 3), and such a technical matter as social research (item 8), could hardly be expected to appeal to practical-minded constituents.

Participation in movements for community improvement in turn (item 4) can easily be thought of as somewhat off the main track of federation responsibility, as well as something in which the churches could rarely take original leadership.

It is nothing less than conspicuous, however, that the three phases of social service that have to do with the guidance and education of Christian attitudes in the largest of social interests, those of industrial, international, and interracial relationships (items 5, 6, and 7), should fall at the unpopular end of the scale. These three interests are declared unimportant, questionable, or improper by a distinctly larger proportion of constituents than oppose most of the other forms of service.

Commenting on this discovery in the reactions of his own constituency, a federation secretary gave what is probably the general explanation: "The places where public opinion is still in a controversial state are the points where the program of the council is most severely criticized. Even at these places the number of adverse criticisms is apparently small."

Eleven of the twenty-three kinds of social service are regarded as highly important by between 70 and 80 per cent. of the constituents who replied. Of the more frequent activities of church federations the conspicuous items are, coöperation of the local social agencies (item 10), promotion of social and moral legislation (item 12), the advocacy of social morality (item 15), organized political action (item 16), and philanthropic work in hospitals and similar public institutions (item 18).

Finally, four types of social-service work stand at the head of the list as favored by more than four-fifths of all constituents who replied. These fall under two closely related types. The first includes coöperation in reform movements, which is scarcely

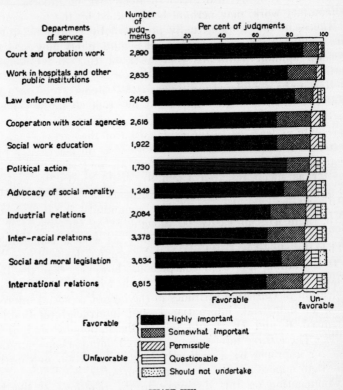

CHART XIV

Distribution of judgments of Church Federation constituents with respect to importance and appropriateness of specified elements of social service programs—16 federations

distinguishable from law enforcement; and the second, general individual and family case-work, together with similar work in connection with the courts and probation systems. In brief, the two aspects of social work that have the most complete backing of constituencies are (1) that focussing of organized Protestant influence upon the State in behalf of compulsion toward right conduct in the sphere of social morality, and (2) philanthropy in the form of direct personal work, especially for unfortunate children and youth.

The strong and steady total backing of social-service programs as revealed by this test, and the significant variation of judgment from item to item, are both to be regarded as significant. The first constitutes the substantial practical sanction of social-service work; the second shows the fluctuating limits within which this sanction pertains.

The social-service work of church federations proceeds in such fields and through such activities as Chapters XX and XXI presented. It is accompanied and supported by such sentiment as has been here described. It should be no surprise if such essentially ragged thinking and uneven support should result in a program of action that is fragmentary and none too well-rounded.

CHARACTERISTICS

A COOLED-OFF MOVEMENT

Some of the more salient characteristics of social service as developed by the federations emerge from the foregoing evidence. In the light of its history, the mood of current social service as carried on by church federations appears as a distinct let-down. Gone are the glow and assurance of the originators of this emphasis in modern Christianity. Its first fires have cooled. "Bliss was it then to be alive": routine it is now.[11] The present movement is more traditional or technical than it is inspired.

This verdict is not incompatible with the fact that the general attitude of the federation with respect to social service is still too advanced for considerable elements of the Protestant constituency. The federation movement in general is a middle-of-the-road phenomena. Of all its concerns, it is scarcely too much to say that social service alone shows any distinct trend toward innovation or radicalism; and it is only by virtue of this element within the total federation program that the movement as a whole bears just a little to the left in the march of American Protestantism.[12]

Obviously, so slight a tendency cannot please advanced social radicals. The evidence found an occasional militant constituent raising his voice to accuse the federation movement—and the Church in general—of being "mere stretcher-bearers on the battlefields of acquisitive civilization." In the main, however, genuine social radicalism merely passes the church federation by

[11] Cf. Chapter III.
[12] P. 276.

as something to be disregarded because it cannot possibly escape the bonds of its essentially conservative ecclesiastical connections.

But the present cooled-off mood of social service is no more scientific than it is prophetic. It falls between these two extremes; it lacks the authentic flavor of either. It neither fulfills the promise of its youth, nor has it achieved distinguished wisdom and excellence along objective lines.

Some extenuation for the changed atmosphere that surrounds social service, may be found in considering that learning to walk or to talk is a romantic adventure to the child; and it is no more necessarily a discredit for a movement to reach a certain maturity than for a man to do so. In the social-service field, as in others, the opportunity available to the federations is one of practical leadership rather than of notable originality. Conciliators of conflicting interests and effective administrators are wanted, rather than men of innovating minds. If, then, the fathers of the social-service movement have no body of successors, it may partly be because "new occasions teach new duties," and because their particular phase of service does not need to be repeated.

But even when this is said, one is not left exactly easy in mind. No good course occurs to the present writer except for the church federation movement to pray for more prophets, or to go about it to employ more scientists, or both. In other words, the movement needs in one way or another to get back into a more dynamic phase.

NON-ECCLESIASTICAL TENDENCY

Although attached to a federation movement whose antecedents and psychology are essentially ecclesiastical and largely fixed along denominational lines, social service shows an inherent tendency towards non-ecclesiastical and non-denominational direction. It is the most novel and challenging of the major federation interests. It puts forward their least churchly side. Evangelism, religious education, and church extension all fall within the realm of traditional religious concern. Social service, on the contrary, represents viewpoints not universally accepted; some of its very postulates are still under debate. While all the other offspring of the federation nest stay on safe shores, this odd duck of an interest takes to elements not recognized as proper and safe.[13]

---

[13] P. 275.

But social service is not only less at home with ecclesiastical traditionalism than any other federation interest; it is also less domesticated within denominationalism. One of the most illuminating discoveries of the investigation is that the federation movement is quite as much a means of protecting denominations against unacceptable and premature versions of coöperation as it is an expression of the coöperative spirit itself. As embodied in the federations, coöperation walks, if not in a straight, at least a narrow way. It is continually being warned off of fields preëmpted by the parochial or denominational church. It gets only crumbs from the ecclesiastical table.

Now social service began historically with a different and challenging viewpoint.[14] It is still somewhat strongly inclined to start its thinking with the welfare of communities, rather than with the conservation and convenience of denominational interests. It has saved a trace of innovating genius and is surrounded with an atmosphere of unrest not found about those interests with which federations are more familiarly at home.[15] It is actually the field in which the most frequent clashes between departmental commissions and the boards of directors of federations occur.

This means that social service actually performs a distinctive spiritual function within the federation movement. Besides helping the poor and needy, it ministers to the movement itself. It keeps one field of activity unusually sensitive to motives arising beyond the bounds of ecclesiasticism. It goes on challenging denominationalism in the name of the community. It remains the particularly drafty corner within the snug federation fold, the one through which outdoor winds blow most freely.

LACK OF A COMPREHENSIVE THEORY

The loose group of undertakings comprehended under the term social service, does not reflect any clear-cut doctrine as to what ends of social effort are held by federations in common, to say nothing of the agreement as to the means of attaining them. The movement lacks a comprehensive theory.[16] The supposed implications of Christianity are almost always announced piecemeal. These separate discoveries are not integrated with one another, nor are they systematically organized, so as to cover even the narrower fields to which they immediately refer.

On the one hand, this condition is another reflection of the

---

[14] P. 45.
[15] P. 276.
[16] P. 258.

non-ecclesiastical tendency of social service. It puts much less stress on systems of thought than the churches generally do. At the same time it has not made conscious connections with such formulations of social doctrine as have been made by secular thinkers, either the systematic sociologists or the practical reformers.

There is not only no pretense that the federations have achieved a final social doctrine, but there is to be found no generally accepted positive formulation of convictions held in common. The movement has recorded its own uneasiness upon this point in the following:

> Let it not be forgotten that the social question is primarily one of social thought. It is a philosophy before it is an activity. The modern socialists have seen this, and hence they have spent their lives in seeking to mold the thought life of men and communities. They have been social teachers rather than social workers in all our great centers. We cannot expect to have a social order based on Christian principles, so long as our social philosophy is made by men who hold materialistic principles. The times are appealing to the churches to inspire the thought of the social movement, and to reconstruct the economic code of modern society on that industrial and economic philosophy which is germinal to Christianity.[17]

Such philosophy is found in practical use either as a point of departure or as a device whereby other views can be checked, classified and discussed. (It may perhaps go without saying that such a formulation should be tentative and perpetually kept under active criticism.) The federation movement is virtually without any such instrument.

It lacks even a vigorous analysis of the purposes and undertakings of actual coöperative social service, as disclosed by the present study. It is preaching much, working a good deal, but integrating its thinking a very little.

INADEQUATE CONSOLIDATION OF CONVICTION

Following perhaps from its lack of intellectual background, social service as carried on by federations is greatly handicapped by an inadequate consolidation of conviction on the part of its constituent group. As is the case with the movement as a whole, complete agreement of the Protestant body is by no means essential. Thus, denominational differences remain in spite of the fact that the meaning has so largely been dissolved out of them and actual assimilation of thought and mood are far

---

[17] *Community Programs For Coöperating Churches* (New York: Association Press, 1920), Chapter IV, p. 88.

advanced. Even so, churches uniting in federated movements virtually have to agree in advance not to discuss one another's doctrinal and ecclesiastical positions.[18] There is much of humor, therefore, in the fact that these same churches sometimes assume to have reached agreement in realms involving sharp social conflict, realms as vitally difficult as theology ever was, where differences are exceedingly sharp, and Christian conviction far less standardized. Even in the more traditional realms of moral reform to which the Church has long been devoted, and in movements nearest to the Church in antecedents, many variations in emphasis and policy appear. Social service frequently tries to ignore differences that cannot successfully be ignored; and is attempting to go forward without the necessary consolidation of conviction on the part of its constituents.

OUTSIDE STIMULUS AND LEADERSHIP

On the other hand, in no other sphere of its activity does the local federation appear so largely in the rôle of agent for a centrally conceived and inspired program. The initiative of the Federal Council in much of the federation's program, and its continuous prodding in behalf of particular social interests, are written pretty fully into the evidence as presented.[19] The records on the one hand include cases of vigorously expressed resentment over this fact, and of the very willing evasion of local responsibility on the other. Not infrequently the Federal Council's suggestions are followed out by means of a series of rather perfunctory gestures, rather than taken to heart as matters of urgent concern for the particular community involved.

In special social issues, the initiative is occasionally taken by state federations and passed down for action to local ones, especially where state federations are strong, as in Massachusetts. The local federations, as clearing houses, in turn pass along to the local churches the matters involved. The result of this system, all told, is that social service generally has not been taken hold of from the local angle nor understood and applied as it would have been if it had started with concrete near-by issues.

PROBLEMS

PROPAGANDA OUTRUNS EDUCATION

Certain practical problems—of method, of scope, of direction, of performance, and of relationship—follow pretty definitely

---

[18] P. 254.
[19] Pp. 205 and 206.

from the characteristics just enumerated. The first to be mentioned is a problem of method—at bottom one of moral outlook. It relates to propaganda and education.

Federation activities are either forms of coördination and facilitation of denominational plans and programs; or specialized services performed through paid professionals; or incidental services in connection with a central office; or propaganda in some form. Propaganda,[20] in this connection, means trying to spread ready-made opinions; for example, about the Church's duty in social relations, in particular legislation, in policies and methods of law enforcement, in industrial justice, international relations, and world-peace. The frequency of effort of this kind will be impressed upon any one who will review the actual lists of social-service activities carried on by twenty-nine federations,[21] or who will reconsider the criticisms of social service, originating within federation constituencies themselves.

Educational processes, on the other hand, in their more systematic and unhurried form (to say nothing of education as the exercise of the inquiring spirit, and the acquisition of techniques necessary to discover truth) are on a very low level either from the standpoint of interest or of the time and money devoted to them.

There may be a short way—which is at the same time both righteous and effective—of getting people to accept, believe and act upon convictions the grounds of which they have not examined. It may be that their own good or the good of the community justifies such an attempt. At least the federations generally are acting this assumption.

This substitution of propaganda for education, it may be noted, takes place in a realm in which the extensive social verification of the past is lacking. Many of the issues of social righteousness are new. They could not have originated before the coming of the modern age. They are beyond easy personal apprehension; but must be investigated from the outside, and by means of extensive samplings of facts. Whatever may be true of individual ethics, bare principles simply will not apply themselves to social life. The writer personally questions whether at least two-thirds of the effort of federations to line up the Protestant constituency in support of specific movements, formulas, or causes, should not be spent upon study-classes and discussion-groups of intelligence, within which convictions could be formed.

---

[20] P. 374 f.
[21] P. 491.

LITTLE PROGRESS TOWARD COÖRDINATING PROTESTANT
SOCIAL AGENCIES

A second problem relates to the scope and direction of social service. If the analogy of other phases of federation work were to govern, it would be most natural to find these agencies making active effort to correlate the work of the entire body of Protestant philanthropies, most of which are denominational. Philanthropies of the institutional sort exist in great numbers. They are frequently duplicatory and competitive. If churches were found in this condition, comity would promptly intervene to prevent or reduce rivalry. It might even venture upon a positive version of coöperative churchmanship, attempting to meet the total need of the community in behalf of the combined Protestant forces.[22]

But the federations have rarely ventured upon similar attempts in the field of the Protestant philanthropies, and no federation has carried coördination in this field through to any degree of completion comparable to that which the more positive examples of comity have achieved in the ecclesiastical field.

Yet every motive operative in the case of comity suggests that church federation might well work out common plans and common standards for the philanthropic agencies of their member denominations. The issue is particularly pertinent in view of the prevailing critical attitude of the social agencies, the acknowledged difficulty of securing competent paid leaders for denominational social work, and the frequent failure to do work of standard quality in this field.

Comity was first worked out on its negative side, and is only now becoming more positive. It takes time to create the sense of any new problem and to force the conviction of its importance into action. Thus the federations spent twenty years in coming as far as they have come in the coördination of the strictly ecclesiastical forces. It ought not then to be regarded as an unheard-of task if they should be starting on another twenty-year job in this similarly important line.

A SECONDARY PROTESTANT SYSTEM OF SOCIAL AGENCIES

Is a separate Protestant system of social-welfare agencies desirable in any sense? One need not reopen the question of a complete and rounded system of Protestant philanthropy,

[22] See the companion volume of this report, *Church Comity*, especially Chapter II.

paralleling the State and secular systems, to realize that there is a lesser, but a real, problem of the existing agencies. With the rapid growth especially of city populations, social need is forever outstripping the development of forces adequate to deal with it. There will have to be more agencies, and undoubtedly the best available social intelligence will conclude that some of them should be Protestant, as in the case of the Detroit Hospital Foundation.[23]

In view of this inevitable prospect, a number of questions arise with respect to the Protestant agencies as a group: can denominationalism, as related to them, properly be controlled except through the development of the coöperative spirit within the Protestant body? Have these agencies common interests that will find it natural to integrate first under their own auspices? Might not a coördinating agency of their own lead them forward faster and more comprehendingly than an alien movement such as a secular Council of Social Agencies? Are there occasions in which the strength of the Protestant ecclesiastical group will need to be exercised as an entity parallel with the Catholic and Jewish systems? Might there be impositions on the part of secular social agencies and exactions on the part of the Community Chests which could best be resisted in this way, and compelled to become reasonable?

These questions conspire to raise the more general issue of a Protestant ecclesiastical system of the second order; a system within a system, by means of which the coöperating forces can better proceed to occupy whatever field falls to them in the division of responsibility.

COMMITTEE PERFORMANCE BELOW AVERAGE

The actual record of social-service committees constitutes a fourth problem. With the single exception of committees of religious education, they register a poorer attendance-average than is found in any department of federation work, or of boards of directors.

With respect to attendance, the membership of social-service committees divides into two contrasting groups, one of which attends frequently, the other not at all. In view of the low average attendance, it is most striking that no other group of committees shows so high a percentage of members attending more than half of all meetings; and at the same time, none shows so high a percentage of members who never attend. This highly exaggerated situation may be due to the mixture on the

---

[23] P. 401.

same committees of paid professional advocates of social reform—Mr. Mencken's "wowsers"—and laymen who are no match for the professionals technically, yet who may not be convinced of the righteousness of their more extreme positions. At any rate, this anomaly with respect to attendance constitutes one of the high spots of the evidence.

UNDER SHARP CRITICISM BY SOCIAL AGENCIES

Membership in the larger world of social-welfare effort also discovered another problem for federation social service. It frequently falls under the disapproving attention of the agencies that do the thinking and set the standards in that round. In considerably more than half the cities where the social work of federations is extensive enough to enter into the consciousness of the social agencies at all, the prevailing attitudes of these agencies (as revealed in direct interviews with representative leaders) impressed the investigator as distinctly unfavorable. Their disapproval was generally dispassionate and coupled with the desire to help the situation to improve; but a few cases were clearly antagonistic. In one or two cities the critical attitude was more moderate and somewhat constructive. The social agencies were already helping the federations to better technical standards. Finally, in a distinct minority of cases, the attitude toward federation work on the part of social agencies was positively favorable. This was specially true in some of the smaller cities where the social agencies were more directly dependent upon church sentiment for financial support.

Now even when these critical attitudes are sharply discounted, as sometimes based on partisan assumptions and at others because merely academic or possibly jealous, their force is by no means overcome. One is left at least suspecting that the agencies are partly right; and whether they are or not, their attitude constitutes an important element in the situation.

The alleged grounds of the critical attitude of social agencies are in general three: first, that the paid social workers of the federations are inadequately prepared; second, that their technique is deficient and that they do not coöperate loyally with the other agencies in the use of common instruments such as the social-service exchange; and, third, that the churches are attempting work in inappropriate fields properly belonging to other agencies. Back of this criticism is the fact that while somewhat general acceptance has been won for the formula that all social issues involving definite human and moral values are the concern of the Church, the gravest differences remain in concrete issues relating to the Church's consequent responsibility.

SUGGESTIONS

So great a fund of information concerned social service as now presented may naturally be expected to throw light upon the practical conduct of this interest by federations. Seven ways in which the investigator thinks current methods might be improved, are suggested in the following section. Other ways will occur to the reader.

REDUCE THE NUMBER OF COMMITTEES AND INTEGRATE THEIR WORK

The average federation has four social-service committees, large ones many more. The committee system cuts up the general field into disconnected and sometimes competitive phases of social interest. Progress, then, is made by segments rather than as a whole. Something is needed to synthesize the separate fragments of service and bring them within an effectively unified program. The problem is primarily one of unified thinking which would be necessary to achieve positive integration even if rigid departmentalization were abandoned.

The author, therefore, suggests both a reduction of the number of committees and some coördinating agency in case several committees are still to be maintained. This agency might be an interdepartmental committe covering the whole social-service field. It would be especially valuable in integrating the work of women's departments with the main body of social service, and would be greatly strengthened by competent professional leadership.

SUPERVISE PAID WORKERS BETTER

There is scarcely any institution that might not improve its administrative supervision of subordinate workers. At this point appears a glaring contrast between the elaborate (sometimes too elaborate) devices of the more progressive secular agencies and those of many federations. This comes out when federation workers are supported on Community Chest funds. They then have to fill out extensive records with quite unaccustomed accuracy. Their results are mere continuously checked. It is not too much to say that an entirely different atmosphere of fidelity and precision in supervision pertains in the better type of social agencies than is found in church federations. He will be a good friend of the federation who urges them to put in more time and more money at this point.

USE OF REFERENDUM

It seems reasonable to suggest that federations explore the possibilities of the referendum as a test of their actual representativeness on particular issues. This was sometimes suggested by constituents, and was occasionally used. The experience of the present investigation in measuring constituents' judgments on specific propositions tends to indicate that a fairly strong majority would probably be found in favor of almost anything on which the officers of a federation might find enough agreement to submit it for popular approval. A federation would be actually stronger with the public if it could say, "Sixty per cent. of our constituents are with us on this point and the remainder vary on either side of the dominant positions in such and such proportion." As it is now, when the federation says, "We speak for a united Protestantism," the world doubts whether it has even a 60 per cent. agreement. In brief, the facts are likely to be more effective than the most extreme claim without the facts can possibly be.

ACCEPT TECHNICAL STANDARDS OF SOCIAL WORK

It can hardly be other than good counsel to urge federations to adopt the current standards of social service, as developed by the most reputable administrative and educational agencies of progressive communities, both as relates to the preparation of workers and to the conduct of any types of welfare work for which accepted standards exist.

Whatever be the additional virtues that ecclesiastical auspices and conscious Christian motive bring to the situation, they need not conflict with the acceptance of these more external and technical standards.

Such a position is necessary to give the Church's social workers equal standing in the councils of organized social work, and to secure for their work the prestige and respect it deserves. The lack of technical preparation on the part of workers, and the frequently low quality of work under religious auspices, have been amply demonstrated in the text. What, then, is the need of going on to appoint still more workers who lack the traditional training? The urban church is especially clear-cut in its demands for full professional training on the part of the ministry. Why should it not show equivalent regard for the criteria of professional fitness which the social-work field has evolved?

MODIFY THE RÔLE OF THE FEDERAL COUNCIL

One may even venture to suggest that a more satisfactory rôle for the Federal Council in the field of social service would be that of technical assistant to, and constructive critic of, the local federations, rather than that of the promoter of fixed programs. While a process of give-and-take between the central national agencies and the organizations of the local communities is entirely normal and most desirable, would it not be better if the Federal Council secretaries functioned as evangelists, experts, and reporters upon facts, rather than as departmental administrators? They might then work at the call of local federations under a flexible system for the mutual exchange of experience. Why, at least, should it be any part of their business to put over upon local communities administrative schemes of merely departmental scope, disregarding the total social-service problems as they exist concretely in any community?

TRAIN FOR SOCIAL SERVICE

As the vehicle of the thinking and integrating process, a system of social education under federation auspices might well be attempted. It should be as far-reaching as the effort to train workers in the theory and practice of religious education, and indeed might be institutionally associated with that process. The so-called leadership-training school would much more nearly justify its name if it were equally a school of religious education and of social work, with parallel types of instruction and an equal range of courses. In brief, a great extension of popular education in the social sphere is not at all beyond the characteristic methods, and the contemporary resources, of coöperative Protestantism. And such a system merits an equal claim with religious education, when relative emphasis on the two fields in the actual federation scheme is considered.

ENLARGE THE RÔLE OF DENOMINATIONAL SOCIAL WORKER

The investigator was especially impressed by a few cases in which a denominationally supported court worker or chaplain had been recognized as representing the entire Protestant group, and in which the cost of his support had been credited to his denomination as a contribution toward the federation. Might there not be other profitable experiments of the same sort? Four general conditions would seem to be implied: (1) Representatives of the employing denomination should participate in the corresponding committee of the federation where their viewpoints and policies as related to the worker would be subject to general discussion and the pressure of collective opinion. (2) The agency employing the denominational worker should report the results of his work to the federation, with sufficient definiteness so that the federation could interpret it as a coöperative activity. (3) The worker's personal version of his ministry must be catholic in spirit and capable of expressing the consensus of the Protestant group. (4) Finally, there should be initial agreement covering the terms on which the arrangement should be stated to the public as at the same time denominational and interdenominational.

If these conditions were met, the actual administrative control of the denominational worker might continue to rest in his denomination, just as though the denomination constituted a subcommittee of the federation. The relationship would then have representative quality, and the results in service would be just what they would be if the worker were a federation employee, pure and simple.

This suggestion might well apply to institutions as well as to single workers. For example, denominational hospitals or homes might be interdenominationalized on these terms.

Such an arrangement might permit denominations like the Protestant Episcopal and Lutheran, which have relatively numerous philanthropies, to find a distinguished place in the federation movement on the side of social service, a place commensurate with their position in the total work of American Protestantism.

STRESS SERVICE DISTINCTIVE OF THE CHURCH

Any agency seeking to determine its particular share in a common task may well consider what native gifts it has to bring, and what the areas are within which it can act with the greatest facility.

The Church as represented by the federation movement, has not closely observed this principle in the field of social service. In casting about for easy solutions within its practical limitations, and especially under the crowding of other agencies, it has deflected the Church from its most appropriate emphases. While, therefore, one may be entirely willing for the Church to accept the humbler rôle of an assistant rather than a principal in social work, one can scarcely be wholly pleased with conditions that make it difficult for the Church to assert its own genius.

Now one of the primordial strains in the Church's general outlook is the prophetic one; and all along this strain is so characteristic that one expects to find it asserted continuously. One might well urge, then, that as a permanent part of its program, the Church should undertake pioneering experiments in social work, particularly as related to the use of religious feeling and motive as a social force. Within this area it would not be difficult to keep ahead both of the public and the private social agencies. Here the Church could find its most congenial and least competitive rôle, one that would take it out of merely traditional rounds and make it more than an ancillary agency.

Again the Church cherishes a deep-seated pastoral instinct. It seems logical to suggest that a permanent phase of its effort should directly concern the more directly psychological and spiritual aspects of social case-work, where this instinct could find fullest play. Why should not the Church set itself to discern the symptoms of social disaster and specialize on borderland cases; that is to say, the cases of people who are slipping, but who have not yet fallen over the line into the hands of the charities and the courts? Here the Church would find a free and distinctive field, and could direct its energies straight at the point where religion ought to count the most. Would it not be better to put major emphasis in an area where the Church has natural and prescriptive rights, where it could avoid embarrassing organizational alliances or conflicts with respect to prerogative, where, in brief, its energies would be expended to the best result?

All this is not to suggest any lessening of effort at other points, but merely to introduce a principle of selection, and to point out the grounds on which federations might follow it.

Chapter *XXII*

COÖPERATION BY PROTESTANT WOMEN

Twelve of the twenty-two federations studied reported women's departments; but the actual frequency of these adjunct organizations of women is difficult to calculate because of the widely differing relations they sometimes bear to the major bodies. The ways in which the coöperative movement among Protestant women are related to the federation movement in general have been carefully set forth in Chapter X.[1] The present chapter accordingly undertakes to generalize broadly as to this type of coöperative work, not narrowly limiting its cases to those that bear the label, "Women's Department."

ORGANIZATIONS

Beginning with the more formal factors of women's organizations, it is natural to consider first the official statement of their objectives.

OBJECTIVES OF WOMEN'S INTERCHURCH ORGANIZATIONS

These statements are made in exceedingly varied terms. They differ from corresponding statements by federations in being much more frequently specific rather than general. In the simplest case they enumerate particular kinds of service which the organization aims to perform; for example, work in hospitals and courts, or the promotion of interracial goodwill. More often the general sphere of the intended service is indicated but not the particular form. Thus, numerous constitutions declare that social work, law enforcement, child welfare, etc. are the objectives of the organization. Sometimes, however, the formal statement consists merely of highly general phraseology indicating moral purpose, as when an organization declares it exists to further the "application of the gospel to every relation of life," or to "enlist women in coöperative work for the extension of Christ's Kingdom." Even to such loose—and frequently borrowed—phraseology, a hint of particular method is sometimes attached, as in a constitution which declares that the purpose of

---

[1] Pp. 169 ff.

the organization is "to unite participating churches in community programs of Christian service."

In connection with these statements of ultimate objective, five types of formulae are used, indicating larger spheres and relationships in which the particular objectives are to be sought. These are: (1) "to unify women for Christian service, or some of its variations; (2) to organize women "in their own fields of activity"; (3) to coöperate with church councils or federations of churches; (4) to coöperate with the social agencies of the community; and (5) to be affiliated with national councils of women for home or foreign missions. Only occasionally does one find a somewhat comprehensive statement of objective, such as "to promote home and foreign missions, to engage in social work and to coöperate with the church federation."

MEMBERSHIP AND PARTICIPATION

In the discussion of federation membership and participation,[2] it has been pointed out that certain departments are characteristically broader in the terms of membership and actually get a wider participation on the part of constituents than the federation itself does. Women's departments present one of the outstanding examples of this situation.[3]

The constitutional formula providing for inclusive membership runs typically as follows: "Any church of a denomination affiliated with the federation or of any other denomination" may be a member of the women's interchurch organization. An alternative formula is, "Each church (of the community) shall be entitled to representation whether it belongs to the church federation or not." Such provisions allow the women's organization to take in non-evangelical groups in some cases, as well as to secure the coöperation of evangelical groups who are self-excluded from the general federations. Thus, in New York city, Unitarians, Universalists, Lutherans, and Friends elect delegates to the women's division, though outside of the membership of the federation. As was also pointed out in an earlier connection, women's organizations also sometimes draw on a larger geographical area than is served by the federation itself.[4]

UNITS OF MEMBERSHIP

From the standpoint of kinds of units out of which they are constituted, women's interchurch organizations fall into three types.

---

[2] P. 100.
[3] Ibid.
[4] Ibid.

(1) In the majority of cases the unit of membership is the women's society in the local church. Local churches may of course have both foreign and home missionary societies, or a combined society, and there may or may not be additional organizations of the "Ladies' Aid" type, or for other purposes. In this form of organization each of these societies elects its own delegates to the women's interchurch organization. These delegates, in turn, elect the governing body. There is no body of individual members apart from the aggregate membership of the women's organizations.

(2) In the second type of organization, the local church is the unit rather than the individual women's society. In this case, the whole female membership of the Protestant churches is generally conceived of as constituting the ultimate membership of the organization, and delegates are then elected from each church as in the previous case.

(3) In the third and rarer type of organization, financial contributors constitute the membership of the organization and elect its governing body.

In the composition of boards of directors or other governing bodies, denominations are almost always equally represented. This is in contrast with the usage of church federations which generally make representation proportionate to the size of the denomination.

Compared with church federations, women's organizations run to a larger number of committees relative to the number and kinds of work they undertake. The major functions are naturally represented by standing committees, but there is little uniformity in nomenclature, and no definite tendency as to departmentalization.[5]

RELATION TO OTHER TYPES OF WOMEN'S ORGANIZATION

Ten of the twenty-one women's organizations studied, reported affiliation with the National Councils of Women for Home and Foreign Missions. Many others have organizational membership in local federations of social or religious agencies. Some of these federations are constituted on the interconfessional basis, and representatives of Protestant women thus become fellow members on their boards with women of Catholic and Jewish faith. Indeed it is often urged as a reason for having a Protestant interchurch organization that it enables the evangelical forces to be equally represented with other communions in moral

---

[5] For a statement of the system of committee organization of general federations, see Chapter XVI.

and civic movements, as they cannot be in their denominational separation.

This direct connection of Protestant women with systems of coöperation outside the local and Protestant ranks, contributes to the independence and distinctiveness of their organizations within the federation system.

FUNCTIONS

A classified list of the more frequent activities of women's departments, showing the number of federations that actually carry on each as a distinct function, appears in Appendix III, and the typical program is characterized in Chapter VII.[6] These enable the reader to compare the content and variety of the distinctive women's organizations with those of the movement as a whole.

FUNCTIONAL TYPES

The coöperative organizations of Protestant women, whether departments of federations or independent affiliated organizations, fall into five types with respect to function. Each has its corresponding requirements as to staff, resources, and administrative methods:

(1) The first type is concerned primarily with interests outside the local community, in the sphere of home or foreign missions. Its functions are necessarily limited to those of advocacy, promotion and very incidental financial support. The only cost of these processes is that involved in the holding of certain meetings, and of limited publicity and educational processes. All the work talked or learned about is ordinarily carried on denominationally. Work on this level is nationally administered and has very slight local roots.

(2) The second type of women's organization undertakes to educate church women in the social needs and concerns of their own communities, and to connect them helpfully with the work of social agencies through various means of service and support. The activities involved are essentially those of the other agencies. To these the church women's organization constitutes a sort of auxiliary at large for securing voluntary participation, and a clearing house for parceling out minor responsibilities to groups or individual volunteers. The function of the women's department is thus administrative, relating to this recruiting and parceling out process. The ultimate responsibility both for management and support remains with the several agencies.

---

[6] Pp. 117 f.

(3) In a third and more developed type of organization the women's department, in addition to the functions previously enumerated, also undertakes temporary responsibility of its own for social case-work in limited fields, particularly those of Protestant juveniles in courts and Protestants in hospitals. At these points, they operate through professional representatives in meeting the needs of persons undergoing crises. The primary work of the women's organization is the support of these workers, who may or may not be administratively controlled by committees of the women's department. Almost always, representative status in the courts and hospitals is secured by the general federation and not by the women's department exclusively. In other words, such major social agencies of the community virtually require that united Protestantism shall enter into relations with them through some single representative agency inclusive of the entire Protestant body and not merely through one representing a sex segregation. Accordingly, women's organized work in this phase tends to become more closely integrated than usual with the total Protestant coöperative program.

(4) In the fourth type of organization, the women's department adds a body of permanent case-work under its own auspices. Cases originating in courts or hospitals, or initiated in any other way, for example, by reference from the churches, are undertaken for continuous treatment and solution; whereas, in the previously described type, they are handled by the church forces only at a certain critical period and then turned over to other agencies for final solution. This fourth type requires a varied staff of social case-workers with differentiation of responsibility. Thus, the problems of juveniles and of aged persons are different from those presented by family case-work in general. Organizations of this type generally work in close coöperative relations with the great voluntary case-work agencies of their communities; but they maintain their work out of their own resources and carry it on through their own workers and according to their own standards and methods.

(5) The fifth type takes on the large additional responsibility of conducting some philanthropic institution under its own auspices; for example, the Girls' Club of the St. Louis Board of Religious Organizations, the temporary Old People's Receiving Home of the women's division of the Greater New York Federation, and the Mexican settlement of the Wichita women's department. Institutional work obviously involves an additional specialized staff of workers; it implies peculiar administrative

problems and large additions to the financial burdens of the organization.

With minor variations, these five types comprehend all the women's coöperative organizations met with in the study of twenty-one cities. It is only fair to add that, relative to the total problem of Protestant philanthropy, the most extensive work yet developed by any women's organizations carries only a very small proportion of the total burden of the community. Most of the social work for needy Protestants everywhere is carried on through public and voluntary agencies, not under ecclesiastical administration or support.[7]

FUNCTIONAL RELATIONSHIPS WITH FEDERATIONS

Comparing the functions performed by the women's organizations with the general functions of church federations, three types of relationship occur. Certain elements in the work of women are distinctive and not paralleled by anything generally undertaken by the federations. Missions and personal social work belong in the main to this category. The promotion of ideals by women is paralleled by the promotion of the same ideals by the federation. This occurs in the fields of international and interracial relationships, moral reform, and citizenship, where women's groups pass resolutions, circulate petitions, and issue appeals as representing their particular constituency. The third type of relationship is one in which women's departments coöperate with the federations in the maintenance and management of paid representatives in their distinctive fields of service.

It is a fair question at any time, and with respect to any federation, whether the distinctive and unduplicated, the parallel and the duplicated, and coöperative phases of work are suitably proportioned one to another. This appears not always to be the case.

AGENCIES AND RESOURCES

COMMITTEES

The fact that the committee records of women's departments were generally not kept in the federation files but were in the hands of volunteer secretaries, made it difficult to secure an adequate sampling as a basis for a study of committees and their work. But the executive committees of eight women's departments, including those in Chicago, Detroit, Minneapolis, San

---

[7] Pp. 395 f.

Francisco, Washington, and the Massachusetts State Federation, were studied in detail; and on certain points data concerning additional committees were secured.[8]

COMPOSITION AND CHARACTERISTICS

The study revealed the following characteristics:

Fifty-three per cent. of the membership was over fifty years of age and none was under thirty. No traceable correlation was found between age and program or emphasis. In the large, the younger women of the churches were inadequately represented.

With the exception of one Negro and one Japanese woman, the membership was confined to white Americans.

Ninety-one per cent. of the members had been on their respective committees three years or less, while only one in every thirty had had more than five years of committee service. The committees of no other department showed so low an average of experience—a fact partly explained by the relative newness of some of the women's departments.

The overwhelming majority of committee members came from the home-making classes. Out of an aggregate of 257 members whose occupations were recorded, only nineteen belonged to the professions, while three were in business, and two others occupied some status other than that of housewife.

As compared, however, with other committees of federations, the average attendance on women's committees made a better showing.[9] This is perhaps partly chargeable to the greater leisure of women committee members as indicated by their age-tendencies and occupational classification.

Only eleven out of a sample of 143 members belonged to any other committee of their respective federations. Even this small showing is partly explained by the fact that the presidents of women's departments often have constitutional place in boards of directors of the general federations. On the whole, the women's committee membership is much less integrated with other federation responsibilities than is true of other committees. This is simply another evidence of the essentially separate character of this phase of the coöperative movement.

PAID DEPARTMENTAL WORKERS AND FACILITIES

In contrast with the relatively large number of women employed as paid workers in the general federation movement,[10]

---

[8] Pp. 296 and 298 ff.
[9] P. 298.
[10] P. 148.

women's departments themselves rarely have paid executives. Their characteristic mark is that they are administered by unpaid workers, some of whom contribute very large amounts of time to this service. Office secretaries are, however, employed in one or two instances. In one or two others the name of a social worker supported primarily by the women's department appears on the letterhead as the employee of that department, though her standing with the court, or other institution served, is as a representative of the federation at large.

The rare cases in which a salaried executive was found are those of organizations whose previous federation affiliation has been relaxed until they are essentially independent.

Except for special facilities used by social workers, women's departments have no special equipment other than office space for their volunteer or salaried administrators. In certain cases, they even assist the federation in paying the rent of the quarters they use.

FINANCES

The expenditures of women's departments naturally reflect the nature of the programs undertaken. Where salaried social workers are employed, the budgets for this purpose run from $1,200 to $2,800. In the few cases where women's departments operate philanthropic institutions, the cost runs from a modest $2,200 to nearly $20,000 annually.

Income is chiefly secured from individual subscriptions and organizational contributions. Federations that make the women's society in the local church their unit of organization commonly attempt to get the uniform minimum payment from each member organization. Income from lectures or entertainments to which admission is charged constitutes a subordinate resource of the women's department, while the costs of educational institutes are partially met by fees, and those of meetings by loose collections taken on the spot.

The women's departments are in all cases self-financing; and, except as related to coöperative work, their receipts and expenditures frequently do not go through the books of the church federation. It seems obvious that they should do so, to afford a true statement of the amount spent coöperatively by the Protestant community.[11]

PUBLICITY

As instruments of publicity, the women's departments generally share the printed organ of the federation in which they

---

[11] P. 457.

sometimes conduct a separate column or department in behalf of women's interests. They also keep up an active circularization of constituent bodies through mimeographed or leaflet matter, and find the usual publicity opportunities through the public press. Only a single organization (now independent of the local federation) was publishing a monthly bulletin of its own.

CONSTITUENTS' ATTITUDES

In connection with the investigation of the constituent's reactions to federations and their programs, a separate calculation was made covering constituents' attitudes toward women's departments. As is shown on page 134, the constituencies at large view women's work with just about average favor. On the total body of returns it rates below comity and religious education, but above social service and evangelism.

As part of the larger investigation reported on page 133, a limited calculation was also made of the attitudes of women constituents toward the federation movement.[12] The results showed that relatively more women expressed the highest degrees of loyalty to the movement than was true of constituents in general.

In brief, the federations appreciate the women to an average degree, and the women reciprocate just a little more warmly.

TENDENCIES AND CHARACTERISTICS

Like the general federation movement, the interdenominational organizations of church women disclose themselves as tentative in method and opportunistic spirit. No strongly dominating trends have yet developed. Nevertheless, certain fairly consistent characteristics have emerged and one begins to feel that one can guess which way the movement is going.

DIVERSE ANTECEDENTS AND INTERESTS

Here are movements with different historical motives and antecedents. A poorly defined but strong impulse is leading them toward a larger integration. The effort is to affect such combinations as will give these movements a more adequately representative character with respect to united Protestant womanhood. There is a tendency for programs to broaden. For example, missionary interests are being socialized under the conception of world-friendship, besides being given local content

---

[12] Based on 300 cases of women in Boston, Chicago, Detroit, Washington, and Wichita.

under the aspect of community service. All these characteristics are essentially paralleled by the federation movement at large.

DISTINCTIVE ATTITUDES

The interdenominational movement of Protestant women is, however, marked by distinctive attitudes. It is sensitive; it is aggressive; it reveals itself as a phase of contemporary femininism. In this aspect it is not always being fairly dealt with. An occasional federation has attempted to meet the situation by platitudes, such as that "men and women share equally with all the privileges and responsibility of the coöperative movement", when women are not by any means proportionately represented either in its basic membership, on committees, or in staffs. Against such an attitude the movement necessarily protests, and may easily pass over into active opposition.

RECENT SITUATIONS

A review of situations occurring in the immediate past shows with considerable definiteness the terms upon which women's organizations have or have not been willing to enter into closer organic relationships with federations. As the price of surrendering organic independence, they have commonly insisted that women have more recognition in the basic structure of the federation, and that more women be placed on committees, etc. The responses of certain federations that have tried to meet this demand by compromise, have not gone to the bottom of the matter. Thus, to the formal condition "that women should be named on the various standing committees of the church federation, not relegated to any one department or committee," a certain federation made the counter-proposal, "that women should be named on committees of the federation in which it would appear after conference that the Council of Church Women had interests that would be involved." Now, what women are contending for is, that they are involved in all the interests of the Church. When such situations have been met flatly the response of the women has been the logical expression of this position, namely, that they desire proportionate representation in all the concerns of the federation, not merely in those labeled as "women's sphere"; and, in addition, opportunity to conduct work under their own initiative in any sphere which they may regard as distinctively theirs.

Equally illuminating are certain recent cases in which women's organizations have forced a loosening of their previous relationships with church federations. Here the insistence has been on "our own activities, which we are usually willing to consult about provided the constitution does not say that we must consult about them." Such a note as the following has been frequently sounded: "We propose to discuss and take our own action on public questions."

In the matter of relationships with church federations, the worst, however, that must be said is that the technique of adjustment between them and the women's organizations is imperfectly developed, and that occasionally the will to coöperate is not sincerely present. The official position of the women's organization as nationally federated is definitely for remaining in affiliation with the federation movement, both local and national, on terms yet to be explored and agreed upon.[13]

CHARACTERISTICS OF COÖPERATIVE WOMEN'S WORK

Some of the outstanding characteristics of coöperative movement among Protestant women, as the investigation has discovered them, may now be briefly summarized:

(1) The movement represents an apparently irrepressible segmentation in the Church along sex lines.

(2) The exact relationships of the movement to the federation movement are still doubtful and subject to further evolution.

(3) The movement is less ecclesiastical in impulse and instinct than the general federation movement.

(4) Its methods are less unified and less standardized than those of the federation movement in general.

(5) It is more broadly inclusive and less sensitive to the theological grounds of eligibility in vogue in the general federation movement.

(6) The women's coöperative movement exhibits certain apparently feminine traits, such as larger use of the motive of social prestige in cultivating a following. Leadership not infrequently is in the hands of women of wealth, and other women are invited in the name of coöperation to social events which their individual status in society would not accord them. These factors play a part in the women's movement which they do not in the federation movement at large. Apparently, there is also a tendency to multiply machinery relative to the magnitude of the programs, even beyond the probably excessive example of the federations themselves. In brief, the mechanics of women's coöperative organizations appear to be very much out of proportion.

---

[13] Action to this end was taken at a meeting held in Boston in 1929.

PROBLEMS

Generalizing the situation thus summarized, it appears that the outstanding problems of adjustment for the women's departments lie in two areas. In the first place, they are organizational and administrative. In this age, which is continually calling out new specialization with a corresponding complexity of machinery, the essential demand is that integration shall somehow more than keep up with separation; so that the net result will be fewer and better organizations, rather than more and poorer ones. Feminism in the Church with its tendency of sex separation, runs counter to this principle. Women's departments are in danger of developing parallel and unrelated programs, even when they nominally group themselves within the federation organization. Duplicate, perplexing, and sometimes conflicting approaches are being made to local churches. Numerous adjustments along this line will be called for before the total movement has reached consistency.

On the psychological side, the essential problem is "within what bounds will feministic tendencies be kept by their own instincts and reason?" In the case of the federations, organized women are dealing with a weak movement. They are sometimes compelling it to grant them recognition which they cannot at present get from the denominations to which the women belong. There is continued insistence on recognition and position, which adds considerably to the difficulties of an already hard-pressed movement.

Attacking federation tendencies from another angle, the organized feminine mind is impatient of their slow pace as an ecclesiastical movement. It does not regard as important many venerable considerations which churchmen in office cling to. Psychologically speaking, it is a more adventurous movement— and one more willing to ignore theological and traditional distinctions for the sake of the values of coöperation as it sees them.

CONCLUSIONS

Despite its problems, the women's coöperative movement expresses a definite urge toward Protestant integration. It is of commanding importance because it stands for another serious way of taking the problem of interchurch relationships. Even the formal loosening of previous ties with federations and the growing instability of old relations, mean progress in this sense. The situation grows in part out of the fact that the federation movement has been too slow and uncommanding. Besides insisting on what their peculiar status impels them to ask for themselves, women want greater unity in the Church. They feel that, potentially, they are able to muster coöperative forces so numerous and strong as to make it ludicrous and unfitting that they should figure at the small end of the so-called general movement. The only way in which the federation movement at large can, or perhaps should, hold the woman's movement as part of itself, is by expanding commensurately with the ideas it professes.

Finally, in harmony with the initial hypotheses of the investigation, the author's judgment is that it is wholesome and necessary for all vital aspects of the women's movement to get into organized expression. Even if it should be temporarily disruptive of the larger coöperative effort at certain points, it is better for the separatist movement to be brought out into the open; to have its day; and then to re-enter into such combinations as prove to be still more vital and masterful. There should be no attempt to thwart it in any degree. One may regard it as a bit ungallant for the ladies to use the formula of coöperation and unity when some of their attitudes and measures are non-coöperative: but one may, at the same time, hold that their logic is sound. Quite likely the reasons why women should separate themselves from the federation movement are more vital than are any reasons for denominations remaining apart from one another. Might it not be better, however, to assert outright the righteousness of women's position and of the cause which the women's movement represents, than to talk "union in Christian service" when temporary separation, at least, from the main movement is intended?

Last of all, as a challenge to the traditional masculine ecclesiastical leadership which has made the Church what it is, one must welcome the women's movement; even though suggesting in the same breath that its issues had better be fought out in the arena of the denominations rather than in that of the comparatively feeble federation movement for which it may constitute too strong an explosive.

Chapter XXIII

FINANCES AND FACILITIES

With this chapter the report turns to a technical consideration of the material resources by means of which the work of federations is carried on.

FINANCES

The chief difficulty of reaching a fair basis for exact financial statements lies deep in the structure of the federation movement. The local federation is frequently a loose alliance of affiliated organizations and quasi-independent commissions whose finances are not raised in common, do not pass through a central treasury, and consequently are never completely aggregated for purposes of reporting. Even when centralized financing is adopted, curious other minor exceptions occur. Thus the women's department under the Chicago federation regularly merges its finances with those of the federation except for small sums which it retains as a species of philanthropic pin money. It is still further to be considered that a great part of the work of federations is the coördination of denominational programs that are separately financed.

In view of these considerations, it is probable that the federation's own summaries of finances, reported in Chapter IX, considerably understate the financial magnitude of the total enterprise.

The finances of twenty federations were studied intensively, including those of all agencies functionally identified with the federations so far as they could be ascertained. The present chapter is based upon these twenty cases.

SOURCES OF SUPPORT

Like all Church enterprises, federations are voluntarily supported; but unlike a considerable proportion of city churches they have no backing in accumulated wealth. No federation reports any income from endowment, though beginnings of endowments have been made in a few cases.

Inasmuch as federations are composed of ecclesiastical units, one might expect denominational treasuries to furnish much support. As a matter of fact, however, the denominations strongly incline to send the federations back to their individual constituents for contributions. Taking the entire twenty cases, 29 per cent. of the total receipts come from churches and denominational sources, and 35 per cent. from individuals. Other sources of support are collections at public meetings, income from minor business transactions and services, community funds, and temporary loans.

The distribution of income for the twenty cases, according to source, is given in Table XXIX and Chart XV (p. 450).

TABLE XXIX—SOURCES OF INCOME IN 20 FEDERATIONS

Sources	Income Amount	Per Cent. Distribution	No. of Federations Receiving Income from This Source
Total	$444,338	100	20
Individual churches	109,011	25	20
Denominational and coöperating agency subsidies	42,027	9	10
Individuals	154,906	35	19
Endowment	0	0	0
Other sources	138,394	31	20
Business or services, admissions, fees, etc.	*23,137*	*5*	15
Collections	*21,518*	*5*	12
Community chest	*31,033*	*7*	3
Loans	*21,186*	*5*	9
Departments (direct transfer of funds)	*31,108*	*7*	8
Unclassified	*10,412*	*2*	12

But these totals and averages throw little light upon the distribution of income with a given federation. Some of the sources are essentially alternative. Thus, large denominational subsidies preclude any general financial appeal to churches, and are so intended. Community Chest appropriations are apt to be conditioned upon agreement not to engage in a general solicitation of individuals.

Support by Individual Churches

Considering church sources of all sorts, it is noteworthy, first, that, though local churches constitute the units of membership in the great majority of federations, the modal situation (applying to over one-third of the cases) is one in which only about 25 per cent. of the federation's total income is received from individual churches. However, in about one-fourth of the cases the ratio rises to between 40 and 50 per cent. Only three federations receive more than 50 per cent. from this source. The extremes are those of Youngstown, which gets only 5 per cent. from churches, and Louisville, which gets 78 per cent.

Denominational Subsidies

Appreciable denominational subsidies are naturally to be expected primarily in federations constituted out of denominational units: notably those of Detroit, Chicago, and Pittsburgh. But even so, a large federation with many departments is apt to

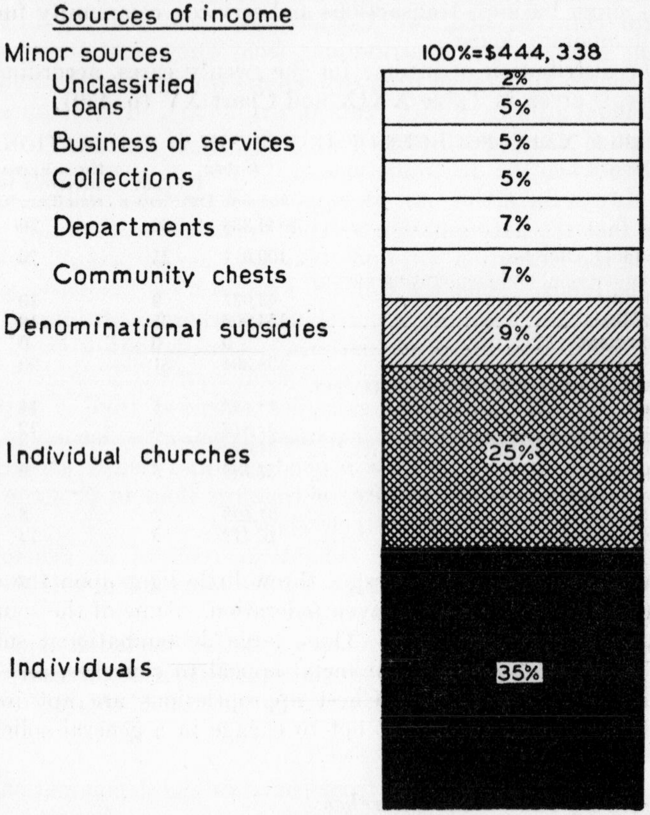

Sources of income

Minor sources	100%=$444,338
Unclassified	2%
Loans	5%
Business or services	5%
Collections	5%
Departments	7%
Community chests	7%
Denominational subsidies	9%
Individual churches	25%
Individuals	35%

CHART XV

Distribution of annual income according to source—20 Church Federations

receive not more than 20 to 30 per cent. of total income from denominational sources. Departmental budgets are rarely entirely covered by denominational subsidies. Thus Detroit, while financing its central budget denominationally, had nevertheless to get contributions from forty-nine churches of ten denominations and from 139 individuals, to carry out its religious-education budget in a recent year.

Again, denominationally supported federations get additional support from churches of denominations not in formal membership. These contribute to particular phases of work from which they benefit. For example, the Pittsburgh Federation social work for Negroes is financed outside of denominational subsidies. In a recent year it was supported by gifts from thirty-nine Negro churches and two Conferences, collections from three public services, and contributions from forty-eight individuals. The church gifts range from two dollars to forty dollars, and the individual gifts from fifty cents to ten dollars. This implies the receipt of many small sums.

Even when the denominations is the unit of membership, it is not always the active unit of support. What the situation comes to is that the denomination accepts financial responsibility providing the federation will undertake the duty of actually soliciting the funds. Thus, the Chicago Federation is the active agent in approaching the individual churches whose contributions are then credited to the denominations.[1] Occasionally a small and struggling federation composed of local churches is largely sustained by denominational subsidies extended from a sort of missionary motive; or, in a few cases, because the leaders of the denominations wish to show a good will and find it simpler to get the money from the central treasury than to promote the federation idea throughout their churches.

All told, nearly half the federations received no denominational funds at all. Pittsburgh, on the other hand, gets 83 per cent. of all income from this source.

Besides denominational subsidies, rather negligible amounts are received by three or four federations from the treasuries of non-church organizations attached to their memberships.[2]

Total Support from Church Sources

Adding together receipts from churches and denominations to get total receipts from church sources, the modal condition is found to be one in which a federation received from 45 to 58 per cent. of its support directly from the agencies that constitute its membership. But even so, about a third get not more than 25 per cent. in this way.

With respect to support from the contributions of individuals (exclusive of collections at public meetings), the modal condition

---

[1] In the case of Chicago, certain denominational subsidies for social service are credited outside the budget. These are not recognized in the above statement.

[2] For constitutional provision for membership by non-church organizations, see p. 80.

is one in which the federation gets from one-fifth to one-fourth of its support from this source. This accounts for a third of all cases. An additional fourth of the cases get from 36 to 46 per cent. from individuals, while New York gets 60 per cent., Sacramento 63, and Youngstown 88 per cent. Each of the three, however, represents a highly peculiar situation. The large individual gifts in New York come from committees in support of national radio broadcasting; in Sacramento, from a single "angel"; in Youngstown, from a general community campaign.

At the other extreme, as already noticed, are such cities as Indianapolis, St. Louis, and Detroit which get Community Chest funds; and Pittsburgh, which is mainly supported by denominational subsidies. These methods of securing support preclude any large appeal to individuals. St. Louis, for example, gets only a few hundred dollars by solicitation of individuals for its outdoor preaching. Louisville is the only city so well provided for by the churches as not to have to depend on income considered from individual support.

Incidental Business Income

Federations, of course, are in business only incidentally. Many of them, however, operate educational courses for which fees are charged. They take in money and may make slight profits on lunches or on the sale of books. In one or two cases, small tuitions charged in week-day schools of religious education are brought into the central treasury of the federations. Very infrequently, federations do for churches technical services for which they are paid; such as making surveys. New York and Brooklyn operate service bureaus that furnish temporary pulpit supplies, and church musicians and other workers. These services are free to churches, but bring in incidental income. Finally, some of the smaller federations bring distinguished speakers or musical events to their communities and charge admission fees. They sometimes make an appreciable proportion of their income in this way. But income of these sorts averages only 1 per cent. in the median case.

Collections

Twelve federations report that from 1 to 17 per cent. of their total receipts are from collections taken at public services. The median and mode both fall at 11 per cent.

The primary occasion of these collections is found in the series of Lenten or Holy Week services, which sometimes draw very large congregations, and, to a lesser degree, the Thanksgiving or similar undenominational celebrations. Occasionally, receipts from these sources more than pay for the cost of the particular activity involved, and help finance other departments.

Community Chest Funds

Receipts from Community Chests are enjoyed by only three of the twenty federations studied. In these cases they constitute 16 per cent., 46 per cent. and 48 per cent. of the total receipts respectively. To justify so large a proportion of support from community funds, a federation obviously must lay great stress on social service relative to its total program. In the extreme case, that of Indianapolis, the arrangement with the community fund even permits partial use of its appropriation for salaries and overhead expenses of the federation. The grounds on which such an appropriation for work under undenominational religious auspices is justified, may be judged from the following statement of policy:

> The social service department, outside of such service as the executive secretary may give to this department proposes to work along the following lines:
>
> (a) First, that of relating the different social agencies of the city to the churches. This will be accomplished by securing volunteer workers from the churches who may assist in the social service work, and placing these volunteers directly under the various social service agencies for guidance, and also by interpreting the work of the social agencies of the city to the churches through such means as addresses, institutes, and appropriate literature;
>
> (b) Second, through the performance by a paid worker of actual probation work in conjunction with the Criminal Court, Juvenile Court, City Court, or any or all of them, the object of this work being actually to serve the needs of such persons and families as may be brought into court, and also to demonstrate the value of making use of volunteer services from the churches in this field.

Federations that receive Community Chest funds render such technical reports as are required of all beneficiaries, and make annual reports showing the relation of their social work to their total programs, as a justification for continued assistance.

Loans

During the year preceding the study, eight federations had been compelled to supplement their current income by loans to amounts equaling from 6 to 29 per cent. of their total incomes. Occasional loans smaller than these were regarded as negligible. The larger loans were, of course, symptoms of serious financial difficulty. In one case, a well-to-do secretary was presumed to have met a large deficit out of his own pocket. In another, workers remained incompletely paid for as long as six months. In a third case, complete financial disaster was barely averted; while in a fourth, the loan tided over a period preceding to an extensive financial campaign, which in turn failed to secure sufficient funds to meet the deficit and cover the following year.[3]

Departmental Funds

The central treasury of a federation may support its departments wholly, in part, or not at all. A few departments on the contrary, turn over to federations funds to be expended by the central administration on types of work not directly falling to them, but in which they are interested. That is to say, they act as financial auxiliaries. This is true of women's departments or councils of religious education in a total of seven cases. The departments in turn get these funds from their special constituents: church societies, individuals, or collections at public meetings may all be involved.

Unclassified miscellaneous income averaging 2 or 3 per cent. of the total budget is also reported by twelve federations.

EXPENDITURES

Considered in detail, the more outstanding facts with regard to expenditures are the following.

Administrative Salaries

These absorb from one-seventh to two-thirds of the total expenditures of the federations. In nearly half the cases, they take from a third to half the budget. Relatively speaking, the largest federations spend the least on this item. A high showing of expenditure for administrative salaries is definitely correlated with low departmental expenses. The cause is self-evident. When departments are not separately staffed, leadership falls on the central administration and entails increased salary costs at this point. A federation with the modal staff of three workers may expect to spend approximately half its income upon administrative salaries.[4]

Rent

Of the federations that pay rent, nearly two-thirds devote from 4 to 6 per cent. of their income to this item; about 5 per cent. being strongly modal.[5]

---

[3] For further light on financial problems of federations, see p. 459.
[4] P. 309.
[5] For conditions under which federations receive free rent, see p. 465.

Relatively speaking, less than average rent is paid by such large federations as those of New York, Chicago, and Detroit, which employ the largest staffs. Small programs and meagre staffs involve relatively higher rent. Within the space that such federations require as a minimum, considerably more work could be carried on without adding to the rental charges. Under ordinary conditions the modal rent of 4 to 5 per cent. of the expenditure budget may be regarded as reasonable.

General Operating Expenses

These absorb from 4 to 20 per cent. of federation budgets. With about half the cases, this item ranges between 8 and 12 per cent., with 10 per cent. very strongly modal.

Relatively speaking, high costs of operating expenses are associated with low departmental costs. This is really a matter of lack of differentiation in bookkeeping. When work is not departmentalized, and falls under the central administrative staff, it is customary to charge its operating costs to the central budget. The lowest rate of operating costs is found in federations where semi-independent subsidiaries accept a proportionate share of the overhead charges and include them in their own budgets.

Even in such a case, operating expenses may be high because the activity of the central administrative staff is unusually extensive. Very infrequently, too, an operating budget has been loaded with the costs of a defunct department which started out to pay its own way and failed.[6]

Departmental and Other Specially Budgeted Activities

Considering all expenditures of this character, the proportionate cost ranges from 2 per cent. to virtually two-thirds of the total federation budget. No strongly modal tendency appears. There is some tendency, however, for departmental expenses to absorb from one-fifth to one-third of the budget, or else from one-third to two-thirds. The most conspicuous federations whose operating expenses fall within the former range, lack religious-education departments; while almost all of the latter group stress religious education. When there is similar emphasis on other departments, coupled with large staffs, the highest ratio of departmental expenses is naturally found.

Religious Education

Considering separate departments, religious education, as just indicated, tends to be most expensive. In twelve federations

[6] P. 462.

that budget this interest separately, the cost ranges from 1 per cent. to just under 50 per cent. of the total expenditures of the federation. Within this range, relative costs are widely scattered. For religious education to get about one-fourth of the total federation budget is slightly characteristic. In general, however, specific explanations relate to the degree of development of this department. Where religious education costs only 1 or 2 per cent. of the budget, it is a mere gesture or a transient phase. Where it costs 4 or 5 per cent., it is limited to some single features such as a training school. It will cost approximately one-fourth of the federation's total resources when the total program is large and relatively well balanced, as is the case in Detroit, Rochester, and New York City. Costs will rise to over one-third of the budget when they include the expenditures of local day-schools of religious instruction, or of training schools, that do not pass through the federation treasury. Finally, moderate-size cities whose relatively small federations operate extensive systems of religious day-schools, may require as much as half the total resources to maintain this interest. The facts then seem to warrant the rough generalization that a large federation may normally spend one-fourth of its resources on an all-round program of religious education, and a smaller one as high as one half.

Evangelism

This department is separately budgeted in only fourteen federations. It costs on an average of 7 per cent. of the total budget. Cases in which this average is exceeded are where very extensive Easter or Lenten services, or joint evangelistic campaigns, are carried out. The extreme costs, reaching 20 and 24 per cent. respectively, of the total budget, are found where street and shop meetings in one case, and radio services in another, are staffed by full-time secretaries. The other extreme appears in a majority of federations that leave the management of evangelistic activities to a competent committee and the executive secretary.

General Social Service

In its general and undifferentiated phase, social service is separately budgeted in only six of the twenty cases studied. The cost is relatively trivial (1 or 2 per cent. of the total budget) except in two cases; one in which a half-time worker is employed particularly for social service education, and one in which an interested individual as chairman of the committee personally contributes to its work what amounts to 40 per cent. of the total budget.

Court and Hospital Work

These special phases of social service are carried on by a minority of federations; but generally involve the employment of paid professionals, and are consequently relatively expensive. In seven cases of court work, cost ranges from 4 to 23 per cent. of the budget. Smaller per cents. are found in very large federations with many interests. The other factor governing the ratio of expenditure on this interest, is that costs are less where part-time, or women, workers are employed. The same principle governs variations in the cost of hospital work, which in the eight cases separately budgeted range from 3 to 39 per cent. of the budget, with 8 or 9 per cent. rather strongly modal.

Industrial, Interracial and International Committees

These phases of social-service work are separately budgeted in only four cases, and absorb only from 1 to 3 per cent. of the budget. Their work lies primarily in the spheres of conference and education, and is carried on by competent committees.

Comity and Research

In only one case does a federation employ a research secretary primarily concerned with comity studies. In the two others in which this interest is separately budgeted, the costs are respectively 1 and 6 per cent. of the total budget.

Women's Departments

A discussion of the finances of women's departments relative to the total budgets of federations is difficult: first, because the more distantly coöperating women's organizations do not report financially to the federation; and, second, because the more strictly auxiliary group of women's organizations raise money, but transfer it to the federations for spending (largely in the field of hospital and other social work). Expenditures covering the remaining budgets of the women's organizations range from 1 to 37 per cent. of the total federation budget, with 3 to 6 per cent. as the most frequent range. This roughly represents the relative costs of women's departments when they concern merely the missionary and educational activities of women constituents. As the educational program becomes systematic, the ratio of expenditure rises. In the extreme case, where a women's department absorbs more than half the total federation budget, it has not only a salaried worker but an institutional program carried out under its separate auspices.

Other departmentalized activities are separately budgeted in six federations and cost from 1 to 6 per cent. of the total budget. The only outstanding novelty in this list is the department of church athletics in the Detroit federation.[7]

Publicity and Financial Campaigns

These activities are separately accounted for in only a minority of federations, chiefly those that publish elaborate organs, and raise large sums of money by intensive effort. When the federation organ is strongly featured, the cost of publicity may be 4 or 5 per cent. of the total budget. In federations that stress campaigns, the cost may be from 4 to 6 per cent. Expenditures under these heads are, however, usually covered under general operating costs.

In eleven federations, from 1 to 7 per cent. of the total budget remains unaccounted for under the head of miscellaneous expenditures. This indicates a relatively small area of loose bookkeeping, and has no great influence upon the previous showing.

Four federations, during the year studied, had to spend from 2 to 9 per cent. of their incomes to meet past indebtedness.

Summarizing: expenditures for administrative salaries and overhead costs obviously must be invariable items. Departmental expenditures (most frequently for evangelism and religious education) and rents are frequently budgeted separately. Women's departments come in with moderate frequency, while undifferentiated social service, court, hospital, and other committees on social work have very infrequent budgetary recognition. Least frequent of all are expenditures for comity and young people's departments.

Very small miscellaneous expenditures occur almost invariably.

Two aspects of expenditures are worthy of separate comment. First, all things being equal, the ratio of the cost of each phase of federal activity to total expenditures depends upon the size of the total enterprise. Administrative salaries, rents, and general operating expenses are inordinately high in the smaller federations. Central budgets of a given size can carry on more work at relatively less cost when the total enterprise is large enough to be efficient.

---

[7] The rural-church department of the Massachusetts State Federation is not strictly comparable. This absorbs 49 per cent. of the total budget of that federation.

Whatever be the distribution of costs, the main expenditure of federations is for paid workers. Nowhere are they dealing extensively with material interests or even with institutions. They are essentially investments in personality and leadership, either for the general direction of the work or for personal ministries, such as those of court workers, chaplains, and teachers.

HOW FINANCIAL SUPPORT IS SECURED

Finance Committees

Financial responsibility primarily attaches to the board of directors of federations, and constitutions sometimes so specify. About half the federations studied, however, maintain separate financial committees whose duty is to secure the resources which the directors proceed to administer. The composition and characteristics of these committees have been studied in comparison with others in Chapter XVI,[8] but certain special characteristics deserve further stress.

During the year covered by the study, they met infrequently or not at all, except in two cases. The two exceptions included one very large and highly organized federation, and one that engaged in an extensive financial campaign in coöperation with other agencies. It looks as though financial committees knew that theirs was a thankless job and acted accordingly.

Naturally a majority of members are drawn from the money-making and money-controlling classes in business and industry. The proportion of ministers greatly declines. While more than half the members of these committees belong to no other committees of the federation, one-fifth belong to one other, and nearly another fifth to at least two others. Members of finance committees thus stand in only fairly close relations with other phases of federation interests. Few get appointed on these committees who have not had some considerable apprenticeship in federation service; and there is a considerable old-guard of federation workers.

From the standpoint of attendance, members of the committees fall into two groups—the very faithful, and the rest.

Methods

Financial methods in general follow familiar patterns. First of all, a federation naturally makes a theoretical division of expected income among the several sources on which it is able to draw. With respect to churches, denominations, and indi-

---

[8] P. 298.

viduals, quotas are likely to be assigned in denominational terms. As to the basis of these apportionments, some formula will naturally be adopted, and modified in accordance with previous experience of the unequal giving capacity of different elements of the constituency. Directors will be asked to accept the duty of raising their respective denominational quotas, either formally or informally.

Simultaneous campaigns to secure individual gifts follow the now standardized routine of such efforts. Prospect lists will be prepared, and solicitation by teams organized, in an attempt to cover the whole matter within a given period, ordinarily a week. To facilitate the work of the solicitors, a barrage of publicity will be laid down in advance. It will consist of a variety of personal communications of the adroitly forceful type, the circulation of printed matter, the use of the press or special organs; and in a few instances of window placards. Special committees of men whose names carry financial weight may be organized for use in connection with such campaigns. The morale of the solicitors will be supported by dinners and competitive reports. The campaign is sometimes initiated by Federation Sunday, in which the claims of the federation are presented in pulpits or by church notices throughout the city.

Occasionally such campaigns are jointly undertaken by a group of Protestant agencies. When the campaign method is not used, the same elements will naturally enter into the continuous cultivation of individual constituencies through recurrent appeals.

In the approach to churches for support, the effort is to get a federation regularly included as an item in the church's budget. The approach is primarily undertaken by denominational delegates who appeal to churches of their own communion. The following is a somewhat typical agreement illustrating such an arrangement:

1. That each denominational representative would assume the responsibility for raising the amount of the Federation budget assigned to his denomination. This amount is calculated on the basis of current expense of the various churches of his denomination.
2. Each denominational representative agreed to appoint one laymen in each of his churches who would see that his respective church pledged and raised its portion of the budget.
3. These local church committeemen are to be appointed upon their consent to serve, and the names to be reported to the Federation Office inside of one week.
4. The committee agreed that this work could be entirely cleaned up and the budget provided for in thirty days, in order that the

Federation might know its resources for the year, and that finances might be out of the way.

It was further agreed, informally, to make an effort to secure at least some contribution from every church, as nearly as possible an amount equal to 5% figured on the current expense budget, this current expense budget to be the amount left after deducting any principal payment on a mortgage indebtedness or interest on that mortgage indebtedness.

It was further advised and generally agreed that each denominational representative should call together his committeemen from the local churches as early as possible after they are appointed, in order to make perfectly plain to them the proposition, and to have a general understanding as to spirit and method, amount to be raised, and the time of doing the work.

The members of the federation staff frequently seek opportunity to present the financial claims of the federation in the most important pulpits; and churches occasionally take special collections on the spot. The cultivation of denominational subsidies is naturally undertaken through officials responsible for budgets, as already explained. The acceptance of financial responsibility by denominations varies as to degree. In some cases it amounts merely to approbation and willingness to have the church credited on denominational apportionments for its gifts to federations. On the other hand, the denomination sometimes constitutes its own collecting agent, and merely transmits to the federation the funds it directly secures.

When collections at public services constitute an important element of federation support, there is sometimes a definite effort to make the financial appeal as indirect as possible so that it will not detract from the more exalted moods of the occasion. Thus at Lenten services, an informal offering is sometimes taken at the door rather than by the usual method of passing collection plates.

Whatever be the initial financial plan, to turn pledges into cash requires follow-up methods. The responsibility of the federation secretary and office becomes acute at this point. These paid workers must also seek to capitalize piecemeal support by the recurrent cultivation of contributors. Renewals of expiring subscriptions are sought by written communication or interview; and the insistent checking up of sources of income constitutes a central concern of every federation office.

Policies

Of general financial policies, the most significant concerns the relation of the central to the departmental budgets. Two distinct tendencies are at work; the one to unify all appeals and to try to raise money enough for all expenditures through a single approach to the constituency, the other to expect the larger departments to finance themselves. The first tendency goes with the smaller federations or those in which one or two departments absorb a very large part of the total resources. In such cases a unified appeal is indicated. The other tendency goes with the existence of several semi-independent subsidiary departments that possess strongly marked separate constituencies. This is likely to be the case with the larger federations in the larger cities. The problem is not only to avoid duplication of appeal but to reach each special constituency with special cultivation.

It has frequently been proved that financial cultivation incidental to specific activities can be economically carried out with constituencies it would not be economical to cultivate directly. It simply becomes natural to ask them for money while the activities are in process. Thus, for example, appreciative letters for radio broadcasting may be replied to in such a way as to give the person benefited a chance to share the cost of the service. Naturally, the two tendencies are mingled in the case of most federations.

Debt

Of the federations studied, about four-fifths were at least getting by financially. By diligent use of such methods, they had been able to go on for a series of years without serious financial difficulty. Disregarding debts of less than 10 per cent. of the total budget (which could ordinarily be absorbed into the financing of the following year), the study found four federations that had accumulated indebtedness equaling from 20 to 33 per cent. of annual costs. The situation led in one case to unpaid salaries; in another, it was rescued by denominational subsidies. In a third there had to be a great reduction of program. In the fourth an intensive campaign took care of the immediate exigency, but involved financial uncertainty for the following year.

The causes of debt were in most cases entirely discernible. There was either an abnormally small proportion of individual gifts, or too few churches supporting, or both; or else certain departments had heaped up deficits that swamped the central treasury. In future financing by federations, the ratios discovered in the present study will at least prove suggestive. New federations especially must have considerable individual backing beyond what they can possibly secure from church sources. Without this assurance it is foolhardy to start. But they must equally secure from the outset the support of a reasonable proportion of the churches; and they must not let the departments run away with them before their central financial resources are well established.

In happy contrast with the story of indebtedness was the fact that five of the federations studied carried surpluses equaling from 15 to 25 per cent. of the cost of the current budget. These were mainly the result of campaigns which were intended to start the succeeding year. In one case, however, specially large receipts were made the ground of a large expansion of program.

FINANCIAL PROBLEMS

Apart from the serious handicap which financial burdens imposed upon the morale and spirit of many federations, the outstanding problems that occur to the observer are the following.

Psychology of Appeal

First, of course, comes the underlying question of an effective psychology of appeal. The quality of federation publicity will bear reconsideration from this viewpoint. Relatively little of it consists of a definite reporting of results. Generally the constituency is not taken into the financial confidence to the extent of receiving a detailed budget of income and costs. Boosting without a budget is the rule. When the nature of the loyalties upon which federations rest is considered, along with the hazy knowledge of them on the part of their constituents which the study revealed, it may be questioned whether supporters are interested in details. Perhaps they wish to be appealed to in round and high-sounding periods. It is also barely possible that much of their haziness results from the failure of current publicity to bring the compelling facts home to them.

Better and Broader Non-financial Cultivation

This is essentially a question of better and broader non-financial cultivation. A city with 100,000 Protestants does well if it has 2,000 names on the federation mailing list. A general extension of the federation's appeal would create a ground-work for its financial cultivation. The entire fabric of its life and influence is after all of one weave; and in large measure, educational processes must precede the specifically financial ones.

Duplicating Appeal

The most difficult problem is that of avoiding internal rivalry and duplication of appeal to the common constituency, while at the same time reaching the natural constituencies of each major activity. The writer inclines to the judgment that the separate constituency must be counted on in spite of the duplicate appeal involved—which, of course, must be minimized in every way possible.

Division of Financial Responsibility

Another problem concerns the division of financial responsibility between individuals and churches. The individual has already supported his church, which may then turn over part of his money to the federation treasury. The federation then proceeds also to approach the individual directly. No solution of this problem appears to the author except to explain patiently to individuals that this is an inherent condition in the financing of religious work. He is particularly unimpressed by the hope of certain secretaries that financial support may in time become completely provided by routine processes. It is his suspicion that a movement involving prophetic initiative, and pioneering in certain areas in advance of the main movement of the Church, can never be supported as a by-product of ecclesiastical systems. The situation calls permanently for a goodly company of financial adventurers who will make personal investments in their own ideals and dreams.

FACILITIES

As is shown in Chapter IX,[9] the greater part of federation facilities is comprehended by an administrative office and its meagre equipment, together with certain housing and apparatus borrowed on occasion from the coöperating churches. The present chapter shows how these facilities are related to the various classes of workers who use them, and to the public.

DESIRABILITY OF LOCATION AND QUALITY OF HOUSING

A strong majority of federation offices are advantageously located in central down-town districts and at points of convenience and accessibility. The exceptions tend to be those housed in buildings belonging to philanthropic or religious bodies. Though such agencies must necessarily be fairly near city centers, they do not always command the most central sites for themselves. In rather more than half the cases in which federations are lodged in rented office buildings, poverty has compelled them to put up with a rather out-of-date or inferior type of building, considering the standards of the particular city. This leaves rather less than half occupying property of the more

---

[9] P. 150.

modern and up-to-date type. No federation has, however, a downright unworthy or undesirable location.

SIZE AND ARRANGEMENT OF OFFICES

With respect to size and arrangement, the facilities of federations are not so uniformly satisfactory. The free quarters are all bad. One is merely desk-space in the game-room of a boys' department of a Young Men's Christian Association; another, a suite of dark dormitory rooms; the third, a large room shared by four workers with a desk in each corner. The rented quarters range from mere desk-space to thirteen rooms; while St. Louis in its own quarters has also thirteen rooms. Suites of three rooms are more numerous than those of any other size but nearly half the federations have more than three.

The one-room offices will necessarily have to serve a mixture of functions. The two-room arrangements generally consist of a general office and a combination work-and-storage-room. The three-room arrangements generally consist of a general office, a private office for the executive secretary and one for a specialized departmental worker. If there are four rooms, the fourth will go to a second departmental worker. The larger suites of six or more rooms pretty definitely tend to include: (1) a lobby or reception room in charge of a clerical worker who meets callers; (2) a series of private offices for executive and departmental secretaries; (3) general stenographer's workroom in which (4) there will also be desk space for part-time social or subordinate religious-education workers; and (5) separate storerooms.

FACILITIES AS RELATED TO PAID WORKERS

The adequacy of any given set of facilities, of course, depends on the number of workers and the character and magnitude of the work to be carried on. The total facilities have accordingly been studied with reference to the provision made for each class of paid workers.

Executive secretaries are supplied with private offices almost invariably, except in the case of one-, or two-room suites. Only one executive secretary is habitually compelled to use artificial light.

Assistant secretaries and departmental secretaries for religious work, religious education, and social service, as well as the few secretaries of women's departments, also tend strongly to be supplied with private offices (except in the one-, or two-room arrangements), with a few somewhat unexplained exceptions. One of these workers also has to use artificial light habitually.

Religious-education supervisors and directors (of week-day schools, children's divisions, etc.) do not fare so well. They usually have to share a general departmental office along with some of its clerical workers.

Office secretaries generally have desks in reception rooms or lobbies which, in more than half the cases, they share with other clerical workers. As was shown in the discussion of this type of worker,[10] there is a tendency for a few office secretaries to develop into unacknowledged executive assistants or office managers. This is reflected in the fact that a few workers of this kind also have private offices. In a few such cases some subordinate clerical worker is stationed in the reception lobby and makes the first contact with the public.

General and departmental clerical workers almost invariably have to share their quarters with other clerical workers when there is more than one; or they work in rooms that are also devoted to storage; or that contain desks of part-time executive workers or those whose duties are chiefly outside the office. Six out of twenty-four such workers habitually have to use artificial light.

Chaplains and court and social case-workers almost never have private offices in federation headquarters, and only about half of them have desks for their exclusive individual use. One is assigned a cell in a jail as his office. As a partial offset, in somewhat more than half the cases they have desk space, or occasionally private offices, in the courts or institutions in which they work. In a typical case, three social workers occupy one desk in catch-as-catch-can fashion. Such arrangements frequently cause dissatisfaction. They are at the same time sometimes deliberately maintained in the attempt to keep the worker out on the job, and to minimize the tendency to dawdle away time in an easy chair.

Some of the workers of this type complained, and with apparent reason, that they are afforded no adequate possibility of privacy in interviews of the most confidential character.

Part-time workers, employed on retainers as are a number of publicity men, or seasonally as are the directors of vacation schools, also commonly have to use desks in the general stenographer's rooms in turn with other workers.

SUMMARY

Generalized, the above facts come to something like this: the smaller and poorer federations have poor and cluttered quarters.

---

[10] P. 119.

Most of the others have fairly suitable quarters commensurate with the size and scope of their work. About the same type of provision for the different ranks of workers is supplied that would be expected in a commercial office. In attempting economy, a number of the federations have subdivided their space by more or less temporary partitions and in ways rather lacking in beauty. Certain obvious possibilities have rarely been utilized. Thus, in only one case is there a glazed partition with a movable opening that would permit the office secretary to command the entrance lobby and meet callers without delay, and at the same time to enjoy the equivalent private room with its necessary working facilities. Many other minor improvements in office arrangement could easily be made. But no case was found in which a federation was prevented from doing an essentially high quality of work for lack of proper quarters.

The problem of providing space for part-time workers and those whose duties lie chiefly outside the office is one of policy, and not primarily a question of equipment.

Common conveniences for workers are generally simply those afforded by the building in which the federation offices are located. They consequently vary with the quality of the building. Inadequate coat-closets are frequent. Less than one-third of the federations have any washstand within their own office suites. Only one provides space for a ladies' rest-room. Toilet arrangements sometimes leave a good deal to be desired and are rarely provided for the exclusive use of the federation employees.

FACILITIES FOR VOLUNTEER WORKERS AND THE PUBLIC

In spite of the enormous number of the federation committees, only three federations maintain special boardrooms or committee rooms as part of their office equipment. Eight others, which are tenants of Young Men's Christian Association or denominational headquarters buildings, are entitled to the incidental use of some of the committee rooms of the plant. More than half, however, must take their committees outside their own walls for meetings, or else must crowd their sessions into reception lobbies, private offices, or workrooms, where they greatly interfere with the regular use of the space. The preference of the committees for meeting at meal-times in hotels or restaurants is a partial extenuation of the lack of special committee rooms. The small average attendance at committee meetings also helps make it possible to get along with the special facilities. It is a question, however, whether lack of facilities may not figure as a contributory cause of small attendance. It is with difficulty that a committee chairman finds space in federation headquarters for any special committee meeting that he may wish to call on short notice. In only two or three instances is even desk-space provided for the president or other voluntary officers of the federation who may be willing to contribute considerable time to its work.

Of arrangements for the convenience of the public, eight federations out of twenty-three have lobbies or outer offices primarily devoted to use as reception rooms. In three others, the room so functioning is in part-time use as a workroom; while in three others its primary use is that of a workroom. This leaves more than half the organizations ushering their callers directly into private offices or rooms that are in constant use for general purposes. This condition is scarcely in keeping with standards of urban office practice.

GENERAL INDEX OF QUALITY

A still more general index of the quality of federation housing is the very general shortage of special storage space, and the consequent cluttering of office rooms with all manner of apparatus and supplies. Only about a third of the federations have separate storage-room. The rest must do with closets or movable cupboards. One may even find the stock of supplies and apparatus for seasonal activities, such as a system of daily vacation schools, without any storage-space. They occupy the chairs and tables of the stenographer's workroom for the entire term of the school. Under these conditions, even the meagre satisfaction of bare orderliness cannot be attained. Here again, however, the architect's layout, as well as the refinement of his details, goes far toward determining the underlying conditions. Few federations, however, have made any attempt toward consistency in furnishings, to say nothing of aesthetic effectiveness.

A rough standard of the equipment demanded by efficiency and convenience in modern office practice may be assumed to be generally established. But the investigation could not have determined the adequacy of any particular set of equipment without an elaborate technical comparison of the exact kinds and amounts of work to be done. Thus, whether a given federation could better afford an addressograph or send its work out, was beyond the present investigation. Some note was, however, made of the frequency of the more important facilities, with the following results:

Besides universal equipment, such as desks, typewriters, telephones and files (not really so universal in federation offices as might be assumed), nearly all these organizations have one or more bookcases, and a map locating the churches of the city. Only a very few, however, indulge in sets of maps adequate for making social studies or surveys, or in a filing system for maps. About two-thirds of the federations possess mimeographs or multigraph outfits. About half have addressographs; but one finds only four or five safes in more than twenty cases. The total value of movable equipment is believed not to exceed $1,000 or $1,500; but the figures are not really comparable for lack of cost inventories or means of calculating depreciation.

In view of what has been said about free rents and concessions, as well as of the varying qualities of buildings and the influence of the size of the city upon rents, it is obvious that no direct comparison of expenditure for this item would be significant, even if reduced to rates per cubic foot of office space. Rents range from nothing to $466 per month. Where commercial rates are charged, three-, to five-room suites tend to cost from $75 to $100 a month, and six-, to nine-room suites from $100 to $200 a month. As has already been noted, most of the latter have been provided by the temporary subdivision of larger rooms. New York, paying the maximum rent per month for its thirteen rooms, gets a good deal more space for its money than does Louisville, which puts up with part of one room.[11]

CONCLUSION

Except for the salaries of paid workers, the service of federations is carried on at very small expense. Sources of support are rather unsettled, but fairly numerous. Even salaries are often separately budgeted and raised from sources outside those regularly depended upon; for example, from women's organizations in local churches. Denominations, as such, also sometimes make special supplementary appropriations. A few federations get grants from Community Chests.

Where no paid workers are employed, expenditures of commissions and committees are generally covered in the central administrative budget of the federation. On the basis of a few cases involving separate accounting, they appear to spend about $130 per committee on the average. It becomes possible to do with these small amounts because the Federal Council and other specially organized interests contribute so many speakers and so much literature for propaganda; also because study courses, lectures, and dinners in behalf of various interests are paid for by fees or charges upon the participants.

---

[11] For the proportion of total expenditures which goes to rent, see p. 454.

Much volunteer work is contributed and much service secured from professionals paid by other organizations. In brief, the secret of the federation's economy in social work is that it operates coöperatively, and that it is only one part of a system whose general overhead charges it does not directly pay for. While consequently a good deal of the cost of federation service cannot be separately accounted for, what impresses one most is that a work so vast in the aggregate is carried on at so little local expense.

Other than a modest headquarters, with desk facilities, files for records and reports, occasional separate offices for paid social workers, and automobiles for those whose duties involve travel, very few special facilities are required by the present development of the work. At this point again, the few institutions directly operated by federations constitute exceptions. In view of the literally awe-inspiring total of expenditures for church edifices in American cities, the virtually complete lack of urban investment in anything visible and material to symbolize Protestant fraternity and unity gives one pause.

Chapter XXIV

PROMOTION AND PUBLICITY

Federations attempt to secure the interest and support of their special constituencies and of the more general public chiefly through individual communications, for which they rely upon interviews, the telephone, and the mails; by the use of printed matter in various forms, especially in the newspapers; and by having members of the paid staff or volunteers establish personal contacts with groups and deliver addresses. To these methods are to be added miscellaneous forms of publicity found here and there, incidental or experimental devices proving more or less useful.

INDIVIDUAL AND INTIMATE CULTIVATION OF CONSTITUENTS

The attempt to commend their institution to constituents and the public, runs as a persistent undertone through all the contacts of secretaries and paid workers. The strictly promotional element cannot be isolated from functional or merely business transactions. Neither the more incidental cultivation of supporters, nor the more intimate sort shrouded in the privacy of personal letters, can be quantitatively estimated. But the large blocks of the secretary's time habitually devoted to interviews, small committees, and public meetings, suggests how vital a part of promotion lies in this realm. Formal means of individual promotion appear first in connection with concrete issues.

CIRCULAR LETTERS

The circular letter is the nearly universal method of putting such matters before constituents; especially letters to pastors of the coöperating churches. These communications are usually mimeographed or multigraphed and sent to a general address-list. All such letters sent out for a period of one year by several federations were analyzed, especially with reference to the number and status of persons addressed, the subjects covered, and the persons who signed the letters. Notices of meetings were found to be most numerous; after which came communications in departmental promotion of the various programs. The largest number of letters relating to a single department were in the

471

interests of religious education. Next come financial appeals. The remainder of the communications were distributed over a great many subjects, a letter or two perhaps on each. They ranged from Christmas greetings or the sale of Christmas seals, to the use of family worship; the promotion of Bible week; the state Sunday-school convention; coöperation with the Young Men's Christian Association; and, finally, to political propaganda and the duty of getting out the church vote.

Communications were addressed to groups of persons of many kinds; some to single committees, some to all committeemen, to all ministers, to ministers and Sunday-school workers, or to all constituents. They were generally signed by the executive secretary, but often by other members of the staff or chairmen of commissions.

FEDERATION PUBLICATIONS

Three kinds of printed matter are exceedingly important and in general use as means of promotion and publicity; the federation organ, annual reports, and occasional pamphlets. Federations that do not use all three are those financially unable to do so.

THE FEDERATION ORGAN

Of the twenty-nine federations concerning which information was obtained, twenty-one were maintaining an organ of some sort, issued regularly. Of the twenty-one organs, four were weeklies; one appeared fortnightly; nine, monthly; four, bimonthly; and three, quarterly. In general there are three types: the newspaper type, illustrated in *The Chronicle* of the Wichita Council of Churches, and found in four cases; the magazine type, used by three federations, of which *The Pittsburgh Christian Outlook* is a good example; and the bulletin type, used in various forms by fourteen of these organizations. Of bulletins, several distinct kinds were found, ranging from the Chicago Federation's very large one to the rather small one of the Boston Federation. Of the medium-sized bulletin, the finely printed *Cooperator* of the Baltimore Federation of Churches is a good example. A number of federations get along with single-page sheets printed to carry an address for mailing on one side when folded. This type originated with the Rochester Federation. Its supposed merit is indicated in its slogan, "All the news a busy man will read." A few of the federations issue mimeographed bulletins—in some cases very attractively executed. These have paved the way to a printed bulletin in at least two instances.

One of the most interesting of bulletins is found in New Bedford. Here the federation secretary edits a twenty-page, magazine type bulletin for a printing concern which sells it to the various churches as a weekly church calendar. Its first and last pages are printed for the individual church. Once a month the bulletin is largely given over to the news of the federation. The cost is met by advertising, except for the individual pages. A number of churches that could not otherwise afford calendars have thus been able to have them; and this has provided a large circulation to the federations' medium.

Quality of Federation Organs

Needless to say, some of these organs are better than others. No attempt has been made to grade them technically; but from a general survey of them certain factors of importance in judging their value have emerged.

First to be considered are the mechanical features, including the form of the pages, the type and set-up used, and the general attractiveness. Again, style is obviously important. The paper must be made interesting with due consideration to literary merit and conciseness. The most important single feature is, of course, the content. An analysis was made of a year's file of several federation organs. A résumé of their most recurrent features indicates that the promotion of the principle of coöperation and the cause of federation ranks first in importance. Next comes news of past activities of the federation and the announcement and promotion of the program of the future. Third in rank comes news of various coöperative interest, both local and of wider range; then news of general interest of the local churches and the denominations. Inasmuch as the organ is primarily for the purpose of local promotion, it makes many direct approaches to its readers and calls for participation in the various programs. The organ finds occasional use as a vehicle for expressing the needs or wants of various coöperating groups. Certain departments maintain their own columns. A number of organs also carry regularly a calendar of religious events both local and coöperative.

For filling, most federation papers frequently include little essays on religious or social truth or duty. They are for the most part merely fugitive utterances with no genuine local flavor.

Circulation

The circulation of the organs varies greatly. Some are mailed to all who happen to have their names on the mailing list of the particular federation office. In other cases contributor's pledge cards specify that a certain part of the contribution is for a subscription to the federation organ. A few have separate paid subscriptions. The Wichita Council belongs to the latter class. Its paper has a subscription list of between 5,000 and 5,500 in a city of 100,000. This gives it proportionately the largest circulation of any federation organ in the country. The Secretary of the Wichita Council of Churches says, "The Chronicle is worth $10,000 a year to the coöperating spirit of the churches of Wichita. Two things," he continues, "are necessary to create such a paper: first, a publisher with nerve and a generous policy; and second, at least one available person with a flair for journalism."

The Federation News of the Brooklyn Federation of Churches has the largest actual circulation, some 20,000; but with the population of two and a quarter millions this is proportionately a very much smaller circulation than that of Wichita.

ANNUAL REPORTS

Of the twenty-nine federations studied, only nineteen issued annual reports to their constituents. Twelve of these were published in separate form, and seven were carried in the federation organ.

The important features of the annual report are its general attractiveness and its circulation. It is valuable in proportion as its distribution is extensive and systematic, and as a basis for newspaper publicity. Here again, however, content is the most important factor. Such a report generally covers a statement of receipts and expenditures; and detailed reports of the commissions and committees, and of the general program carried out. An important feature often omitted from annual reports is a statement of the progress of the organization, especially in increasing the coöperation of constituents and in the progressive fulfillment of objectives. The best reports make comparisons with former years, and thus measure advance objectively.

OTHER PROMOTIONAL LITERATURE

The minor promotional literature of the federations is extensive and varied. Each organization uses as much printed material as it can afford in general promotion, and as a background for financial appeal. Departments and commissions issue reports and pamphlets appealing for participation and attendance in activities and upon classes and programs. There are posters and leaflets and schedules and handbills. Some are excellent; others are almost valueless. Many are very attractive, their content presenting a specific point of information or attitude in adequate and interesting fashion, with definite solicitation of interest and support. Not all are carefully and thoroughly distributed. One of the Chicago Federation's leaflets presents an example of the better promotional literature. Its cover pictures Chicago's loop district at night, with its blaze of myriad lights; it bears the inscription "I see the lights of the city." Within is found a brief story of the federation's ministry, a chart of its organizations and functions, and an effective appeal. Most of the promotional literature of the religious-education department is well worked out, particularly the schedules of classes of the community-training schools. On the other hand, some examples of shockingly poor material are found. One single sheet covering week-day church schools in a certain city tells only a piece of a story and ends with a good appeal; but nowhere is the name or address of the organization given. Another leaflet has a picture of a pile of locks and a ring and keys on its cover; but the keys fit a different kind of lock from that shown in the picture! The content of this particular leaflet tells of the activities of the executive group and outlines the federation's program; but it in no way carries a report of the functioning of the organization as representative of the Protestant group. The constituency appears to be outside looking on rather than inside making the federation go.

The Public Press

Because of wide fields of federation activity and interest, the newspaper provides them an especially available medium of publicity. This opportunity is capitalized in many ways. Several of the federations have publicity men experienced in newspaper work, who are thus able to keep up a rather steady stream of material acceptable to the newspapers. Other federations attempt—usually less successfully—to do this from their own offices. In Wichita the reporters from the two city papers visit the federation office nearly every day for news. Too many federations, however, send material to the newspapers only occasionally. In a few instances—as in Kansas City and Minneapolis—an agreement has been made with one of the local papers to carry a special box with a message from the federation in the weekly "church news" page. A few federations use paid newspaper advertising in connection with special events such as noon Lenten meetings and union Thanksgiving service.

One of the smaller federations, that of Oakland, California, in checking up its newspaper publicity for a year, found that there had been some 900 column-inches, and at least fifteen pictures, some of which were several columns wide. The Ohio State Federation reports that in the course of a recent year it was instrumental in having published in the newspapers of the state more than 2,000 news stories of its work. This is in no way an unusual instance where the newspapers are cultivated; and this has been found by many federations to have a splendid basis for the development of the general prestige of the organization.

PERSONAL PUBLICITY

Part of the job of the executive secretary of a federation is to promote the organization and its work through addresses and contacts whenever opportunity affords. The addresses of ten executive secretaries for one year were classified. They totalled 271 addresses in promotion of the federation work, an average of twenty-seven each. The numbers ranged from none in the case of one of the better established federations to 113 in the case of the secretary of the Massachusetts Federation. These same secretaries, as easily available persons, were called on to preach and make addresses in 486 cases, more than twice as often as they had opportunity to talk for the benefit of their organizations. The indirect publicity value of these latter occasions is nevertheless highly significant.

Addresses made by fourteen other staff members during one year, were also classified. This group was called on, as a matter of convenience to others, for 315 addresses; while the promotion of the general work or the work of their departments, special addresses in line with their specific duties, and the teaching of classes, jointly account for 778 addresses, or about three times as many as the promotional addresses of the executive secretaries.

A few federations maintain something of a speakers' bureau; they make engagements for famous visiting speakers; maintain lists of available local speakers, and are constantly asked to suggest competent speakers for various occasions. In a few of the cities, a Federation Sunday has been set apart. All of the churches have been asked to make the federation and its needs the subject of one service on that day—the federations furnishing special literature and speakers.

A really comprehensive program of promotion through direct personal presentation of the work apparently has not yet been adequately developed in any city.

MISCELLANEOUS PROMOTION

Of the numerous forms of miscellaneous promotion, two or three have more general promise and deserve special mention.

CHURCH DIRECTORIES

The publication of church directories is primarily a matter of service to the coöperating churches; but it serves admirably as federation publicity. Such directories are issued by several federations. Some are put out in a rather pretentious book form with many illustrations and considerable information of permanent value concerning the churches. This type of directory generally must be paid for by advertising. Another type consists of a small booklet merely giving the name, address, and position of each church, and similar information about religious societies. Such directories are often published in coöperation with some local newspapers. A few federations get out large poster cards carrying a directory of the churches to be placed in public places, such as hotel lobbies.

RADIO

As used by church federations, the radio is primarily a vehicle for the evangelistic message. Seventeen of the twenty-nine federations broadcast in some form. This ranges from the very extensive program of several hours of chain broadcasts, as conducted by the Greater New York Federation of Churches, to the regular teaching of the Sunday-school lesson, and the occasional conducting of an hour of prayer. By means of this service to the community, the sponsoring federations are becoming better and more favorably known, just as the commercial advertisers are.

OTHER FORMS

Thirty-one items, all told, make up the publicity programs of one or more federations. The more important and frequent items have now been considered. The remainder occur only in a few cases and range from the coöperation with advertising clubs and poster advertising companies to editing the Monday church news of the local paper and the holding of a religious art exhibit.

PUBLICITY AGENCIES

COMMITTEES

Nine of the federations studied maintain publicity committees. Small or medium-sized committees usually have few meetings, related to specific tasks rather than convened regularly. Their scope of activity shows but slight variation. Their primary responsibility is generally publicity in connection with financial campaigns; secondly, for federation organs and for special pieces of promotional literature. In a few cases, these committees have assisted with the publicity of other coöperative agencies. They rarely consider or determine the total promotional policy of their respective organizations.

One of the chief considerations of these committees is the obtaining of better newspaper publicity for the churches of their cities. The opening paragraph of the annual report of the publicity committee of the Washington Federation might have been from the report of almost any of the committees:

> It would seem that advertising, publicity, and the use of the press as a means of creating public sentiment, has come to play an increasingly important part in nearly every line of human activity, and that this is particularly true as regards the Church. The Church today is competing, in its efforts to draw all men unto it,' with the theatre, the athletic event, and a thousand and one other counter attractions, practically all of which are using the newspapers for advertising and publicity appeals. Why not meet modern competition with modern methods? With these thoughts in mind, your publicity committee has devoted its efforts this winter to giving the work of the Federation, and other church matters, as extensive publicity as possible.

PUBLICITY DIRECTORS

In line with this philosophy, three federations have employed part-time publicity directors for the purpose of assisting the churches in planning better publicity and more effective and more attractive advertising in the newspapers. These directors are experienced newspaper men with entrée to the newspapers. They are paid for their service by the churches who use them— the theory being that the churches can get value received in the increased amount and better quality of advertising.

THE PUBLICITY CONFERENCE

In a few of the cities, publicity committees have undertaken to conduct publicity conferences, sometimes in coöperation with local advertising clubs. Chicago made such a conference a big annual event for ten years. It has become an occasion of national importance in the field of church publicity. An all day session is held and the best church publicity men in the nation are imported to direct the consideration of the various phases of publicity and advertising available to and practical for the use of the churches. The New York Federation has sponsored extended courses in advertising for ministers.

Constituents' Judgments

Eight thousand and forty-two judgments of federation constituents were obtained on fifty-six items of publicity of sixteen federations. Of these judgments, 92 per cent. were favorable to the activity of the given federation in its various phases of publicity, while less than 1 per cent. felt that these activities should not be undertaken. The judgments on the whole program were 91 per cent. favorable and 2 per cent. against, which by comparison shows that publicity and promotion is one of the most generally accepted points of federation programs.

Problems

The more obvious problems in the realm of publicity and promotion are of two orders: first, technical psychological; second, practical.

How to write a forceful advertisement, and how to balance the several elements in a promotional program, are problems of the first order. A partial solution may be found in the study of current advertising methods and theory, such as some of the federations are attempting. More of a solution might be reached as the result of coöperative experimentation over a period of time, with various forms of publicity, the cost and results of which should be very carefully recorded. Federations might then know what they could expect for their money from the use of different types of approach to the constituency—say from circular letters as against newspaper announcements. It is a matter of common knowledge that advertising doctors find plentiful disagreement, and a large area of uncertainty would be left. Nevertheless, some gain of precision and certainty would be made from such a first-hand study of federation promotion.

The overwhelming practical problem of promotion is that the federations have, at best, an exceedingly small degree of direct contact with their constituencies. An average of not more than 2 per cent. of nominal Protestants of a city gets into the typical mailing list. It is sometimes questioned whether churchmanship as such can ever be made of interest to the average layman. Perhaps it is inherently a matter for a relatively few leaders and followers closely identified with the operation of the machinery. Many political analogies would suggest this verdict. At the same time, some margin of improvement is clearly possible; and to achieve this is very important. Wider promotion, rather than greater stress on promotion with the consequent danger of overstatement, is the outstanding necessity.

It may be questioned, however, whether the limited understanding of the federation movement will not have to continue
until a larger body of work is federated. This matter lies primarily in the hands of ecclesiastical leaders already in touch
with the movement. If they would allow federations wider
functions, they could probably impress themselves on a larger
proportion of people. A more massive phenomenon would attract the eye and command the imagination of the masses as the
present limited agencies never can.

A still deeper promotional issue, that of propaganda in contrast with inquiry and education, is essentially moral. This has
already been dealt with in another connection.

APPENDICES

Appendix I

(Chapter I)

ORGANIZATION OF THE ROMAN CATHOLIC ARCHDIOCESE OF NEW YORK

Territory covered—Boroughs: Manhattan, Bronx, Richmond; Counties: Dutchess, Orange, Putnam, Rockland, Sullivan, Ulster, Westchester; also, the Bahama Islands.

Total Catholic population, 1,273,291.

Organization—Cardinal: Patrick Cardinal Hayes, Archbishop of New York, 452 Madison Avenue, New York City. Other officials: Bishop Auxiliary; Vicar Apostolic of Jamaica; Vicar General; Chancellor; Assistant Chancellors; Officialis; Synodal and Pro-synodal Judges; Secretary; Diocesan Consultors; Defender of the Marriage Bond; Auditor; Notaries; Promotor of Justice; Examinatores of Pro-synodales; Parochi Consultores; Examiners of the Clergy; Theological Censor Librorum; Moderator of Theological Conferences; Urban Deans; Rural Deans; School Board; Superintendent of Schools; Board for Catechetical Schools; Catholic Charities of the Archdiocese; Archdiocesan Managing Director of Cemeteries; Commission for the Seminaries; Church Music Committee; Diocesan Committee on Literature; Pontifical Society for the Propagation of the Faith; Archdiocesan Union of the Holy Name Societies; Priests Eucharistic League; Officers for each county.

INSTITUTIONS		STATISTICS
Churches		440
Churches with resident priests..........................		*358*
City churches	*204*	
Outside of city	*154*	
Missions with churches		*82*
Chapels		208
Stations without churches..............................		31
Priests		1,314
Secular	*830*	
Religious	*484*	

EDUCATIONAL INSTITUTIONS	No.	PUPILS
Theological seminaries	2	273
Preparatory	1	459
Colleges for boys	3	3,974
High schools for boys....................................	1	200
Academies for boys	28	4,871
Colleges for girls	4	1,778
Academies for girls......................................	46	7,286
Parish Schools—New York City		
Boys	129	41,378
Girls	129	45,085
Parish Schools—Outside the city		
Boys	69	8,852
Girls	69	9,358
(Total in Parish Schools)................................		(104,673)

Division of Charities	Number of Institutions
Protective agencies	18
Child-caring institutions	24
Day nurseries and settlements	38
Summer camps for girls and boys	13
Summer homes for children	13
Clubs for Young People	10
Homes for the aged	6
Homes and residences for women and men	28
Correctional homes for women	2
Hospitals, sanitariums and convalescent homes	29
Immigrant homes	12
Nursing sisterhoods	7
Other missionary works	14
Administrative offices	8

(Total number of young people under Catholic care). (178,177)

Orphan Asylums		25
Number of orphans	3,500	
Hospitals		23
Number of beds	3,798	
Students in training school	503	
Religious	*14*	
Lay	*489*	
Personnel	661	
Religious	*388*	
Religious (R. N.)	*106*	
Internes	*55*	
Lay (R. N.)	*112*	

Appendix II

THE INVESTIGATION OF RELIGIOUS DISTANCE

(Chapter II)

The instrument by means of which the problem of religious distance was explored was the accompanying questionnaire.

This questionnaire was used to ask constituents of church federations to indicate the degree of readiness or unreadiness they felt toward entering into each of fifteen more or less intimate social and religious relationships with the members of twenty-two different religious denominations and communions, as follows:

Baptist	Christian Science
Congregational	Pentecostal
Disciple	Salvation Army
Friend	Spiritualist
Methodist Episcopal	Greek Orthodox
Presbyterian	Jewish
Lutheran	Roman Catholic
Protestant Episcopal	Mormon
Unitarian	Buddhist
Universalist	Mohammedan
Adventist	Atheist

The relationships with respect to which the feeling of "distance" was registered were expressed in brief form in the first column of the questionnaire as follows: (1) Pray with; (2) Admit to Sacrament of the Holy Communion in your church; (3) Vote for as candidate for President of the United States; (4) Permit to deliver religious address at service of worship in your church; (5) Marry; (6) Discuss religious beliefs with; (7) Recognize as possibly "saved"; (8) Recognize as possibly "Christian"; (9) Coöperate with in efforts for community welfare; (10) Attend service at his place of worship; (11) Employ in an important and confidential position; (12) Appoint as guardian of your child; (13) Approve as day-school teacher for your child; (14) Accept employment from; (15) Admit to United States as resident.

The person filling out the questionnaire indicated his attitude toward persons of other faiths and denominations with respect to the relationships enumerated by making entries in the various columns of the questionnaire wherever he felt any sense of hesitancy or a positive unwillingness to enter into the particular relationship involved. In case of hesitancy, the indication was "H," in the case of refusal "R." In scoring the results, each hesitancy counted one, and each refusal two. The results themselves were regarded as measuring the sense of religious distance or antipathy between those replying and members of different faiths and denominations.

The questionnaires were filled out in the manner above described and tabulated for 1,780 constituents of nine federations as follows: Boston 180, Chicago 279, Detroit 187, Minneapolis 271, Pittsburgh 159, Rochester 186, St. Louis 162, Washington 146 and Wichita 210.[1]

DENOMINATIONAL COMPOSITION OF THE SAMPLE

The 1,780 Protestants who thus registered their religious distance feelings were divided denominationally in Table 1.

The large measure of agreement in the results obtained from city to city which the text shows make it probable that this rather small but widely scattered sampling of church federation constituencies is reasonably representative. The questionnaires were sent out to constituency lists just as they stood in each city. The only principle of selection in responses was that it was the more interested constituents who made the returns. It may be assumed that this principle operated equally among the denomi-

---

[1] See p. 64.

nations. The returns in general are fairly indicative of the relative size of the denominations, four-fifths being from five major ones. Denominations of equal size are, however, not always equally coöperative, and this factor also entered into the distribution of the returns.[2]

TABLE 1—DENOMINATIONAL DISTRIBUTION OF FEDERATION CONSTITUENTS WHO REPLIED TO THE "RELIGIOUS DIS-TANCE" QUESTIONNAIRE

Denominations	Total	4 Cities	5 Cities
Total	1,780	778	1,002
Baptist	251	109	142
Congregational	224	80	144
Disciples	78	38	40
Evangelical	40	28	12
Lutheran	67	39	28
Meth. Epis.	464	178	286
Meth. Prot.	9	9	0
Presbyterian	309	182	127
Prot. Epis.	100	43	57
Reformed	15	6	9
United Presb.	31	31	0
All Other	192	35	157

Instructions printed on the back of the questionnaire required the constituent to fill it out rapidly, so as to catch the first reaction of his mind toward the several faiths and denominations as listed. No time was to be left for rationalization or for the consideration of exceptions. Naturally this requirement was frequently resented. Such answers as "I would worship with some Jews sooner than with some Christians," or "I have known Catholics whom I would rather marry than one of my own faith," were fairly frequent. Exceptions like these would of course occur to anyone who took time for consideration.

The justification of the questionnaire is of course the fact that the human mind inevitably devises general terms to stand for what it thinks to be the major tendencies of groups that bear common names. Thus, the word "United States" arouses an immediate emotional reaction in the native citizen's mind— whatever be his partizan brand—different from that aroused in him by the name of any other country. So, in the politician, does the name of his political party. Indeed "blonde" is sure to have a more or less pleasant halo than "brunette," even though anyone would find plenty of exceptions to his like or dislike of either type. Accordingly, the constituent who really

[2] Certain small denominations separately tabulated in Table 1, and some of the following tables, present too few cases to be at all conclusive. The results are introduced however because they appear to suggest certain denominational trends.

registered his instinctive reaction toward the names of the various denominations and faiths was revealing his habitual attitudes toward persons of the different religious types. These attitudes are measurable realities; and the high degree of consistency found in the returns prove that the majority of the average answers tended to be reliable.

TABLE 2—COMPARISON OF NINE RELATIONSHIPS ACCORDING TO DEGREE OF RELIGIOUS "DISTANCE" ATTACHED TO THEM BY PROTESTANT CONSTITUENTS OF CHURCH FEDERATIONS WITH RESPECT TO MEMBERS OF OTHER FAITHS AND DENOMINATIONS

Relationships	Per Cent. of Possible Distance Feeling
Appoint as Guardian of your child	29.2
Marry	26.2
Vote for as candidate for President of the United States	18.1
Approve as day school teacher for your child	17.4
Average	15.2
Permit to deliver religious address at service or worship in your church	13.3
Admit to Sacrament of the Holy Communion in your church	11.7
Employ in an important and confidential position	7.8
Recognize as possibly "saved"	6.6
Pray with	6.5

SOCIAL AND RELIGIOUS RELATIONSHIPS TO WHICH DISTANCE FEELINGS ATTACH THEMSELVES

The fifteen relationships with respect to which the Protestant constituencies registered feelings of distance toward persons of the twenty-two faiths and denominations were selected with the idea of including all degrees of reactions, from mild to extreme; but the labor of tabulation proved too great for each relationship to be dealt with separately. The results were tabulated, however, according to the method previously described, on nine relationships for 1,002 Protestants in five cities (Boston, Chicago, Detroit, Washington and Wichita).

There is, it will be noted, nearly five times as much disinclination to choose the representative of some faith or denomination as guardian for one's child as there is disinclination to pray with him or to recognize him as possibly "saved"; four times as much disinclination to marrying him; and two-and-one-half times as much to voting for him as President of the United States. The implicit logic behind these distinctions of feeling is not hard to trace. The greatest sensitiveness is with respect to entering into intimate domestic relations typified by marriage and child nurture. There is almost as much sensitiveness as to who shall occupy the office of President of the United States, presumably because, as the last election undoubtedly showed, it is regarded as the symbol of the ideals in the nation. In intimacy of responsibility for childhood, the school-teacher obviously stands next to the home. These four relationships accordingly arouse the greatest disinclination to participation with respect to persons of other faiths and denominations. No one of them is ostensibly a religious relationship; and it is a striking fact that no relationship that does take direct ecclesiastical form arouses disinclination to any such degree. Thus, to allow the member of another faith to make a religious address in one's church, or even to partake of the sacrament as there administered, involves less than half as much disinclination as to marry one of another faith, or make him guardian of one's child. Economic relations expressed in the employment of one of another faith even in a confidential nature, arouse little sense of difficulty. Nearly all those responding to the questionnaire declared themselves broad enough to pray even with a heathen, and to leave the question of his being "saved" to the divine wisdom.

TABLE 3—SPECIFIED RELATIONSHIPS WITH OTHER FAITHS AND DENOMINATIONS RANKED BY CITIES ACCORDING TO DEGREE OF "DISTANCE" FELT

RELATIONSHIPS	PER CENT. OF POSSIBLE DISTANCE	RANK OF ALL	RANK BY CITIES				
			Boston	Chi.	Detroit	Wash.	Wichita
Appoint as guardian of your child	29.2	1	1	1	1	1	1
Marry	26.2	2	2	2	2	2	2
Vote for as candidate for President of the United States	18.1	3	3	4	4	3	3
Approve as day-school teacher for your child	17.4	4	4	3	3	4	4
Permit to deliver religious address at service of worship in your church	13.3	5	6	5	5	6	5
Admit to Sacrament of the Holy Communion in your church	11.7	6	5	6	6	5	7
Employ in an important and confidential position	7.8	7	7	7	8	8	6
Recognize as possibly "saved"	6.6	9	8	8	7	9	9
Pray with	6.5	8	9	9	9	7	8

Participation with persons of another religion in the six relationships in connection with which returns were not tabulated involved less disinclination on the average than did participation in the nine relations already reported upon. As has been seen,[3] the inclusion of the six additional relationships in the totals consequently tended to dilute the feeling of distance. One can conceive on the contrary of devising a list including a larger rather than a smaller number of very intimate relations. Such a list would probably result in a great increase of the feeling of distance.

Consistency of Returns by Cities

The substantial and relatively fixed character of the distinctions of feeling attached to the relationships under discussion is proved by comparison of the returns for the several cities. All cities show that Protestants have greater disinclination to relationships with persons of other religions with respect to the guardianship of children and marriage. While the order of antipathy is not identical in the other relationships, the shift from the average is never more than one place in the ranking scale, except in a single instance. This is shown in Table 3.

TABLE 4—SPECIFIED RELATIONSHIPS WITH OTHER FAITHS AND DENOMINATIONS RANKED BY DENOMINATIONS ACCORDING TO DEGREE OF "DISTANCE" FELT

RELATIONSHIPS	PER CENT. OF POSSIBLE DISTANCE	RANK OF ALL	RANK BY DENOMINATION									All Other
			Bapt.	Cong.	Disc.	Evan.	Luth.	ME.	Pres.	P.E.	Ref.	
Appoint as guardian of your child	29.2	1	1	1	1	2	1	1	1	1	1	1
Marry	26.2	2	2	2	3	1	6	2	2	2	2	2
Vote for as candidate for President of the United States	18.1	3	4	3	4	3	7	4	3	4	6	4
Approve as day-school teacher for your child	17.4	4	3	4	2	5	3	3	4	3	7	3
Permit to deliver religious address at service of worship in your church	13.3	5	5	6	5	4	2	5	5	6	3	5
Admit to Sacrament of the Holy Communion in your church	11.7	6	6	5	8	6	4	5	6	5	4	7
Employ in an important and confidential position	7.8	7	8	7	7	9	9	7	7	7	9	6
Recognize as possibly "saved"	6.6	9	7	9	6	7	8	8	9	9	5	9
Pray with	6.5	8	9	8	9	8	5	9	8	8	8	8

---

[3] Chapter II.

CONSISTENCY OF DENOMINATIONAL ATTITUDES

Denominations from which returns were received for fifty or more constituents show about the same degree of consistency of attitude, as is shown by the different cities. Congregationalists, Methodists, Presbyterians, Episcopalians, with the denominations included in "All Other" classification, never vary by more than one place in the distance rank which they ascribe to a given relationship. Denominations represented by less than fifty cases, on the contrary, while evidencing the same general tendencies show much more erratic ranking tendencies. In their cases it is impossible to say how far actual divergence of denominational judgments explain the showing and how far it is due to the fact that the small number of cases do not furnish a representative sampling.

Appendix III

FREQUENCY OF PARTICULAR ITEMS IN FEDERATION PROGRAMS, BY MAJOR DEPARTMENTS (29 FEDERATIONS)

(Chapter VII)

A. EVANGELISTIC ACTIVITIES

Over ¾

	No. of Federations
Hold Lenten or Holy Week services	25
Supply pulpits for coöperating churches	23
Hold conferences on evangelism	21
Make comprehensive plans for community evangelism	21

½ to ¾

Operate home visitation plan of evangelism	20
Hold interdenominational Good Friday services	19
Conduct surveys to find unchurched	19
Conduct week of prayer in January	16
Make annual survey of growth of churches	15
Promotes daily Bible reading	14

¼ to ½

Broadcast daily religious service or Scripture reading	13
Coöperate with the Y.M.C.A. in Evangelism	13
Conduct street and park meetings	12
Furnish religious speakers in philanthropic institutions	12
Promote national evangelistic conventions, etc.	12
Hold pre-Easter evangelistic campaigns	11
Help organize district evangelistic campaigns	11
Arrange yearly retreat for pastors	11
Distribute the Scriptures	10
Circulate devotional literature	9
Promote church-attendance campaigns	8
Broadcast Sunday service	7

Less than ¼

Hold schools of personal work for laymen; hold Easter Sunrise service; promote special forms of evangelism for age- and sex-groups.

B. RELIGIOUS EDUCATION

Over ¾

Conduct training schools for Church Vacation School Workers.... 19

½ to ¾

Maintain general Community Training Schools of Religious Education 17
Coöperate with State Councils of Religious Education............ 16
Promote improved administration of Religious Education........ 13

¼ to ½

Maintain Central Library on Religious Education................ 12
Maintain Speaker's Bureau 12
Promote Church Vacation Schools............................... 11
Make Religious-education surveys................................ 11
Conduct young people's leadership-training courses.............. 10
Maintain District Conference on Religious Education............ 9
Promote father and son, or mother and daughter, activities....... 8
Maintain children's workers conference.......................... 8
Promote annual Sunday-school rally-day.......................... 8
Instruct Protestant children in public institutions................ 8

Less than ¼

Promote religion in the home; conduct normal classes; support special paid supervisors of church vacation schools; and five additional activities each carried on by five or more federations.

C. SOCIAL SERVICE

I. *Systematic Advocacy of Social Ideals and Values*

Less than ¼

1 activity

II. *Non-Institutional Social Service under Federation's Own Auspices* (Case Work, Neighborhood Work and Miscellaneous)

Less than ¼

17 activities

III. *Participation in Voluntary Social and Reform Organization*
(1) Social Organization
Coöperation with voluntary agencies

More than ⅔

Promotes coöperation of churches with social agencies of the community...................... 22

½ to ⅔

Coöperates with relief agencies in foreign lands (Near East Relief, Red Cross, etc.).............. 18

¼ to ½

Promotes coöperation of churches with Council of Social Agencies 15
Promotes coöperation of churches with Community Chest 14

Recruits volunteer workers for social agencies from
the churches 13
Federation executives serve on committees of social
agencies 13

Less than ¼
13 additional activities
(2) Reform Organization
Advocacy and promotion

More than ⅔
Agitates for reform in specific issues............... 25

¼ to ½
Registers Protestant sentiment on public issues..... 14
Coöperates with law enforcement or good govern-
ment agencies

Less than ¼
10 additional activities
IV. *Coöperation with Institutional Social Agencies*
(1) Social Service in Courts and Penal Institutions

¼ to ½
Conducts religious services in jails and prisons..... 10
Attempts to bring families of court cases under
church care 9
Employs worker in adult courts.................... 8
Relates paroled children to some church............ 8
Employs worker in juvenile court.................. 7
Advocates prison reform........................... 7

Less than ¼
11 additional activities
(2) Social Service in Hospitals and Public Philanthropic
Institutions

¼ to ½
Supports pastoral visitor in hospitals.............. 12
Conducts regular religious services in Hospitals and
institutions 9
Answers calls for special ministries in Hospitals..... 7

Less than ¼
10 additional activities
V. *Organization to Influence or Control Government*
(1) Legislation

½ to ⅔
Promotes worthy and opposes undesirable legislation 18

Less than ¼
2 additional activities
(2) Administration
¼ to ½
Coöperates with officials in law enforcement....... 12
Investigates alleged violations of law.............. 10
Files information of violations of law with enforcement officials 10

Less than ¼
3 additional activities
(3) Voluntary Political Action

¼ to ½
Promotes the exercise of the franchise (special attention to women)............................... 11

Less than ¼
4 additional activities
VI. *Education in Larger Group Relationships*
(1) Industrial

¼ to ½
Promotes celebration of Labor Sunday............. 14
Coöperates with Federal Council's Industrial program 11
Holds conferences on industrial relations.......... 7

Less than ¼
10 additional activities
(2) International

More than ⅔
Gives publicity to movements for international good will and world peace........................... 23
Advocates specific measures...................... 22
Promotes projects for world friendship among children 21

½ to ⅓
Expresses Protestant sentiment on international questions 18
Promotes observance of Armistice Sunday by churches 14

¼ to ½
Promotes community celebration of Armistice Sunday in interest of peace........................ 12
Opposes militarism 13
Gives social recognition to foreign representatives.. 8
Promotes systematic lectures or occasional addresses on international problems...................... 7

Less than ¼
6 additional activities
(3) Interracial

½ to ⅔
Promotes friendly relations between whites and Negroes 17
Advocates interracial good will.................... 14

¼ to ½
Coöperates with Federal Council interracial program 13
Promotes friendly relations between Jews and Christians 12
Promotes exchange of pulpits between white and Negro ministers 12
Promotes interracial Sunday...................... 11
Institutes interracial commissions................. 9
Conducts interracial conferences.................. 8

Less than ¼
10 additional activities

VII. *Research, Education and Technical Services*
   (1) Research

Less than ¼
   1 activity
   (2) Education

Less than ¼
   6 activities
   (3) Technical Services

Less than ¼
   2 activities

VIII. *Borderland Activities*
   (Missionary, rural, recreational and educational activities
having social service aspects are not enumerated because
considered under other topics)

D. WOMEN'S DEPARTMENTS

(Frequency of activities in eighteen departments found in
twenty-nine federations)

I. *Missions*

Over ¾
Celebrate World's Day of Prayer for Missions..............   15

½ to ¾
Conduct missionary education institutes...................   10

¼ to ½
Hold interdenominational missionary rallies...............   9

II. *Social and Community Service*

¼ to ½
Attempt to educate church women in social work...........   8
Study social problems of their own communities...........   6
Support paid worker in the courts (under church federation)   5
Conduct religious services in philanthropic institutions......   5

III. *Citizenship, Legislation and Law Enforcement*

¼ to ½
Advocate good citizenship

IV. *Internationalism*

¼ to ½
Promote international good will projects for children.......   5

Less than ¼
Recruit church women as volunteer social workers; assist
work of particular social agencies; recruit women for technical training in social work; maintain neighborhood clubs;
carry on social case-work; distribute food, clothing and other
relief to the needy; maintain volunteer court worker; support hospital chaplains; place dependents in institutions;
maintain own philanthropic institution; promote education
in social hygiene; coöperate in law enforcement measures;
publish the records of candidates for office; help get out the
women's vote; promote desirable legislation; investigate
commercialized amusements; study international relationships; promote interracial good will; conduct Americanization classes and make friendly contacts with the foreign
born; promote vacation Bible schools.

Appendix IV

CONSTITUENTS' JUDGMENTS REGARDING FEDERATION PROGRAMS

(Chapter VIII)

TABLE 5—CONSTITUENTS' JUDGMENTS REGARDING APPRO-PRIATENESS AND IMPORTANCE OF PROGRAMS IN 17 FED-ERATIONS, BY CITIES

CITY	No. OF CONSTIT- UENTS ANSWERING	No. OF JUDG- MENTS	"Should Not Under- take"	"Ques- tion- able"	"Permis- sible but Not im- portant"	"Some- what Impor- tant"	"Highly Impor- tant"
Total	2,884	134,280	2,040	2,661	7,223	26,012	96,344
Baltimore	203	6,723	148	185	566	1,613	4,211
Boston	168	6,024	231	273	544	1,722	3,254
Chicago	279	14,162	72	200	680	2,774	10,436
Detroit	160	8,390	137	187	410	1,488	6,168
Indianapolis	31	2,237	26	59	112	505	1,535
Minneapolis	249	10,791	102	152	479	1,534	8,524
New York	190	8,870	201	200	585	2,037	5,847
Oakland	98	2,810	43	100	180	504	1,983
Philadelphia	216	4,725	183	210	298	933	3,101
Pittsburgh	183	8,550	167	155	317	1,470	6,441
Portland	41	1,128	7	19	34	261	807
Rochester	205	14,474	100	174	575	2,704	10,921
St. Louis	207	13,044	201	249	523	1,940	10,131
Washington	191	8,247	131	197	701	2,106	5,112
Wichita	159	8,789	70	69	353	1,480	6,817
Youngstown	127	4,983	26	32	291	894	3,740
Massachusetts State	177	10,333	195	200	575	2,047	7,316

TABLE 6—CONSTITUENTS' JUDGMENTS REGARDING APPRO-PRIATENESS AND IMPORTANCE OF PROGRAMS IN 10 FED-ERATIONS, BY DENOMINATIONS

DENOMINATION	No. OF JUDG- MENTS	"Should not un- dertake"	"Ques- tionable"	"Permissible but not important"	"Somewhat important"	"Highly Important"
Total	99,092	1,371	1,817	4,994	18,587	72,323
Baptist	15,800	177	335	659	2,803	11,826
Congregational	16,989	146	331	1,010	3,661	11,841
Disciples	5,303	60	98	195	911	4,039
Evangelical	3,028	23	27	127	619	2,232
Lutheran	3,149	70	57	179	576	2,267
Meth. Epis.	18,717	199	259	850	3,290	14,119
Meth. Prot.	470	0	3	17	100	350
Presbyterian	18,536	238	306	956	3,395	13,641
Prot. Epis.	5,209	195	169	390	992	3,463
Reformed	364	6	12	16	73	257
United Pres.	1,758	64	20	43	280	1,351
All Other	9,194	193	198	534	1,774	6,495
Federated Community Church	575	0	2	18	113	442

Appendix V

BIBLIOGRAPHY

BOOKS

Atkins, *Modern Religious Cults and Movements* (New York, Fleming H. Revell Company, 1923).

Bass, *Protestantism in the United States* (New York, Thomas Y. Crowell Company, 1929).

Brown, *The Church In America* (New York, Macmillan Company, 1922).

Cavert, "Twenty Years of Church Federation," *Report of Federal Council of Churches, 1924-1928* (New York, 1929).

Coe, *What Is Christian Education?* (New York, Charles Scribner's Sons, 1929).

Douglass, *Church Comity* (New York, Institute of Social and Religious Research, 1929).

Douglass, *The City's Church* (New York, Friendship Press, 1929).

Douglass, *The Springfield Church Survey* (New York, Institute of Social and Religious Research, 1926).

Douglass, *The St. Louis Church Survey* (New York, Institute of Social and Religious Research, 1924).

Elliott, *The Process of Group Thinking* (New York, Association Press, 1928).

Fry, *The U. S. Looks At Its Churches* (New York, Institute of Social and Religious Research, 1930).

Guild, *Community Programs for Coöperating Churches* (New York, Association Press, 1920).

Guild, *Practicing Christian Unity* (New York, Association Press, 1919).

Hallenbeck, *Minneapolis Churches and Their Comity Problems* (New York, Institute of Social and Religious Research, 1929).

Johnson (ed.), *The Social Work of the Churches* (New York, Department of Research and Education, Federal Council of Churches, 1930).

Macfarland, *The Progress of Church Federation* (New York, Fleming H. Revell Company, Revised edition, 1922).

McGarrah, *Practical Interchurch Methods* (New York, Fleming H. Revell Company, 1919).

Niebuhr, *The Social Sources of Denominations* (New York, Henry Holt & Company, 1929).

Sanford, *History of the Federal Council of the Churches of Christ in America* (Hartford, S. S. Scranton Company, 1916).

Sears, *City Church Planning* (Boston, Judson Press, 1928).

Slosser, *Christian Unity: Its History and Challenge in All Communions, In All Lands* (New York, E. P. Dutton & Company, 1929).

PERIODICALS

"Federal Council Bulletin," a Journal of Interchurch Coöperation; New York, The Federal Council of the Churches of Christ in America, Monthly.

"Church Council News Letter," New York, The Federal Council of the Churches of Christ in America, Monthly.

INDEX

Activities,
    characteristic federation, by major departments, 111
    evangelism, 112
    federations ranked by scope of program, 108
    frequency of particular, 106
    habitual and exceptional elements of programs, 106
    relative frequency of fields of, 105
    religious education, 113
    scope and variety of programs compared, 108
    scope of federation programs, 104
    service functions of federations, 118
    social service, 113
    social welfare, 116
    standard, by departments of work, 108
    women's departments, 117
Adjustment, of conflicting interests of groups within the larger group, needed, 14
Administration, the church, 19
Administrative machinery,
    committees, 84
    "executive committee," 86
    the board of directors, 85
    the "council," 84
Affiliation,
    actual coöperation, 157
    adjustments with major agencies, 158
    combination or incorporation of organizations, 158
    councils of religious education,
        adequacy of solution, 168
        distinctiveness, 162
        historic relationships, 162
        increasing denominational control, 164
        independent movements of, 164

Affiliation—cont'd
    councils of religious education—cont'd
        internal organization, 167
        temporary adjustments, 169
        the new religious education, 163
    devices for, 157
    federations as amalgamations of previous interdenominational movements, 156
    historic relationships with federations, 159
    ministers unions, 158
        affiliating devices and organic combinations, 160
        characteristics bearing on relationships, 161
        functional unification, 160
        historic relationships with federations, 159
        present relationships, 160
    of other types of interdenominational agencies, 180
    types of adjustment attempted, 156
    women's interdenominational organizations, 169
        antecedents, 170, 171
        banded for moral reform, 171
        denominational organizations, 170
        present relationships, 172
        local women's interchurch organizations, 173
        modifying factors, 175
        status of women within federation movement, 172
    young people's organizations,
        adjustments attempted with, 177
        coöperation without combination, 178
        divisions in departments of religious education, 178

Affiliations—*cont'd*
young people's organizations—
cont'd
facilitation of community
councils of, 179
formal coöperative alliances,
178
youth and the church, 176
Agencies,
affiliations adjustments with major, 158
federation finances, 148–151
federations relationships with
other, 200
non-ecclesiastical, 18
paid workers, 142, 146
classification of, 147
number of, 146
problem of federation's relationship with other, 182
publicity and promotion, 152
scheme of internal organization
and how it works, 139
officers and directors, 140
paid professional employees,
142
standing committees and commissions, 141, 143
standing committees and commissions, 143–146
exceptional committees, 145
number of, 143
overorganization and underorganization, 144
types of internal organization,
143
women on committees, 145
summary, 153
women, 145, 148
Agitation, as means of arousing
sentiment to influence government, 115
Allegiances, prior, not affected by
federation, 77
Appeal, financial, 463
duplicating, 463
psychology of, 463
Assimilation, the essence of unity,
277
Authority, of federations,
ecclesiastical, 280
prophetic, 281

Authority of federations—*cont'd*
third possibility, 281
Autonomy, assertions of, 205

Baltimore Ministerial Union, 41
Behavior, coöperative, 9
Board of directors, of federations,
85
Boy Scouts, 19
Broadcasting of services, 330
Budgets, size and range of, 148

Camp Fire Girls, 19
Catholic Church,
coöperation in religious education, 216
coöperate in week-day schools
movement, 354
Chaplains, 332, 409
Characteristics, organizational, of
federations, 254–271
functional, 254
actual scope opportunistically
determined, 255
coöperative service limited to
"lines agreed upon," 255
gradual emergence of conventional areas of activity,
256
limitation to coöperative service, 254
natural history of federation
functions, 256
program ragged and unbal-
anced, 256
thinking related to particular
issues, 257
of federation evangelism, 341
of religious education organization, 367
practices and policies,
a slenderly supported movement, 265
departmentalization, 263
inexpert professionals, 264
inflated promotional claims,
266
large use of untrained volunteers, 264
uncritical acceptance of committee system, 263
uneven promotion, 266

Characteristics, organizational, of
federations—*cont'd*
practices and policies—*cont'd*
unstandardized methods, 265
traits of the group mind, 257
accumulation of taboos, 262
defensive thinking meeting
specific attacks, 261
fear of commitment, 257
generalization by dramatization, 260
genius of movement not philosophical but practical, 258
practical thinking negative in
tendency, 260
small use of ready-made formulas, 259
superficial restatements of conventional morality, 262
tendency to concession and
compromise, 262
verdict, 266
a versatile and unexhausted
movement, 268
dependable loyalty of constituents, 267
practical virtues outweigh intellectual and moral qualities, 268
relation of results to resources,
266
vitality heightened by selective
mortality, 268
vocational, of directors of religious education, 318
vocational, of paid staff, 315
vocational, of social service
workers, 322
women's departments, 443
Charity, 393
Chicago Church federation, and
commission on interracial
relations, 386
Chicago Race Commission, 386
China Famine Relief, 390
*Christian Unity: Its Problems and
Possibilities*, 41N
Church, the,
administrative machinery, 19
any member church may be
dropped from association
for non-coöperation, 82

Church, the—*cont'd*
non-ecclesiastical extensions and
allies, 18
representation of individual
churches and persons in
federation, 83
résumé of, in fifty largest cities,
15
"Church and community convention," 61
Church Comity, Douglass, 76N,
107N, 110N, 374N
Church directories, 477
Church federations,
activities, coöperative, 104–126
(see also "Activities")
administrative machinery, 84
affiliation of other interdenominational organizations, 155
agencies, 139–143
and attempted governmental influence, 374–380
and Federal Council, 204 (see
also "Federal Council")
and State Councils of Churches,
206
and the "council," 84
attempted solutions of coöperation, 184
case study of membership, 96
characteristic activities by major
departments, 111
church school, the, 346
claims and recognitions, 56–75
announced objectives, 57
churches in simultaneous common action, 61
fundamental principles of coöperative work, 61
how impress their constituencies, 64
moral authority of federations,
69
official expositions, 61
official pronouncements, 60
slogans and sales talk, 62
summary, 74
committees, 86
conclusions on denominational
differences and partisan-
ship as regards coöpera-
tion of, 38

Church federations—*cont'd*
  criticism of social service and its
    limitations, 247
  designations of, 5N
  distribution by size of city, 3
  distribution of those studied, 4
  district federations, 87
  evolution, trends of, 50 (see also
    "Evolution")
  evolutionary process of move-
    ment,
    assimilation the essence of
      unity, 277
    federation as symbol of com-
      mon feeling and aspira-
      tion, 278
    future extension of organized
      coöperation, 277
  facilities, housing, 464–468
  fallacy of regarding, "as just an-
    other organization," 10
  finances, 148–151, 448–470 (see
    also "Finances")
  forces unifying and enlarging
    movement, 203–227
  form and structure,
    administrative machinery, 84
    form, nature and consequences
      of act of association, 81
    geographical jurisdiction of
      federations and denomi-
      nations as locally organ-
      ized, 79
    limited participation provi-
      sions for, 82
    nature of association involved,
      76
    non-ecclesiastical organizations
      representation, 80
    organizational relations with
      denominations as locally
      organized, 79
    recognition of local churches
      when denomination is unit
      of membership, 78
    representative persons, 83
    units of association, 77
    secondary membership, 80
    withdrawal from, provisions
      for, 82
  industrial relationship, 384
  interracial relationships, 386–388

Church federations—*cont'd*
  limited participation, provisions
    for, 82
  major problems that underlie
    local coöperative experi-
    ments, 13
  membership and participation,
    89–103
    eligibility, 89
    financial participation of
      churches, 97
    habitually non-coöperative ele-
      ments, 101
    measuring total participation,
      100
    membership in church federa-
      tions, 92
    partial membership, 99
    participation without mem-
      bership, 100
    summary, 102
  moral authority of, 69
  more ultimate problems, 280
    a third possibility, 281
    authority, 280
    ecclesiastical authoritarianism,
      281
    prophetic authoritarianism,
      281
    regulative devices, representa-
      tive democracy, 283
    representativeness, 283
    significance of position with
      respect to authority, 282
  movement, 41–54
    amalgamation of previously
      independent, 52
    attitude toward church unity,
      44
    capitalization of experience, 54
    effect of evangelical alliance
      on church policies, 43
    evolutions of programs, 53
    historical summary, 42
    history by epochs, 43
    ideals and institutions of
      founders, 43
    is voluntary, 76
    leadership, 54
    local federations antedating
      federal council, 47
    organization of federal coun-
      cil, 48

Church federations—*cont'd*
movement—*cont'd*
origins and course of development, 41
progress selective rather than inclusive, 51
promotion of local federation, 49
rapid growth of surviving organization, 52
recent history, 50
social gospel, 45
World War, the, 49
number and location of, 3
organizational characteristics, 254–271
other major Protestant alliances, 211
religious education, 211
women's national interchurch organizations, 212
paid workers, 142, 146–148
practical problems of, 39, 279
complexity and competition, 279
present limits of coöperation, 182–202
problem of relationship with allies, 182
problems of national system from local viewpoint, 210
national promotion in local communities, 211
representation and share of control in council, 210
ranked by scope of program, 108
ranking of 26, according to scope of program, 109
recognition of unique functions of, 396
regionality, 4
relative importance of, in community social effort, 395
relatively small per cent of Protestant denominations belonging, 95
relationships with other organizations, 159, 160
relationships with other Protestant agencies, 200
representation of individual churches, 83
scope of programs, 104

Church federations—*cont'd*
secular alliances, 218
service functions of, 118
standing committees, 143–146
summary of, 285
the conditional outcome, 286
the historic movement, 272
a reminiscently prophetic movement, 275
achievement of a dominant temper, 273
actual ecclesiastical dominance, 274
ecclesiastical order guaranteed by national relationships, 275
numerical preponderance of clergy on federation committees, 274
the "Y" as an initiator of federations, 188
thinking, currents and eddies, 229–253
vacation Bible schools as an activity of, 348
withdrawal from, 82
Church organs, 472
Church School, the, 346
Circulation, of church organs, 473
Cities, direct denominational membership in certain specified, 94
Clergy, the,
numerical preponderance of, on federation committees, 274
Collections, 452
Comity, 329N
defined, 111N
does not flourish in the south, 110
expenditures for, 457
importance of, in constituents' judgment, 135
one of big five of federation activities, 105
Committees,
Boards of Directors and equivalent organizations, 291
attendance, 294
characteristics, 293
composition of, 292
executive committee, 295

Committees—*cont'd*
  size and frequency of meetings, 292
  conclusions as to, 304
    more general suggestions, 307
    practical considerations, 306
  conduct of, 301
    committee decisions, 304
    forms in which business is presented, 303
    minutes, 304
    notice of meetings, 302
    preparation, 302
    the rôle of chairman, 303
    time, place, and duration, 301
  departments and commissions headed by, 86
  exceptional, 145
  executive, 86, 295
  finance committee, 459
  number of, 143
  numerical preponderance of clergy on federation, 274
  of women's departments, 440
  overorganization and underorganization, 144
  performance of, in social service, below average, 428
  publicity, 477
  responsible for conduct of religious education, 363
  social service, 412–416
  standing committees,
    age, sex and race of, 298
    attendance, 297
    component elements, 298
    duration of service, 300
    frequency of meeting, 297
    occupation, 300
    number of members, 296
    relation to enterprise as a whole, 301
  the system of, 291–308
  types of internal organization, 143
  uncritical acceptance of committee system, 263
  women on, 145
Community, the, federation identified with, 76
Community Programs for Coöperating Churches, Guild (Ed.), 62N, 371, 371N

Competition, federations as a cure for, 66
Community Chest, 397, 453
Complexity of religious organizations, 75
  concern with, and competition, 279
  degree varies with size and character of city, 20
  increased by denominational divisions, 22
  problem identified, 14
  shown by inventory of Protestant organizations in cities, 17
  suburban exaggeration, 20
Conflict of religious groups, hypothesis of coöperation explains decline, 11
Confidential advice, furnished by federation, 119
Conflict, of religious groups, problem identified, 14
"Conservation," plan of, 51
Constituents,
  and religious education, 365
  attitude on coöperation with social agencies, 398
  attitudes on women's departments, 443
  attitudes toward departments of work, 134
  attitudes toward interconfessional coöperation, 215
  criticism of federations, 228–253
  distribution of judgments according to classes of, 133
  federations an accepted common agency, 66
  five practical reasons for favoring federation, 67
  how reactions of, secured, 64
  how they regard service program of federations, 120
  judgments on publicity, 479
  judgments upon current programs, 127–138
    by cities, 128
    by denominations, 130
    criteria of, 129
  judgments upon proposed programs, 136

Constituents—*cont'd*
judgments upon proposed programs—*cont'd*
contrasting attitudes, 136
explanations, 138
reactions to specific proposals,
137
opinions on social service, 230
reactions summarized, 65
referendum, on governmental
matters, 380
regard federations as cure for
competition, 66
returns from Philadelphia constituents, 68
sense of obligation to coöperate,
69–71
verdict of, on evangelism, 340
verdicts on social service, 417
judgments regarding importance of phases of social
service, 418
Constitutions, of federations,
common sources and elements,
59
federations and church unity, 60
frequency of mention of specific
objectives, 58
occasional balanced statements,
58
proposed activities listed, 59
Coördination, of separate units
making up church, needed,
14
Coöperation (see also "Church
Federations")
activities, coöperative, 104–126
(see also under "Activi-
ties")
annual evangelistic programs,
339
as practiced, 9
attempted solutions, 184
relationships with Y. M. C. A.,
184 (see also under "Y.
M. C. A.")
behavior of churches more significant than pronounce-
ments, 56
complexity of religious organizations, 14

Coöperation—*cont'd*
conclusions on denominational
differences and partisan-
ship as regards problem
of, 38
coöperation rather than formal
membership should be
heart of movement of,
103
fallacy of regarding movement
"as just another organization," 10
form, nature and consequences
of act of association, 81
fundamental principles, 61
future extension of organized,
277
habitually non-coöperative elements, 101
hypothesis of Protestant coöperation, 11
ideal vs. institutions, 7, 8
idealizing formulas and utterances, 7
interconfessional, 213
constitutents' attitudes, 215
directions and limitations of,
216
occasional, 215
relations with Greek orthodox
church, 215
significance of, without affiliation, 214
major problems, identification
of, 13
meaning of, for ultimate participant, 6
phenomena of, 3
practical problems of, 39
present limits of, 182–202
problem of relationship with allies, 182
Protestants coöperate, 121
in areas of activity not controlled by clerical and ecclesiastical tradition, 124
in situations controlled by
forces outside church willing to recognize coöpera-
tive method of service but
not a sectarian method,
124

Coöperation—*cont'd*
Protestants coöperate—*cont'd*
in spheres not previously occupied denominationally, 123
in work requiring an exceptionally exacting technique, standards of which are set by forces outside ecclesiastical field, 124
where high symbolic significance of an occasion requires gesture of united action, 125
when an accepted and unchallenged generality needs particular reinforcement, 123
when feeling need of united forces to win particular issue or plan, 125
when it is a habit and original motive obscured by tradition, 122
when practical convenience coupled with small ecclesiastical implications are found, 123
when process is profitable and safeguarded, 123
where new and poorly established interchurch movements find they can strengthen themselves, 124
where type of activity and characteristics of persons concerned do not constitute field for denominational service, 123
secular alliances, 218
sense of obligation to coöperate, 69–71
denominational variation in, 72
social agencies, methods of, 394
the federation movement, 272, 287
the viewpoint, 10
when and why Protestants coöperate, 121
Council of Churches (see also "Church Federation")
Council of Social Agencies, 393

Council, the, of federations, representation on, 84
Court work, of social service, 403
continuous case work, 404
finances and expenditures, 457
social workers and constituents' attitudes, 405
Curriculum, of vacation schools, 351
Criticism, pro and con, of federations,
actual misrepresentation of church is rarely charged, 239
constructive, 240
federations must not outstrip churches, 239
local or incidental grounds of, 232
approval conditioned upon leadership, 234
cautionary counsels, 234
criticism of federation practice, 233
federation locally unacceptable, 232
results not worth effort, 235
major sensitive points, 235
authority, 235
inclusiveness, 237
representativeness, 238
need of federation as common organ for Protestantism, 243
significance for church unity, 240
of social service, 247–253
official thinking, 243
unequal distribution of dynamic thinking, 244
unofficial thinking, 229
minor issues expressive of constituents' moods, 231
opposition without explanation, 231
superfluous and burdensome, 232
sources of data, 230

Debt, 462
Decentralization,
city federations and recognition of suburbs, 76

Decentralization—*cont'd*
constitutional provision for district federation, 87
federations of cities coördinate in membership with suburban congregations (Boston), 81
Denominationalism,
barriers of, 23
central problem, 23
comparisons, as regards federation membership by city, 94
fugitive illustrations of extreme, 24
Denominational differences,
conclusions as bearing upon problem of coöperation, 38
generalization, 37
in acuteness of feeling of religious distance, 25
consistency of attitudes, 37
measure of partisanship, 37
between given denominations and all others, 26, 32
by cities, 34
by denominations, 31
by particular denominations, 32
in sense of obligation to coöperate, 69
explanations of, as revealed, risky, 74
measure of partisanship, 37
by geographical regions, 34
by sex and ecclesiastical status, 35
marriage and the presidency, 29
summary of factual findings, 36
Denominations (see also "Denominational differences," and "Denominationalism")
classification, 16
comparison of federation membership, by city, 94
constituents' judgment on current program by, 130
ranking tables for, 131, 132
sentiment vs. judgment, 132

Denominations—*cont'd*
coöperating in religious education, 368
denominational machinery, 25
direct membership, in federations, 94
number in cities, 16
Departmentalization, 263
Designations, of federations, 5N
Directors, Boards of, 291–296
Directory, of pastors and churches, 118
District federations, 87
Ecclesiastical inhibitions, 122

Ecclesiastical traits,
actual ecclesiastical dominance, 274
preponderance of clergy on federation committees, 274
Economic order, relationships within, 115
Eligibility, to federation membership, 89
evangelical limitations, 90
grounds of, 89
limitation of, and size of group, 91
modification, by usage, 90
negro churches, 91
Employment bureaus, 393
Endorsement of special interests, 119
Evangelical Alliance, the, 41
Evangelism,
a practical suggestion, 344
activity in Philadelphia and Louisville, 110
annual coöperative programs, 339
characteristics of, 341
constitutes one of big five of federation activities, 105
continuous activities, 330
broadcasting of services, 330
coöperative discussion of plans, 330
institutional chaplaincies, 332
finances and expenditures, 456
limitation as to federation membership, 90
occasional activities, 335
concomitant activities, 338

Evangelism—*cont'd*
evangelistic campaigns, 335
extra-parochial ministry, 337
problems, 342
program of, 112
radio broadcasting, 113, 330, 477
recurrent activities, 333
celebration of Christian year
and nation, 333
Lent and Holy Week, 333
seasonal pastoral ministries,
335
summer evangelism, 334
scope and magnitude, 329
summary of activities, 340
technical surveys, 113
verdict of constituents, 340
ranking of items of program
according to, 341
Evolution, trends of, in church
federations,
amalgamation of previously independent movements, 52
capitalization of experience, 54
leadership, 54
of programs, from original germs,
53
progress selective rather than inclusive, 51
rapid growth of surviving organizations, 52
typical life-cycle, 50
Expenditures, 150, 454–457 (see
also under "Finances")
Extra-parochial ministry, 337

Facilities, federation,
desirability of location and quality of housing, 464
facilities as related to paid workers, 465
facilities for volunteer workers
and public, 467
general index of quality, 468
size and arrangement of offices,
465
summary, 466
Federal Council of Churches of
Christ in America,
Church Council News Letter,
N167
organization of, 42, 48

Federal Council of Churches of
Christ in America—*cont'd*
promotion of local federation by,
47
relationships of local federations
with federation move-
ment, 49
representation and share of control in, 210
present relationships with, 204
actual relationships varying in
different departments, 205
assertions of autonomy, 205
constitutional recognition of,
204
national relationships as represented to local constituencies, 205
representation in federal council, 206
Federation of churches (see also
"Church Federation")
Federation of Protestant Child-
Caring Agencies, 399
Finances,
campaigns, 458
collections, 452
community chest funds, 453
contributions to phases of federation work through sub-
sidiaries, 98
debt, 462
departmental funds, 454
expenditures, 150, 454
administrative salaries, 454
comity and research, 457
conclusions, 469
court and hospital work, 457
departmental and specially
budgeted activities, 455
evangelism, 456
general operating expenses,
455
general social service, 456
industrial, interracial and international committees,
457
publicity and financial campaigns, 458
religious education, 455
rent, 454
women's departments, 457
federation facilities, 464

Finances—*cont'd*
finance committees, 459
financial policies, 461
how financial support is secured,
459
incidental business income, 452
individual gifts, 460
loans, 453
methods of obtaining, 459
of women's departments, 442
participation of churches, 97
problems, 463
better and broader non-financial cultivation, 463
duplicating appeal, 463
division of financial responsibility, 464
psychology of appeal, 463
secondary types of support, 98
size and range of budgets, 148
sources of support, 150, 448, 450
support by individual churches,
449
tenure, 151
total support from church sources, 451
Financial participation, of churches
to federation, 97
Formulas, idealizing, in coöperation, 7

Geographical jurisdiction, of federations and denominations as locally organized,
79
Girl Scouts, 19
Government,
attempt by church to influence
action of, 115, 374
complexities and difficulties,
380
law enforcement, 382
legislation, 379
outcomes and problems of, 383
pitfalls and attempted safeguards, 378
planes of social action involving, 375
referendum as a method, 380

*History of the Federal Council of
Churches,* Sanford, 41N

Homogeneity, of religious bodies,
trend toward, 12, 14
Homogeneous America, Bertrand
Russell, 11N
Hospital work, 406
expenditures for, 457
Housing, 464
Hypothesis, concerning organized
Protestant coöperation, 11
trend toward homogeneity of all
religious bodies, 12

Individual gifts, 460
Industrial committees, expenditures, 457
"Industrial Week," in Boston, 384
Information, furnishing of, 118
Institutional service, and non-institutional, 116
International Committees, expenditures, 457
Interdenominational organizations,
17
International relations, one of big
five of federation activities, 105
International relationship, education of social attitudes on,
115, 116
International Council of Religious
Education, 203
Interracial Committees, expenditures, 457

Jewish churches,
coöperate with week-day schools
movement, 354
coöperation in religious education, 216
coöperation with Christian federation, 213
Jury duty, 381

Ku Klux Klan, 37

Law enforcement, by federations,
382
methods and their theoretical
justifications, 382
spheres of churches special concern, 382

Leadership (see also "Paid Staff")
   discontinuity of, 54
   inexpert professionals, 264
   professional, 368
   training, 359 (see also under
      "Religious Education")
League of Nations, 381
Legislation, of federations, 379
Limited participation, provisions
   for, 82
Loans, 453

Mailing lists, federations, 119
Marriage and the Presidency,
   faiths and denominations
   ranked by degree of "distance" felt toward them,
   29
Membership, in federation,
   acid test of, whether it causes
     church to transfer money
     to treasury of federation,
     97, 98
   case study of, 96
   churches participating in, larger
     than average, 93
   current participation really
     ground for, 93
   delegates, appointment to gov-
     erning body, 92
   denominational comparisons, 94
   direct denominational, 94
   eligibility, 89
   financial participation of church-
     es, 97
   habitually non-coöperative ele-
     ments, 101
   measuring total participation,
     100
   membership in church federa-
     tion, 92
   no official list of member-
     churches, 93
   partial membership, 99
   participation without member-
     ship, 100
   specific conclusions, 103
   success in securing, 93
   summary, 102
Minutes, of committee meetings,
   304
Ministers unions, 158–162 (see also
   under "Affiliations")

Morality, conventional, 262
Mormonism, 46
National system of church federations, 203
Near East Relief, 393
Negro churches,
   and eligibility to federation, 91
   exclusion of, and size of Protes-
     tant group, 92
   finances, 451
   interracial relationships, 386
   on committees concerned with
     race relations, 413
   "usage" as limitation to federa-
     tion membership of, 91
Newspapers, 475
Non-coöperative elements, habitually,
   adverse attitude of certain de-
     nominations, 101
   conditions tending to keep
     churches out of federa-
     tions, 101
     churches of alien antecedents,
       102
     extreme parties withhold
       membership, 102
     geographical conditions, 102
     weak churches of coöperating
       denominations, 102
Non-ecclesiastical extensions, 18
Non-ecclesiastical organizations,
   secondary membership
   and representation, 80

Objectives, of federations, limita-
   tion of, 77
Offices, 465
Old people's homes, 400
Our Country, Dr. Josiah Strong,
   45

Paid staff, 142, 146
   assistant and departmental sec-
     retaries, 315
   characteristics of workers, 318
   directors vs. supervisors, 321
   duration and variety of work,
     316
   executive secretaries, 310
     age, 310
     attendance at meetings, 313
     duties, 312

Paid staff—*cont'd*
 period of service, 311
 perquisites, 311
 executive secretaries—*cont'd*
 salaries, 311
 summary, 314
 training, 310
 general and departmental clerical workers, 317
 in social service, 321
 differentiation from other types of federation workers, 324
 hours of labor, 323
 kinds of work, 323
 variation according to position, 324
 vocational characteristics, 323
 kinds of duties, 319
 management, 327
 of women's departments, 441
 pay, 327
 recruiting of workers, 326
 selection of, 326
 size of, 309
 training, 326
 women's assistants and office secretaries, 315
 workers at work, 319
 workers in religious education, 317
 vocational characteristics, 315
 vocational characteristics of directors of religious education, 318
 vocational problems of, 325
Partial membership,
 causes of, 99
 does not commit a church to entangling alliances, 100
Participation, of federation membership,
 habitually non-coöperative elements, 101
 measuring total, 100
 without membership, 100
Partisanship, religious,
 central problem, 23
 measurement of, 37
Pay, of paid workers, 327
Persons, representative, in federation, 83
Phenomena, of coöperation, 3

Phenomena, of coöperation—*cont'd*
 coöperative behavior, the central, 9
 federation presents itself as essentially a congregational and low-church, 88
 inherent complexity of, 75
Political action, on part of federations, 226
Programs,
 annual coöperative, 339
 compared as to scope and variety, 108
 constituents' judgments upon current, 127–138
 federations ranked by scope of, 108
 problems for consideration, 111
 problems of, 120
 ragged and unbalanced, 256
 scope of, 104
Project; present study,
 character and limitations, vii
 demand for investigation, 3
 method and spirit of investigation, x
 narrative of, viii
 published results, ix
Promotion, of federations, 152
 Federal Council as an external promotional agency, 266
 federation publications, 472
 annual reports, 474
 circulation, 473
 federation organ, 472
 promotional literature, 474
 quality of organs, 473
 individual and intimate cultivation of constituents, 471
 circular letters, 471
 miscellaneous, 476
 of national agencies in local communities, 211
 personal publicity, 476
 problems, 479
 public press, 475
Propaganda, 389
 in social service, 426
Protestant Children's Homes, 400
Protestants, when and why they coöperate, 121
 absence of guiding principle or agreement, 121

Protestants, when and why they
coöperate—*cont'd*
conditions of, 122
ecclesiastical inhibitions diminished, 122
re-enforced impulses, 124
under internal pressure, 125
Public agencies, coöperation with
church agencies, 402
Public institutions, social service
in, 405
correlation of Protestant effort
in, 408
federation methods, 406
hospital work, 406
public support of chaplains, 409
religion in, 406
Publicity,
agents, 477
committees, 477
publicity conference, 478
publicity directors, 478
expenditures for campaigns, 458
importance of, in constituents'
judgment, 135
judgment of constituents, 479
of federations, 152
of women's departments, 442
personal, 476
problems, 479
Pupils, 360

Questionnaire,
on "sense of obligation to coöperate," etc., 26, 69–71

Racial groups, and education of
social attitudes, 115
Radio broadcasting, and evangelism, 113, 477
Red Cross, 393
Referendum, the, 431
as method of referring controversial matters to sections
of constituency, 380
Religious distance questionnaire
and results, 26
Religious education,
as a major Protestant alliance,
211
characteristics of organization
as bearing on relation-
ships, 367

Religious education—*cont'd*
characteristics of organizations
as bearing on relation-
ships—*cont'd*
coöperating denominations,
368
dual affiliations, 367
high degree of development,
367
professional leadership, 368
standardized field, 367
church school, the, 346
committees and committee performance, 363
constituents' opinions on, 365
ranking of items, according to
judgments regarding ap-
propriateness and impor-
tance, 366
councils of, 162–169
historic relationships, 162
present relationships, 165
federations have departments
for, operating under their
own by-laws, 81N
finances and expenditures, 455
grading and age-adoptions, 362
interconfessional relationships
on, 216
leadership training, 359
auspices and location, 359
curriculum, 361
divisional committees, 360
organizational and institutional characteristics, 360
teachers and pupils, 360
one of big five of federation activities, 105
overlapping of fields, 363
paid workers in, 317
problems of, 369
program for, in Wichita and
Toledo federations, 110
program more clear-cut and
standardized than evan-
gelism, 113
program of, 113
scope and magnitude, 345
causes of variation in, 346
separate basic organization, 369
vacation Bible schools, 348
as a federation activity, 349

Religious education—*cont'd*
vacation Bible schools—*cont'd*
curriculum, 351
facilities and costs, 351
organization, 350
quantitative measurement, 351
week-day church schools, 352
educational characteristics, 355
organization aspects, 353
problems, 357
Rent, 454

"Sabbath" observance, 398
Salaries, administrative, 454
Sales talk, 62
Scope,
actual, of federations, opportunistically determined, 255
federation programs, 104
genesis in American Protestantism, 45
problems of federation programs, 120
Secular alliances, 218
increasing recognition by social agencies, 220
problems growing out of, 221
"Christian" social service, 225
dignity of ancillary rôle, 225
ecclesiastical vs. private nonsectarian social agencies, 221
how ought responsibility be divided, 221
political action, 226
private welfare agencies vs. the state, 223
voluntary social agencies, 219
Slogans, 62
Social agencies (see also "Social Service")
conflict or competition of, 400
correlation of work of Protestant, 399
creation of new interdenominational, 401
resources and facilities, 412
Social Gospel,
concept of, 246
content in thought of founders, 43
place in federation history, 47

Social Gospel—*cont'd*
qualifications and limitation of social service, 247 (see also "Social Service")
Social Service,
advocacy and promotion of reform organizations, 398
advocacy of general social ideals, 115
agencies, resources and facilities, 412–416
committees, 412
committee processes, 414
attempts to influence action of governments, 374
complexities and difficulties, 380
law enforcement, 382
legislation, 379
outcomes and problems of, 383
pitfalls and attempted safeguards, 378
planes of social action involving, 375
attitudes including larger group relationships, 384
characteristics, 421–425
a cooled-off movement, 421
inadequate consolidation of connection, 424
lack of comprehensive theory, 423
non-ecclesiastical tendency, 422
outside stimulus and leadership, 425
China Famine Relief Fund, 390
conflict or competition of agencies, 400
constituents' attitudes, 398
constituents' verdicts, 417
coöperation with public agencies and institutions, 402
correlation of work of Protestant agencies, 399
court work, 403
continuous case work, 404
social workers' and constituents' attitudes, 405
creation of new interdenominational social agencies, 401

Social Service—*cont'd*
  education of attitudes involving
      larger group relationships,
      115
  finances and expenditures, 456
  for needy, is carried on mostly
      by public agencies, not
      under ecclesiastical sup-
      port, 440
  in federation thinking, 245
  in public institutions, 405–410
  industrial relationships, 384
    relative weakness and outside
        stimulation of interest in,
        385
  interracial relationships, 386
    a typical interracial commis-
        sion, 386
    constituents' attitudes, 388
    other methods and condition-
        ing factors, 388
  international relationships, 388
    constituents' attitudes and or-
        ganized criticism, 390
    methods, 389
    propaganda and taking sides,
        389
  machinery, 372
  magnitude and importance, 371
  methods of coöperation, 394
  most problematical and least
      well-established program,
      113
  one of big five of federation ac-
      tivities, 105
  paid workers in, 321
  participation in voluntary social
      and reform organizations,
      393
  Pittsburgh federation strong in,
      110
  problems, 425
    a secondary Protestant system
        of agencies, 427
    committee performance below
        average, 428
    little progress toward coördi-
        nating agencies, 427
    propaganda outruns education,
        425
    under criticism by social agen-
        cies, 429

Social Service—*cont'd*
  proclamation and advocacy of
      social ideals, 374
  program of, 113
  qualifications and limitations of,
      acute controversy on, 252
    church's business, but only in
        one aspect, 249
    church's business, but second-
        ary one, 248
    concrete attempts to apply
        principles to issues, 249
    not the church's business, 247
    sacred vs. secular, the, 247
  recognition of federation's unique
      function, 396
  relative importance of federa-
      tions in community effort
      at, 395
  semi-welfare activities, 391
    miscellaneous services, 393
    neighborhood and community
        work, 392
    non-institutional social service
        directly under federation
        auspices, 391
  social welfare activities, 116
    coöperation with institution-
        alized activities of gov-
        ernment, 116
    institutional service, 116
    non-institutional service, 116
    participation in work of vol-
        untary social organiza-
        tions, 116
    technical and marginal activi-
        ties, 117
  suggestions for improvement of
      methods of, 430
    accept technical standards of
        social work, 431
    enlarge the rôle of denomina-
        tional social workers, 432
    modify rôle of federal council,
        432
    reduce number of committees
        and integrate their work,
        430
    stress service distinctive of
        church, 433
    supervise paid workers better,
        430

Social Service—*cont'd*
   suggestions for improvement of
      methods of—*cont'd*
      train for social service, 432
      use of referendum, 431
   systematic organization for co-
      öperation, 394
   technical and marginal activities,
      410–412
      borderland activities, 412
      endorsement of financial ap-
         peals of social agencies,
         411
      social education and research,
         410
   types of activity, 114
   welfare activities, 116
Social Work of the Churches, 371N
State Councils of Churches,
   activity in initiating state coun-
      cils, 206
   association of church-federation
      secretaries, 207
   concurrent action of federative
      agencies, 208
   determination of relations of
      state and city federations,
      206
Summer camps, 393
*Survey of Higher Education for
   the United Lutheran
   Church in America,* Leonard, N225
Synthesis, need of instrument of,
   270

Taboos, accumulation of, 262
Teachers, of religious education,
   360
Technical surveys, to measure
   evangelistic needs, 113
Tenure, 151
The Challenge of The City; Dr.
   Josiah Strong, 45
Theology,
   only admitted grounds of feder-
      ation eligibility are theo-
      logical, 89
   taboo on theological discussion,
      41
   theological basis of Evangelical
      Alliance, 43

Theology—*cont'd*
   theological basis of Federal Coun-
      cil, 47
   theological basis of local federa-
      tions, 47
Training, of paid staff, 326

Units, of association, 77
   organizational relations with de-
      nominations as locally or-
      ganized, 79
   primary, 78
   recognition of local churches
      when denomination is, 78
   secondary membership, 80
"Usage,"
   and limitation on negro churches
      to federation membership,
      91
   as a limitation to federation
      membership, 90
Utterances, on coöperation, 7

Vacation Bible Schools, 348
Visitation Evangelism, Kernahan,
   336N
Voluntary Social organizations, 116

Week-day Church Schools, 352
   educational characteristics, 355
   organization aspects, 353
   problems, 357
Wichita,
   experiment of relationships be-
      tween Y.M.C.A. and local
      federation in, 194
   provision of, with reference to
      week-day schools, 353
Withdrawal, provisions for, 82
Women's departments,
   agencies and resources, 440
      committees, 440
      composition and characteris-
         tics, 441
      constituents' attitudes, 443
      finances, 442
      paid departmental workers
         and facilities, 441
      publicity, 442
   conclusions, 446
   expenditures for, 457

Women's departments—*cont'd*
  federations and, operating under
      their own by-laws, 81N
  functional relationships with
      federations, 440
  functional types, 438
  functions, 438
  generalization, 117
    scope of programs of, 118
  in executive positions, 148
  interdenominational organiza-
      tions, 169–176
  membership and participation,
      436
  objectives of organizations, 434
  on committees, 145
  on social service committees, 413
  problems, 446
  relation to other types of wom-
      en's organization, 437
  tendencies and characteristics,
      443
    characteristics of coöperative
        women's work, 445
    distinctive attitudes, 444
    diverse antecedents and inter-
        ests, 443
    recent situations, 444
  units of membership, 436
World Court, 381
"Wowsers," 414
World War, the, 49

Yearbook of the Churches, 41N
Young Men's Christian Associa-
    tion, 19, 42
  and closer alliance of young peo-
      ple's movement, 46

Young Men's Christian Associa-
    tion—*cont'd*
  and court work in Pittsburgh,
      400
  and federations,
    actual relationships, 188
    administrative unification, 194
    facts bearing on relationship,
        184
    attempted statement of rela-
        tionship, 185
    churches' reaction, 186
    competition of, 191
    coöperation between, 188
    general conclusions as to rela-
        tionships, 196
    organizational membership,
        188
    "Y" as an initiator of federa-
        tions, 188
  and financial appeals, 396
  as non-ecclesiastical organiza-
      tions, 81
  doing special work in religious
      education, 164, 165
  federations as tenants of, 151
  membership in federation's
      boards of directors, 85
  young people's organizations in,
      179
Young Women's Christian Associ-
    ation, 19, 42
  and federations, 197
    exchange of service and coöp-
        erative activities, 198
    potential competition, 199
  (and see also items under "Young
      Men's Christian Associa-
      tion")